Grade 3
Teacher Edition

Spelling

purposeful design
publications
A Division of ACSI

Colorado Springs, CO

Development Team

First Edition

Editorial Team

Dr. Sharon Berry	*Managing Editor*
Dr. Barry Morris	*Content Manager*
Dr. Ollie Gibbs	*Project Manager*

Author Team

Sharon Bird	Linda Miller
Cathy Guy	Nancy Wetzel
Eunice Harris	Connie Williams

Project Consultants

Dr. Barbara Bode	Ruth McBride
Dr. Richard Edlin	Dr. Connie Pearson
Dr. Omer Bonenberger	Patti Rhan
Dr. Linda Goodson	Dr. Milton Uecker
Dr. Alex Lackey	Dr. Ray White

Second Edition

Editorial Team

JoAnn Keenan	*Managing Editor*
Maria L. Deckard	*Editor*
Cynthia C. Shipman	*Editor*
Lorraine Wadman	*Editor*
Dr. June Hetzel	*Senior Content Editor*

Design Team

Monica Starr Brown	*Graphic Designer, Photographer*
Susanna Garmany	*Graphic Designer*
Leslie E. Swift	*Graphic Designer*

Project Consultants

Dr. Derek Keenan	*ACSI Vice President for Academic Affairs*
Steven Babbitt	*Director, Purposeful Design Publications*
Don Hulin	*Assistant Director, Textbook Development*

Purposeful Design

Grade 3
Teacher Edition

Spelling

shuttle

balloon

skateboard

sailboat

locomotive

Managing Editor
JoAnn Keenan

Editors
Maria L. Deckard
Cynthia C. Shipman
Lorraine Wadman

Designers
Monica Starr Brown
Susanna Garmany
Leslie E. Swift

Senior Content Editor
Dr. June Hetzel

Purposeful Design Publications is the publishing division of the Association of Christian Schools International (ACSI) and is committed to the ministry of Christian school education, to enable Christian educators and schools worldwide to effectively prepare students for life. As the publisher of textbooks, trade books, and other educational resources within ACSI, Purposeful Design Publications strives to produce biblically sound materials that reflect Christian scholarship and stewardship and that address the identified needs of Christian schools around the world.

References to books, computer software, and other ancillary resources in this series are not endorsements by ACSI. These materials were selected to provide teachers with additional resources appropriate to the concepts being taught and to promote student understanding and enjoyment.

Unless otherwise identified, all Scripture quotations are taken from the Holy Bible, New King James Version (NKJV), © 1982 by Thomas Nelson, Inc. Used by permission. All rights reserved.

Photograph of David Paulus used by permission.
Photograph of Joe Lortie used by permission.
Photographs of Chris Reifel used by permission.

Illustration on Student Edition page 112 by Aline Heiser, North Ridgeville, OH

Printed in the United States of America
17 16 15 14 13 12 11 10 09 08   1 2 3 4 5 6 7

Spelling, grade three
Purposeful Design Spelling series
Second edition
ISBN 978-1-58331-241-4   Teacher edition   Catalog #7412

Purposeful Design Publications
A Division of ACSI
PO Box 65130 • Colorado Springs, CO 80962-5130
Customer Service: 800-367-0798 • www.acsi.org

Table of Contents

Lesson		Page

Teacher Resources

Blackline Master List

Transparency List

Poster List

Foreword

The fourfold educational mission of Christian schools is to prepare young people as disciples of Christ who are spiritually-formed thinkers. Education implies the development of the mind by the acquisition of knowledge and the ability to think and understand. Schools also equip students with a set of skills that are essential for life and vocation. In addition, the training process seeks to ground pupils with a worldview that is biblical and that shapes their lives into a God-pleasing spiritual pattern. In order to fulfill this Kingdom mandate, schools need to do their educational work carefully and responsibly. Purposeful Design Publications exists to assist educators in the fulfillment of that mission.

Over the past decades there continues to be a plethora of approaches to many aspects of the language arts. The research literature is somewhat conflicted about what is most effective in preparing students to be good readers, but it is quite clear about developing strong spellers. We have been through an era where spelling did not need to be taught explicitly but as an outgrowth of reading (Smith 1971). Several things from the research about spelling instruction are quite clear:

- Effective spelling instruction strengthens reading
- There are multiple benefits to explicit spelling instruction
- Strategies must be matched according to the age and level of spelling ability
- Well-developed and current spelling resources incorporate comprehensive tested strategies that match a variety of learners

(Gentry 2004)

The revised Purposeful Design Spelling series approaches spelling as a critical literacy skill that strengthens reading and writing ability. Spelling strategies such as word sorting by phonetic pattern, developing vocabulary through word study, and using the writing process to compose original stories pervade the books. Each of these strategies has a direct correlation to more effective and efficient reading and writing. Just as manipulatives are critical to mathematics understanding, spelling activities are crucial to the long-term acquisition by students of a significant bank of words they can spell correctly.

Each grade level and each lesson in the series has been thoroughly revised with updated strategies and research-based activities. Every page has been redesigned for readability, instructional flow and sequence, and attractive pictures and illustrations that draw students into and through each lesson.

Purposeful Design Publications, the publishing division of the Association of Christian Schools International, is indebted to a fine team of consultants, editors, and contributors who have invested themselves in this revision project. It was clear from the outset that some of the core concepts of the original spelling series were sound, but this team, backed by extensive research findings, has thoroughly revised these books into an outstanding series.

Your students will be well served by utilizing Purposeful Design Spelling in your classroom. We are certain that it will assist you to produce students who know how to spell, enjoy the activities of learning to spell, and embed in their minds a growing bank of words that support and strengthen vocabulary acquisition and reading skills.

Derek J. Keenan, Ed.D.
Vice President, Academic Affairs

Gentry, J. Richard. 2004 *The Science of Spelling*. Portsmouth, New Hampshire: Heinemann.

Smith, F. 1971 *Understanding Reading: A Psycholinguistic Analysis of Reading and Learning to Read*. New York: Holt, Rinehart and Winston.

Lord, there are many words to spell,
Guide me as I learn them well.
Help me choose the words to write,
So in my work
You'll take delight.
Amen.

Preface

The Purposeful Design Publications Team carefully crafted this revised spelling series with you and your Christian School students in mind. The philosophical underpinnings of this grades 1–6 series are as follows:

The ultimate aim of Christian education is to bring students to a saving knowledge of Jesus Christ, to know His Word, and to live Christianly in right relationship with God and others. Therefore, literacy contributes to a child's spiritual maturity as he or she develops as a reader and a writer, processing the truths of Scripture. Mastery of conventional spelling and word study become critical subsets of the writing branch of literacy, sharpening the student's literacy tools and his/her ability to accurately convey love and truth to others through the written word.

Conventional spelling contributes to the accuracy with which a writer can convey his message. Therefore, this series provides delightfully interesting and varied word study activities for both phonetically-consistent pattern words as well as high-frequency words. Study of phonetically-consistent pattern words supports students' acquisition of spelling generalizations, and study of high-frequency words promotes writing fluency with high-utility words. Writing assignments provide opportunities for learners to apply spelling in context, accurately conveying messages to readers through the encoding process.

Children are unique image bearers of God. Therefore, the learning process must take into account child development, academic strengths and weaknesses, learning styles, learning modalities, and learning rates. The Purposeful Design editorial team has ensured that you have straightforward methods to differentiate the learning process for high achievers, average performers, and struggling learners. Each lesson provides opportunities for high achievers to study challenge words and for struggling learners to receive additional spelling support. Additionally, a website has been developed to provide a plethora of resources to assist you in strategically planning for all learners.

Parents and teachers jointly share the responsibility of the child's education. Therefore, this series provides spelling study activities for both school and home, conceptualizing the training of the child as a partnership between parents and teachers.

Learning should satisfy the God-given curiosity of a child and inspire increased desire for learning. Therefore, the creative design team of Purposeful Design Publications has provided inviting images of God's creation and attractive layouts of student workbook pages and blackline masters. Additionally, the editorial team has carefully crafted lessons to include games, puzzles, stories, poems, and other inspiring, fun activities.

The Purposeful Design Publications Team desires that this series ministers to the educational needs of your students and that spelling becomes a favorite part of their day and your day as students study spelling "their way"—actively and joyfully! May the Lord bless you as you continue to press on in the name of the Lord Jesus Christ, training the next generation of Kingdom writers.

June Hetzel, Ph.D.
Professor of Education
Biola University

Acknowledgments

The Peer Review process is an important step in the development of this textbook series. ACSI and the Purposeful Design staff greatly appreciate the feedback we receive from the schools and teachers who participate. We highly value the efforts and input of these faculty members; their recommendations and suggestions are extremely helpful. The institutions listed below have assisted us in this way.

Calvary Christian Academy, Philadelphia, PA

Cedar Park Christian School, Bothell, WA

Cincinnati Hills Christian Academy, Cincinnati, OH

Colorado Springs Christian Schools, Colorado Springs, CO

Cypress Christian School, Houston, TX

Evangelical Christian Academy, Colorado Springs, CO

Faith Christian Academy, Arvada, CO

Faith Christian School, Rocky Mount, NC

Fresno Christian Schools, Fresno, CA

Greenbrier Christian Academy, Chesapeake, VA

Harvest Christian Academy, Elgin, IL

Jupiter Christian School, Jupiter, FL

Kodiak Christian School, Kodiak, AK

Light and Life Christian School, Escondido, CA

North Cobb Christian School, Kennesaw, GA

North County Christian School, Florissant, MO

North Heights Christian Academy, Roseville, MN

Northwest Christian School, Phoenix, AZ

Oak Park Christian Academy, Oak Park, IL

Rocky Bayou Christian School, Niceville, FL

Santiam Christian School, Corvallis, OR

Schenectady Christian School, Schenectady, NY

Smithtown Christian School, Smithtown, NY

The Pilgrim Academy, Egg Harbor City, NJ

Traders Point Christian Academy, Indianapolis, IN

Tri-City Christian Schools, Vista, CA

Trinity Christian Academy, Jackson, TN

Trinity Christian School, Addison, TX

West Bay Christian Academy, North Kingston, RI

West-Mont Christian Academy, Pottstown, PA

Spelling Series Task Force

June Hetzel, Ph.D.
Biola University

Pam Levicki
St. Stephen's Episcopal Day School

Anne Lichlyter
Evangelical Christian Academy

Victoria Lierheimer
Evergreen Academy

Keith McAdams
Cornerstone University

Rebecca Pennington
Covenant College

Julia Taves
Colorado Springs Christian School

Carolyn Ware
North Cobb Christian School

Amy Young
Rocky Mountain Christian Academy

Using the Teacher and Student Editions

Welcome to Purposeful Design Grade Three Spelling!

We believe that you will enjoy the new format, including beautiful, full-color photographs, well-researched word lists, and teacher-friendly lesson instructions. The curriculum components, comprised of a Teacher Edition, Student Edition, Blackline Masters CD, Color Transparencies, and Posters, are all designed to assist you in engaging and challenging your students to become excellent spellers.

Visit www.acsi.org/~spellingresources for a listing of a wide variety of resources specifically selected to provide you with classroom tools in support of spelling and language arts instruction. Resources listed, although not endorsed by Purposeful Design Publications, are recommended by local educators for supporting grade three spelling.

Grade three of the revised spelling series consists of 36 lessons, primarily using whole-group activities; however, guidance for supporting students who struggle as well as students who are advanced is also included. Each weekly word list lesson is designed for five days, 20–30 minutes of instruction per day. After each five-week set of word list lessons, a review lesson is provided.

Teacher Edition

Each Teacher Edition lesson includes an instructional "Objective," lesson "Introduction," and "Directed Instruction" in a step-by-step format. All the materials needed to teach each lesson are listed in the Lesson Materials. Instructional objectives and lesson content meet the criteria set by state and national language arts standards.

The five-day instructional format of the word list lessons begins with the "Warm Up" (Pretest) on Day 1 and concludes with the "Wrap Up" (Posttest) on Day 5. Day 2 is reserved for "Phonics" instruction, Day 3 for "Word Study," and Day 4 for "Writing." Lesson activities strengthen the students' skills in decoding, encoding, vocabulary, word building, proofreading, and creative word application in daily writing.

The "Warm Up" is an ungraded pretest. Each "Warm Up" assesses current skill levels of individual students, as well as the skills of the entire class, in the context of the list words provided. If your students miss several words on the "Warm Up," more practice will be needed throughout the week. It is important to teach your students to check the accuracy of their own "Warm Up" test so that they strengthen proofreading skills and understand their own error patterns. An extremely helpful tool for spelling practice is "A Spelling Study Strategy" found on a poster (P-1), color transparency (T-1), and blackline master (BLM SP3-01A). "A Spelling Study Strategy" is also found on the inside cover of the Student Edition. Demonstrate the use of the Spelling Study Strategy before beginning Lesson 1.

On weekly "Wrap Ups" (Posttests), students write their spelling words and dictated sentences containing the spelling words. Dictation is an excellent way to integrate auditory and visual memory skills, as well as writing skills and conventions, such as capitalization and punctuation. Dictation also provides a model of a complete sentence. We suggest that you read each sentence slowly, have the students repeat the sentence, and then read it once again before the students begin to write the sentence. It is perfectly acceptable for students to subvocalize as they write. Students take the "Warm Up" and "Wrap Up" tests on their own paper. Score the dictation sentences as a part of the overall grade on the "Wrap Up"; however, the scoring procedure is up to you.

The "Assessment" for each review lesson is given on Day 5. It is cumulative, covering words from the five previous lessons. Each "Assessment" is helpful in preparation for achievement testing since it is in standardized test format; words are presented in the context of a sentence that contains three underlined words, one of which may be misspelled, and a fourth choice of *All correct*. Students fill in the circle below a misspelled word or choose *All correct* if there are no misspellings. To extend each "Assessment," you may choose to have the students rewrite each misspelled word correctly.

The "Student Spelling Support" appears as a sidebar. The "Student Spelling Support" contains suggested activities to extend the spelling lessons, provides additional ideas for different learning styles, and incorporates spelling with other curriculum areas, including biblical worldview. There are writing challenge activities suggested for advanced students as well as suggested literature. You will not be able to use every suggestion listed for each lesson; however, a rich selection of spelling support strategies enables the teacher to pick and choose as he/she carefully crafts activities tailored to student needs. All materials needed for the "Student Spelling Support" are listed in "Student Spelling Support Materials."

One of the "Student Spelling Support" suggestions calls for starting and adding words to a classroom "Word Wall." Develop student-generated "Word Walls," using rimes (e.g., **-en**) or patterns (e.g., /ō/ spelled **ow**). For example, the teacher writes "-en." Then students brainstorm words that rhyme with "-en," such as ten, men, or pen. Students might also brainstorm words with **-en** as the final syllable (e.g., open, glisten, or sunken). Guide students to brainstorm words that follow generalizations (e.g., **hard** and **soft c**), and add these to the Word Wall. Words are posted vertically on the Word Wall to emphasize the pattern. Posting each list of words categorized by pattern is recommended for each lesson.

Word Wall

-en	/ō/ spelled **ow**	**Hard c** and **Soft c**	
open	below	cabin	cities
glisten	follow	clothes	notice
sunken	throw	colorful	advice

Blackline Masters and Other Resources

Each lesson includes one or more blackline masters. You will find the title and other useful information in the upper right-hand corner. The title is in the uppermost box. The second box contains the abbreviation, BLM SP3, followed by the lesson number and a letter. For example, BLM SP3-06C indicates that this blackline master is found in grade three (SP3), lesson six (06), and is the third (C) blackline master in that lesson. Additionally, each blackline master has a circled letter code that indicates the primary use for the blackline. **A** stands for Assessment, **G** for Games, **H** for Homework, **P** for Practice, and **T** for Teacher Tool.

- The blackline masters labeled **A for Assessment** are needed for the Review Assessment. Day 5 of each review lesson indicates the blackline masters needed for the "Assessment."

- The blackline masters labeled **G for Games** provide game boards, game cards, game pieces,

and instructions. These are file folder games and may take some time to assemble the first time you use them. Laminate the games and accessories for durability.

- The blackline masters labeled **H for Homework** provide practice with the skills taught in class. Homework suggestions are given for three nights per week to accommodate evening worship schedules. Prior to each set of five lessons, there is a blackline master listing the words for the next set of five lessons. Add the Challenge Words and test dates before duplicating to inform parents of the words and test dates. Refer to this take-home list as the "fridge" list and remind students that it is to be kept accessible for home study.

- The blackline masters labeled **P for Practice** mirror the concepts and skills taught in the Student Edition. Answers are provided on the blackline master CD.

- The blackline masters labeled **T for Teacher Tools** are to be used as visual aids in instruction. We suggest attaching Teacher Tools to the board, bulletin board, felt board, or classroom wall with magnets, double-sided tape, pushpins, or hook and loop tape.

Color transparencies are coded with *T* plus a number and posters are coded with *P* plus a number for identification. Transparencies and Posters are used in different lessons, and instructions for their use are included in the Teacher Edition.

Student Edition

The theme of grade three is Transportation. Throughout the lessons, students are introduced to various modes of transportation, ranging from simple stilts to manned space flight. These lessons provide an opportunity for you to help your students see how God has blessed them with many inventions in the area of transportation. The ingenuity of these inventions reflects the working principles of nature.

The handwriting styles presented in the lessons include both standard manuscript and cursive forms commonly used in Christian schools. Word lists are presented in a manuscript form on odd-numbered pages; word lists are presented in a standard cursive form on each even-numbered page. Either handwriting form can be viewed by flipping the page or looking at the adjacent page. Please note that most visual memory and recall of spelling words is in manuscript. However, for those schools that have already introduced cursive, these lists can serve as a penmanship model. Students struggling with spelling should study their words exclusively in manuscript. It would be helpful to copy and paste manuscript lists over cursive lists for students with visual perceptual disorders.

Each word list lesson is organized around phonetic or structural generalizations. An understanding of these generalizations will give your students knowledge of the spelling patterns required to spell phonetically-consistent words in their written work. The target generalizations presented in the lessons are found in frames with a compass on the student pages as well as on posters for frequent review. Word lists also incorporate High-Frequency Words. High-Frequency Words seldom follow a phonetic pattern, but are often used in writing. High-Frequency Words were chosen from up-to-date compilations. Lists also include space on the student pages for the assignment of Challenge Words. You may choose Challenge Words based on the phonetic pattern targeted in the lesson, words previously misspelled, or content area words from other subjects you are studying, including reading, science, and Bible. Students are often motivated to spell content words by their interest in those subjects.

"My Words for Writing" is found in the back of the Student and Teacher Editions. In this section, students add Challenge Words that serve as a reference for their writing. Following this section is the "Spelling Dictionary," which is needed for the completion of several student pages. The pronunciation(s), part(s) of speech, definition(s), and sentence(s) are provided for each third grade spelling word.

Pages are perforated so that each lesson may be removed from the Student Edition. A line is provided for students to write their name on the front of each odd-numbered page. Colored boxes at the top of the page highlight the skill(s) practiced on each page. Some of the instructions suggest the use of colored pencils. Although colored pencils are preferred, crayons or markers may be used.

Differentiated Instruction

We have included options for differentiated instruction because no textbook series is "one size fits all." These suggestions for "Differentiated Instruction" include changing the number of spelling words for learners who are either behind or ahead of their peers so as to secure an appropriate level of difficulty for each student.

There are important considerations when spelling is differentiated. The first is clear communication with parents, and the second is evaluation and grading. Parents need to be partners in the differentiation process. Parents need to know which words their child will be responsible for learning and how he or she will be evaluated. We suggest that you hold a meeting early in the school year with parents of students whose skills were below grade level expectations, or who missed more than half of the words on the first two or three spelling list lessons. Let the parents know that students acquire skills at different rates, and that phonetic spelling skills and visual memory skills should improve throughout the third grade year, paralleling developmental progress. Assign more words as each student's progress dictates. Develop a method of communicating with parents which words students need to study (e.g., highlight specific words on the "fridge" lists).

If you have several students who have differentiated lists, a weekly e-mail will keep parents updated. It is also suggested that, if possible, the students attempt to spell every word on the "Warm Up" and "Wrap Up" tests, even though they will be graded only on words that they were assigned. This is not only good practice for the students, but it reduces the chance of students being questioned or ridiculed for having fewer words on their tests. All students should complete every page in the Student Edition in preparation for the weekly "Wrap Up." The "Assessment" for the review lessons is cumulative and has been organized so that the first ten sentences contain the spelling words that have been assigned to students who have reduced word lists.

For students who are ahead of their peers, we suggest that Extra Challenge Words be assigned. The words suggested are taken from the lesson theme and lists of High-Frequency Words that are ranked by usage and grade level. You may use the words suggested, develop your own list from content area study, or invite advanced students to suggest their own Extra Challenge Words. Extra Challenge Words may be written on the "fridge" list or sent home via e-mail. Decide with parents whether or not to include these words in each student's overall spelling grade.

Discuss the evaluation and grading of students who have differentiated lists with your administrator and teammates to provide grade level and/or schoolwide consistency.

Finally, enjoy using Purposeful Design *Spelling Grade Three*. It has been our pleasure to receive teacher input and revise this series to better meet your students' needs. Enjoy the journey.

Preparing a Lesson

Read through the lesson and make notes regarding preparation.

Read the lesson objective so that it is clear in your mind.

Note the materials needed to teach the lesson as well as where and how each item is used.

Read the Transportation theme presented on the sidebar.

Locate definitions of new terms printed in blue italics.

Take note of the suggestions given in the Differentiated Instruction section if you plan to differentiate instruction.

Review the Directed Instruction section to become familiar with the sequence of procedures to follow.

Lesson 9 — Consonant Blends

Student Pages
Pages 33–36

Lesson Materials
BLM SP3-09A
BLMs SP3-09B–C
BLM SP3-09D
Card stock
T-14
BLM SP3-09E
BLM SP3-09F
Encyclopedia
T-15
BLM SP3-09G
BLM SP3-01A
Whiteboards

Transportation
The theme of this lesson is Aircraft Carriers and Submarines. An aircraft carrier is a large ship with a flight deck that supports the takeoff and landing of military aircraft. Submarines are able to stay below the surface of the water for long periods of time without being seen. These naval vessels keep our nation safe in times of war.

Day 1 Warm Up
Objective
The students will accurately spell and write words with **consonant blends**. They will spell and write high-frequency words and challenge words.

Introduction
Before class, select Challenge Words for numbers 21 and 22 from a cross-curricular subject, words misspelled on previous assignments, or words that interest your students. The word *Scripture* has the **blend scr** and is suggested for number 21. Administer the Warm Up. Encourage students to write all the list words to the best of their ability.

Directed Instruction
1 Say each word, use it in a sentence, and then repeat the word.

Pattern Words

1. kept	Sam kept his promise to be ready.	kept
2. clasp	The girls will clasp hands.	clasp
3. craft	Origami is a Japanese paper craft.	craft
4. asks	Marcus always asks good questions.	asks
5. behind	My best friend sits behind me in class.	behind
6. drifted	The boat drifted along the river.	drifted
7. risk	Soldiers risk their lives for their country.	risk
8. interesting	The Bible is the most interesting book.	interesting
9. subtract	Did you subtract to find the difference?	subtract
10. gifts	The wise men brought gifts to Jesus.	gifts
11. facts	Joshua knew his math facts very well.	facts
12. actor	An actor played the part of the king.	actor
13. meant	She never meant to hurt your feelings.	meant
14. except	Everyone is going except Mark.	except
15. speech	Mr. Davis gave a nice speech in chapel.	speech
16. skipper	The skipper commanded the crew.	skipper
17. present	All members of the class were present.	present
18. understand	I cannot understand Spanish.	understand

High-Frequency Words

19. toward	The little dog made its way toward home.	toward
20. finally	We finally finished our math assignments.	finally

Challenge Words
21. _____
22. _____

2 Allow students to self-correct their pretest, following this procedure:
a. Write each word on the board. Discuss the letter/sound relationships in each word. Define *consonant blends* as a group of two or three consonants together in a word or syllable. Each consonant sound is heard in a blend. Blends can come at the beginning, middle, or end of words. The word *interesting* has four syllables and is often misspelled; pronounce each syllable distinctly and have students repeat after you.
b. As a class, read, spell, and read each word again. Direct students to circle misspelled words with a colored pencil and rewrite them correctly.

3 Proof each student's Warm Up. This becomes an individualized study sheet that can be used at school or at home.

34   © Spelling Grade 3

---

4 Homework suggestion: Use **BLM SP3-09A Submarines** to practice the words in this lesson.

Day 2 Phonics
Objective
The students will complete words by writing the missing **consonant blends**. They will write high-frequency words, and replace letters with **consonant blends** to make list words.

Introduction
Before class, duplicate one copy of **BLMs SP3-09B–C Lesson 9 Spelling Words I, II** and **BLM SP3-09D Sorting Mat** on CARD STOCK for each student. The High-Frequency and Challenge Words are not needed for this activity. The word *understand* can be sorted under **st** and/or **nd**. *Interesting* cannot be sorted under **nt** because *n* and *t* are in separate syllables. Provide the students with a second flash card of *understand* by writing *understand* on an empty flash card. Cut the flash cards apart. Place **T-14 Lesson 9 Sorting** on the overhead. The **consonant blends cl, cr, tr, dr,** and **pr** are shown on the side of a submarine. Have volunteers draw a line from each blend to a word that has that blend. In the lower portion of the transparency, the **consonant blends sk, nd, nt, st, ft, ct, sp,** and **pt** are shown. Pronounce each consonant blend and draw students' attention to exercises 6–13. Ask a volunteer to read the words and find the blend that is the same in each exercise. Write the blend on the line. Refer to **BLM SP5-09E T-14 Answer Key**. Remove the transparency before distributing the flash cards and a sorting mat for each student to place on his/her desktop. Allow students to sort the flash cards. The sorting mat focuses on the following blends: **sk, nd, nt, st, ft, ct, sp, pt.**

Directed Instruction
1 Proceed to page 33. Say, spell, and say each Pattern and High-Frequency Word. Provide this week's Challenge Words and have students write them in the spaces provided. Clap out the syllables in each word. Ask volunteers to tell you which words have one, two, three, or four syllables.

Differentiated Instruction
- For students who spelled all the words correctly on the Warm Up, select and assign three Extra Challenge Words from the following list: submarine, aircraft, scheme, specialize, dangerous, Colossians.
- For students who spelled less than half correctly, assign the following Pattern and High-Frequency Words: asks, facts, craft, meant, behind, present, subtract, understand, finally, toward. On the Wrap Up, evaluate these students on the ten words assigned; however, encourage them to attempt to spell all the list words to the best of their ability. They are also responsible for writing the dictated sentences.

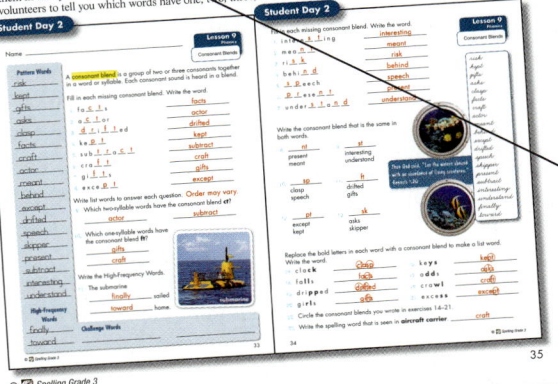

Look at the Student Spelling Support section of suggested activities to extend the spelling lessons, provide additional ideas for different learning styles, and incorporate spelling with other curriculum areas, including biblical worldview.

Note the blackline masters, posters, and color transparencies provided.

Look at the lesson Introduction for ways to engage the students' interest in the lesson.

Prepare the classroom for the activity noted in the lesson Introduction.

Use the suggestions listed for assessment to monitor student progress.

Use the answers provided on the reduced student pages for correction and evaluation of student work.

Student Spelling Support Materials

BLMs SP3-09B–C
Card stock
BLM SP3-01A
Ping-pong balls
Empty milk carton

Student Spelling Support

1. Write this week's words categorized by patterns on a large piece of paper and attach to the Word Wall.
2. Duplicate **BLMs SP3-09B–C Lesson 9 Spelling Words I and II** on CARD STOCK for students to use as flash cards at school or at home.
3. Use **BLM SP3-01A A Spelling Study Strategy** in instructional groups to provide assistance with some or all of the words.
4. Assist students in writing the Challenge Words, numbers 21 and 22, in the section called My Words for Writing, in the back of their textbook.
5. For kinesthetic learners, play Spell and Roll with two teams or two players. You will need a list of the Pattern Words in this lesson, 13 PING-PONG BALLS, and a clean, EMPTY MILK CARTON. Open one end of the milk carton. Use a black marker to write each of the following **consonant blends** on a ping-pong ball: **sk, nd, nt, st, ft, ct, sp, pt, cl, cr, tr, dr, pr.** Place the ping-pong balls on the carpet in a line about a yard away from the milk carton with the open end facing the line of ping-pong balls. Say one of the Pattern Words, allow the student to spell the word, and identify a consonant blend in the word.
Cont. on page 37

2 Allow students to supply the missing blends, write the words, and answer the questions independently. In exercise 11, students write the High-Frequency Words to complete a sentence.
3 Proceed to page 34. In exercises 1–7, students write the missing blends to complete words. They write the blend common to two words in 8–13. Students replace bold letters with **consonant blends** to make Pattern Words in 14–21. Select a volunteer to read the verse on the page.
4 Homework suggestion: Use **BLM SP3-09F Sorting Consonant Blends** to review **consonant blends** and High-Frequency Words.

Day 3 Word Study
Objective
The students will write a word to match each definition or description. They will use the context of a sentence to determine the meaning of a list word and use the words to complete cloze sentences.

Introduction
Write the list words *speech, facts, understand, drifted, craft,* and *gifts* to one side of the board and the following definitions in another area of the board:
- a talk given to a group (**speech**)
- things known to be true (**facts**)
- things given as presents (**gifts**)
- floated along (**drifted**)
- a type of artwork often made with paper (**craft**)
- grasp the meaning of something (**understand**)

Read the definitions and invite students to tell you a word that fits each definition. Remind students that words may have more than one definition and that the Spelling Dictionary can help them to determine the appropriate definition for the word they want to use.

Directed Instruction
1 Write the following sentence on the board:
- The soldier will <u>risk</u> his life to save others.
Read the sentence. Explain that the meaning of the underlined word can be learned from the context of the sentence. *Risk* in this context means to take a dangerous chance. Ask a volunteer to tell what *risk* means and use it in an original sentence.
2 Proceed to page 35. Read the directions and let students know that they may use the Spelling Dictionary for help with any unknown words. Remind students that antonyms are opposites. Define *periscope* before students complete the page.

Day 4 Writing
Objective
The students will sequence a series of notes taken from an encyclopedia article.

Introduction
Display an ENCYCLOPEDIA. Explain that information found in encyclopedia articles is nonfiction material. Encyclopedias give facts about a number of different subjects. Diagrams may be used to add information or assist in understanding the facts. Many subjects can be found listed alphabetically in various volumes within a set of encyclopedias. Taking notes from encyclopedia articles helps to prepare for a written report.

Directed Instruction
1 Place **T-15 Encyclopedia Article** on the overhead. This transparency is a partial replica of student page 36. Read the article together. Ask, "What is the first thing that has to happen before the submarine dives?" Number and record the response on the transparency below the text.

36

Continue, "Then what happens?" Continue the list on the transparency. Refer to **BLM SP3-09G T-15 Answer Key.** Remove the transparency.
2 Proceed to page 36. Choose a volunteer to read the directions. Point out that there is an order to the events involved in a submarine's dive and rise that makes sense. Encourage students to read the entire text before attempting to order the sentences in Steven's notes.
3 Homework suggestion: Read the submarine text on page 36 to an adult. Take a practice spelling test at home or use **BLM SP3-01A A Spelling Study Strategy** for additional practice.

Day 5 Wrap Up
Objective
The students will correctly write dictated spelling words and sentences.

Introduction
Provide a review, utilizing WHITEBOARDS or Student Spelling Support suggestions.

Directed Instruction
1 Dictate the list words by using the Warm Up sentences or developing original ones. Reserve *craft, subtract,* and *finally* for the dictation sentences.
2 Follow this procedure for the dictation sentences: read the sentence, invite the class to say the sentence with you, then read the sentence again. Dictate the following sentences:
- Jane made a <u>craft</u> from paper and string.
- I will <u>subtract</u> five from ten.
- The lost dog <u>finally</u> reached his home.
3 If assigned, dictate Extra Challenge Words.
4 Score the test, counting each misspelled word as an error. Correct the dictation sentences as follows: grade only the spelling words or grade the complete sentences, including capitalization and punctuation.

Student Spelling Support
Cont. from page 36

If the student correctly spells the word and identifies the blend, allow him/her to get down on hands and knees and blow the ping-pong ball with the matching blend into the milk carton. Follow the same procedure for the other team/player. Continue until all the words or ping-pong balls have been used. The winner is the team or player who has blown the most ping-pong balls into the milk carton.

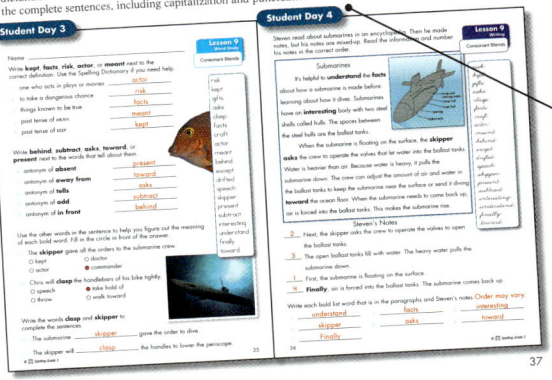

37

A Spelling Study Strategy

Teacher Note: Instruct students in the use of **A Spelling Study Strategy** prior to Lesson 1.

Display the poster.

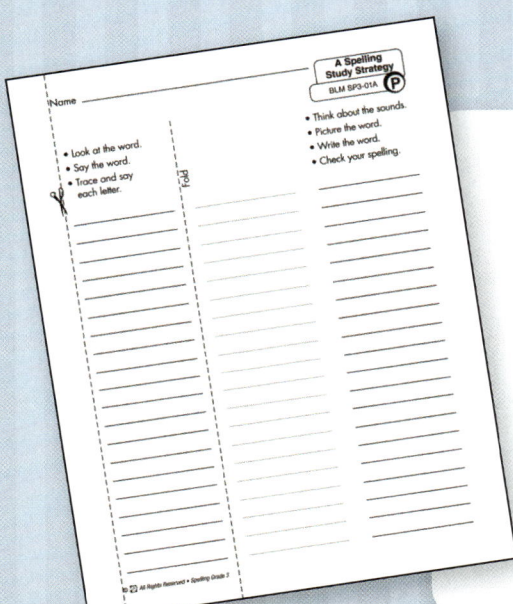

Duplicate one copy of **BLM SP3-01A A Spelling Study Strategy** for each student. Write *legs, skill, crush, jacket,* and *wobble* in the left-hand column. Model each step.

- Look at the first spelling word, say it, and then trace and say each letter.
- Fold the paper.
- Think about the sounds in the word, picture the word in your mind, and write the word.
- Unfold the paper.
- Use a colored pencil for checking and making corrections. If a word is misspelled, direct students to circle it, go back to the first column, retrace the word, and write it in the faded column.

Consonants and Short Vowels

Student Pages

Pages 1–4

Lesson Materials

BLM SP3-01B
BLM SP3-01C
P-3
BLM SP3-01D
P-11
T-2
BLM SP3-01A
Whiteboards

Transportation

Lessons 1–5 utilize the theme of different modes of people-powered transportation. Lesson 1 begins with Scooters, Pogo Sticks, and Stilts. Children have been getting around on some of these people-powered devices for over one hundred years. Entertainers have delighted crowds by walking on stilts. Scooters and pogo sticks have been enjoying a surge in popularity in recent years.

Day 1 Warm Up

Objective

The students will accurately spell and write words with **consonants and short vowels**, high-frequency words, and challenge words.

Introduction

The Warm Up (Pretest) is an ungraded assessment to assist students in studying the list words—Pattern, High-Frequency, and Challenge. To meet your students' needs, select Challenge Words from a cross-curricular subject, common misspellings for third graders, or words that interest your students. The word *saddle* has **short a** in the first syllable and is suggested for number 21. Encourage students to position their paper properly, hold their pencil correctly, and sit with correct posture. Explain that they are to attempt to write all the spelling words. If they cannot spell a particular word, they should try to write down all the letters that they hear. Students take the Warm Up on their own paper.

Directed Instruction

1 Use the sentences that follow or develop original ones.

2 Say each word, use it in a sentence, and then repeat the word.

Pattern Words

1. hundred	A century is one <u>hundred</u> years.	hundred
2. wobble	The baby may <u>wobble</u> when learning to walk.	wobble
3. pocket	My <u>pocket</u> has a hole in it.	pocket
4. gutter	Water filled the <u>gutter</u>.	gutter
5. jacket	Antonio zipped his <u>jacket</u> before leaving.	jacket
6. block	Can you ride around the <u>block</u> on a scooter?	block
7. crush	Please don't <u>crush</u> the pages of your book.	crush
8. stilts	Akeelah learned to walk on <u>stilts</u>.	stilts
9. skill	It takes lots of <u>skill</u> to juggle.	skill
10. led	Don <u>led</u> the class in a prayer.	led
11. address	My <u>address</u> includes the zip code.	address
12. matter	No <u>matter</u> what happens, trust God.	matter
13. yellow	<u>Yellow</u> is a light color.	yellow
14. tennis	You'll need a racket to play <u>tennis</u>.	tennis
15. never	Jesus will <u>never</u> leave you nor forsake you.	never
16. stick	Anita used a <u>stick</u> to hit the piñata.	stick
17. legs	His <u>legs</u> were strong and muscular.	legs
18. sniff	The puppy began to <u>sniff</u> its food.	sniff

High-Frequency Words

19. during	Nicodemus came to Jesus <u>during</u> the night.	during
20. eye	If dirt gets in your <u>eye</u>, do not rub it.	eye

Challenge Words

21. _____ **(Insert your choice.)**
22. _____ **(Insert your choice.)**

3 Allow students to self-correct their pretest, following this procedure:

   a. Write each word on the board. Discuss the letter/sound relationships in each word. Point out the short vowel spellings in each word. Remind students that in words with double consonants, the double consonants make only one sound. The word *address* is used as a noun and is pronounced /'a dres/.

b. As a class, read, spell, and read each word. Direct students to circle misspelled words with a colored pencil and rewrite them correctly.

4 Proof each student's Warm Up. This becomes an individualized study sheet that can be used at school or at home.

5 Add the Challenge Words and Test Dates before distributing a copy of **BLM SP3-01B Lessons 1–5 Spelling Lists** to each student for home study.

6 Homework suggestion: Use **BLM SP3-01C Poems** for extra practice with the double **consonant** and **short vowel** spellings in this lesson.

Day 2 Phonics

Objective
The students will sort short vowel words by vowel sound. They will write rhyming words and add missing letters to complete words. They will write high-frequency words.

Introduction
Third graders are developing their skills by spelling multisyllable words. Define a *syllable* as <u>a word or part of a word with one vowel sound</u>. Review the short vowel sounds. Write each vowel on the board. Ask volunteers to say the name of the letter, to pronounce the short vowel sound, and provide an example of a word having that sound; *a* makes the /a/ sound in *ant*.

Directed Instruction
Teacher Note: In the student edition, statements about phonetic or structural principles appear in a frame with a compass. While it is appropriate to refer to these statements as rules, they are actually generalizations that are true in most cases, but not all cases. The rules are found on student edition pages as well as on the posters.

1 Proceed to page 1. Define the following categories of words: Pattern Words—words with similar spellings or sounds; High-Frequency Words—words used often in writing and do not always follow a pattern; and Challenge Words—words that may be harder to spell. Say, spell, and say each Pattern and High-Frequency Word. Provide this week's

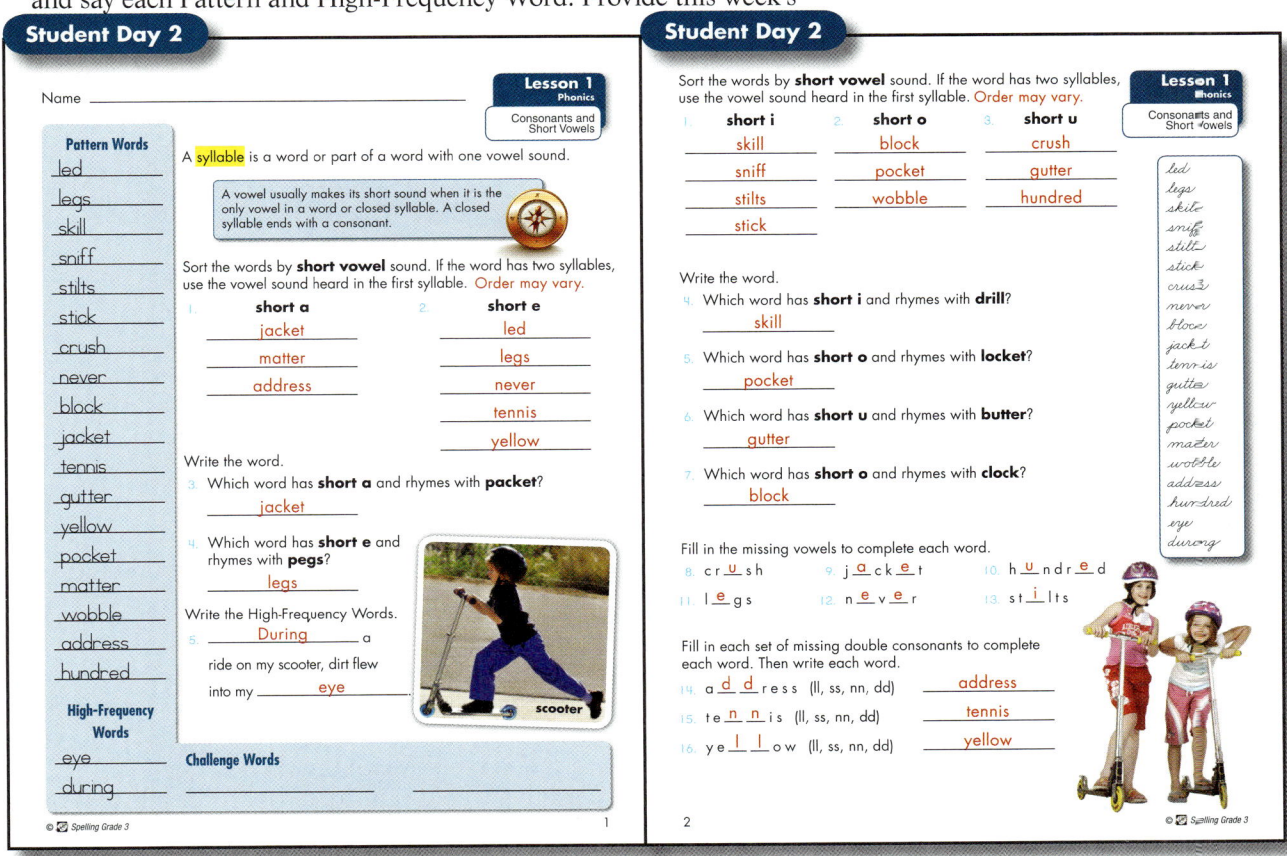

2 Direct students' attention to the definition of a syllable at the top of the page. Explain that one-syllable words have one vowel sound, and two-syllable words have two vowel sounds, one for each syllable. Use *led*, *legs*, *pocket*, and *yellow* to demonstrate this by pronouncing each word and having students hold up one finger for each vowel sound heard.

3 Display **P-3 Spelling Rules**, and read the following rule: A vowel usually makes its short sound when it is the only vowel in a word or closed syllable. A closed syllable ends with a consonant (rule number 1). Words that follow this rule are spelled in a CVC pattern—a short vowel between two consonants or consonant sounds. Choose volunteers to give examples of spelling words with a short vowel sound in the first syllable. Allow students to complete the page, including the High-Frequency Words.

4 Proceed to page 2. In exercises 1–7, students sort by short vowel pattern and complete rhymes. In exercises 8–16, they add the missing letters.

5 Homework suggestion: Use **BLM SP3-01D Riddles** to practice the words in this lesson.

Day 3 Word Study

Objective

The students will complete a cloze activity involving two missing words in each sentence, determine the definitions of spelling words, and divide words into syllables between unlike consonants or double consonants.

Introduction

Display **P-11 Syllables** to discuss the following syllabication generalizations:
- Divide after a consonant or consonant sound in a closed syllable (example number 1). Write *hundred*, *jacket*, and *pocket* on the board and solicit volunteers to make a vertical line between syllables. (**hun|dred, jack|et, pock|et**)
- Divide between double consonants (example number 2). Write *tennis*, *gutter*, and *wobble* on the board. Have volunteers divide these words between the double consonants. (**ten|nis, gut|ter, wob|ble**)

Be sure students understand that words with only one vowel sound, such as *sniff*, are one-syllable words and cannot be divided into syllables.

Directed Instruction

1 Proceed to page 3. Choose a volunteer to read the directions. Explain that a *cloze activity* consists of a sentence or passage with a blank(s). In exercises 1–4, each sentence has two blanks; stress the importance of completing the first blank correctly before proceeding to the second blank. Instruct students to read each completed sentence.

2 In exercises 5–7, students read each sentence and find the group of words that have the same meaning as the bold word. Students divide words into syllables in exercises 8–13. Provide guidance as needed. Encourage students to refer to **P-11 Syllables**.

Day 4 Writing

Objective

The students will write the spelling words that best complete a passage written in a cloze format.

Introduction

Display **T-2 People-Powered Transportation** on the overhead projector. Say, "Let's talk about transportation—ways of going from place to place. Many kinds of transportation are powered by motors, but people-powered transportation is still very important today." Ask, "Which kind of transportation would you like to try? Which is best to go around the block?" Record several responses on the board.

Student Spelling Support Materials

BLMs SP3-01E–F
Card stock
T-1
Whiteboards
Letter tiles
BLM Parent Letter
P-2

Student Spelling Support

1. Make a Word Wall using this week's spelling words. Categorize the words by phonograms or short vowel sounds, write them on a large piece of paper, and attach to the wall. Posting words by patterns helps students internalize generalizations.

a	**e**	**i**
jacket	led	skill
matter	legs	sniff
address	never	stilts
	tennis	stick
	yellow	

o	**u**
block	crush
pocket	gutter
wobble	hundred

2. Duplicate **BLMs SP3-01E–F Lesson 1 Spelling Words I** and **II** on CARD STOCK for students to use as flash cards at school or at home.

3. Use **T-1 A Spelling Study Strategy** for students who demonstrate the need for additional practice with some or all of the words. Write the words in the left-hand column, place on the overhead, and model the steps of learning to spell a word.

4. Assist students in writing the Challenge Words, numbers 21 and 22, in the section called My Words for Writing, in the back of their textbook.

Cont. on page 5

Directed Instruction

1 Proceed to page 4 and select a volunteer to read the directions. Students determine the list word that best completes each sentence and write those words on the lines with the corresponding numbers.

2 Lead a discussion of the questions at the bottom of the page. Allow time for students to put their answers in writing.

3 Homework suggestion: Read the journal entry on page 4 to an adult. Take a practice spelling test at home or use **BLM SP3-01A A Spelling Study Strategy** for additional practice.

Day 5 Wrap Up

Objective

The students will correctly write dictated spelling words and sentences.

Introduction

Provide a review, utilizing WHITEBOARDS or Student Spelling Support suggestions.

Directed Instruction

1 Dictate the list words by using the Warm Up sentences or developing original ones. Reserve *sniff*, *never*, and *hundred* for the dictation sentences.

2 Follow this procedure for the dictation sentences: read the sentence, invite the class to say the sentence with you, then read the sentence again. Dictate the following sentences:
- The shy puppy will <u>sniff</u> my hand.
- You must <u>never</u> forget that God loves you.
- One <u>hundred</u> is ten times ten.

3 If assigned, dictate Extra Challenge Words.

4 Score the test, counting each misspelled word as an error. Correct the dictation sentences as follows: grade only the spelling words or grade the complete sentences, including capitalization and punctuation.

Student Spelling Support

Cont. from page 4

5. For auditory learners, practice phoneme sequencing. A *phoneme* is <u>the smallest phonetic unit with a distinct sound</u>. Dictate each Pattern Word by saying only the phonemes, for example, /l//e//d/. Invite students to write each word on their WHITEBOARD or build each word with LETTER TILES.

6. Provide a copy of the **BLM Parent Letter** for each student to take home. This will inform parents about their child's spelling class

7. Display **P-2 High-Frequency Words** for students to reference when writing.

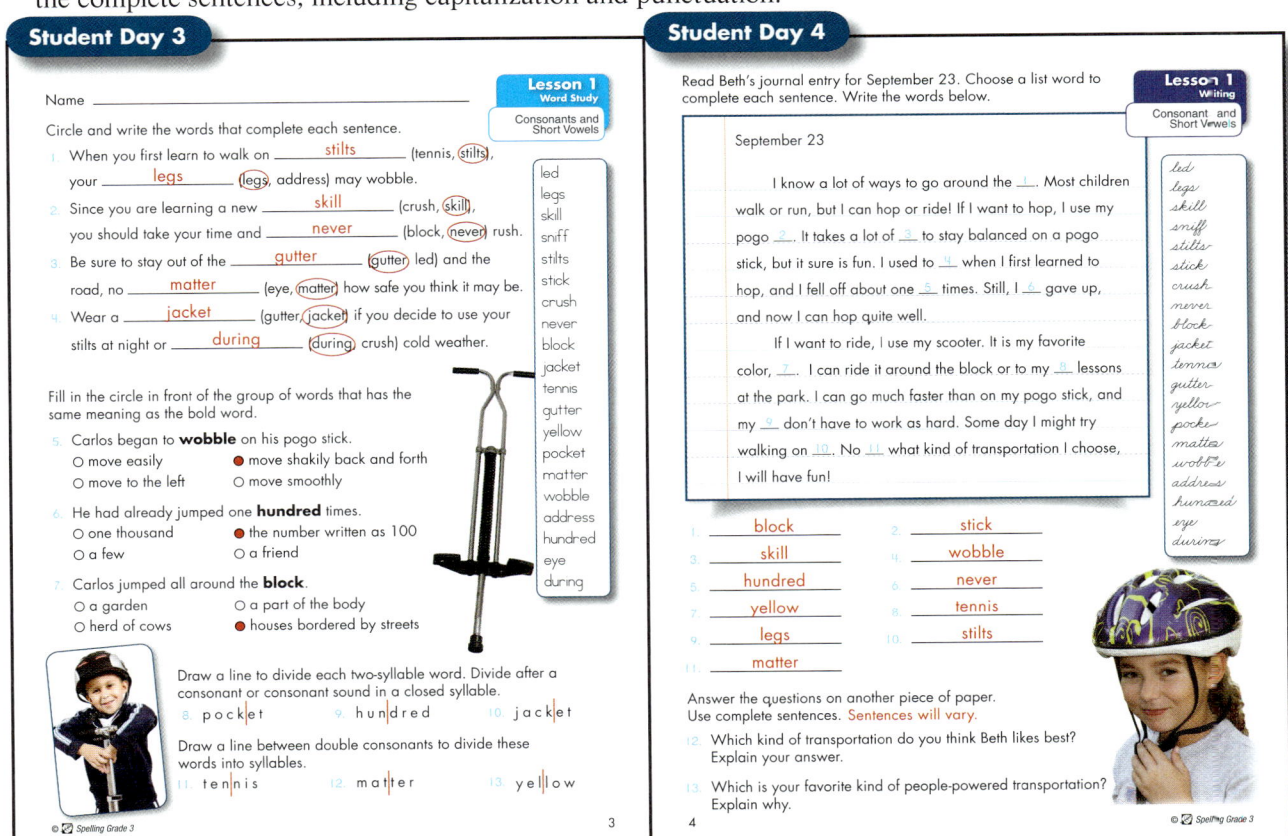

© *Spelling Grade 3*

Student Pages
Pages 5–8

Lesson Materials

B_M SP3-02A
P-3
P-4
B_M SP3-02B
P-11
5' × 8" Index cards
T-3
Transparency Pen
B_M SP3-02C
B_M SP3-01A
Whiteboards

Transportation

The theme of this lesson is Skates and Skateboards. Roller skates initially began as in-line skates but later developed into quad skates. In the 1980s, in-line skates made a comeback. Skateboards got their design from surfboards. In the 1950s surfers realized they could simulate their technique on two-by-four pieces of wood and roller skate wheels.

Day 1 Warm Up

Objective

The students will accurately spell and write words with **long a**. They will spell and write high-frequency words and challenge words.

Introduction

The Warm Up (Pretest) is an ungraded assessment to assist students in studying the Pattern, High-Frequency, and Challenge Words. To meet your students' needs, select Challenge Words from a cross-curricular subject or words misspelled on previous assignments. The word *quake* has **long a** spelled a_e and is suggested for number 21. Remind students of proper posture and check for correct positioning of their paper. Explain that they are to attempt to write all the spelling words. If they cannot spell a particular word, they should try to write down all the letters that they hear.

Directed Instruction

1 Use the sentences that follow or develop original ones.

2 Say each word, use it in a sentence, and then repeat the word.

Pattern Words

1. eighty	Grandpa Brown is <u>eighty</u> years old.	eighty
2. playing	Jeanie enjoys <u>playing</u> the piano.	playing
3. acorn	An <u>acorn</u> can grow into a big oak tree.	acorn
4. they	Mom and Dad said that <u>they</u> were tired.	they
5. safety	It is important to wear a <u>safety</u> helmet.	safety
6. mistake	Mike had one <u>mistake</u> on his math test.	mistake
7. lady	The nice <u>lady</u> smiled at me.	lady
8. explain	Will you <u>explain</u> how to do this?	explain
9. neighbor	God's Word tells us to love our <u>neighbor</u>.	neighbor
10. delay	The storm caused a <u>delay</u> to our trip.	delay
11. break	"Did you <u>break</u> this cup?" asked Phil.	break
12. skateboard	Billy likes to ride on his <u>skateboard</u>.	skateboard
13. afraid	When I am <u>afraid</u>, I will trust God.	afraid
14. maybe	<u>Maybe</u> it will rain today.	maybe
15. forgave	Mindy <u>forgave</u> Anna for telling a lie.	forgave
16. training	An athlete spends hours in <u>training</u>.	training
17. steak	The <u>steak</u> tasted delicious.	steak
18. weigh	Do you know how much you <u>weigh</u>?	weigh

High-Frequency Words

19. months	How many <u>months</u> equal one year?	months
20. because	We love God <u>because</u> He first loved us.	because

Challenge Words

21. _____ (Insert your choice.)
22. _____ (Insert your choice.)

3 Allow students to self-correct their pretest, following this procedure:

a. Write each word on the board. Discuss the letter/sound relationships in each word. Point out the **long a** spelling patterns—a, a_e, ai, ay, ea, eigh, ey—and circle each one in the Pattern Words.

b. As a class, read, spell, and read each word. Direct students to circle misspelled words with a colored pencil and rewrite them correctly.

4 Proof each student's Warm Up. This becomes an individualized study sheet that can be used at school or at home.

5 Homework suggestion: Distribute a copy of **BLM SP3-02A Skateboards** to each student to review **long a** spelling patterns.

Day 2 Phonics

Objective
The students will accurately sort and write words that contain spellings for **long a**, identify other words with the same **long a** sound, and write high-frequency words.

Introduction
Write the following **long a** spellings and Pattern Words on the board. Choose volunteers to circle the **long a** pattern in each word. (Keep this chart on the board for use later.)

<u>a_e</u>	<u>ai</u>	<u>ay</u>	<u>a</u>	<u>ea</u>	<u>eigh</u>	<u>ey</u>
safety	afraid	delay	lady	steak	weigh	they
forgave	explain	maybe	acorn	break	eighty	
mistake	training	playing			neighbor	
skateboard						

Directed Instruction

1 Display **P-3 Spelling Rules** to teach the following rule: A vowel is usually long when it is followed by one **consonant** and **silent e** (rule number 2). *Safety* is an example of an **a_e** word.

2 Display **P-4 Spelling Rules** to teach the following rule: A vowel is usually long when it is followed by another vowel. The second vowel is silent (rule number 3). *Afraid* and *delay* are examples. Point out the position of **ai** in *afraid* and *explain* and **ay** in *delay* and *playing*. In the spelling pattern **ay**, the letter *y* is a silent vowel that makes the letter *a* say its long sound. Note that the **ai** and **ay** spellings follow rule number 3, but **ea**, **eigh**, and **ey** do not follow this rule.

3 Share the following rule: A vowel usually makes its long sound when it is

Differentiated Instruction

Differentiating spelling instruction is an option to consider.
- For students who spelled all the words correctly on the Warm Up, select and assign three Extra Challenge Words from the following list: quad, technique, brochure, embarrass, appreciative, Philippians.
- For students who spelled less than half correctly, assign the following Pattern and High-Frequency Words: they, lady, steak, eighty, acorn, playing, mistake, training, months, because. On the Wrap Up (Posttest), evaluate these students on the ten words assigned; however, encourage them to attempt to spell all the list words to the best of their ability. They are also responsible for writing the dictated sentences.

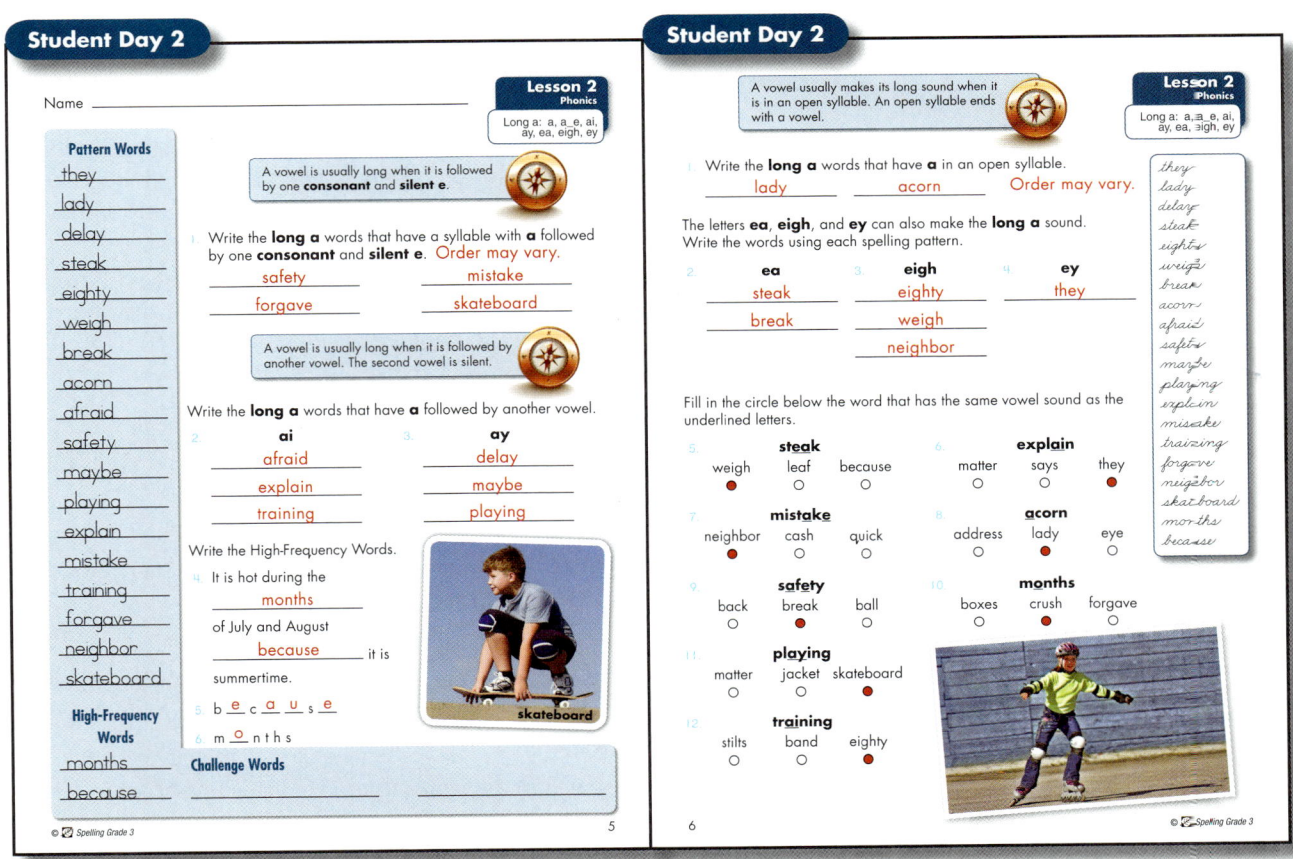

in an open syllable. An open syllable ends with a vowel (rule number 4). Divide *lady* and *acorn* into syllables. Point to the letter *a* in *lady*, explaining that **long a** is heard at the end of the first syllable, which makes it an open syllable. Relate that *a* in *acorn* is a syllable all by itself. Be aware that the first *a* in *afraid* is pronounced /ə/.

4 Ask if **ea**, **eigh**, and **ey** come at the beginning, middle, or end of the words in the chart on the board. (**ea—middle; eigh—beginning, middle, end; ey—end**)

5 Proceed to page 5. Say, spell, and say each Pattern and High-Frequency Word. Provide this week's Challenge Words and have students write them in the spaces provided.

6 Select a volunteer to read the directions aloud. Answer any questions before allowing students to complete the page independently.

7 Proceed to page 6. Provide assistance as students complete the page.

8 Homework suggestion: Distribute a copy of **BLM SP3-02B Word Switch** to each student to practice writing words with **long a**.

Day 3 Word Study

Objective

The students will divide **long a** words with prefixes and compound words into syllables, alphabetize groups of words, and write homophones.

Introduction

Write *maybe*, *forgave*, and *skateboard* on the board. Draw a vertical line between the two smaller words within each compound word and explain that compound words are divided between each word part. Refer to **P-11 Syllables** to reinforce the following generalization: Divide between two smaller words in a compound word (example number 3). Write *be-*, *de-*, *ex-*, and *mis-* on the board and relate that they are prefixes. Teach the following generalization: Divide between a prefix and a base word (example number 4). Write *because*, *delay*, *explain*, and *mistake* on the board. Have students divide the words into syllables.

Directed Instruction

1 Before class, write the following words on 5" x 8" INDEX CARDS: afraid, acorn, ankle. Select three volunteers to come to the front of the room, distribute the cards in the order listed above, and have students hold the cards for the class to read. Lead students to alphabetize the words by the second letter since all the words begin with the same letter. Underlining the second letter will assist with focus.

2 Define homophones as words that sound the same but have different meanings and spellings. Write the following sentences on the board and select volunteers to find the homophones:
- I like to see a pretty sunset over the sea. (**see, sea**)
- Do you write with your right or left hand? (**write, right**)

3 Proceed to page 7. Allow students to complete the page independently.

Day 4 Writing

Objective

The students will complete a graphic organizer by circling list words in given sentences and writing about skateboard safety tips.

Introduction

Ask students if they have a skateboard or have ever ridden on one. Select a few students to give a short description of their skateboard experience.

Directed Instruction

1 Display **T-3 Parts of a Skateboard**. Explain that this is a graphic organizer showing how the different parts fit together to make a skateboard. A *graphic organizer* is a drawing that shows how words or ideas fit together.

2 Read each sentence and select volunteers to choose the word that best completes the sentences. Solicit a volunteer to dictate a sentence about skateboard wheels. Write the sentence on the overhead using a TRANSPARENCY PEN. Refer to **BLM SP3-02C T-3 Answer Key**.

3 Proceed to page 8 and allow students to work independently.

4 Homework suggestion: Read the graphic organizer on page 8 to an adult. Take a practice spelling test at home or use **BLM SP3-01A A Spelling Study Strategy** for additional practice.

Day 5 Wrap Up

Objective

The students will correctly write dictated spelling words and sentences.

Introduction

Provide a review, utilizing WHITEBOARDS or Student Spelling Support suggestions.

Directed Instruction

1 Dictate the list words by using the Warm Up sentences or developing original ones. Reserve *they*, *steak*, and *training* for the dictation sentences.

2 Follow this procedure for the dictation sentences: read the sentence, invite the class to say the sentence with you, then read the sentence again. Dictate the following sentences:
- They saw a hundred birds flying in the sky.
- Derek ate a steak for dinner.
- Pam is training to become a nurse.

3 If assigned, dictate Extra Challenge Words.

4 Score the test, counting each misspelled word as an error. Correct the dictation sentences as follows: grade only the spelling words or grade the complete sentences, including capitalization and punctuation.

Notes

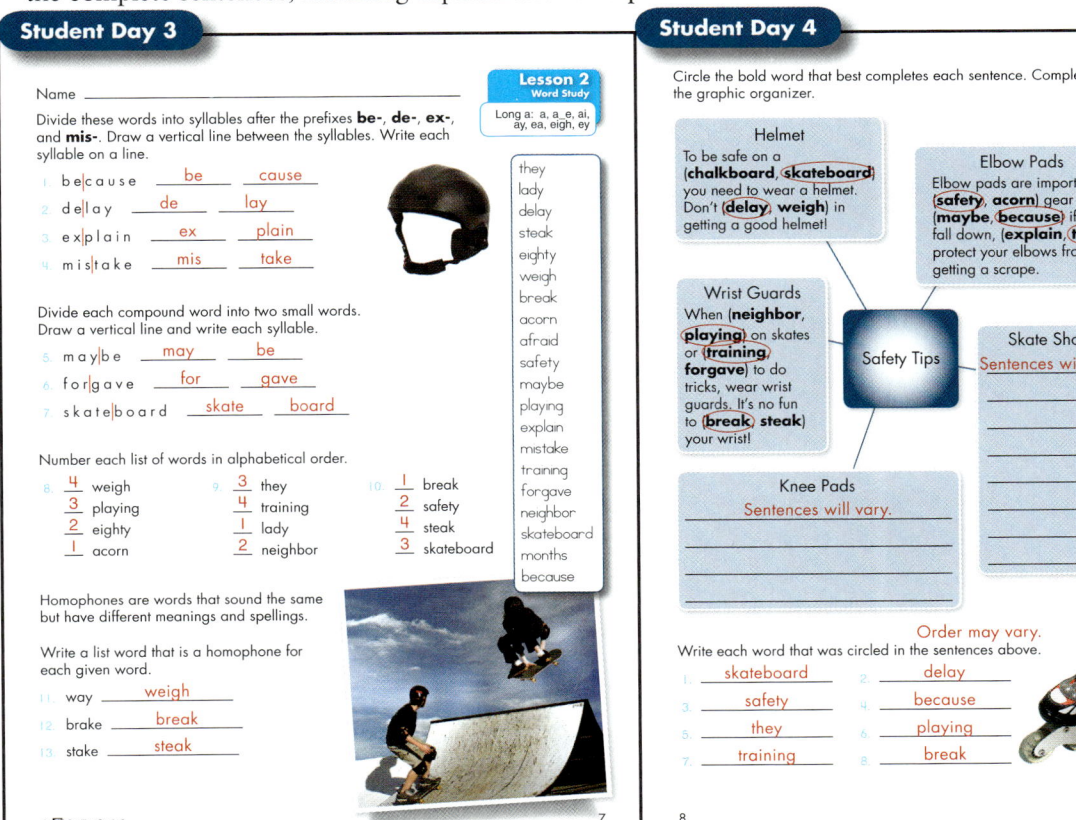

Long e: ea, ee, ei

Student Pages

Pages 9–12

Lesson Materials

BLM SP3-03A
BLMs SP3-03B–C
Card stock
P-4
P-5
BLM SP3-03D
Tennis shoes
T-4
BLM SP3-01A
Whiteboards

Transportation

The theme of this lesson is Running. Running is an excellent way to stay in shape and to do something fun outdoors. When running, one should wear comfortable clothes, have a good pair of running shoes, and warm up thoroughly to prevent muscle injuries.

Day 1 Warm Up

Objective

The students will accurately spell and write words with **long e** spelled **ea**, **ee**, and **ei**. They will spell and write high-frequency words and challenge words.

Introduction

The Warm Up (Pretest) is an ungraded assessment to assist students in studying the Pattern, High-Frequency, and Challenge Words. To meet your students' needs, select Challenge Words from a cross-curricular subject or words misspelled on previous assignments. The word *breathe* has **long e** spelled **ea** and is suggested for number 21. Remind students of proper posture and check for correct positioning of their paper. Explain that they are to attempt to write all the spelling words. If they cannot spell a particular word, they should try to write down all the letters that they hear.

Directed Instruction

1 Use the sentences that follow or develop original ones.

2 Say each word, use it in a sentence, and then repeat the word.

Pattern Words

1. street	Rose walked across the <u>street</u>.	street
2. easy	The math problem was very <u>easy</u>.	easy
3. queen	Do you know the name of the <u>queen</u>?	queen
4. leaf	Emilio found a beautiful oak <u>leaf</u>.	leaf
5. between	Can you run <u>between</u> the cones?	between
6. breeze	The cool <u>breeze</u> felt wonderful.	breeze
7. jeans	Alyssa bought a new pair of <u>jeans</u>.	jeans
8. speed	The track team ran at a good <u>speed</u>.	speed
9. deceive	It is not good to <u>deceive</u> anyone.	deceive
10. eager	Sean was <u>eager</u> to begin his project.	eager
11. steep	The hiking trail was very <u>steep</u>.	steep
12. beat	Will Tara <u>beat</u> the other contestants?	beat
13. receive	Ian will <u>receive</u> a trophy for first place.	receive
14. cleaned	The volunteers <u>cleaned</u> up after the race.	cleaned
15. please	Could you <u>please</u> help me lift the box?	please
16. reach	Paula will <u>reach</u> the end of the trail soon.	reach
17. mean	Do not be <u>mean</u> to your friends.	mean
18. really	I <u>really</u> wanted to buy the gift.	really

High-Frequency Words

19. said	Jesus <u>said</u> to love one another.	said
20. says	The sign <u>says</u>, "Keep out!"	says

Challenge Words

21. _____ **(Insert your choice.)**
22. _____ **(Insert your choice.)**

3 Allow students to self-correct their pretest, following this procedure:

a. Write each word on the board. Discuss the letter/sound relationships in each word. Point out the **long e** spelling pattern—ea, ee, ei—in each Pattern Word.

b. As a class, read, spell, and read each word. Direct students to circle misspelled words with a colored pencil and rewrite them correctly.

4 Proof each student's Warm Up. This becomes an individualized study sheet that can be used at school or at home.

5 Homework suggestion: Use **BLM SP3-03A Shoelaces** to review the **long e** spellings of **ea**, **ee**, and **ei**.

Day 2 Phonics

Objective
The students will correctly sort words by **long e** spellings of **ea**, **ee**, and **ei**. They will write words with two syllables, words that rhyme, and high-frequency words.

Introduction
Before class, duplicate one copy each of **BLMs SP3-03B–C Lesson 3 Spelling Words I** and **II** on CARD STOCK, cut the cards apart, and place them facedown in a pile. Write the following column headings on the board: ea, ee, ei, no long e. Select a word card, dictate the word, and return the card to the bottom of the pile. Allow students to spell the dictated word. Write the word under the indicated column—even if the spelling is incorrect. Repeat this procedure for all the word cards. When complete, place the word cards under the correct column to use as a checklist for the written columns. Correct any misspelled words.

ea		ee		ei	no long e
leaf	beat	steep	queen	receive	said
easy	jeans	speed	street	deceive	says
really	mean	breeze	between		
eager	reach				
please	cleaned				

Directed Instruction
1 Chorally read and clap out the syllables in each word. Select volunteers to come to the board, read a word, and circle the **long e** spelling pattern.

2 Display **P-4 Spelling Rules** to review the following rule: A vowel is usually long when it is followed by another vowel. The second vowel is silent (rule number 3). This rule applies to the **ea**, **ee**, and **ei** spellings for **long e**.

3 Display **P-5 Spelling Rules** to teach the following rule: The letter **i** comes

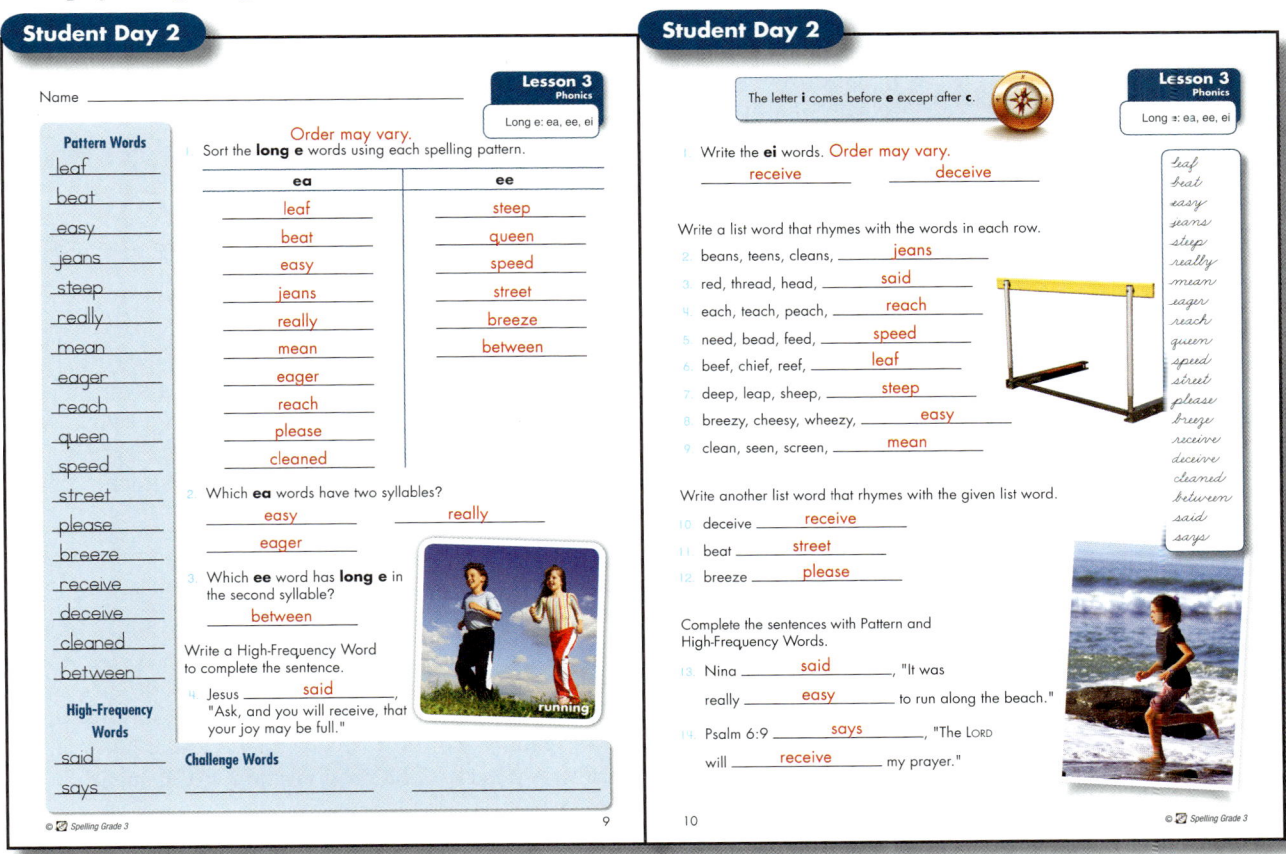

Student Spelling Support Materials

BLMs SP3-03B–C
Card stock
BLM SP3-01A
Construction paper
Letter tiles

Student Spelling Support

1. Write this week's words categorized by patterns on a large piece of paper and attach to the Word Wall.

2. Duplicate **BLMs SP3-03B–C Lesson 3 Spelling Words I** and **II** on CARD STOCK for students to use as flash cards at school or at home.

3. Use **BLM SP3-01A A Spelling Study Strategy** in instructional groups to provide assistance with some or all of the words.

4. Assist students in writing the Challenge Words, numbers 21 and 22, in the section called My Words for Writing, in the back of their textbook.

5. For visual and kinesthetic learners, write incomplete Pattern Words on CONSTRUCTION PAPER, leaving an empty space for the **ea**, **ee**, and **ei** in each word. Allow students to use LETTER TILES with e, a, and i to complete the **long e** spelling for each word.

6. Read 1 John 1:8 to students: "If we say that we have no sin, we **deceive** ourselves, and the truth is not in us." Discuss with students the dangers in thinking that we have no sin. The Lord sent Jesus to die for our sins and we are to honor Him with living our lives honestly.

---

before **e** except after **c** (rule number 5). Ask students to identify which list words follow this rule. (**receive, deceive**)

4 Proceed to page 9. Say, spell, and say each Pattern and High-Frequency Word. Provide this week's Challenge Words and have students write them in the spaces provided. Allow students to complete exercises 1–4 independently. Read the directions at the bottom of the page and the sentence for exercise 5. In John 16:24, Jesus said, "Ask, and you will receive, that your joy may be full." Remind students that Jesus said these words when He was alive on the earth. Assist students to fill in the answer line with *said*, the past tense of *say*.

5 Continue to page 10 and select a student to read the rule in the frame with the compass. Remind students that the letters **ei** come after the letter *c* in a **long e** word. Assist students in completing the page.

6 Homework suggestion: Use **BLM SP3-03D What Did You Say?** to review **long e** spellings and High-Frequency Words.

Day 3 Word Study

Objective

The students will match words to the correct definitions, choose a list word that best completes a sentence, and write the word to complete the sentence.

Introduction

Before class, write the following words on the board: cleaned, jeans, queen, receive, leaf, steep. Write the following incomplete sentences and definitions on the board:

- My blue ____ got dirty. (**jeans**)
- A red ____ fell from the tree. (**leaf**)
- The ____ wore a crown. (**queen**)
- sloping very sharply (**steep**)
- to get or accept something (**receive**)
- past tense of CLEAN (**cleaned**)

Select students to complete the sentences with the correct word and match definitions to the correct word.

Directed Instruction

1 Invite a volunteer to come to the board and circle the **long e** spelling in each answer word.

2 Proceed to page 11 and read the directions. Allow students to complete the page independently.

Day 4 Writing

Objective

The students will use proofreading marks to identify mistakes in a letter. They will correctly write misspelled words.

Introduction

Display a pair of TENNIS SHOES and say, "Running is a great way to exercise. We should wear a good pair of running shoes when running." Ask students to describe places where one would go running. (**park, playground, etc.**) Discuss with students the reasons why a good pair of shoes is essential in preventing injuries. (**ankle support, shock absorption, etc.**)

Directed Instruction

1 Draw the Proofreading Marks box on the board and write the following sentences:
- Cole was eeger to begin his run. (**Cole was eager to begin his run.**)
- He will stay stay out of the streit. (**He will stay out of the street.**)
- cole will run at a good speed. (**Cole will run at a good speed.**)

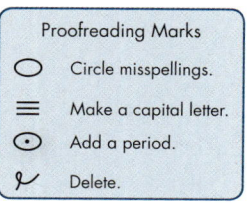

Proofreading Marks	
◯	Circle misspellings.
≡	Make a capital letter.
⊙	Add a period.
ℓ	Delete.

Inform students that the sentences contain mistakes and allow volunteers to identify the mistakes. Use correct proofreading marks and rewrite the sentences correctly.

2 Proceed to page 12. Select a volunteer to read the sentences at the top of the page. Assist students to make sure that all errors are corrected. (**9 misspellings; 5 capital letters needed; 3 periods needed; 3 deletes**)

3 Use **T-4 Proofreading a Letter** to correct the exercise on page 12.

4 Homework suggestion: Read the letter on page 12 to an adult. Take a practice spelling test at home or use **BLM SP3-01A A Spelling Study Strategy** for additional practice.

Day 5 Wrap Up

Objective
The students will correctly write dictated spelling words and sentences.

Introduction
Provide a review, utilizing WHITEBOARDS or Student Spelling Support suggestions.

Directed Instruction

1 Dictate the list words by using the Warm Up sentences or developing original ones. Reserve *leaf*, *steep*, and *queen* for the dictation sentences.

2 Follow this procedure for the dictation sentences: read the sentence, invite the class to say the sentence with you, then read the sentence again. Dictate the following sentences:
  - The <u>leaf</u> fell into the gutter.
  - They were afraid of the <u>steep</u> hill.
  - The <u>queen</u> was playing tennis.

3 If assigned, dictate Extra Challenge Words.

4 Score the test, counting each misspelled word as an error. Correct the dictation sentences as follows: grade only the spelling words or grade the complete sentences, including capitalization and punctuation.

Notes

Student Day 3

Name _____

Lesson 3
Word Study
Long e: ea, ee, ei

Write a word that matches each definition. 
1. a public road ___street___
2. not hard to do ___easy___
3. a king's wife ___queen___
4. a part of a plant ___leaf___

Write the letter of the definition that matches each word.
d 5. breeze   a. to trick somebody
c 6. jeans   b. rate at which something moves
b 7. speed   c. a pair of pants
a 8. deceive   d. a gentle wind

Fill in the circle next to the word that best completes each sentence. Write the list word on the line.
9. Evan was ___eager___ to start the race.
   ○ mean   ● eager
   ○ please ○ said
10. Evan ran up a ___steep___ hill.
   ○ really ○ between
   ● steep   ○ deceive
11. Will Evan ___beat___ the other runners?
   ○ says   ○ jeans
   ○ leaf   ● beat
12. Evan will ___receive___ a ribbon.
   ● receive ○ breeze
   ○ queen   ○ easy
13. Evan ___cleaned___ the mud from his shoes.
   ○ reach   ● cleaned
   ○ street ○ speed

leaf
beat
easy
jeans
steep
really
mean
eager
reach
queen
speed
street
please
breeze
receive
deceive
cleaned
between
said
says

© Spelling Grade 3   11

Student Day 4

Clay went for a run. He wrote a letter to his cousin, Matt, telling him about it. Clay made some mistakes in his letter. Find his mistakes. Use proofreading marks.

Lesson 3
Writing
Long e: ea, ee, ei

July 5, 2008

Dear Matt,

today I went for a long run with some friends. We drove down the the streat to a park. I was so eiger to reach the trail to begin our adventure! The trail was pretty flat, but it had a steap hill at the end. i reely thought that I would not be able to make it up the hill. We all decided to stay together and run at the same speid before I knew it, we all made it up the hill! It was a pretty day day, and there was a nice breaze.

I am so glad that you shared your love of running with me. Running is so much fun! will you please write and tell me about where you have run lately? I can't wait to to receave your letter.

Sincerely,
clay

Proofreading Marks
○ Circle misspellings.
≡ Make a capital letter.
⊙ Add a period.
✃ Delete.

leaf
beat
easy
jeans
steep
really
mean
eager
reach
queen
speed
street
please
breeze
receive
deceive
cleaned
between
said
says

Write the correct spellings on the lines below. Order may vary.
1. ___street___   2. ___eager___
3. ___reach___   4. ___steep___
5. ___really___   6. ___speed___
7. ___breeze___   8. ___please___
9. ___receive___

© Spelling Grade 3

12

© Spelling Grade 3

13

Student Pages

Pages 13–16

Lesson Materials

BLM SP3-04A
BLMs SP3-04B–C
Card stock
P-5
BLM SP3-04D
T-5
BLM SP3-04E
BLM SP3-01A
Whiteboards

Transportation

The theme of this lesson is Snow Skis, Sleds, and Snowshoes. Popular winter sports using these things originated in Nordic countries where rock carvings of people wearing skis have been dated to be between 4,000 and 5,000 years old. The carvings show that snowshoes, sleds, and skis were originally used for hunting and transportation.

Day 1 Warm Up

Objective

The students will accurately spell and write words with **long e** spelled **e**, **ey**, **ie**, and **y**. They will spell and write high-frequency words and challenge words.

Introduction

The Warm Up (Pretest) is an ungraded assessment to assist students in studying the Pattern, High-Frequency, and Challenge Words. To meet your students' needs, select Challenge Words from a cross-curricular subject or words misspelled on previous assignments. The word *relief* has **long e** spelled **ie** and is suggested for number 21. Remind students of proper posture and check for correct positioning of their paper. Explain that they are to attempt to write all the spelling words. If they cannot spell a particular word, they should try to write down all the letters that they hear.

Directed Instruction

1 Use the sentences that follow or develop original ones.

2 Say each word, use it in a sentence, and then repeat the word.

Pattern Words

1. brownie	Jan chose to eat a <u>brownie</u> for dessert.	brownie
2. monkey	The little <u>monkey</u> chattered and chattered.	monkey
3. secret	It's no <u>secret</u> that Jesus loves you!	secret
4. pieces	Does your puzzle have over 500 <u>pieces</u>?	pieces
5. honey	<u>Honey</u> is sweet and golden.	honey
6. equal	Five plus five is <u>equal</u> to ten.	equal
7. grief	Mary experienced <u>grief</u> when Jesus died.	grief
8. yield	A <u>yield</u> sign tells drivers to wait for others.	yield
9. only	She had <u>only</u> five cents in her pocket.	only
10. icy	Will the <u>icy</u> roads make driving dangerous?	icy
11. keys	I'll loan you the <u>keys</u> to the storage room.	keys
12. busy	Martha was <u>busy</u> with many things.	busy
13. chief	A fire <u>chief</u> directs the operations at a fire.	chief
14. valley	The <u>valley</u> is lower than the mountains.	valley
15. sleepy	Jeff felt <u>sleepy</u> after taking a warm bath.	sleepy
16. snowy	He saw footprints on the <u>snowy</u> ground.	snowy
17. beyond	Do not go <u>beyond</u> the safety line.	beyond
18. believes	Whoever <u>believes</u> in Jesus has eternal life.	believes

High-Frequency Words

19. favorite	My <u>favorite</u> ice-cream flavor is chocolate.	favorite
20. against	Mack put his finger <u>against</u> his forehead.	against

Challenge Words

21. _____ (Insert your choice.)
22. _____ (Insert your choice.)

3 Allow students to self-correct their pretest, following this procedure:

a. Write each word on the board. Discuss the letter/sound relationships in each word. Point out the spelling pattern for **long e**—e, ey, ie, y—in each Pattern Word. Explain that the letter **y** is a suffix in the words *icy, snowy,* and *sleepy*. It is not a suffix in the words *busy* and *only*.

b. As a class, read, spell, and read each word. Direct students to circle misspelled words with a colored pencil and rewrite them correctly.

4 Proof each student's Warm Up. This becomes an individualized study sheet that can be used at school or at home.

5 Homework suggestion: Use **BLM SP3-04A Jesus and Lazarus** to practice the words in this week's lesson.

Day 2 Phonics

Objective

The students will correctly sort words with **long e** spelled e, ey, ie, and y. They will write words with **long e** in the first and second syllables, rhyming words, missing vowels, and high-frequency words.

Introduction

Before class, duplicate one copy of **BLMs SP3-04B–C Lesson 4 Spelling Words I** and **II** on CARD STOCK for each student. Cut the flash cards apart. Distribute a set of flash cards to each student. Write the list words in a column and the headings **ie, e, ey, y,** and **no long e** across the board. Say, "The **long e** sound may be spelled different ways. This week's words have four spellings for the **long e** sound. We will sort the words by spelling patterns." Direct students' attention to the board. Begin sorting by asking a volunteer to suggest a word with an **ie** spelling for **long e**. Write the word under the **ie** heading. Choose a second volunteer to suggest a word with **long e** spelled **e**. Continue in the same manner with the **ey** and **y** spellings, writing several list words under the proper headings before allowing students to sort their flashcards on their desktop. Check for correct sorting.

ie		e	ey	y	no long e
yield	grief	equal	keys	icy	against
chief	pieces	secret	valley	only	favorite
believes	brownie	beyond	honey	busy	
			monkey	sleepy	
				snowy	

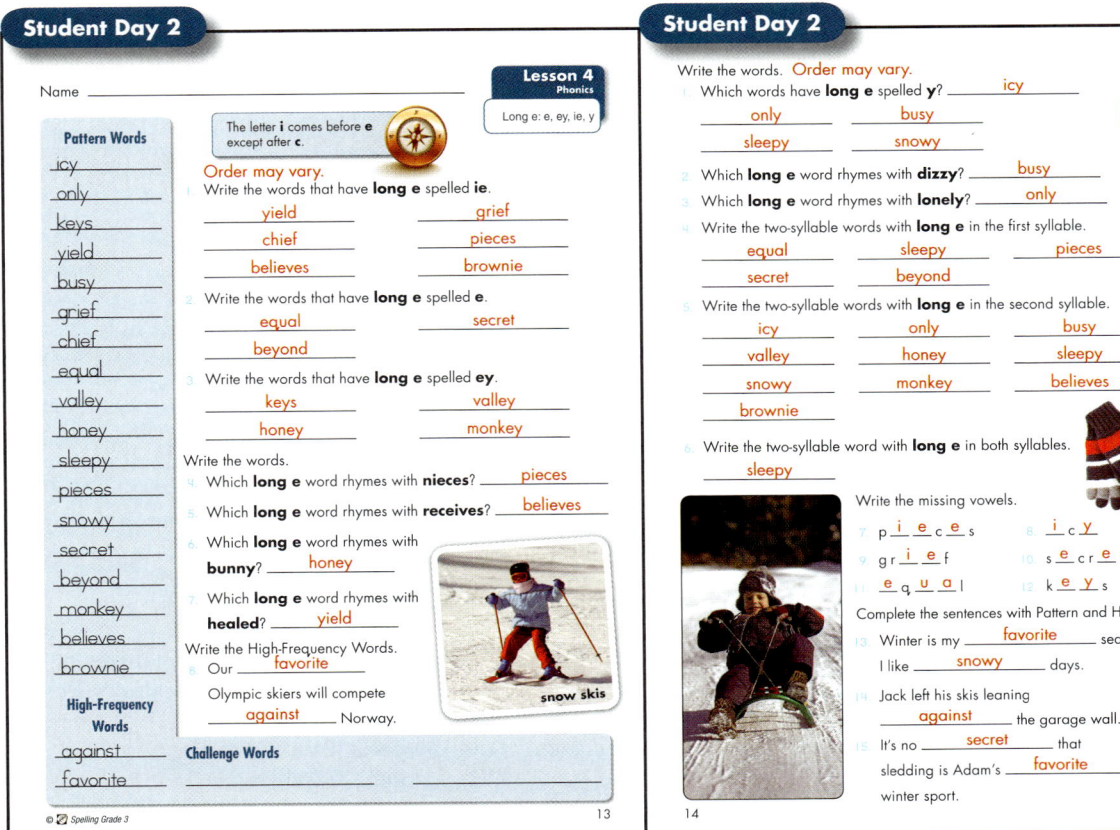

Student Spelling Support Materials

BLMs SP3-04B–C
Card stock
BLM SP3-01A
3" × 5" Index cards
File folder
Envelope
Flash cards from Lessons 2 and 3
BLMs SP3-04F–H

Student Spelling Support

1. Write this week's words categorized by patterns on a large piece of paper and attach to the Word Wall.

2. Duplicate **BLMs SP3-04B–C Lesson 4 Spelling Words I and II** on CARD STOCK for students to use as flash cards at school or at home.

3. Use **BLM SP3-01A A Spelling Study Strategy** in instructional groups to provide assistance with some or all of the words.

4. Assist students in writing the Challenge Words, numbers 21 and 22, in the section called My Words for Writing, in the back of their textbook.

5. For auditory learners, play Sounds Alike. Write the following words on 3" × 5" INDEX CARDS: pricey, lonely, bees, field, dizzy, leaf, reef, sequel, rally, bunny, weepy, leases, showy, chunky, receives, downy. Provide each player with a list of Lesson 4 Pattern Words. (*Secret* and *beyond* do not have rhymes listed.) Shuffle the index cards and slowly pronounce each word for the group. The first player to find a list word that rhymes with the word called raises his/her hand. Have the player spell the word without looking at the list. One point is scored

Cont. on page 17

Directed Instruction

1 Proceed to page 13. Say, spell, and say each Pattern and High-Frequency Word. Provide this week's Challenge Words and have students write them in the spaces provided. Lead students to clap out the number of syllables in each word.

2 Display **P-5 Spelling Rules** to reinforce the following rule: The letter **i** comes before **e** except after **c** (rule number 5). Ask students to identify which list words follow this rule. (**yield, grief, chief, pieces, believes, brownie**) Students complete the page independently.

3 Proceed to page 14. Tell students that *believes* is pronounced /bə ˈlēvz/. Only the word *sleepy* has a **long e** sound in both syllables.

4 Homework suggestion: Use **BLM SP3-04D Skiers** for practice with the list words.

Day 3 Word Study

Objective

The students will write antonyms and synonyms for list words. They will choose the correct usage for a list word.

Introduction

Write the word *antonym* on the board. Explain that an *antonym* is a word that means the opposite of another word. Turn the lights off and on. Share that *off* and *on* are opposites or antonyms. Write the word *synonym* on the board. Explain that a *synonym* is a word that means the same or almost the same as another word. Select a student to hop up and down. Have another student pantomime jumping a jump rope. Associate the words *hopping* and *jumping* with the actions. Explain that the words *hopping* and *jumping* describe actions that are the same or almost the same, therefore, they are synonyms. Invite students to suggest other antonyms (**Possible answers: up/down, laugh/cry**) and synonyms (**Possible answers: unafraid/brave, little/small**).

Directed Instruction

1 Briefly play a guessing game to reinforce the meanings of some list words and their antonyms/synonyms by writing the following sentences on the board:

- When I have plenty to do, am I busy, or am I idle? (**busy**)
- John is sure that dogs can bark. Does he doubt it, or does he believe it? (**believes**)
- Chocolate ice cream is preferred by third graders. Is it a favorite, or is it disliked? (**favorite**)

Choose volunteers to answer each question.

2 Proceed to page 15. Continue the lesson by reading the definitions at the top of the page. Discuss any unfamiliar vocabulary before allowing students to complete exercises 1–15.

Day 4 Writing

Objective

The students will complete a graphic organizer time line using the events in an article from a reference book. They will find and underline list words located in the text.

Introduction

Place **T-5 Time Line** on the overhead. Say, "This graphic organizer is called a time line. A time line shows a series of events in the order in which they happened. We can use a time line to display the sequence of events in a piece of writing." Read the paragraph above the time line. Select volunteers to tell you which sentences to write on the blanks next to the dates on the time line based on the information in the paragraph. When the time line is complete, reread it to be sure the facts written on the time line agree with the text. Refer to **BLM SP3-04E T-5 Answer Key**.

Directed Instruction

1 Proceed to page 16. Explain that the text found on the page could be taken from an encyclopedia or other reference book. Facts about skiing are written in paragraph form. Have students copy the sentence that contains the date onto the blank line next to that date on the time line.

2 Homework suggestion: Read the paragraphs about skiing on page 16 to an adult. Take a practice spelling test at home or use **BLM SP3-01A A Spelling Study Strategy** for additional practice.

Day 5 Wrap Up

Objective

The students will correctly write dictated spelling words and sentences.

Introduction

Provide a review, utilizing WHITEBOARDS or Student Spelling Support suggestions.

Directed Instruction

1 Dictate the list words by using the Warm Up sentences or developing original ones. Reserve *believes*, *against*, and *favorite* for the dictation sentences.

2 Follow this procedure for the dictation sentences: read the sentence, invite the class to say the sentence with you, then read the sentence again. Dictate the following sentences:

- Jack <u>believes</u> in Jesus with all his heart.
- Our team will be playing <u>against</u> another team.
- Jan wore her <u>favorite</u> yellow jacket and blue jeans.

3 If assigned, dictate Extra Challenge Words.

4 Score the test, counting each misspelled word as an error. Correct the dictation sentences as follows: grade only the spelling words or grade the complete sentences, including capitalization and punctuation.

Student Spelling Support

Cont. from page 16

for each correct word and spelling. The words *grief* and *chief* rhyme and are interchangeable in this game. To make the game more challenging, allow players to score two points if they are able to spell both rhyming words correctly.

6. For a small group activity, play Downhill Racers. You will need a FILE FOLDER, an ENVELOPE, CARD STOCK, **BLMs SP3-04B–C Lesson 4 Spelling Words I** and **II**, FLASH CARDS FROM LESSONS 2 AND 3, and **BLMs SP3-04F–H Downhill Racers I**, **II**, and **III**. Use the instructions on the blackline master.

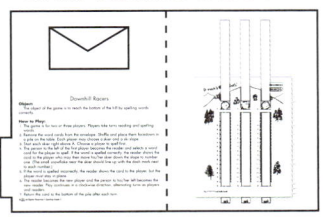

Student Day 3

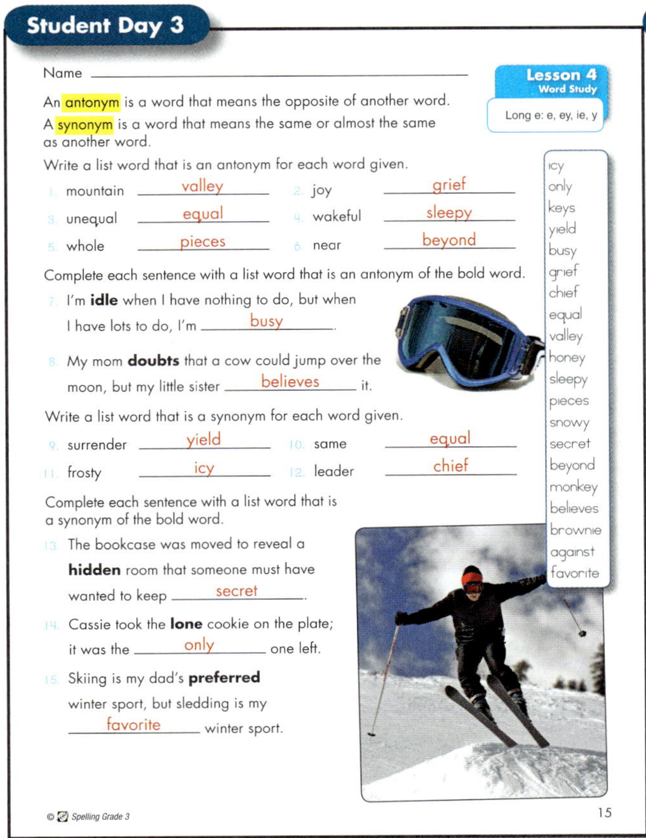

Name _____

An <mark>antonym</mark> is a word that means the opposite of another word. A <mark>synonym</mark> is a word that means the same or almost the same as another word.

Lesson 4
Word Study

Long e: e, ey, ie, y

Write a list word that is an antonym for each word given.

1. mountain	valley	2. joy	grief
3. unequal	equal	4. wakeful	sleepy
5. whole	pieces	6. near	beyond

Complete each sentence with a list word that is an antonym of the bold word.

7. I'm **idle** when I have nothing to do, but when I have lots to do, I'm ___busy___.

8. My mom **doubts** that a cow could jump over the moon, but my little sister ___believes___ it.

Write a list word that is a synonym for each word given.

9. surrender	yield	10. same	equal
11. frosty	icy	12. leader	chief

Complete each sentence with a list word that is a synonym of the bold word.

13. The bookcase was moved to reveal a **hidden** room that someone must have wanted to keep ___secret___.

14. Cassie took the **lone** cookie on the plate; it was the ___only___ one left.

15. Skiing is my dad's **preferred** winter sport, but sledding is my ___favorite___ winter sport.

icy
only
keys
yield
busy
grief
chief
equal
valley
honey
sleepy
pieces
snowy
secret
beyond
monkey
believes
brownie
against
favorite

Student Day 4

Read the paragraphs about skiing. Underline the list words. Write the sentences in each paragraph that tell what happened on the dates shown in the time line.

Lesson 4
Writing

Long e: e, ey, ie, y

Skiing

Swish! Down the <u>snowy</u> slopes come the skiers. They speed down the mountain toward the finish line! Downhill skiing is one of the world's <u>favorite</u> winter sports.

Did you know that ski racing may have begun with a cross-country ski race instead of a downhill race? This race was held in Norway in 1843. Ski racing became popular in countries far <u>beyond</u> Norway's borders. The first ski race with countries competing <u>against</u> each other was held in 1892.

Ski jumping started in 1840. A <u>busy</u> man named Sondre Norheim invented a way to keep the skis fastened to the skier's boots. His invention helped skiers to go down <u>icy</u> slopes quickly and easily.

Men's ski races were held in the Olympic Games in 1924. <u>Only</u> men could ski in those races. Women got an <u>equal</u> chance to compete in 1950.

1840 ★	Ski jumping started in 1840.
1843 ★	This race was held in Norway in 1843.
1892 ★	The first ski race with countries competing against each other was held in 1892.
1924 ★	Men's ski races were held in the Olympic Games in 1924.
1950 ★	Women got an equal chance to compete in 1950.

icy
only
keys
yield
busy
grief
chief
equal
valley
honey
sleepy
pieces
snowy
secret
beyond
monkey
believes
brownie
against
favorite

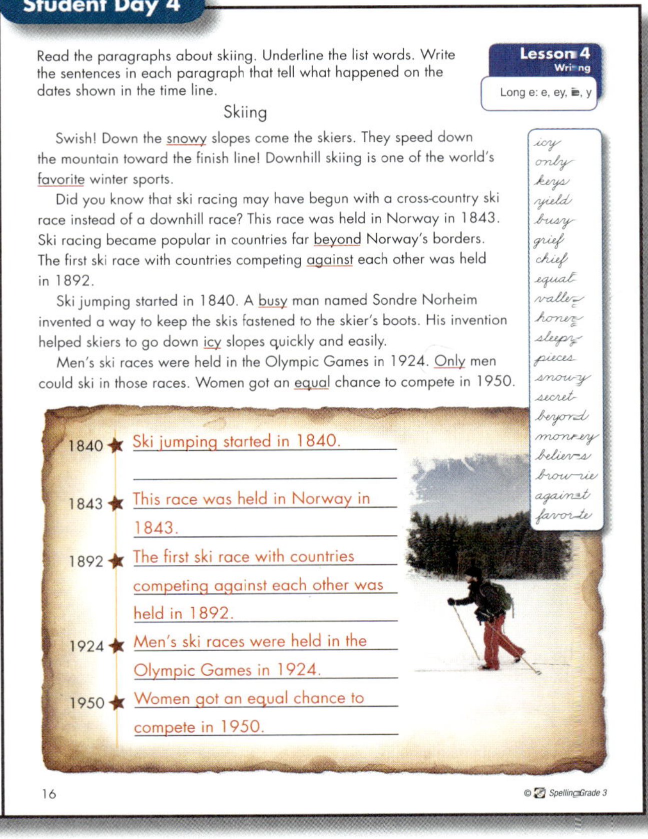

Student Pages

Pages 17–20

Lesson Materials

BLM SP3-05A
P-11
P-3
P-4
BLM SP3-05B
T-6
T-7
BLM SP3-01A
Whiteboards

Transportation

The theme of this lesson is Bicycles, Tricycles, and Unicycles. These three vehicles have seen many changes over the past 100 years. The first bicycle did not have pedals and was simply a walking machine that helped a person glide along as he or she walked. This walking machine was nicknamed "hobby horse." Bicycles preceded tricycles and unicycles.

Day 1 Warm Up

Objective

The students will accurately spell and write words with **long i**. They will spell and write high-frequency words and challenge words.

Introduction

The Warm Up (Pretest) is an ungraded assessment to assist students in studying the Pattern, High-Frequency, and Challenge Words. To meet your students' needs, select Challenge Words from a cross-curricular subject or words misspelled on previous assignments. The word *quiet* has **long i** spelled **i**, and is suggested for number 21. Remind students of proper posture and check for correct positioning of their paper. Explain that they are to attempt to write all the spelling words. If they cannot spell a particular word, they should try to write down all the letters that they hear.

Directed Instruction

1 Use the sentences that follow or develop original ones.

2 Say each word, use it in a sentence, and then repeat the word.

Pattern Words

1.	fright	I ran away in <u>fright</u> from the angry dog.	fright
2.	shine	The sun will <u>shine</u> all day.	shine
3.	childhood	Riding a tricycle is a <u>childhood</u> pastime.	childhood
4.	buying	Mom is at the store <u>buying</u> groceries.	buying
5.	tiny	The <u>tiny</u> baby fell asleep.	tiny
6.	tried	Molly <u>tried</u> to lift the heavy box.	tried
7.	blind	Jesus healed a <u>blind</u> man.	blind
8.	reply	Mrs. Hansen will <u>reply</u> to my question.	reply
9.	skyline	The San Diego <u>skyline</u> looks pretty at night.	skyline
10.	mighty	We have a <u>mighty</u> God.	mighty
11.	lies	Can a person who <u>lies</u> be trusted?	lies
12.	apply	Mr. Larry will <u>apply</u> fresh paint to the wall.	apply
13.	nearby	My grandparents live <u>nearby</u>.	nearby
14.	tired	After a long day, I feel <u>tired</u>.	tired
15.	bicycles	My parents bought us new <u>bicycles</u>.	bicycles
16.	brighter	We need a <u>brighter</u> light for reading.	brighter
17.	lives	<u>Lives</u> are changed when people accept Jesus.	lives
18.	pliers	"Where are my <u>pliers</u>?" asked Dad.	pliers

High-Frequency Words

19.	shoes	Rachel wore her new <u>shoes</u>.	shoes
20.	very	It gets <u>very</u> hot in the summertime.	very

Challenge Words

21. _____ (**Insert your choice.**)
22. _____ (**Insert your choice.**)

3 Allow students to self-correct their pretest, following this procedure:

  a. Write each word on the board. Discuss the letter/sound relationships in each word. Point out each **long i** spelling pattern—i, ie, igh, i_e, uy, y. Explain that *skyline* is a compound word with two different **long i** spellings. In this lesson *lives* is pronounced /līvz/.

  b. As a class, read, spell, and read each word. Direct students to circle misspelled words with a colored pencil and rewrite them correctly.

4 Proof each student's Warm Up. This becomes an individualized study sheet that can be used at school or at home.

5 Homework suggestion: Distribute a copy of **BLM SP3-05A Cycles** to each student to practice writing **long i** words and High-Frequency Words.

Day 2 Phonics

Objective

The students will accurately sort and write words that contain spellings for **long i**, identify other words with the same **long i** sound, and write high-frequency words.

Introduction

On one area of the board, write each Pattern Word. On another area write the column headings shown below. Invite students to come to the board, select, and write a Pattern Word below the correct heading.

i	i_e	y	igh	ie	uy
pliers	lives	reply	fright	lies	buying
tiny	shine	apply	mighty	tried	
blind	tired	skyline	brighter		
bicycles	skyline	nearby			
childhood					

Directed Instruction

1 Display **P-11 Syllables** to reinforce the following generalization: Divide between two vowels only when both vowels are heard (example number 5). Point to *pliers*. Ask how many syllables are in the word, and draw a vertical line to show the division of syllables. Teach that **i** says its long sound at the end of an open syllable and when it precedes the letters *nd* and *ld*.

2 Display **P-3 Spelling Rules** to teach the following rule: A vowel is usually long when it is followed by one **consonant** and **silent e** (rule number 2). Select volunteers to give examples.

3 Teach that **y** often says the **long i** sound when it is at the end of a short word or syllable.

4 Pronounce *fright*, *mighty*, and *brighter*. Ask which three-letter

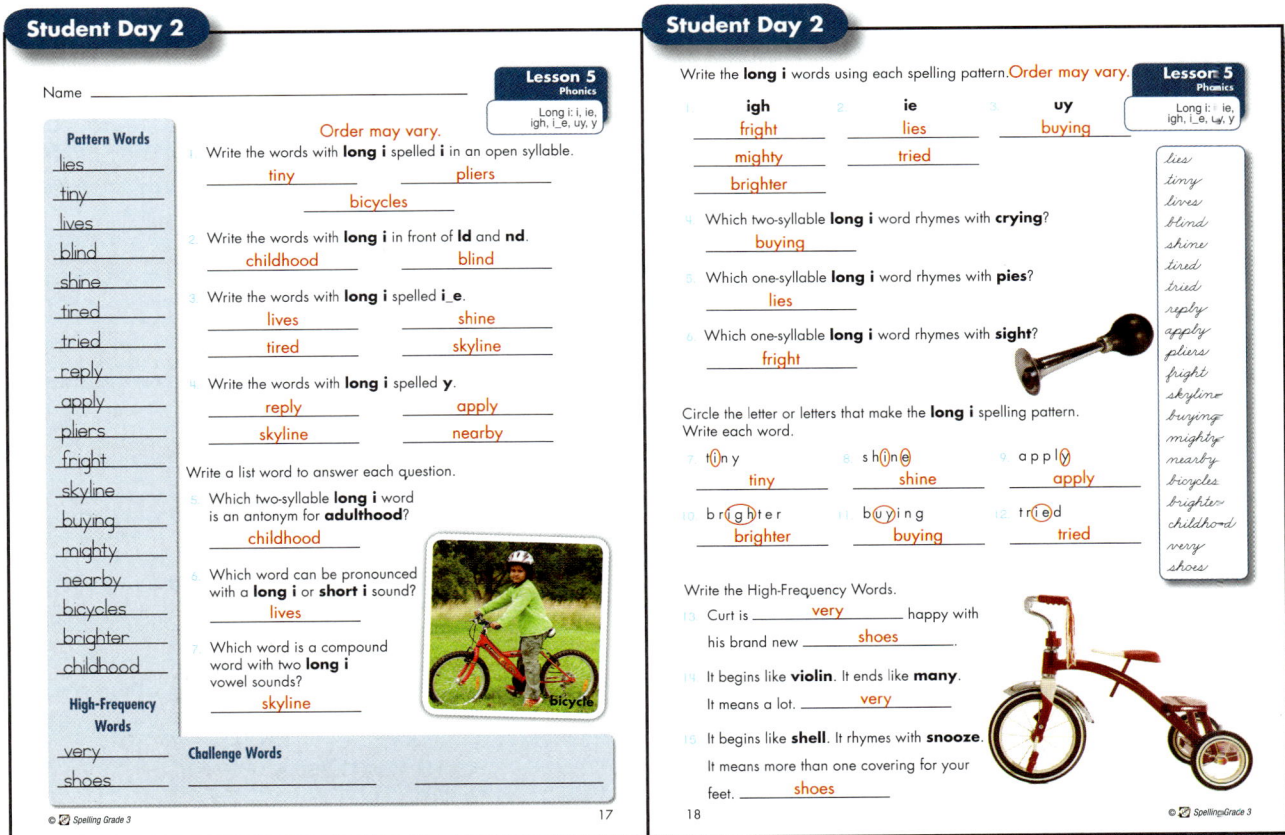

combination makes **i** say its long sound. Select a volunteer to cross out the silent letters *gh*.

5 Display **P-4 Spelling Rules** to review the following rule: A vowel is usually long when it is followed by another vowel. The second vowel is silent (rule number 3). Select a volunteer to give an example of a word that follows this rule. (**lies, tried**) Note that the **uy** spelling does not follow rule number 3.

6 Teach that **uy** says the **long i** sound as in *buying*.

7 Proceed to page 17. Say, spell, and say each Pattern and High-Frequency Word. Provide this week's Challenge Words and have students write them in the spaces provided. Select a volunteer to read the directions aloud. Answer any questions before allowing students to complete the page independently.

8 Proceed to page 18. Provide assistance as students work to complete the page.

9 Homework suggestion: Distribute a copy of **BLM SP3-05B Bicycle Path** to each student to practice writing **long i** words and High-Frequency Words.

Day 3 Word Study

Objective

The students will identify the five parts to a dictionary entry and select list words to complete sentences.

Introduction

Display **T-6 Dictionary Entry**. Point to each part of the dictionary entry, except *n.*, and select a volunteer to correctly identify and explain its purpose.

• An entry word is a word defined in a dictionary.
• The pronunciation shows how to say the entry word.
• The definition tells the meaning of the entry word.
• The sample sentence helps in understanding the definition.

Directed Instruction

1 Point to the *n.* after the pronunciation of *skyline* on the overhead. Teach that *n.* stands for *noun*. A noun is a part of speech. The part of speech indicates whether the word is a noun (*n.*), plural noun (*n. pl.*), (verb (*v.*), adjective (*adj.*), adverb (*adv.*), pronoun (*pron.*), interjection (*interj.*), preposition (*prep.*), or conjunction (*conj.*). Ask the students which part of speech is shown for *skyline*. (**n. which stands for noun**)

2 On the board, write the following sentences and answer choices. Advise students to use the context of the sentences. Select volunteers to complete each one correctly.
• The (blind, skyline) dog lay by the fireplace. (**blind**)
• Grandma will (very, reply) to my e-mail. (**reply**)
• Your (shine, childhood) is the time when you are young. (**childhood**)
• Sam will (apply, fright) glue to the paper. (**apply**)

3 Proceed to page 19. Allow students to complete the page independently.

Day 4 Writing

Objective

The students will complete a story in the context of a cloze activity using pattern and high-frequency words.

Introduction

Display **T-7 Uni-, Bi-, Tri-**. Explain that the prefixes *uni-*, *bi-*, and *tri-* in *unicycles*, *bicycles*, and *tricycles* come from the Latin language and mean "one," "two," and "three." Share a story from your childhood about a bicycle, tricycle, or unicycle. Utilize the transparency to discuss other *uni-*, *bi-*, and *tri-* words. Ask the students if they know what a tandem bike is.

(**A bicycle with two seats for two people to ride.**) Reiterate the importance of wearing safety gear as was presented in Lesson 2.

Directed Instruction

1 Proceed to page 20. Instruct students to quietly read through the paragraphs first to become familiar with them. Invite students to reread the paragraphs and write the word in each blank that best completes each sentence.

2 Homework suggestion: Read the paragraphs on page 20 to an adult. Take a practice spelling test at home or use **BLM SP3-01A A Spelling Study Strategy** for additional practice.

Day 5 Wrap Up

Objective

The students will correctly write dictated spelling words and sentences.

Introduction

Provide a review, utilizing WHITEBOARDS or Student Spelling Support suggestions.

Directed Instruction

1 Dictate the list words by using the Warm Up sentences or developing original ones. Reserve *tiny*, *shine*, and *very* for the dictation sentences.

2 Follow this procedure for the dictation sentences: read the sentence, invite the class to say the sentence with you, then read the sentence again. Dictate the following sentences:
- The <u>tiny</u> leaf fell from the tree.
- The light on the street will <u>shine</u> at night.
- The lady said that the brownie was <u>very</u> good.

3 If assigned, dictate Extra Challenge Words.

4 Score the test, counting each misspelled word as an error. Correct the dictation sentences as follows: grade only the spelling words or grade the complete sentences, including capitalization and punctuation.

Student Spelling Support

Cont. from page 20

6. As a writing extension for advanced learners, have them write and illustrate a book about activities they enjoy. Have them title the book *My Favorite Childhood Pastimes*.

7. For a biblical connection, read Matthew 5:16, "Let your light so **shine** before men, that they may see your good works and glorify your Father in heaven." Mention that the word *light* in the verse has the **igh** spelling pattern. Explain that in all that we say and do, our actions should always please the Lord.

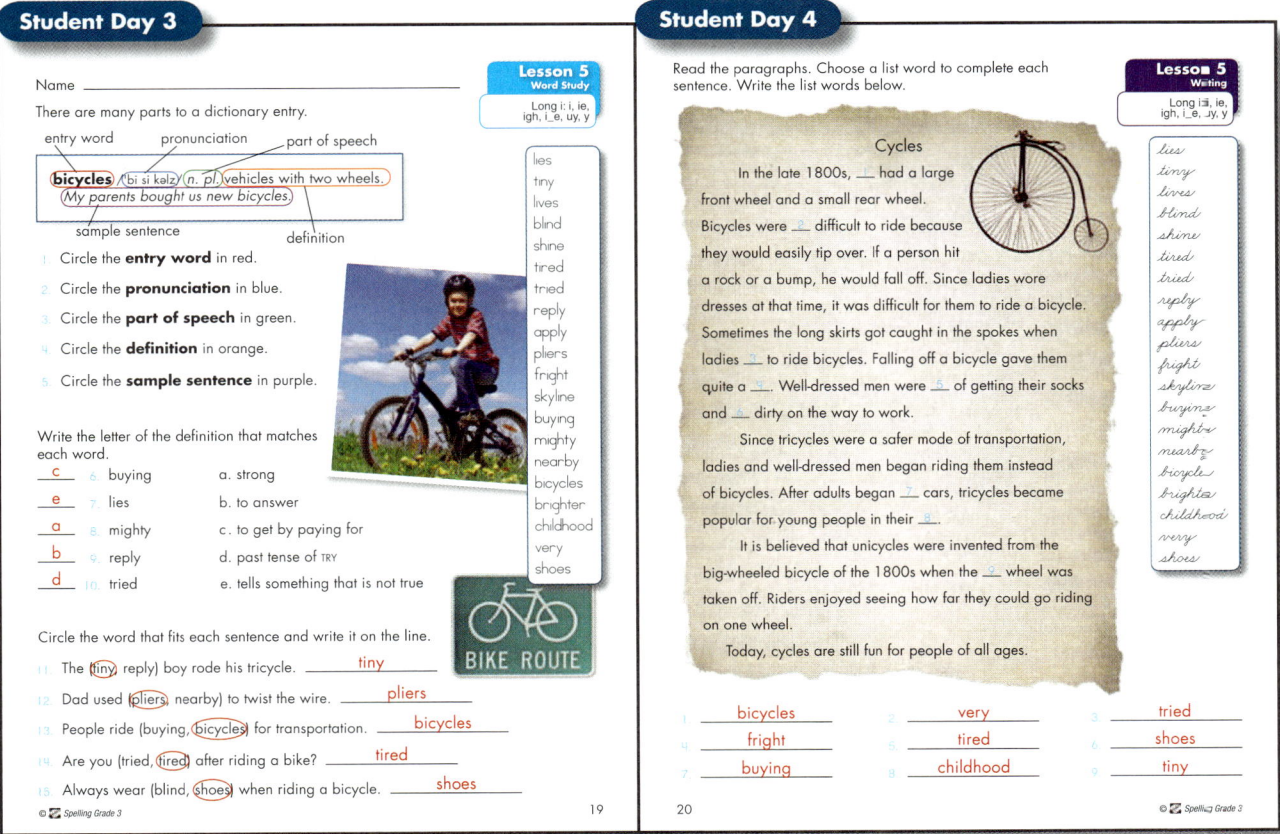

Review Lessons 1–5

Lesson Materials

P-3
T-8
BLM SP3-06A
BLM SP3-06B
P-4
BLM SP3-06C
P-5
T-9
3" × 5" Index cards
BLM SP3-06D
BLMs SP3-06E–F

Day 1 Consonants and Short Vowels

Objective

The students will spell, identify, and circle words with **consonants** and **short vowels**.

Introduction

Teacher Note: This week's lesson incorporates the Pattern and High-Frequency Words taught in Lessons 1–5 using a variety of activities such as sorting, a word search, decoding words, shape boxes, a crossword puzzle, and filling in the correct answer circle.

Review words with **consonants** and **short vowels** by writing the Pattern Words from Lesson 1 on the board. Display **P-3 Spelling Rules** to review the following rule: A vowel usually makes its short sound when it is the only vowel in a word or closed syllable. A closed syllable ends with a consonant (rule number 1). Choose a Pattern Word from the board and dictate a rhyme for that word. Ask students to identify the correct Pattern Word. For example, ask which word rhymes with *batter* (**matter**), *fed* (**led**), *shock* (**block**), *stiff* (**sniff**), *locket* (**pocket**), and *pick* (**stick**).

Directed Instruction

1 Display **T-8 Lessons 1–5 Study Sheet** on the overhead to review Lesson 1 words in unison, following this technique: say the word, spell the word, say the word.

2 Ask students to identify Lesson 1 words that contain double consonants and circle them on the transparency. (**skill, sniff, tennis, gutter, yellow, matter, wobble, address**) Select students to point out the one-syllable words that contain double consonants. (**skill, sniff**)

3 Proceed to page 21. Explain that the box contains all the Pattern and High-Frequency Words in Lessons 1–5. These lists are a review tool and contain the same words that were previously reviewed on the overhead transparency. Allow students to read the directions and complete the page independently.

4 Distribute one copy of **BLM SP3-06A Lessons 1–5 Study Sheet** to each student to take home for study. Each review lesson includes a study sheet for student use.

5 Homework suggestion: Duplicate one copy of **BLM SP3-06B Race** for each student to practice words with **consonants**, **short vowels**, and **long a**.

Day 2 Long a: a, a_e, ai, ay, ea, eigh, ey

Objective

The students will find and circle **long a** words in a word search and write them.

Introduction

Review **long a** words by writing the Pattern Words from Lesson 2 on the board. Dictate a word and select a volunteer to come to the board and underline the word. Ask the student to say the word again, and to underline the **long a** pattern in the word. There will be seven **long a** patterns. (**a, a_e, ai, ay, ea, eigh, ey**) Repeat this process for all the Pattern Words.

Directed Instruction

1 Display **P-3 Spelling Rules** and **P-4 Spelling Rules** to review the following rules: A vowel is usually long when it is followed by one **consonant** and **silent e** (rule number 2). A vowel usually makes its long sound when it is in an open syllable. An open syllable ends with a vowel (rule number 4).

2 Select a few Pattern Words from Lesson 2 that contain similar patterns or letters. Use the words to create a mini word search on the board. Show students how words can intersect and share letters.

t	g	m	l	o
b	r	e	a	k
s	f	z	d	n
t	h	e	y	b
c	i	n	u	z

3 Display **T-8 Lessons 1–5 Study Sheet** to review Lesson 2 words in unison, using the say-spell-say technique.

4 Proceed to page 22 and read the directions. Remind students that words may share letters and allow them to complete the page independently.

5 Homework suggestion: Distribute a copy of **BLM SP3-06C Icy Street** to each student to practice with **long e** words.

Day 3 Long e: ea, ee, ei, e, ey, ie, y

Objective

The students will use a code to spell and write **long e** words. They will write **long e** words in shape boxes.

Introduction

Write the following graphemes and symbols on the board:

ea = ●	ee = ■	ei = ▲

Inform students that the symbols are codes that represent the letters **ea**, **ee**, and **ei**. These graphemes represent a single sound. The **ea**, **ee**, and **ei** words in this list all have the sound of **long e**. Write the following incomplete Lesson 3 words, with symbols, on the board:

- r●lly (**really**)
- str■t (**street**)
- rec▲ve (**receive**)

Invite students to come to the board, decode the word, and write the complete word. Select a student to read the completed words.

Directed Instruction

1 Display **T-8 Lessons 1–5 Study Sheet** to review Lessons 3–4 words in unison, using the say-spell-say technique.

2 Challenge students to identify how many tall letters and tail letters there are in each Lesson 4 **long e** Pattern Word; for example, *sleepy* has one tall letter (*l*) and two tail letters (*p, y*).

3 Display **P-4 Spelling Rules** and **P-5 Spelling Rules** to review the following rules: A vowel is usually long when it is followed by another vowel. The second vowel is silent (rule number 3). The letter **i** comes before **e** except after **c** (rule number 5).

4 Proceed to page 23 and read the directions aloud. Check for understanding and accuracy as students complete the page independently.

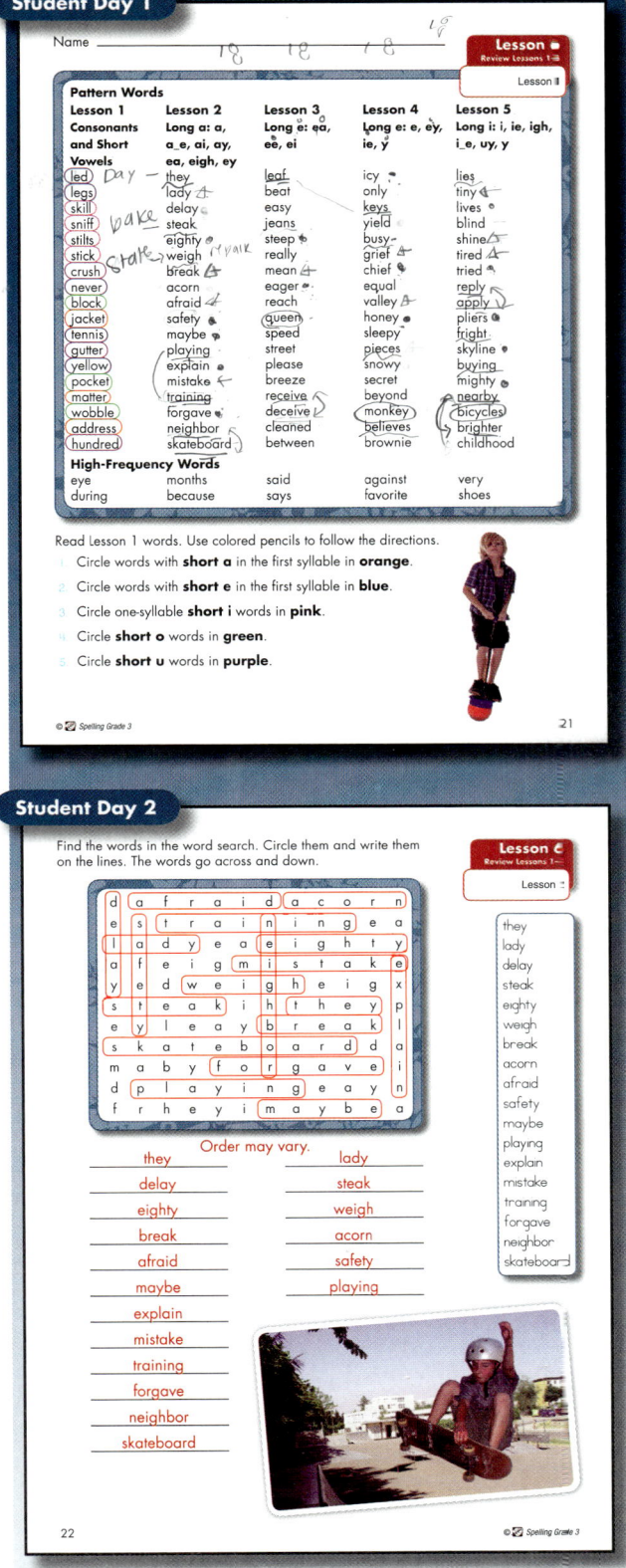

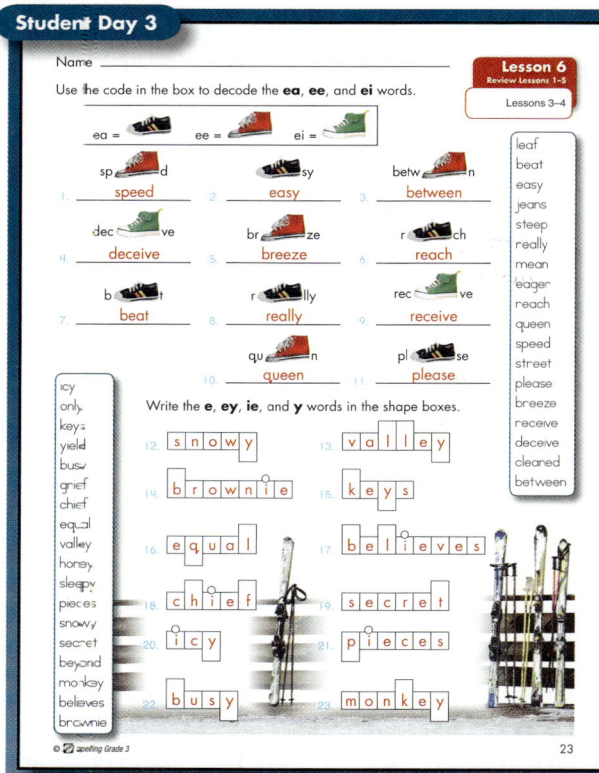

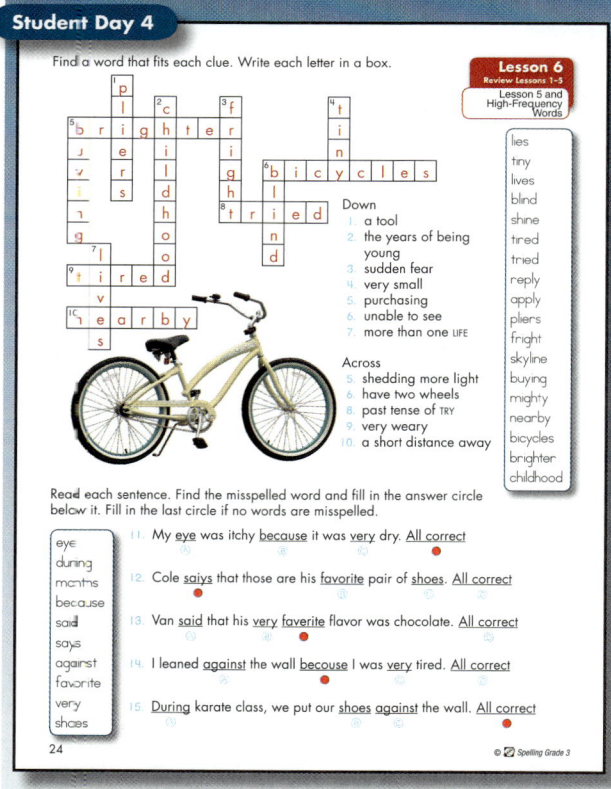

Day 4 Long i: i, ie, igh, i_e, uy, y and High-Frequency Words

Objective

The students will spell and write **long i** words in a crossword puzzle. They will select the appropriate answer circle within the context of a sentence and fill it in.

Introduction

Before class, write the following Pattern Words from Lesson 5 on the board:

- shine (**to give forth light**)
- reply (**to answer**)
- lies (**tells something that is not true**)
- mighty (**strong, powerful**)

Encourage students to listen carefully as you describe each word, using the definitions. Have students identify which word you are defining and then write the definition adjacent to the word. Select students to read each word and its definition.

Directed Instruction

1 Display **T-8 Lessons 1–5 Study Sheet** to review Lesson 5 and High-Frequency Words in unison, using the say-spell-say technique.

2 Proceed to page 24 and allow students to complete the crossword puzzle independently.

3 Display **T-9 Assessment Practice** on the overhead to review an assessment format. This is a partial replica of student page 24. Dictate the following Sample:

<u>Pleaze</u> <u>explain</u> the <u>safety</u> rules. <u>All correct</u>
  ●   Ⓑ   Ⓒ   Ⓓ

Say, "The circle below the first underlined word has been filled in to show that it is the misspelled word. We will continue in the same way. I will read each sentence and you will choose the misspelled word and fill in the circle below it. If all the words are spelled correctly, fill in the last circle underneath *All correct*." Distribute a 3" × 5" INDEX CARD to each student to be used as a marker. Instruct students to place their marker below each number as the test is dictated. Dictate exercises 11–15 and complete page 24 as a class.

4 Homework suggestion: Duplicate one copy of **BLM SP3-06D Bicycles** for each student to practice words with **long i** and High-Frequency Words. Prepare for the Assessment by studying the words on **BLM SP3-06A Lessons 1–5 Study Sheet** that was sent home on Day 1.

Day 5 Assessment

Objective

The students will accurately select the appropriate answer circle within the context of a sentence and fill in the circle.

Introduction

Teacher Note: The Test makes provision for Differentiated Instruction. The first ten sentences include the words assigned to students with shortened lists. Encourage these students to try all the sentences, but only grade the first ten sentences. The first review test is teacher dictated. The Test is found on two blackline masters.

Distribute a copy of **BLMs SP3-06E–F Lessons 1–5 Test I** and **II** to each student and a 3" × 5" INDEX CARD to be used as a marker. Remind students to fill in each answer circle completely and to erase completely if they wish to change an answer.

Directed Instruction

1 Lead students to correctly place their marker below the Sample, listen to the following dictation, and find the correct answer choice:
Sample

It is <u>easy</u> to get <u>tired</u> when <u>trayning</u> for a sport. <u>All correct</u>

Say, "The circle below the third underlined word has been filled in to show that it is the misspelled word. We will continue in the same way. I will read each sentence and you will choose the misspelled word and fill in the circle below it. If all the words are spelled correctly, fill in the last circle underneath *All correct*."

2 Instruct students to move their marker below each number as the test is dictated.

1. Micah tried to reply to the message during the day.
2. They ate their favorite steak for dinner.
3. You should yield while driving on the steep and icy hill.
4. The tall lady wore a yellow jacket.
5. Please help me shine the trophy to make it brighter.
6. The recipe called for equal parts of honey and brownie mix.
7. Queen Cambria owned a hundred pairs of shoes.
8. A light breeze blew the leaf into the gutter.
9. When you receive the keys, put them in your pocket.
10. The Bible says to never let anyone deceive you.
11. What is the address of the neighbor across the street?
12. How soon can the car reach the speed of eighty?
13. I was eager to ride bicycles in my childhood.
14. Brian's legs began to wobble on the skateboard.
15. On snowy days, I feel very sleepy.
16. The busy fire chief used pliers to fix the leaky hydrant.
17. A tiny acorn fell between the roots of the trees.
18. The trained monkey was not afraid to walk on stilts.
19. Follow the safety rules when playing a game of tennis.
20. Eva believes that Jesus forgave her sins and is a mighty God.

Long o: o, oa, oe, o_e, ow

Day 1 Warm Up

Objective
The students will accurately spell and write words with **long o**. They will spell and write high-frequency words and challenge words.

Introduction
Before class, select Challenge Words for numbers 21 and 22 from a cross-curricular subject, words misspelled on previous assignments, or words that interest your students. The word *flotation* has **long o** spelled **o** and is suggested for number 21. Administer the Warm Up. Encourage students to write all the list words to the best of their ability.

Directed Instruction

1 Say each word, use it in a sentence, and then repeat the word.

Pattern Words

1.	post	Dad dug a hole in the ground for the <u>post</u>.	post
2.	coast	Oceanside is a city on the <u>coast</u>.	coast
3.	toe	I stubbed my big <u>toe</u> on a rock.	toe
4.	cove	We rowed passed the <u>cove</u>.	cove
5.	below	The air is cold when it is <u>below</u> zero.	below
6.	mold	The bread with <u>mold</u> was thrown away.	mold
7.	motor	The <u>motor</u> on the lawn mower is loud.	motor
8.	coach	My soccer <u>coach</u> is also my dad.	coach
9.	rope	The <u>rope</u> is very thick and long.	rope
10.	alone	It is not wise to stay home <u>alone</u>.	alone
11.	slowly	The dog walked <u>slowly</u> across the yard.	slowly
12.	throw	Will you <u>throw</u> the ball to me?	throw
13.	chosen	I have <u>chosen</u> two helpers today.	chosen
14.	follow	"Come, <u>follow</u> Me," Jesus said.	follow
15.	stroke	The golfer has a perfect <u>stroke</u>.	stroke
16.	rowboat	We sailed on the lake in a <u>rowboat</u>.	rowboat
17.	tomorrow	<u>Tomorrow</u> we will go on a field trip.	tomorrow
18.	opening	Sue is <u>opening</u> her birthday present.	opening

High-Frequency Words

19.	minutes	How many <u>minutes</u> are in a day?	minutes
20.	pumpkin	The large <u>pumpkin</u> weighs seventy pounds.	pumpkin

Challenge Words

21. _____

22. _____

2 Allow students to self-correct their pretest, using the following procedure:

  a. Write each word on the board. Discuss the letter/sound relationships in each word. Point out each **long o** spelling—o, oa, oe, o_e, ow. Note that **o_e** is visible in *chosen* and *opening*, but each **long o** spelling is in an open syllable.

  b. As a class, read, spell, and read each word again. Direct students to circle misspelled words with a colored pencil and rewrite them correctly.

3 Proof each student's Warm Up. This becomes an individualized study sheet that can be used at school or at home.

4 Add the Challenge Words and Test Dates before distributing a copy of

---

Student Pages
Pages 25–28

Lesson Materials
BLM SP3-07A
BLM SP3-07B
P-11
P-3
P-4
BLM SP3-07C
BLMs SP3-07D–E
T-10
T-11
BLM SP3-01A
Whiteboards

Transportation
Lessons 7–11 utilize the theme of different kinds of watercraft. Lesson 7 begins with Rowboats, Canoes, and Kayaks. Various types of rowboats have been used since ancient times for travel and leisure. Kayaks, although similar in appearance, differ from canoes in that they are not as wide, are more flat-bottomed, and have a covered deck.

© Spelling Grade 3

BLM SP3-07A Lessons 7–11 Spelling Lists to each student for home study.

5 Homework suggestion: Distribute a copy of **BLM SP3-07B Paddle a Canoe** to each student to practice writing list words.

Day 2 Phonics

Objective

The students will accurately sort and write words that contain spellings for **long o**. They will form two- and three-syllable words by combining the correct syllables.

Introduction

On the board, write the following column headings:

o		oa	oe	o_e		ow	
post	mold	coast	toe	cove	rope	below	slowly
motor	chosen	coach		alone	stroke	follow	throw
opening		rowboat				rowboat	tomorrow

Read each **long o** Pattern Word orally in random order. Ask students to identify the pattern and write the word under the appropriate column.

Directed Instruction

1 Instruct the class to read each word on the board, clapping out each syllable.

2 Display **P-11 Syllables** to reinforce the following generalizations. Divide between double consonants (example number 2) as in *follow* and *tomorrow*. Divide between two smaller words in a compound word (example number 3) as in *rowboat*. Divide between a prefix and a base word (example number 4) as in *alone* and *below*. Divide after a long vowel in an open syllable (example number 6) as in *motor*, *opening*, and *chosen*. Divide between a base word and a suffix (example number 7) as in *slowly* and *opening*.

3 Display **P-3 Spelling Rules** and **P-4 Spelling Rules** to review the rules.

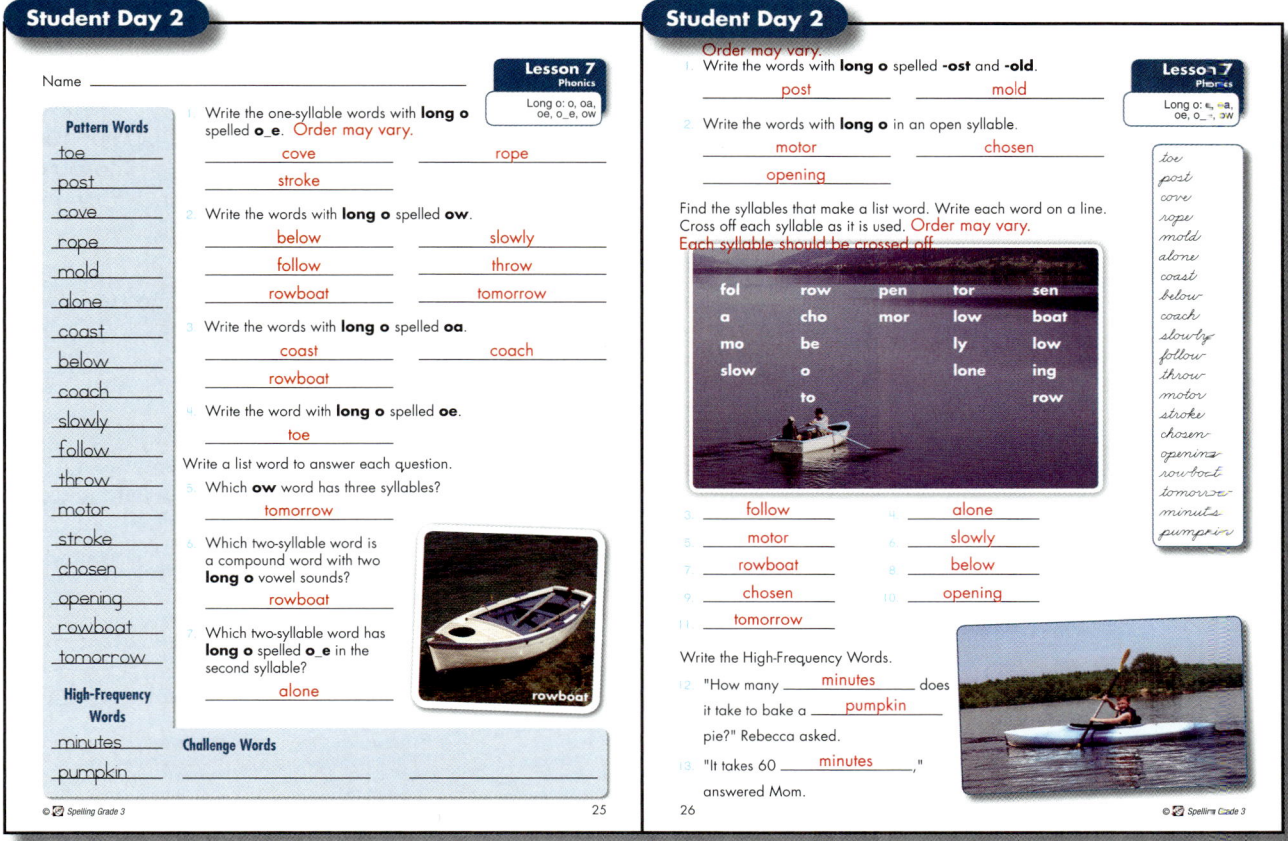

A vowel is usually long when it is followed by one **consonant** and **silent e** (rule number 2). Refer to the o_e column. A vowel is usually long when it is followed by another vowel. The second vowel is silent (rule number 3). Refer to the **oa** and **oe** columns.

4 Explain that *o* makes its long sound in both open and closed syllables. *Post* and *mold* are both closed-syllable words. *Motor, opening,* and *chosen* are words with an open syllable in the first syllable. Refer to **P-4 Spelling Rules** to review the following: A vowel usually makes its long sound when it is in an open syllable. An open syllable ends with a vowel (rule number 4).

5 Teach that the letters **ow** have two pronunciations—/ou/ in *now* and /ō/ in *below*. In this lesson, it is pronounced with the **long o** sound.

6 Proceed to page 25. Say, spell, and say each Pattern and High-Frequency Word. Provide this week's Challenge Words and have students write them in the spaces provided.

7 Proceed to page 26. Provide assistance as needed.

8 Homework suggestion: Distribute a copy of **BLM SP3-07C Boat Phrases** to each student to review multisyllable **long o** words.

Day 3 Word Study

Objective

The students will write list words as nouns and verbs in sentences. They will match sentences with the correct meanings of entry words.

Introduction

Before class, duplicate **BLMs SP3-07D–E Noun, Verb Cards I** and **II** and cut the cards apart. On the board, write the following headings:

Noun—A person, place, or thing		Verb—An action word	
doctor	airport	flying	smelled
paper	shoes	eat	swimming

Teach that a *noun* is <u>a person, place, or thing</u>; a *verb* is <u>an action word</u>. Nouns and verbs are called parts of speech. Randomly select volunteers to attach each card from **BLM SP3-07D Noun, Verb Cards I** to the correct column. Remove the cards from the board.

Directed Instruction

1 Relate that a word can have more than one meaning and be more than one part of speech. *Homographs* are <u>words that are spelled the same but have different meanings</u>. They are different from homophones. Homophones are words that sound the same but have different meanings and spellings.

2 Attach the cards with the word *can* from **BLM SP3-07E Noun, Verb Cards II** under each appropriate column. Explain that *can* is a noun because it is a thing as in *"can of soup"*; it is also a verb because it means *"to be able to,"* as in *"can jump."* *Can* is a homograph. Solicit volunteers to attach the word cards for *bark, seal,* and *slide* in the correct column. Review each meaning.

3 Display **T-10 Multiple Meanings** to show an example of an entry word with multiple meanings and parts of speech.

4 Proceed to page 27. Complete exercises 1 and 2 as a class.

Day 4 Writing

Objective

The students will read a story and write list words. They will write an ending to the story.

Introduction

Display **T-11 Where's My Ending?** and read the story aloud. As a class, brainstorm ideas for an appropriate ending to the story. List the ideas. Choose an ending and write it on the board. Reread the story.

Directed Instruction

1 Proceed to page 28. Students read the story and write each bold list word. They will write an ending to the story on another piece of paper.

2 Homework suggestion: Read the story on page 28 to an adult. Take a practice spelling test at home or use **BLM SP3-01A A Spelling Study Strategy** for additional practice.

Day 5 Wrap Up

Objective
The students will correctly write dictated spelling words and sentences.

Introduction
Provide a review, utilizing WHITEBOARDS or Student Spelling Support suggestions.

Directed Instruction

1 Dictate the list words by using the Warm Up sentences or developing original ones. Reserve *rope*, *coach*, and *chosen* for the dictation sentences.

2 Follow this procedure for the dictation sentences: read the sentence, invite the class to say the sentence with you, then read the sentence again. Dictate the following sentences:
- The monkey tried to climb up the rope.
- The coach put his keys in his pocket.
- The queen has chosen to delay her tennis lesson.

3 If assigned, dictate Extra Challenge Words.

4 Score the test, counting each misspelled word as an error. Correct the dictation sentences as follows: grade only the spelling words or grade the complete sentences, including capitalization and punctuation.

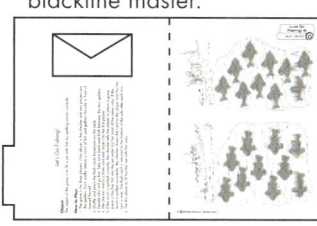

Student Spelling Support

Cont. from page 28

7. For a small group activity play Let's Go Fishing! You will need **BLMs SP3-07H–J Let's Go Fishing! I**, **II**, and **III**, a FILE FOLDER, an ENVELOPE, and CARD STOCK. Follow the assembly instructions on the blackline master.

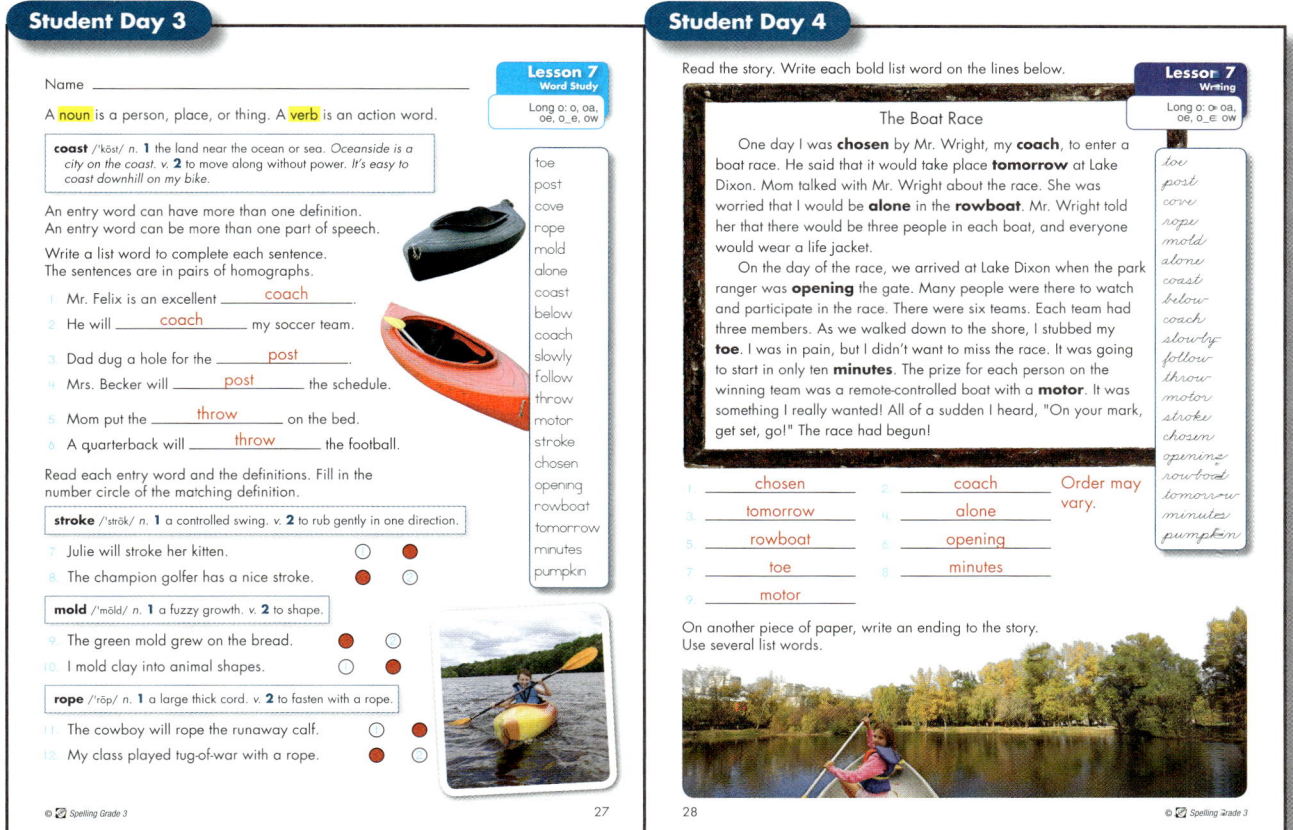

Student Day 3

Name _____

Lesson 7
Word Study

Long o: o, oa, oe, o_e, ow

A noun is a person, place, or thing. A verb is an action word.

coast /'kōst/ n. **1** the land near the ocean or sea. *Oceanside is a city on the coast.* v. **2** to move along without power. *It's easy to coast downhill on my bike.*

An entry word can have more than one definition.
An entry word can be more than one part of speech.

Write a list word to complete each sentence.
The sentences are in pairs of homographs.

1. Mr. Felix is an excellent ___coach___
2. He will ___coach___ my soccer team.
3. Dad dug a hole for the ___post___
4. Mrs. Becker will ___post___ the schedule.
5. Mom put the ___throw___ on the bed.
6. A quarterback will ___throw___ the football.

Read each entry word and the definitions. Fill in the number circle of the matching definition.

stroke /'strōk/ n. **1** a controlled swing. v. **2** to rub gently in one direction.

7. Julie will stroke her kitten.
8. The champion golfer has a nice stroke.

mold /'mōld/ n. **1** a fuzzy growth. v. **2** to shape.

9. The green mold grew on the bread.
10. I mold clay into animal shapes.

rope /'rōp/ n. **1** a large thick cord. v. **2** to fasten with a rope.

11. The cowboy will rope the runaway calf.
12. My class played tug-of-war with a rope.

© Spelling Grade 3 ... 27

toe
post
cove
rope
mold
alone
coast
below
coach
slowly
follow
throw
motor
stroke
chosen
opening
rowboat
tomorrow
minutes
pumpkin

Student Day 4

Read the story. Write each bold list word on the lines below.

Lesson 7
Writing

Long o: o, oa, oe, o_e, ow

The Boat Race

One day I was **chosen** by Mr. Wright, my **coach**, to enter a boat race. He said that it would take place **tomorrow** at Lake Dixon. Mom talked with Mr. Wright about the race. She was worried that I would be **alone** in the **rowboat**. Mr. Wright told her that there would be three people in each boat, and everyone would wear a life jacket.

On the day of the race, we arrived at Lake Dixon when the park ranger was **opening** the gate. Many people were there to watch and participate in the race. There were six teams. Each team had three members. As we walked down to the shore, I stubbed my **toe**. I was in pain, but I didn't want to miss the race. It was going to start in only ten **minutes**. The prize for each person on the winning team was a remote-controlled boat with a **motor**. It was something I really wanted! All of a sudden I heard, "On your mark, get set, go!" The race had begun!

1. ___chosen___ 2. ___coach___ Order may
3. ___tomorrow___ 4. ___alone___ vary.
5. ___rowboat___ 6. ___opening___
7. ___toe___ 8. ___minutes___
9. ___motor___

On another piece of paper, write an ending to the story. Use several list words.

toe
post
cove
rope
mold
alone
coast
below
coach
slowly
follow
throw
motor
stroke
chosen
opening
rowboat
tomorrow
minutes
pumpkin

28 ... © Spelling Grade 3

Student Pages
Pages 29–32

Lesson Materials

BLM SP3-08A
P-3
P-4
BLM SP3-08B
T-12
T-13
BLM SP3-01A
Whiteboards

Transportation

The theme of this lesson is Cruise Ships. Cruise vacations date from the nineteenth century and have recently grown into a booming business industry. Today, cruise ships can accommodate thousands of passengers and are considered floating entertainment centers with spas, swimming pools, movie theaters, and golf courses.

Day 1 Warm Up

Objective

The students will accurately spell and write words with **long u** spelled **ew**, **oo**, **u**, **ue**, **u_e**, and **ui**. They will spell and write high-frequency words and challenge words.

Introduction

Before class, select Challenge Words for numbers 21 and 22 from a cross-curricular subject, words misspelled on previous assignments, or words that interest your students. The word *rescued* has **long u** spelled **ue** and is suggested for number 21. Administer the Warm Up. Encourage students to write all the list words to the best of their ability.

Directed Instruction

1 Say each word, use it in a sentence, and then repeat the word.

Pattern Words

1. huge	Ricky saw the <u>huge</u> ship in the harbor.	huge
2. knew	Max <u>knew</u> the answer to the riddle.	knew
3. clue	Do you understand the <u>clue</u>?	clue
4. crew	The ship's <u>crew</u> stood on deck.	crew
5. loose	The rubber band was <u>loose</u>.	loose
6. choose	Will you help me <u>choose</u> a dessert?	choose
7. root	One <u>root</u> of the tree was above ground.	root
8. fewer	<u>Fewer</u> people came to the pool today.	fewer
9. uniform	Her <u>uniform</u> was clean and ironed.	uniform
10. usual	We will drive the <u>usual</u> way to school.	usual
11. cruise	Vivian went on her first <u>cruise</u>.	cruise
12. suit	Ken bought a new <u>suit</u> for the trip.	suit
13. overdue	The ship was <u>overdue</u> into port.	overdue
14. tube	Anne slid down the <u>tube</u> into the pool.	tube
15. foolish	It is <u>foolish</u> to behave rudely.	foolish
16. fruit	The mango is my favorite <u>fruit</u>.	fruit
17. useful	A compass is a very <u>useful</u> tool.	useful
18. truthful	It pleases God when you are <u>truthful</u>.	truthful

High-Frequency Words

19. Mr.	<u>Mr.</u> Evans will pray during chapel.	Mr.
20. Mrs.	Danielle saw <u>Mrs.</u> Walker today.	Mrs.

Challenge Words

21. _____

22. _____

2 Allow students to self-correct their pretest, following this procedure:

a. Write each word on the board. Discuss the letter/sound relationships in each word. Point out the following **long u** spelling patterns in this lesson: **ew**, **oo**, **u**, **ue**, **u_e**, **ui**. Explain to students that both of the High-Frequency Words, *Mr.* and *Mrs.*, are abbreviations. Define an *abbreviation* as <u>a shortened form of a word</u>. <u>Most abbreviations start with a capital letter and end with a period.</u> Both *Mr.* and *Mrs.* are used as courtesy titles before someone's name.

b. As a class, read, spell, and read each word again. Direct students to circle misspelled words with a colored pencil and rewrite them correctly.

3 Proof each student's Warm Up. This becomes an individualized study sheet that can be used at school or at home.

4 Homework suggestion: Use **BLM SP3-08A Cruise Ship** to review **long u** spelling patterns.

Day 2 Phonics

Objective

The students will correctly sort words by **long u** spellings of **ew**, **oo**, **u**, **ue**, **u_e**, and **ui**. They will write words with more than one syllable, words with the same ending sound, and high-frequency words.

Introduction

Before class, write the **long u** spelling patterns as column headings on the board. Dictate the Pattern Words and invite volunteers to come to the board and write the word below the correct heading.

u_e	ui	ue	oo	u	ew
tube	suit	clue	root	usual	crew
huge	fruit	overdue	loose	truthful	knew
useful	cruise		foolish	uniform	fewer
			choose		

Correct any misspelled words or words written below an incorrect column heading. Chorally read the words while tapping out syllables on desktops.

Directed Instruction

1 Explain to students that **long u** has two pronunciations, /y$\overline{oo}$/ and /$\overline{oo}$/. The /y$\overline{oo}$/ pronunciation is heard in *huge, useful, usual, uniform,* and *fewer.*

2 Display **P-3 Spelling Rules** to review the following rule: A vowel is usually long when it is followed by one **consonant** and **silent e** (rule number 2).

3 Display **P-4 Spelling Rules** to review the following rules: A vowel is usually long when it is followed by another vowel. The second vowel is silent (rule number 3). A vowel usually makes its long sound when it is in

Differentiated Instruction

- For students who spelled all the words correctly on the Warm Up, select and assign three Extra Challenge Words from the following list: passengers, accommodate, scarcity, scheduled, highest, Chronicles.

- For students who spelled less than half correctly, assign the following Pattern and High-Frequency Words: clue, fruit, huge, usual, knew, cruise, choose, truthful, Mr., Mrs. On the Wrap Up, evaluate these students on the ten words assigned; however, encourage them to attempt to spell all the list words to the best of their ability. They are also responsible for writing the dictated sentences.

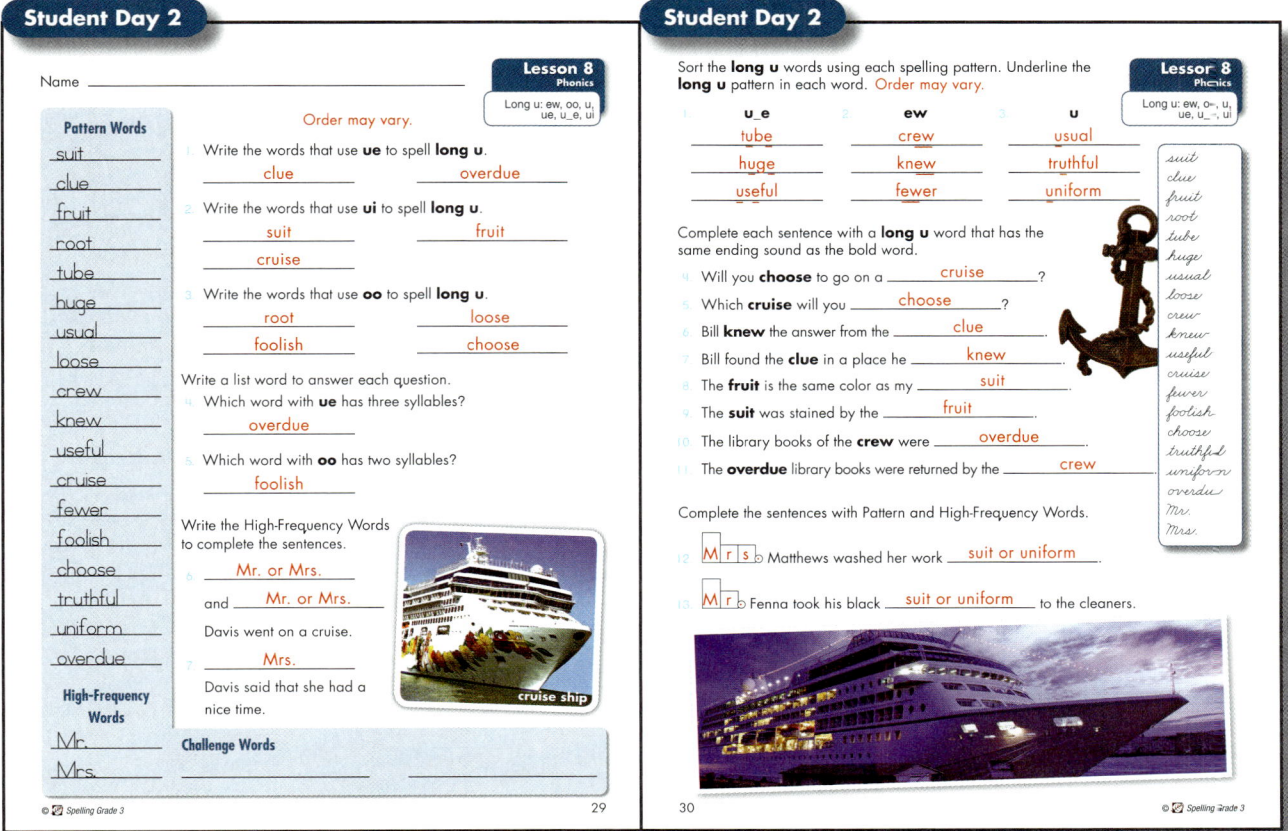

4 Invite students to generate examples for each rule, such as *tube* for rule number 2; *suit*, *clue*, and *root* for rule number 3; and *usual* and *uniform* for rule number 4. Note that *truthful* does not follow rule number 4 because *u* is not in an open syllable.

5 Explain the following spelling generalization for the **ew** spelling: The letters **ew** make the **long u** sound heard in *crew*.

6 Proceed to page 29. Say, spell, and say each Pattern and High-Frequency Word. Provide this week's Challenge Words and have students write them in the spaces provided. Allow students to complete the exercises independently.

7 Proceed to page 30 and select a volunteer to read the directions. Students complete the page independently.

8 Homework suggestion: Use **BLM SP3-08B Fruit** to review **long u** spelling patterns and High-Frequency Words.

Day 3 Word Study

Objective
The students will use their Spelling Dictionary in the back of their textbook to match sentences with identical meanings and match words to the correct definitions.

Introduction
Write the following sentences, with underlined words, on the board:
- Pete will <u>root</u> for his favorite team. (**definition number two**)
- We cut through one <u>root</u> of the tree. (**definition number one**)
- Fred dropped the <u>tube</u> of toothpaste. (**definition number two**)
- Gail waited in line to go down the water <u>tube</u>. (**definition number one**)

Guide students to use their Spelling Dictionary to locate *root* and *tube*. Select students to read the definitions and tell the number of the definition that matches the way the word was used in the sentence on the board.

Directed Instruction
1 Write the following definitions on the board:
- an edible part of a plant (**fruit**)   • not fastened or pulled tight (**loose**)

Dictate the Pattern Words from the lesson and have students raise their hand when they hear a word that matches a definition.

2 Proceed to page 31 and encourage students to use their Spelling Dictionary to assist them as they complete the page independently.

Day 4 Writing

Objective
The students will use proofreading marks to identify mistakes in a travel brochure. They will correctly write misspelled words.

Introduction
Display **T-12 Vacation Cruise** on the overhead. Ask students to share about places they have traveled to for a vacation. Write responses on the board.

Directed Instruction
1 Draw the Proofreading Marks box on the board and write the following sentences:
- (Mrs.) Brown (knue) she had to (t)o pack.
(**Mrs. Brown knew she had to pack.**)
- fewer people vacation during winter
(**Fewer people vacation during winter.**)

Inform students that the sentences contain mistakes and allow volunteers to identify the mistakes. Use correct proofreading marks

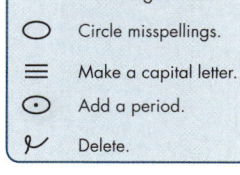

Proofreading Marks
◯ Circle misspellings.
≡ Make a capital letter.
⊙ Add a period.
✔ Delete.

Student Spelling Support Materials

BLMs SP3-08C–D
Card stock
BLM SP3-01A
Construction paper
Letter tiles

Student Spelling Support

1. Write this week's words categorized by patterns on a large piece of paper and attach to the Word Wall.

2. Duplicate **BLMs SP3-08C–D Lesson 8 Spelling Words I** and **II** on CARD STOCK for students to use as flash cards at school or at home.

3. Use **BLM SP3-01A A Spelling Study Strategy** in instructional groups to provide assistance with some or all of the words.

4. Assist students in writing the Challenge Words, numbers 21 and 22, in the section called My Words for Writing, in the back of their textbook.

5. For visual and kinesthetic learners, write incomplete Pattern Words on CONSTRUCTION PAPER, leaving an empty space for the **ew**, **oo**, **u**, **ue**, **u_e**, and **ui** in each word. Allow students to use LETTER TILES with e, i, o, u, and w, to complete the **long u** spelling for each Pattern Word.

6. Share the story of Ananias and Sapphira from Acts 5:1–11. Invite students to write about why being **truthful** is important to God.

and rewrite the sentences correctly.

2 Proceed to page 32. Select a volunteer to read the sentences at the top of the page. Assist students as needed to make sure that all errors are corrected. (**9 misspellings; 4 capital letters needed; 3 periods needed; 4 deletes**)

3 Use **T-13 Proofreading a Travel Brochure** to correct the exercise on page 32.

4 Homework suggestion: Read the brochure on page 32 to an adult. Take a practice spelling test at home or use **BLM SP3-01A A Spelling Study Strategy** for additional practice.

Day 5 Wrap Up

Objective
The students will correctly write dictated spelling words and sentences.

Introduction
Provide a review, utilizing WHITEBOARDS or Student Spelling Support suggestions.

Directed Instruction

1 Dictate the list words by using the Warm Up sentences or developing original ones. Reserve *clue, knew,* and *cruise* for the dictation sentences.

2 Follow this procedure for the dictation sentences: read the sentence, invite the class to say the sentence with you, then read the sentence again. Dictate the following sentences:
- The <u>clue</u> was easy to explain.
- I <u>knew</u> my keys were nearby.
- I will go on the <u>cruise</u> alone.

3 If assigned, dictate Extra Challenge Words.

4 Score the test, counting each misspelled word as an error. Correct the dictation sentences as follows: grade only the spelling words or grade the complete sentences, including capitalization and punctuation.

Notes

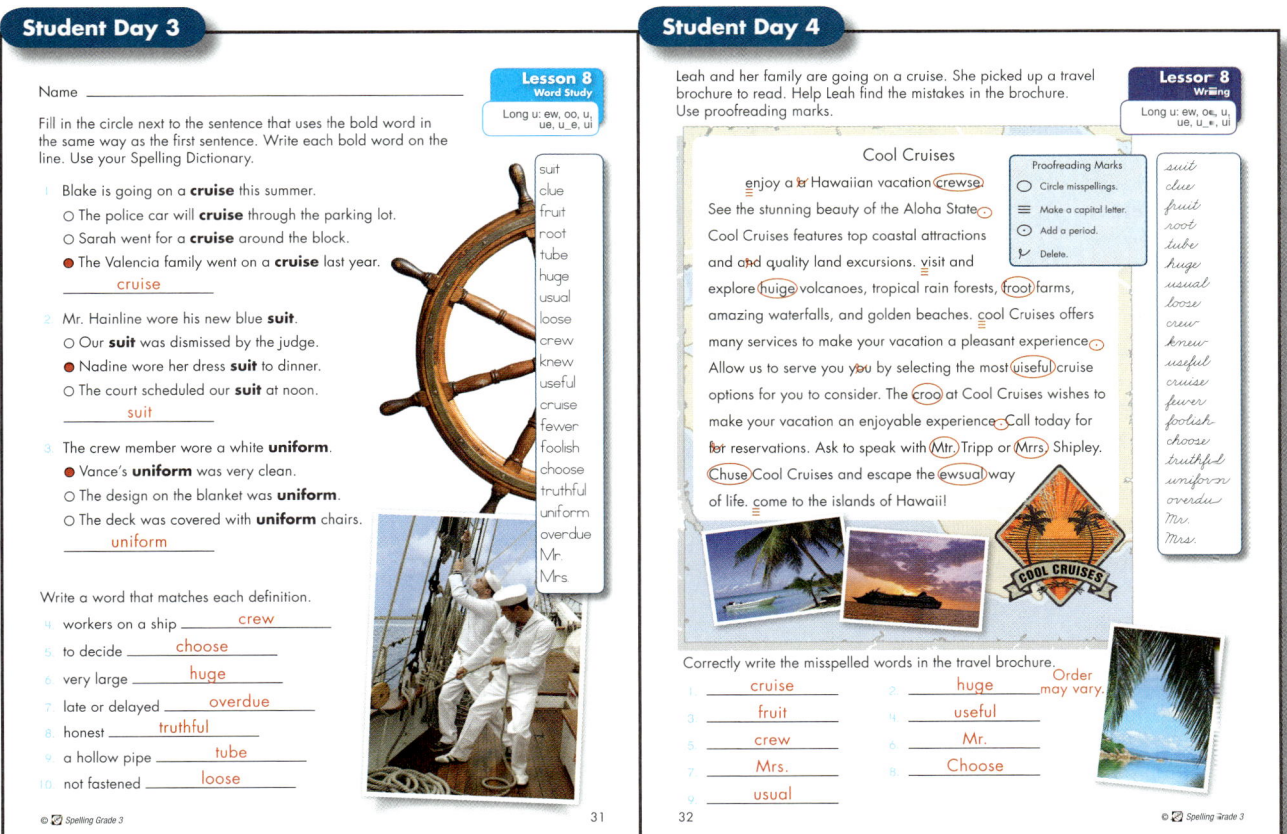

Student Pages

Pages 33–36

Lesson Materials

BLM SP3-09A
BLMs SP3-09B–C
BLM SP3-09D
Card stock
T-14
BLM SP3-09E
BLM SP3-09F
Encyclopedia
T-15
BLM SP3-09G
BLM SP3-01A
Whiteboards

Transportation

The theme of this lesson is Aircraft Carriers and Submarines. An aircraft carrier is a large ship with a flight deck that supports the takeoff and landing of military aircraft. Submarines are able to stay below the surface of the water for long periods of time without being seen. These naval vessels keep our nation safe in times of war.

Day 1 Warm Up

Objective

The students will accurately spell and write words with **consonant blends**. They will spell and write high-frequency words and challenge words.

Introduction

Before class, select Challenge Words for numbers 21 and 22 from a cross-curricular subject, words misspelled on previous assignments, or words that interest your students. The word *Scripture* has the **consonant blend scr** and is suggested for number 21. Administer the Warm Up. Encourage students to write all the list words to the best of their ability.

Directed Instruction

1 Say each word, use it in a sentence, and then repeat the word.

Pattern Words

1.	kept	Sam <u>kept</u> his promise to be ready.	kept
2.	clasp	The girls will <u>clasp</u> hands.	clasp
3.	craft	Origami is a Japanese paper <u>craft</u>.	craft
4.	asks	Marcus always <u>asks</u> good questions.	asks
5.	behind	My best friend sits <u>behind</u> me in class.	behind
6.	drifted	The boat <u>drifted</u> along the river.	drifted
7.	risk	Soldiers <u>risk</u> their lives for their country.	risk
8.	interesting	The Bible is the most <u>interesting</u> book.	interesting
9.	subtract	Did you <u>subtract</u> to find the difference?	subtract
10.	gifts	The wise men brought <u>gifts</u> to Jesus.	gifts
11.	facts	Joshua knew his math <u>facts</u> very well.	facts
12.	actor	An <u>actor</u> played the part of the king.	actor
13.	meant	She never <u>meant</u> to hurt your feelings.	meant
14.	except	Everyone is going <u>except</u> Mark.	except
15.	speech	Mr. Davis gave a nice <u>speech</u> in chapel.	speech
16.	skipper	The <u>skipper</u> commanded the crew.	skipper
17.	present	All members of the class were <u>present</u>.	present
18.	understand	I cannot <u>understand</u> Spanish.	understand

High-Frequency Words

19.	toward	The little dog made its way <u>toward</u> home.	toward
20.	finally	We <u>finally</u> finished our math assignments.	finally

Challenge Words

21. _____

22. _____

2 Allow students to self-correct their pretest, following this procedure:

a. Write each word on the board. Discuss the letter/sound relationships in each word. Define *consonant blends* as <u>a group of two or three consonants together in a word or syllable. Each consonant sound is heard in a blend</u>. Blends can come at the beginning, middle, or end of words. The word *interesting* has four syllables and is often misspelled; pronounce each syllable distinctly and have students repeat after you.

b. As a class, read, spell, and read each word again. Direct students to circle misspelled words with a colored pencil and rewrite them correctly.

3 Proof each student's Warm Up. This becomes an individualized study sheet that can be used at school or at home.

4 Homework suggestion: Use **BLM SP3-09A Submarines** to practice the words in this lesson.

Day 2 Phonics

Objective

The students will complete words by writing the missing **consonant blends**. They will write high-frequency words, and replace letters with **consonant blends** to make list words.

Introduction

Before class, duplicate one copy of **BLMs SP3-09B–C Lesson 9 Spelling Words I**, **II** and **BLM SP3-09D Sorting Mat** on CARD STOCK for each student. The High-Frequency and Challenge Words are not needed for this activity. The word *understand* can be sorted under **st** and/or **nd**. *Interesting* cannot be sorted under **nt** because *n* and *t* are in separate syllables. Provide the students with a second flash card of *understand* by writing *understand* on an empty flash card. Cut the flash cards apart. Place **T-14 Lesson 9 Sorting** on the overhead. The **consonant blends cl**, **cr**, **tr**, **dr**, and **pr** are shown on the side of a submarine. Have volunteers draw a line from each blend to a word that has that blend. In the lower portion of the transparency, the **consonant blends sk**, **nd**, **nt**, **st**, **ft**, **ct**, **sp**, and **pt** are shown. Pronounce each consonant blend and draw students' attention to exercises 6–13. Ask a volunteer to read the words and find the blend that is the same in each exercise. Write the blend on the line. Refer to **BLM SP3-09E T-14 Answer Key**. Remove the transparency before distributing the flash cards and a sorting mat for each student to place on his/her desktop. Allow students to sort the flash cards. The sorting mat focuses on the following blends: **sk**, **nd**, **nt**, **st**, **ft**, **ct**, **sp**, **pt**.

Directed Instruction

1 Proceed to page 33. Say, spell, and say each Pattern and High-Frequency Word. Provide this week's Challenge Words and have students write them in the spaces provided. Clap out the syllables in each word. Ask volunteers to tell you which words have one, two, three, or four syllables.

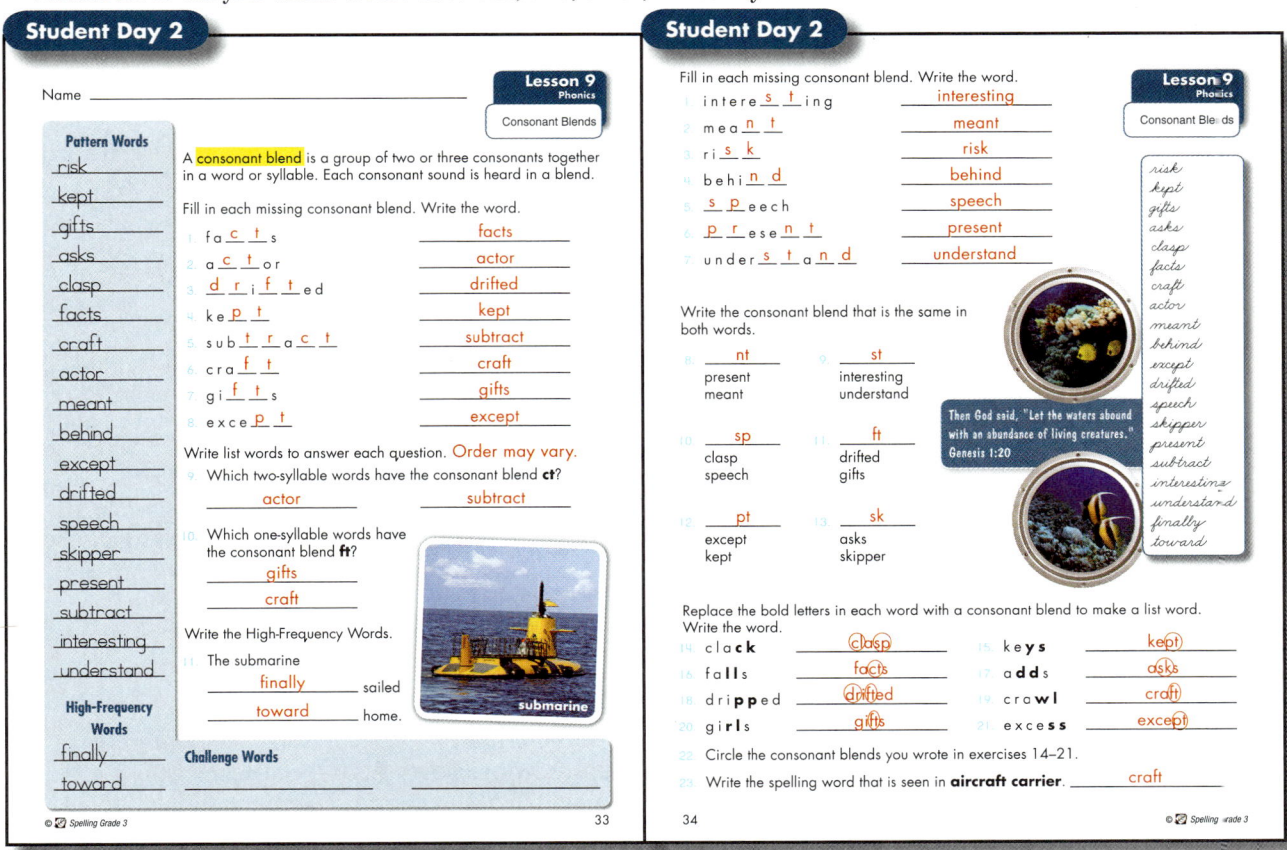

Student Spelling Support Materials

BLMs SP3-09B–C
Card stock
BLM SP3-01A
Ping-pong balls
Empty milk carton

Student Spelling Support

1. Write this week's words categorized by patterns on a large piece of paper and attach to the Word Wall.
2. Duplicate **BLMs SP3-09B–C Lesson 9 Spelling Words I** and **II** on CARD STOCK for students to use as flash cards at school or at home.
3. Use **BLM SP3-01A A Spelling Study Strategy** in instructional groups to provide assistance with some or all of the words.
4. Assist students in writing the Challenge Words, numbers 21 and 22, in the section called My Words for Writing, in the back of their textbook.
5. For kinesthetic learners, play Spell and Roll with two teams or two players. You will need a list of the Pattern Words in this lesson, 13 PING-PONG BALLS, and a clean, EMPTY MILK CARTON. Open one end of the milk carton. Use a black marker to write each of the following **consonant blends** on a ping-pong ball: **sk**, **nd**, **nt**, **st**, **ft**, **ct**, **sp**, **pt**, **cl**, **cr**, **tr**, **dr**, **pr**. Place the ping-pong balls on the carpet in a line about a yard away from the milk carton with the open end facing the line of ping-pong balls. Say one of the Pattern Words, allow the student to spell the word, and identify a consonant blend in the word.

Cont. on page 37

2 Allow students to supply the missing blends, write the words, and answer the questions independently. In exercise 11, students write the High-Frequency Words to complete a sentence.

3 Proceed to page 34. In exercises 1–7, students write the missing blends to complete words. They write the blend common to two words in 8–13. Students replace bold letters with **consonant blends** to make Pattern Words in 14–21. Select a volunteer to read the verse on the page.

4 Homework suggestion: Use **BLM SP3-09F Sorting Consonant Blends** to review **consonant blends** and High-Frequency Words.

Day 3 Word Study

Objective

The students will write a word to match each definition or description. They will use the context of a sentence to determine the meaning of a list word and use the words to complete cloze sentences.

Introduction

Write the list words *speech*, *facts*, *understand*, *drifted*, *craft*, and *gifts* to one side of the board and the following definitions in another area of the board:

- a talk given to a group (**speech**)
- floated along (**drifted**)
- things known to be true (**facts**)
- a type of artwork often made with paper (**craft**)
- things given as presents (**gifts**)
- grasp the meaning of something (**understand**)

Read the definitions and invite students to tell you a word that fits each definition. Remind students that words may have more than one definition and that the Spelling Dictionary can help them to determine the appropriate definition for the word they want to use.

Directed Instruction

1 Write the following sentence on the board:
  • The soldier will <u>risk</u> his life to save others.
Read the sentence. Explain that the meaning of the underlined word can be learned from the context of the sentence. *Risk* in this context means to take a dangerous chance. Ask a volunteer to tell what *risk* means and use it in an original sentence.

2 Proceed to page 35. Read the directions and let students know that they may use the Spelling Dictionary for help with any unknown words. Remind students that antonyms are opposites. Define *periscope* before students complete the page.

Day 4 Writing

Objective

The students will sequence a series of notes taken from an encyclopedia article.

Introduction

Display an ENCYCLOPEDIA. Explain that information found in encyclopedia articles is nonfiction material. Encyclopedias give facts about a number of different subjects. Diagrams may be used to add information or assist in understanding the facts. Many subjects can be found listed alphabetically in various volumes within a set of encyclopedias. Taking notes from encyclopedia articles helps to prepare for a written report.

Directed Instruction

1 Place **T-15 Encyclopedia Article** on the overhead. This transparency is a partial replica of student page 36. Read the article together. Ask, "What is the first thing that has to happen before the submarine dives?" Number and record the response on the transparency below the text.

Continue, "Then what happens?" Continue the list on the transparency. Refer to **BLM SP3-09G T-15 Answer Key**. Remove the transparency.

2 Proceed to page 36. Choose a volunteer to read the directions. Point out that there is an order to the events involved in a submarine's dive and rise that makes sense. Encourage students to read the entire text before attempting to order the sentences in Steven's notes.

3 Homework suggestion: Read the submarine text on page 36 to an adult. Take a practice spelling test at home or use **BLM SP3-01A A Spelling Study Strategy** for additional practice.

Day 5 Wrap Up

Objective
The students will correctly write dictated spelling words and sentences.

Introduction
Provide a review, utilizing WHITEBOARDS or Student Spelling Support suggestions.

Directed Instruction

1 Dictate the list words by using the Warm Up sentences or developing original ones. Reserve *craft*, *subtract*, and *finally* for the dictation sentences.

2 Follow this procedure for the dictation sentences: read the sentence, invite the class to say the sentence with you, then read the sentence again. Dictate the following sentences:
- Jane made a <u>craft</u> from paper and string.
- I will <u>subtract</u> five from ten.
- The lost dog <u>finally</u> reached his home.

3 If assigned, dictate Extra Challenge Words.

4 Score the test, counting each misspelled word as an error. Correct the dictation sentences as follows: grade only the spelling words or grade the complete sentences, including capitalization and punctuation.

Student Spelling Support

Cont. from page 36

If the student correctly spells the word and identifies the blend, allow him/her to get down on hands and knees and blow the ping-pong ball with the matching blend into the milk carton. Follow the same procedure for the other team/player. Continue until all the words or ping-pong balls have been used. The winner is the team or player who has blown the most ping-pong balls into the milk carton.

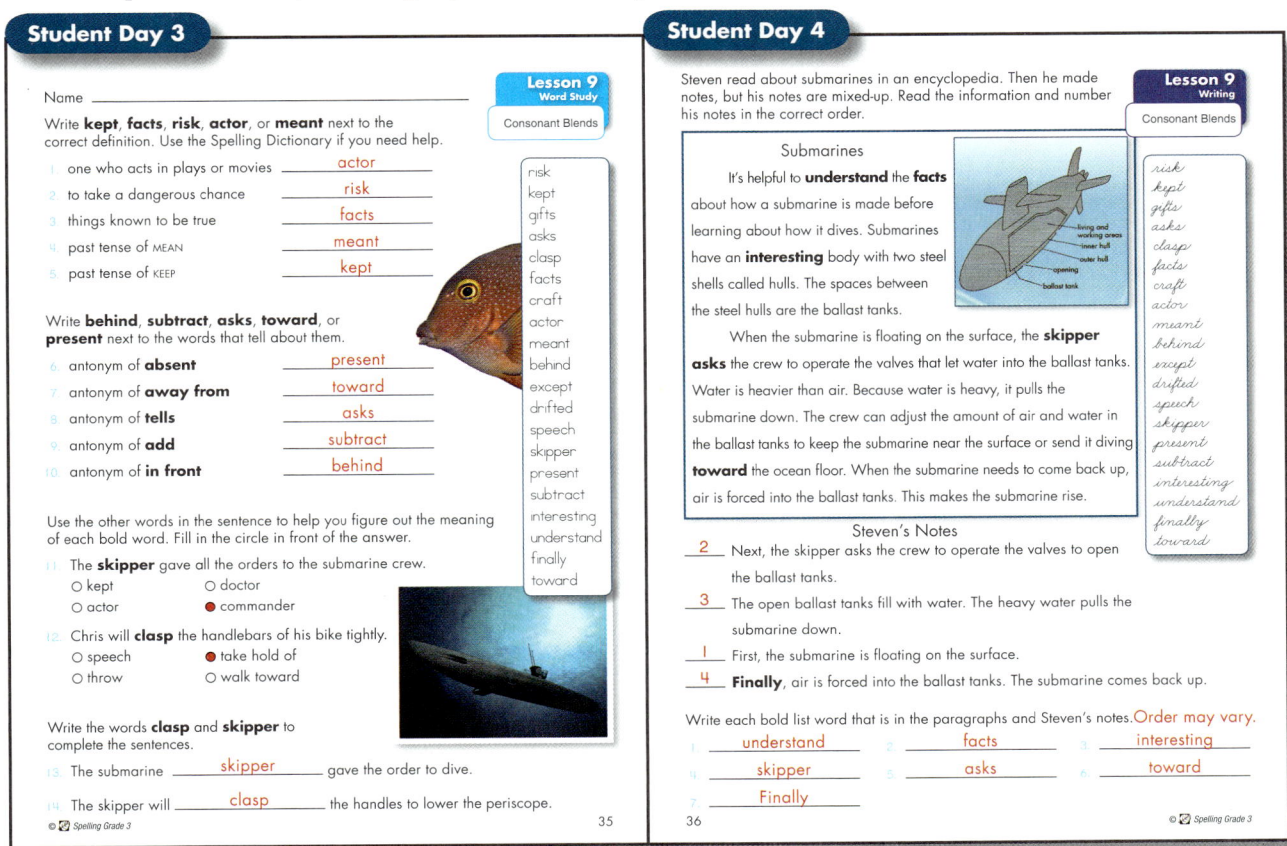

Student Day 3

Name _____

Lesson 9
Word Study

Consonant Blends

Write **kept**, **facts**, **risk**, **actor**, or **meant** next to the correct definition. Use the Spelling Dictionary if you need help.

1. one who acts in plays or movies ___actor___
2. to take a dangerous chance ___risk___
3. things known to be true ___facts___
4. past tense of MEAN ___meant___
5. past tense of KEEP ___kept___

Write **behind**, **subtract**, **asks**, **toward**, or **present** next to the words that tell about them.

6. antonym of **absent** ___present___
7. antonym of **away from** ___toward___
8. antonym of **tells** ___asks___
9. antonym of **add** ___subtract___
10. antonym of **in front** ___behind___

Use the other words in the sentence to help you figure out the meaning of each bold word. Fill in the circle in front of the answer.

11. The **skipper** gave all the orders to the submarine crew.
   ○ kept   ○ doctor
   ○ actor   ● commander

12. Chris will **clasp** the handlebars of his bike tightly.
   ○ speech   ● take hold of
   ○ throw   ○ walk toward

Write the words **clasp** and **skipper** to complete the sentences.

13. The submarine ___skipper___ gave the order to dive.

14. The skipper will ___clasp___ the handles to lower the periscope.

© Spelling Grade 3   35

Word list: risk, kept, gifts, asks, clasp, facts, craft, actor, meant, behind, except, drifted, speech, skipper, present, subtract, interesting, understand, finally, toward

Student Day 4

Steven read about submarines in an encyclopedia. Then he made notes, but his notes are mixed-up. Read the information and number his notes in the correct order.

Lesson 9
Writing

Consonant Blends

Submarines

It's helpful to **understand** the **facts** about how a submarine is made before learning about how it dives. Submarines have an **interesting** body with two steel shells called hulls. The spaces between the steel hulls are the ballast tanks.

When the submarine is floating on the surface, the **skipper** **asks** the crew to operate the valves that let water into the ballast tanks. Water is heavier than air. Because water is heavy, it pulls the submarine down. The crew can adjust the amount of air and water in the ballast tanks to keep the submarine near the surface or send it diving **toward** the ocean floor. When the submarine needs to come back up, air is forced into the ballast tanks. This makes the submarine rise.

Word list (script): risk, kept, gifts, asks, clasp, facts, craft, actor, meant, behind, except, drifted, speech, skipper, present, subtract, interesting, understand, finally, toward

Steven's Notes

__2__ Next, the skipper asks the crew to operate the valves to open the ballast tanks.

__3__ The open ballast tanks fill with water. The heavy water pulls the submarine down.

__1__ First, the submarine is floating on the surface.

__4__ **Finally**, air is forced into the ballast tanks. The submarine comes back up.

Write each bold list word that is in the paragraphs and Steven's notes. Order may vary.

1. ___understand___   2. ___facts___   3. ___interesting___
4. ___skipper___   5. ___asks___   6. ___toward___
7. ___Finally___

36   © Spelling Grade 3

© Spelling Grade 3   **37**

Lesson Materials

BLM SP3-10A
BLM SP3-10B
BLM SP3-10C
T-16
BLM SP3-01A
Whiteboards

Transportation

The theme of this lesson is Sailboats and Personal Watercraft. Egyptians invented sailboats thousands of years ago and built the boats from reeds or imported lumber from Lebanon. Clayton Jacobson II built the first personal watercraft in 1965. Jacobson had enjoyed racing motorcycles and desired a way to race on the water.

Day 1 Warm Up

Objective

The students will accurately spell and write words with **consonant blends and silent letters**. They will spell and write high-frequency words and challenge words.

Introduction

Before class, select Challenge Words for numbers 21 and 22 from a cross-curricular subject, words misspelled on previous assignments, or words that interest your students. The word *vault* has **consonant blend lt** and is suggested for number 21. Administer the Warm Up. Encourage students to write all the list words to the best of their ability.

Directed Instruction

1 Say each word, use it in a sentence, and then repeat the word.

Pattern Words

1. halftime	The band played during <u>halftime</u>.	halftime
2. silky	Mom wore a red, <u>silky</u> scarf with her suit.	silky
3. helper	Mandy is a good <u>helper</u>.	helper
4. lamb	The little <u>lamb</u> lay next to its mother.	lamb
5. crumb	Mark picked up the <u>crumb</u> on the floor.	crumb
6. yourself	You'll complete the project all by <u>yourself</u>.	yourself
7. calf	Did you know a baby whale is called a <u>calf</u>?	calf
8. Psalms	There are 150 chapters in the book of <u>Psalms</u>.	Psalms
9. gulped	Justin quickly <u>gulped</u> the glass of water.	gulped
10. fields	Farmer Jon picked the crops in his <u>fields</u>.	fields
11. building	The tall <u>building</u> is fifty stories high.	building
12. cornstalk	The <u>cornstalk</u> held six ears of corn.	cornstalk
13. melted	The chocolate <u>melted</u> in the hot sun.	melted
14. world	Jesus said, "You are the light of the <u>world</u>."	world
15. built	Noah <u>built</u> the ark according to God's plans.	built
16. climber	Does a mountain <u>climber</u> wear hiking boots?	climber
17. palm	The pitcher held the baseball in his <u>palm</u>.	palm
18. calmed	Jesus <u>calmed</u> the storm on the Sea of Galilee.	calmed

High-Frequency Words

19. nothing	There was <u>nothing</u> left in the cookie jar.	nothing
20. machine	Lorraine enjoys her new sewing <u>machine</u>.	machine

Challenge Words

21. _____

22. _____

2 Allow students to self-correct their pretest, using the following procedure:

   a. Write each word on the board. Discuss the letter/sound relationships in each word. Point out the **consonant blends and silent letters**. Explain that *Psalms* is capitalized because it is a book of the Bible. The High-Frequency Words are difficult to spell since they are nonphonetic. The letters *ch* are pronounced /sh/ in *machine*; this is a new letter/sound relationship for most third grade students.

   b. As a class, read, spell, and read each word again. Direct students to circle misspelled words with a colored pencil and rewrite them correctly.

3 Proof each student's Warm Up. This becomes an individualized study sheet that can be used at school or at home.

4 Homework suggestion: Use **BLM SP3-10A Floating Letters** to review the Pattern and High-Frequency Words.

Day 2 Phonics

Objective

The students will sort and write words according to their **consonant blends and silent letters**, syllables, and ending sounds. They will cross out silent letters and write high-frequency words.

Introduction

Before class, duplicate enough copies of **BLM SP3-10B Blends and Silent Letter Cards** for each student to have one card. Cut apart the cards. On the board, write the headings as shown below.

_lm	_mb	_ld	_lf	_lp	_lk	_lt	**no pattern**
palm	lamb	fields	calf	helper	silky	built	nothing
Psalms	crumb	world	halftime	gulped	cornstalk	melted	machine
calmed	climber	building	yourself				

Distribute one card to each student. Instruct students to listen carefully to the word you say and to raise their card when they hear and identify a word with the same letters on their card. Choose a student to write the word on the board below the correct column. High-Frequency Words will match the "no pattern" card. Collect the cards when finished, but do not erase the board.

Directed Instruction

1 Read each column aloud, clapping for each syllable.

2 Lead students to discover the following letter-sound patterns:
- The letter *b* is silent in *lamb*, *crumb*, and *climber*.
- The letter *l* is silent after short *a*, in *calf* and *halftime*, but heard after short *e* in *yourself*.
- The letter *l* is silent in *cornstalk*, but heard after short *i* in *silky*.
- The letter *l* is silent before *m* in *palm*, *Psalms*, and *calmed*.

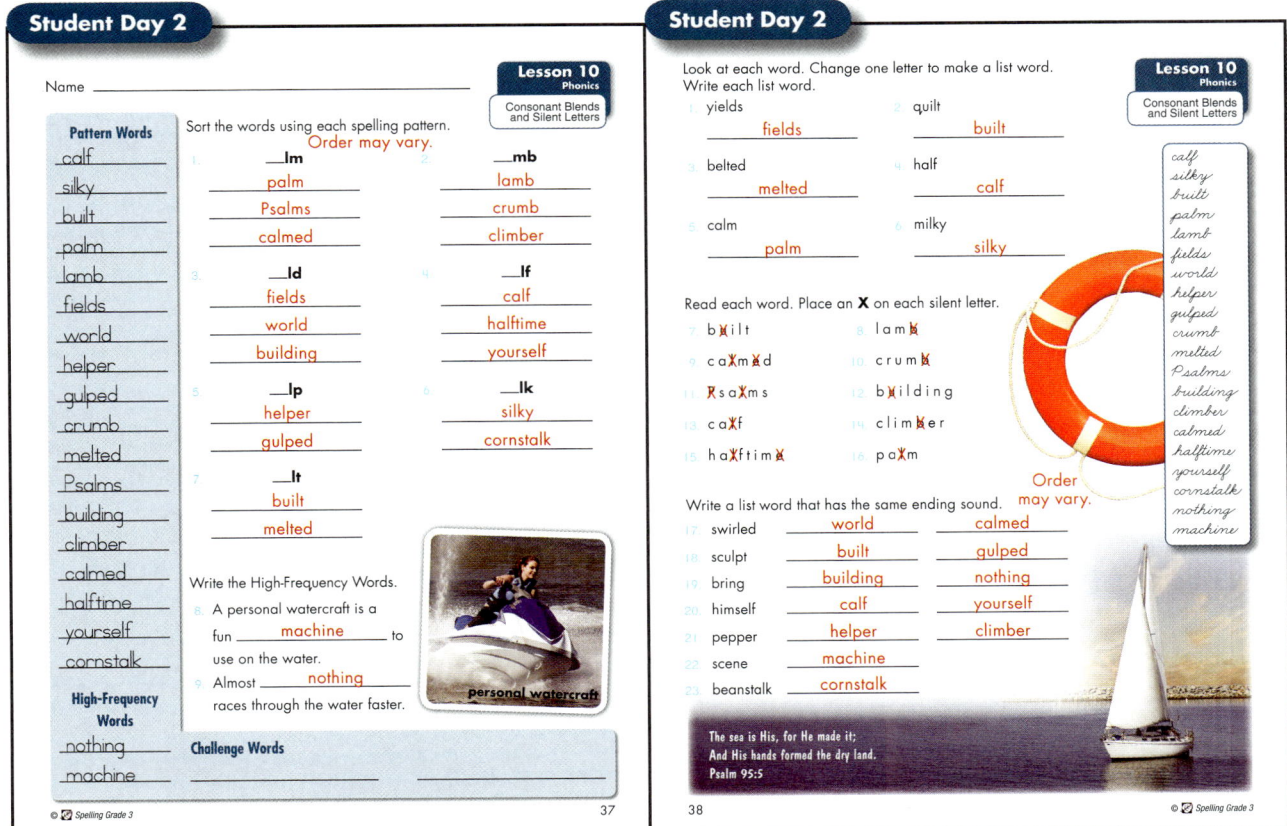

Student Spelling Support

1. Write this week's words categorized by patterns on a large piece of paper and attach to the Word Wall.
2. Duplicate **BLMs SP3-10D–E Lesson 10 Spelling Words I** and **II** on CARD STOCK for students to use as flash cards at school or at home.
3. Use **BLM SP3-01A A Spelling Study Strategy** in instructional groups to provide assistance with some or all of the words.
4. Assist students in writing the Challenge Words, numbers 21 and 22, in the section called My Words for Writing, in the back of their textbook.
5. For kinesthetic learners, have each student take a turn acting out a spelling word in a pantomime. When another student has guessed the word, the "actor" will repeat the word, and then spell it as he/she writes it on the board.
6. For a science and literature connection, have available the book, *Ships and Other Sea Craft* by Nigel Hawkes (Brookfield, CT: Copper Beech Books, 1999). Students can read about how sailboats, personal watercraft, and other water vehicles work, are constructed, and keep afloat.

Cont. on page 41

• The letter *u* is silent after *b* in *built* and *building*. Solicit volunteers to mark an X over the silent letters.

3 On another area of the board, write the words *ball* and *hair*. Explain that these two words will form new words when the first letter is changed. For example, guide students to change *b* to *c* to make *call* and *h* to *p* to make *pair*.

4 Call out the words *wanted* and *follower*. Select a student to name list words that have the same ending sounds. (**Melted ends like *wanted*; helper and climber end like *follower*.**)

5 Proceed to page 37. Say, spell, and say each Pattern and High-Frequency Word. Provide this week's Challenge Words and have students write them in the spaces provided. Select a student to read the directions. Allow students to complete the page independently.

6 Proceed to page 38. Solicit a volunteer to read the directions. Answer any questions before allowing students to complete the page. Select a volunteer to read Psalm 95:5 at the bottom of the page.

7 Homework suggestion: Use **BLM SP3-10C All Mixed-Up** to review the words and the patterns in this lesson.

Day 3 Word Study

Objective

The students will write words with **consonant blends and silent letters** to complete analogies.

Introduction

Before class, write the following incomplete analogies on the board:

• <u>Book</u> is to <u>page</u> as <u>tree</u> is to _____. (**leaf**)
• <u>Hungry</u> is to <u>eat</u> as <u>thirsty</u> is to _____. (**drink**)

Ask the students to raise their hand if they know the name of these kinds of sentences. Guide students to realize that these are analogies. Define an analogy for the students. An *analogy* is <u>made up of two word pairs</u>. <u>Both pairs of words have the same kind of relationship</u>. Read the first analogy and ask a volunteer to state how the words *book* and *page* are related. (**A book has a page.**) Apply the same relationship to *tree* by asking students to tell you what is on a tree. (**A tree has a leaf.**) In the next analogy, assist students in understanding the relationship between *hungry* and *eat*—if you are *hungry*, then you *eat*—before applying it to *thirsty*.

Directed Instruction

1 Proceed to page 39. Reinforce the definition of an analogy. Complete the first analogy together.

2 Allow students to complete the page. Assist as needed.

Day 4 Writing

Objective

The students will read a story and write list words. They will identify sentence parts that compare and contrast sailboats with personal watercraft.

Introduction

Display **T-16 Compare/Contrast**. Discuss how the two pictures are alike and different. Write students' sentences on the board. Possible suggestions are: sailboats and personal watercraft are types of transportation; sailboats and personal watercraft are used on a lake, sea, or ocean; and sailboats get their power from the wind, but personal watercraft get their power from an engine.

Directed Instruction

1 Teach that the previous activity is an example of comparing and contrasting. *Compare* and *contrast* mean <u>to look and see how two or more things are alike or different</u>. Tell students that comparing and contrasting while reading is a useful skill. It helps you remember events, objects, and characters as well as gives you a better understanding of what is read. Instruct students to look for sentences that compare and contrast sailboats and personal watercraft in today's assignment.

2 Proceed to page 40. Allow students to read the paragraphs and complete the page.

3 Homework suggestion: Read the paragraphs on page 40 to an adult. Take a practice spelling test at home or use **BLM SP3-01A A Spelling Study Strategy** for additional practice.

Day 5 Wrap Up

Objective
The students will correctly write dictated spelling words and sentences.

Introduction
Provide a review, utilizing WHITEBOARDS or Student Spelling Support suggestions.

Directed Instruction

1 Dictate the list words by using the Warm Up sentences or developing original ones. Reserve *calf*, *helper*, and *nothing* for the dictation sentences.

2 Follow this procedure for the dictation sentences: read the sentence, invite the class to say the sentence with you, then read the sentence again. Dictate the following sentences:
- The little <u>calf</u> walked toward the barn.
- I was chosen to be a <u>helper</u> this week.
- There is <u>nothing</u> in my pocket.

3 If assigned, dictate Extra Challenge Words.

4 Score the test, counting each misspelled word as an error. Correct the dictation sentences as follows: grade only the spelling words or grade the complete sentences, including capitalization and punctuation.

Student Spelling Support
Cont. from page 40

7. For a biblical connection, read Matthew 7:24–27: "Therefore whoever hears these sayings of Mine, and does them, I will liken him to a wise man who **built** his house on the rock: and the rain descended, the floods came, and the winds blew and beat on that house; and it did not fall, for it was founded on the rock. But everyone who hears these sayings of Mine, and does not do them, will be like a foolish man who **built** his house on the sand: and the rain descended, the floods came, and the winds blew and beat on that house; and it fell. And great was its fall." Relate how our lives need to be built upon God's Word and not on our own feelings and understandings. Display **T-17 The Wise Man and the Foolish Man Lyrics** on the overhead and sing the song.

Student Day 3

Name _____

Lesson 10
Word Study
Consonant Blends and Silent Letters

An analogy is made up of two word pairs. Both pairs of words have the same kind of relationship.

Choose the best word to complete each analogy. Write it on the line.

1. **Full** is to **empty** as **something** is to ___nothing___.
2. **Dog** is to **puppy** as **cow** is to ___calf___.
3. **Grass** is to **lawn** as **crops** are to ___fields___.
4. **Tire** is to **car** as **gear** is to ___machine___.
5. **Cold** is to **hot** as **frozen** is to ___melted___.
6. **Her** is to **herself** as **your** is to ___yourself___.
7. **Cat** is to **kitten** as **sheep** is to ___lamb___.
8. **Street** is to **road** as **Earth** is to ___world___.
9. **Puzzle** is to **piece** as **bread** is to ___crumb___.
10. **Drink** is to **beverage** as **smooth** is to ___silky___.
11. **Waiter** is to **server** as **assistant** is to ___helper___.
12. **Swim** is to **swam** as **build** is to ___built___.
13. **Bean** is to **beanstalk** as **corn** is to ___cornstalk___.
14. **Foot** is to **heel** as **hand** is to ___palm___.
15. **Beginning** is to **kickoff** as **middle** is to ___halftime___.
16. **Sailboat** is to **sailor** as **mountain** is to ___climber___.
17. **Ate** is to **gobbled** as **drank** is to ___gulped___.
18. **New Testament** is to **Matthew** as **Old Testament** is to ___Psalms___.

Word list:
calf
silky
built
palm
lamb
fields
world
helper
gulped
crumb
melted
Psalms
building
climber
calmed
halftime
yourself
cornstalk
nothing
machine

39

Student Day 4

Read the paragraphs. Write each bold list word on the lines below.

Lesson 10
Writing
Consonant Blends and Silent Letters

Sailboats and Personal Watercraft

Did you know that sailboats and personal watercraft (PWC) are two different types of water transportation? People all over the **world** use them.

Sailboats are powered by the wind. To steer a sailboat, you adjust the tiller. While on a sailboat, you should sit down. You can ride alone or with friends.

Personal watercraft were invented by Mr. Jacobson. He liked the idea of riding fast on water. In 1965, he **built** his first personal watercraft. The first PWC was designed for you to steer **yourself** while standing up. Eventually, others were made to include a seat and room for a partner. A PWC gets its power from a **machine** called an engine. To steer a PWC, grip the handlebars.

Both kinds of water vessels, sailboats and PWC, are fun when there is **nothing** to do on a hot summer day. It is best to use them after the winds have **calmed** down and the water is not rough. Whether you are on a sailboat or a PWC, wear a life jacket.

calf
silky
built
palm
lamb
fields
world
helper
gulped
crumb
melted
Psalms
building
climber
calmed
halftime
yourself
cornstalk
nothing
machine

Order may vary.

1. ___world___ 2. ___built___ 3. ___yourself___
4. ___machine___ 5. ___nothing___ 6. ___calmed___

7. Read the phrases that compare and contrast sailboats and personal watercraft. If the phrase tells how sailboats and personal watercraft are the same, write **S** on the line in front of the phrase.

_____ powered by wind
_S_ must wear life jacket
_S_ type of water transportation
_____ invented by Mr. Jacobson
_____ built in 1965
_S_ are fun

40

Three-Letter Consonant Spelling Patterns

Lesson Materials

BLM SP3-11A
BLMs SP3-11B–C
Card stock
BLM SP3-11D
5" × 8" Index cards
BLM SP3-01A
Whiteboards

Transportation

The theme of this lesson is Freighters and Tugboats. Freighters are large, ocean-going cargo vessels. Tugboats are small, sturdy ships used to maneuver large ships within a harbor. Tugboats may also tow barges on rivers. The first tugboat ever, the *Charlotte Dundas*, was built in 1802.

Day 1 Warm Up

Objective

The students will accurately spell and write words with **three-letter consonant spelling patterns**. They will spell and write high-frequency words and challenge words.

Introduction

Before class, select Challenge Words for numbers 21 and 22 from a cross-curricular subject, words misspelled on previous assignments, or words that interest your students. The word *squirrel* has **squ** and is suggested for number 21. Administer the Warm Up. Encourage students to write all the list words to the best of their ability.

Directed Instruction

1 Say each word, use it in a sentence, and then repeat the word.

Pattern Words

1.	splinter	Jana got a <u>splinter</u> in her finger.	splinter
2.	squeak	The little mouse let out a <u>squeak</u>.	squeak
3.	thrill	It was a <u>thrill</u> to hear the orchestra play.	thrill
4.	scratch	My dog began to <u>scratch</u> a flea.	scratch
5.	Christian	Let's say the pledge to the <u>Christian</u> flag.	Christian
6.	splashed	Water <u>splashed</u> against the boat.	splashed
7.	thread	Mom will embroider with <u>thread</u>.	thread
8.	throat	Amesha stayed home with a sore <u>throat</u>.	throat
9.	three	Jesus went to pray with <u>three</u> disciples.	three
10.	Christmas	Have you read the story of <u>Christmas</u>?	Christmas
11.	strong	The <u>strong</u> little tugboat towed a barge.	strong
12.	sprinkle	Rain began to <u>sprinkle</u> down.	sprinkle
13.	shrimp	<u>Shrimp</u> are my favorite seafood.	shrimp
14.	squall	A storm at sea is a <u>squall</u>.	squall
15.	shrink	Some clothes <u>shrink</u> in the dryer.	shrink
16.	struggle	It was a <u>struggle</u> to put on the tight pants.	struggle
17.	spray	I will <u>spray</u> the plants with water daily.	spray
18.	school	<u>School</u> is a place for learning.	school

High-Frequency Words

19.	special	God thinks that you are very <u>special</u>.	special
20.	laugh	A baby's <u>laugh</u> is a delight to hear.	laugh

Challenge Words

21. _____

22. _____

2 Allow students to self-correct their pretest, using the following procedure:

a. Write each word on the board. Discuss the letter/sound relationships in each word. Point out each **three-letter consonant spelling pattern** and pronounce it clearly. The High-Frequency Words may be difficult for students to spell because they are nonphonetic. Explain that the letters *augh* in *laugh* are pronounced /af/. The letters *cial* in *special* are pronounced /shəl/. The words *Christian* and *Christmas* are always capitalized. The letter *u* is not a consonant; however, it goes with *q* to make a three-letter consonant spelling pattern.

b. As a class, read, spell, and read each word again. Direct students to circle misspelled words with a colored pencil and rewrite them correctly.

3 Proof each student's Warm Up. This becomes an individualized study sheet that can be used at school or at home.

4 Homework suggestion: Use **BLM SP3-11A Freighters** to review the Pattern Words and High-Frequency Words in the lesson.

Day 2 Phonics

Objective

The students will write words with **three-letter consonant spelling patterns**, words that rhyme, and high-frequency words. They will identify words with the same sound, write two-syllable words, and write pattern and high-frequency words in sentences.

Introduction

Before class, duplicate **BLMs SP3-11B–C Lesson 11 Spelling Words I** and **II** on CARD STOCK. Cut the cards apart. You will not need the Challenge Words or the High-Frequency Words for this activity. Clearly pronounce each of the following **three-letter consonant spelling patterns: thr, squ, spr, shr, sch, str, spl, scr, chr**. Invite students to hold up a flash card that has that spelling pattern. Select students with the correct spelling pattern to say and spell the word. Since more than one Pattern Word may have a particular spelling pattern, have students who have selected different words, say and spell each word. Write the spelling patterns and Pattern Words on the board after the students have had a chance to respond.

thr	squ	spr	shr	sch
thrill	squall	spray	shrink	school
three	squeak	sprinkle	shrimp	
throat				
thread				

str	spl	scr	chr
strong	splinter	scratch	Christian
struggle	splashed		Christmas

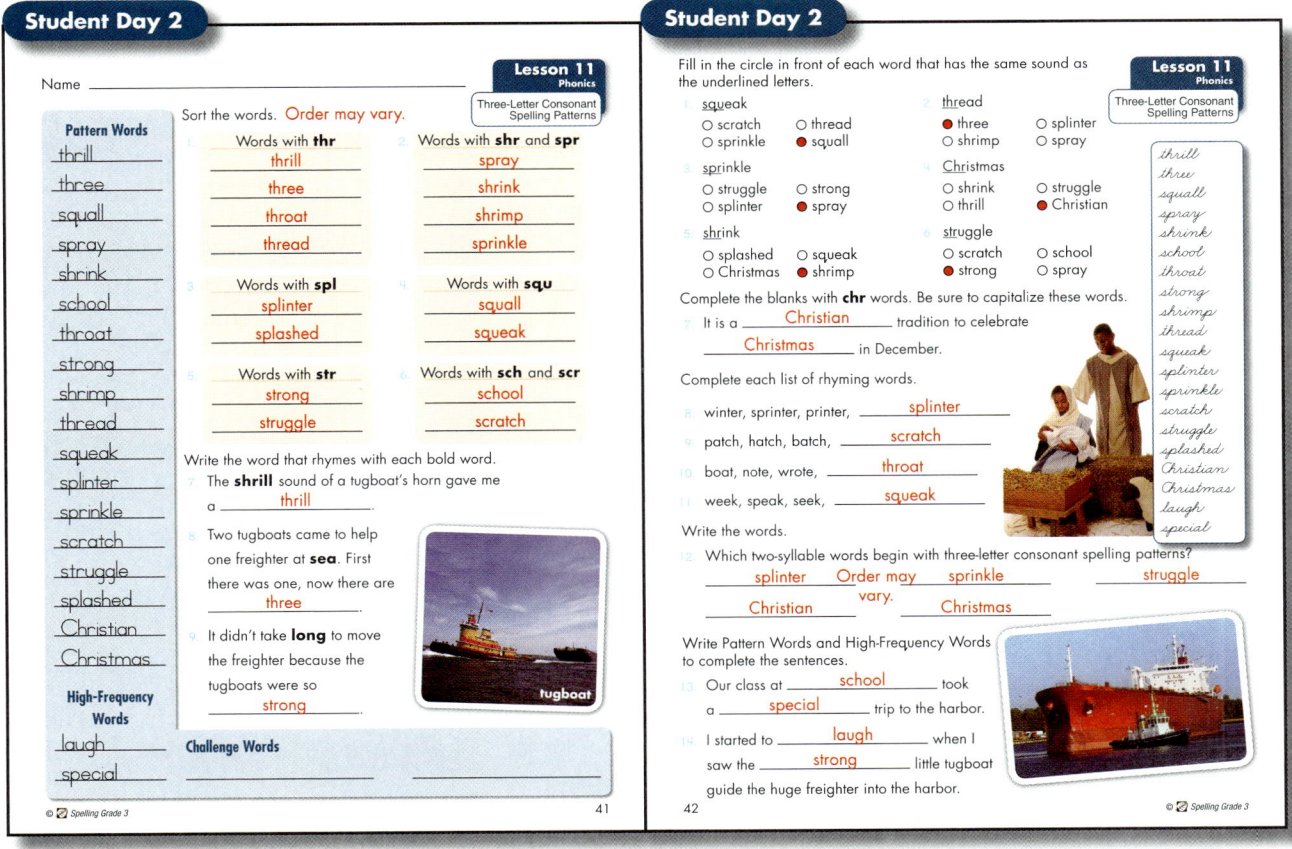

© Spelling Grade 3   43

Directed Instruction

1 Proceed to page 41. Say, spell, and say each Pattern and High-Frequency Word. Provide this week's Challenge Words and have students write them in the spaces provided.

2 Explain that in order for words to rhyme, they must have the same vowel sound and ending sound. Allow students to complete the page.

3 Proceed to page 42. Students identify another word with the same sound as the underlined letters in the target word. Remind students that words may have similar spellings that make different sounds.

4 Use **BLM SP3-11D Tugboats** to review **three-letter consonant spelling patterns**.

Day 3 Word Study

Objective

The students will alphabetize words by the second, third, and fourth letters. They will write list words that would be on the same dictionary page as the sample guide words.

Introduction

Before class, use a black marker to write the words *splinter*, *special*, and *sprinkle* on three 5" × 8" INDEX CARDS. Underline the third letter in each word. Call on three volunteers to come to the front of the room, distribute the cards in the order listed above, and have the students hold the cards for the class to read. Explain that the class will be alphabetizing the words. Note that these words all begin with the letters *sp*. When words begin with the same two letters, the third letter is used to alphabetize the words. Have students identify the third letter in each word, check the alphabet chart, and arrange the volunteers so that they are standing in alphabetical order. Write the words *thread*, *throat*, and *thrill* on three additional index cards. Underline the fourth letter in each word since the first three letters are the same. Repeat the activity.

Directed Instruction

1 Write the words *can* and *cat* on the board. Tell students that these words will be used as *guide words*, the two words at the top of the page in a dictionary. These two words are the first and last words defined on a page. Since both of these words begin with *ca*, the third letter is used to alphabetize the words. Write the words *cab*, *cast*, *cap*, and *call* in a column to one side, underline the third letters, and have volunteers write them under the guide words if they fall alphabetically between *can* and *cat*. (**Cap and cast fall between can and cat.**)

2 Proceed to page 43. Have students underline the second, third, or fourth letter in the words to make it easier to alphabetize.

Day 4 Writing

Objective

The students will complete a cloze activity written in the form of an e-mail. They will match statements that relate a specific cause to a specific effect.

Introduction

Write the following headings and sentences on the board:

Cause (event)
• It began to rain.
• I was late leaving the house.

Effect (what happened)
• I had to run to catch the bus.
• I put up my umbrella.

Define *cause* as an event that leads to another event. Define *effect* as an event that happens as a result of another event. Select volunteers to make a line from the cause in the first column to the effect in the second column.

Directed Instruction

1 Explain that writers use cause and effect relationships to help readers understand the sequence of events in a story or article.

2 Proceed to page 44. Remind students that the numbers in the paragraphs correspond to those below where they write their answers. At the bottom of the page, students match each *cause* to its corresponding *effect*.

3 Homework suggestion: Read the e-mail on page 44 to an adult. Take a practice spelling test at home or use **BLM SP3-01A A Spelling Study Strategy** for additional practice.

Day 5 Wrap Up

Objective

The students will correctly write dictated spelling words and sentences.

Introduction

Provide a review, utilizing WHITEBOARDS or Student Spelling Support suggestions.

Directed Instruction

1 Dictate the list words by using the Warm Up sentences or developing original ones. Reserve *three*, *Christian*, and *special* for the dictation sentences.

2 Follow this procedure for the dictation sentences: read the sentence, invite the class to say the sentence with you, then read the sentence again. Dictate the following sentences:
- Three lambs went into the fields.
- We say the pledge to the Christian flag each day.
- Mom will make a special meal for dinner tonight.

3 If assigned, dictate Extra Challenge Words.

4 Score the test, counting each misspelled word as an error. Correct the dictation sentences as follows: grade only the spelling words or grade the complete sentences, including capitalization and punctuation.

Notes

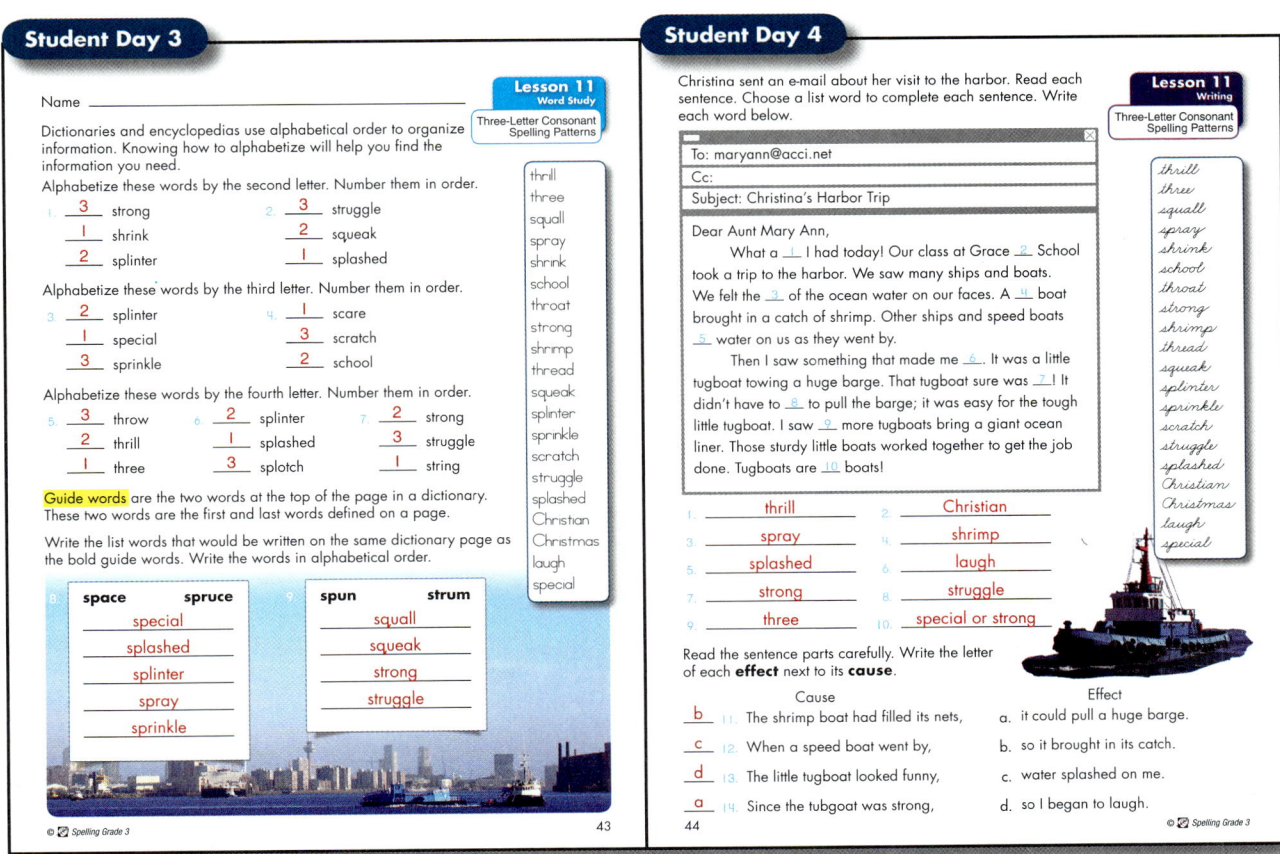

Student Pages
Pages 45–48

Lesson Materials
P-3
P-4
T-18
BLM SP3-12A
BLM SP3-12B
T-19
BLM SP3-12C
BLM SP3-12D
BLMs SP3-12E–F
3" × 5" Index cards

Day 1 Long o: o, oa, oe, o_e, ow

Objective
The students will spell, identify, and circle words with **long o** spelled **o**, **oa**, **oe**, **o_e**, and **ow**. They will identify and write a two-syllable word that contains two spellings for **long o**.

Introduction
Teacher Note: This week's lesson incorporates the Pattern and High-Frequency Words taught in Lessons 7–11 using a variety of activities such as sorting, a crossword puzzle, filling in the correct answer circle, a word search, scrambled words, and shape boxes.

Review **long o** words by writing the Pattern Words from Lesson 7 on the board. Display **P-3 Spelling Rules** to review the following rule: A vowel is usually long when it is followed by one **consonant** and **silent e** (rule number 2). Have students identify Pattern Words that follow this rule. (**cove, rope, alone, stroke**)

Directed Instruction
1 Display **P-4 Spelling Rules** to review the following rules: A vowel is usually long when it is followed by another vowel. The second vowel is silent (rule number 3). A vowel usually makes its long sound when it is in an open syllable. An open syllable ends with a vowel (rule number 4).

2 Have students identify Pattern Words that follow rule number 3. (**toe, coast, coach, rowboat**)

3 Ask students to identify Pattern Words that reflect rule number 4. (**motor, chosen, opening**) Remind students that *post* and *mold* also make the **long o** sound with the **o** spelling, but are closed syllables because they end with a consonant.

4 Display **T-18 Lessons 7–11 Study Sheet** on the overhead to review Lesson 7 words in unison, using the say-spell-say technique.

5 Proceed to page 45. Explain that the box contains all the Pattern and High-Frequency Words in Lessons 7–11. This list is the same list of words that was previously displayed on the overhead. Encourage students to use this list as a review tool. Allow students to complete the page independently.

6 Distribute one copy of **BLM SP3-12A Lessons 7–11 Study Sheet** to each student to take home for study.

7 Homework suggestion: Duplicate one copy of **BLM SP3-12B Missing Letters** for each student to practice with **long o** and **long u** words.

Day 2 Long u: ew, oo, u, ue, u_e, ui and Consonant Blends

Objective
The students will spell and write **long u** words in a crossword puzzle. They will select the appropriate answer circle to indicate if a word with a **consonant blend** is spelled correctly or incorrectly, and correctly write each word.

Introduction
Review the following definition of a **consonant blend**: A consonant blend is a group of two or three consonants together in a word or syllable.

Each consonant sound is heard in a blend. Before class, write the following Pattern Words from Lesson 8 on the board:

- uniform (**an outfit of work clothes; the same in color or design**)
- root (**the part of the plant that absorbs water and nutrients from the soil; to cheer or shout**)
- clue (**an aid in solving a mystery or crossword puzzle**)
- suit (**a set of clothes; a case brought to a court of law**)

Remind students that words may have more than one definition. Ask them to listen carefully as you describe each word by using the definitions. Have them identify which word you are defining and write the definition adjacent to the word. Select students to read each word and its definition(s).

Directed Instruction

1 Display **T-19 Correct or Incorrect?** to teach students how to select appropriate answer circles when identifying a correctly or incorrectly spelled word. Place a piece of paper on the bottom of the transparency to cover the answers. Read each word, indicate if it is spelled correctly or incorrectly, and fill in the appropriate circle. Write each word correctly on the adjacent line. This assessment-style format will help prepare students for achievement testing.

2 Display **T-18 Lessons 7–11 Study Sheet** to review Lessons 8–9 words in unison, using the say-spell-say technique.

3 Proceed to page 46 and allow students to complete the page independently. Encourage them to use their Spelling Dictionary if needed.

4 Homework suggestion: Distribute a copy of **BLM SP3-12C Spell Carefully** to each student to practice with **consonant blends** and **silent letters**.

Day 3 Consonant Blends and Silent Letters

Objective

The students will find and circle words with **consonant blends** and **silent letters** in a word search and write them.

Introduction

Review words with **consonant blends** and **silent letters** by writing the Pattern Words from Lesson 10 on the board. Ask students to identify the following:

- words with **consonant blends** ld, lp, and lt (**fields, world, building; helper, gulped; built, melted**)
- words with **silent** l (**calf, palm, Psalms, calmed, halftime, cornstalk**)
- words with **silent** b (**lamb, crumb, climber**)
- words with **silent** u (**built, building**)

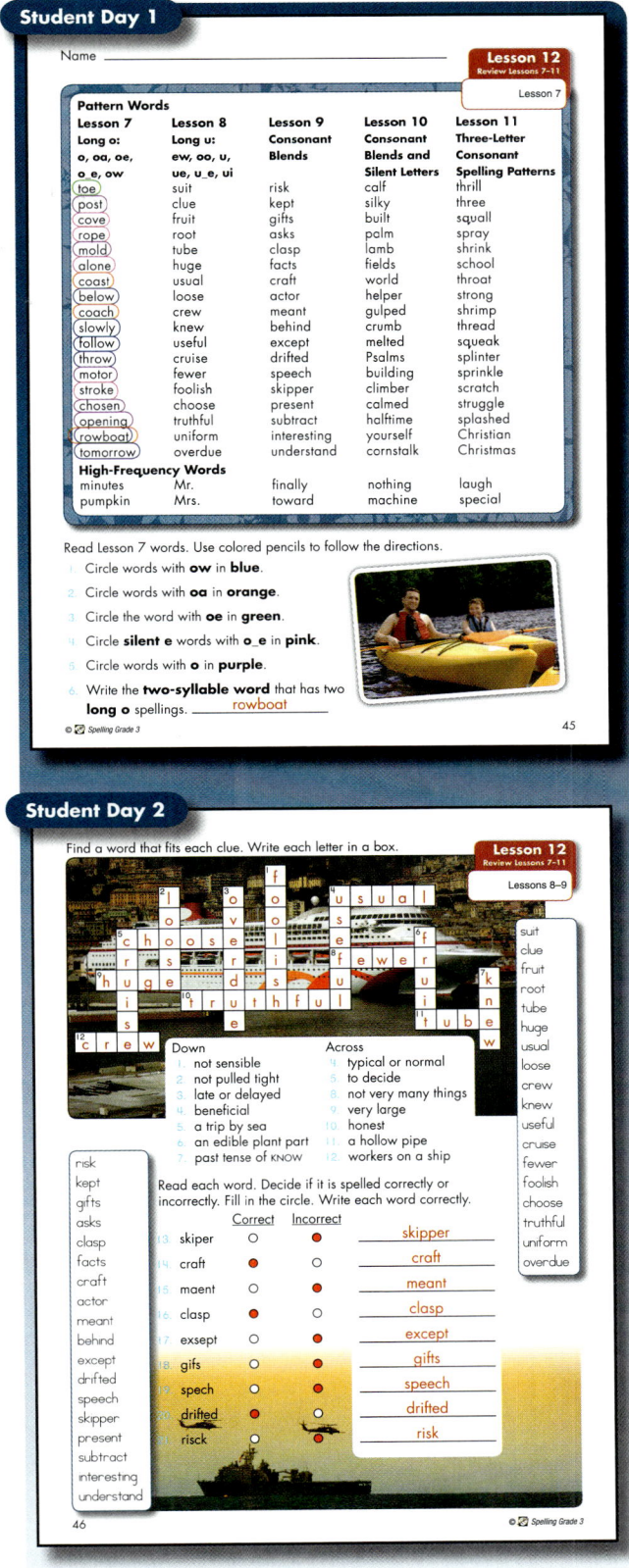

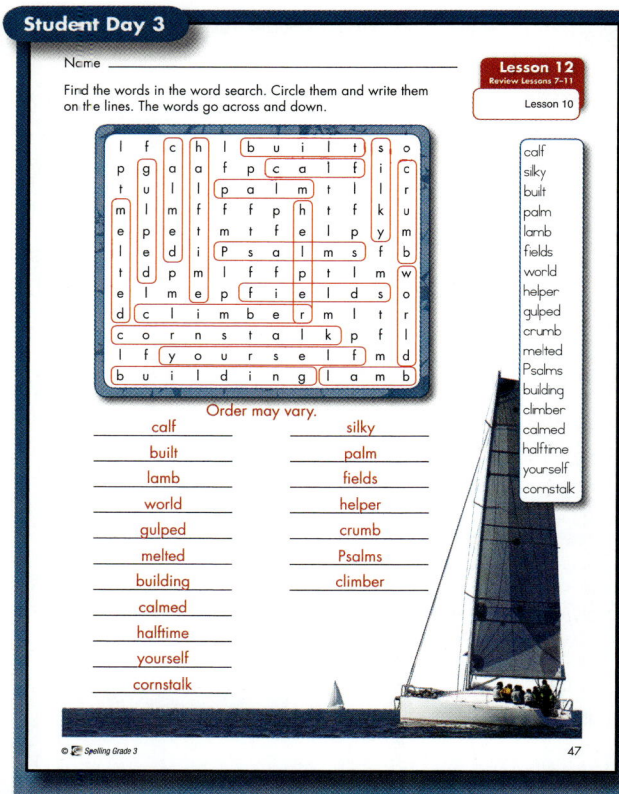

Name _____

Find the words in the word search. Circle them and write them on the lines. The words go across and down.

Lesson 12
Review Lessons 7–11

Lesson 10

Order may vary.

calf	silky
built	palm
lamb	fields
world	helper
gulped	crumb
melted	Psalms
building	climber
calmed	
halftime	
yourself	
cornstalk	

Word list:
calf, silky, built, palm, lamb, fields, world, helper, gulped, crumb, melted, Psalms, building, climber, calmed, halftime, yourself, cornstalk

© Spelling Grade 3   47

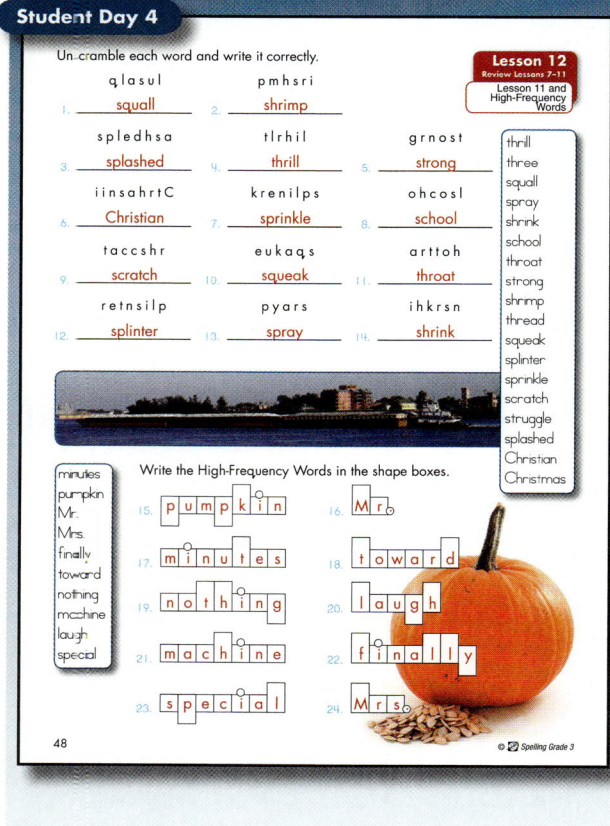

Lesson 12
Review Lessons 7–11

Lesson 11 and High-Frequency Words

Unscramble each word and write it correctly.

1. q l a s u l — squall
2. p m h s r i — shrimp
3. s p l e d h s a — splashed
4. t l r h i l — thrill
5. g r n o s t — strong
6. i i n s a h r t C — Christian
7. k r e n i l p s — sprinkle
8. o h c o s l — school
9. t a c c s h r — scratch
10. e u k a q s — squeak
11. a r t t o h — throat
12. r e t n s i l p — splinter
13. p y a r s — spray
14. i h k r s n — shrink

Word list:
thrill, three, squall, spray, shrink, school, throat, strong, shrimp, thread, squeak, splinter, sprinkle, scratch, struggle, splashed, Christian, Christmas

Write the High-Frequency Words in the shape boxes.

Word list: minutes, pumpkin, Mr., Mrs., finally, toward, nothing, machine, laugh, special

15. pumpkin
16. Mr.
17. minutes
18. toward
19. nothing
20. laugh
21. machine
22. finally
23. special
24. Mrs.

48   © Spelling Grade 3

Directed Instruction

1 Select a few Pattern Words from Lesson 10 that contain similar patterns or letters. Use the words to design a mini word search on the board. Remind students that words can intersect, share letters, and go across or down.

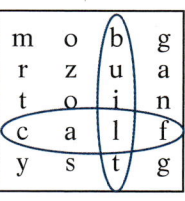

2 Display **T-18 Lessons 7–11 Study Sheet** to review Lesson 10 words in unison, using the say-spell-say technique.

3 Proceed to page 47 and select a student to read the directions. Students complete the page independently.

Day 4 Three-Letter Consonant Spelling Patterns and High-Frequency Words

Objective

The students will unscramble words with **three-letter consonant spelling patterns** and write high-frequency words in shape boxes.

Introduction

Display **T-18 Lessons 7–11 Study Sheet** to review Lesson 11 words. Write the following scrambled words from Lesson 11 on the board:

• h e e r t (**three**)
• t r d h a e (**thread**)
• s s a m i t h r C (**Christmas**)
• g g l e u t r s (**struggle**)

Encourage students to refer to the transparency to find a word that contains the same letters as the scrambled word on the board. Remind students that the words in Lesson 11 begin with a **three-letter consonant spelling pattern** and that they should select three consonants that go together. This will help them to unscramble the words. Select students to unscramble the words and write each word on the board.

Directed Instruction

1 Refer to **T-18 Lessons 7–11 Study Sheet** to review Lesson 11 and High-Frequency Words in unison, using the say-spell-say technique.

2 Challenge students to identify how many tall letters and tail letters there are in each High-Frequency Word.

3 Proceed to page 48. Allow students to read the directions and complete the page independently.

4 Homework suggestion: Duplicate one copy of **BLM SP3-12D Letters and Cake** for each student to practice with **three-letter consonant spelling patterns** and High-Frequency Words. Prepare for the Assessment by studying the words on **BLM SP3-12A Lessons 7–11 Study Sheet** that was sent home on Day 1.

Day 5 Assessment

Objective

The students will accurately select the appropriate answer circle within the context of a sentence and fill it in.

Introduction

Teacher Note: The Test makes provision for Differentiated Instruction. The first ten sentences include the words assigned to students with shortened lists. Encourage these students to try all the sentences, but only grade the first ten sentences. This is the first test that will not be teacher dictated. The Sample will be dictated and the sentences are provided below for reference. The Test is found on two blackline masters.

Prior to handing out the Test, read through the sentences and select words that may be confusing or challenging for students. Inform students that the Test will not be a teacher-dictated test, but that you will be reviewing some difficult words that are in sentences on the test. Write the words on the board and sound them out with students before the Test.

Directed Instruction

1 Distribute a copy of **BLMs SP3-12E–F Lessons 7–11 Test I** and **II** to each student and a 3" × 5" INDEX CARD to be used as a marker. Remind students to fill in each answer circle completely and to erase completely if they wish to change an answer.

2 Lead students to correctly place their marker below the Sample, listen to the following dictation, and find the correct answer choice:

Sample

The <u>calf</u> and <u>lammb</u> were standing by the <u>post</u>. <u>All correct</u>

 Ⓐ ● Ⓒ Ⓓ

Say, "The circle below the second underlined word has been filled in to show that it is the misspelled word. You will continue the test now on your own. Move your marker below each sentence and read each sentence. Choose the word that you think is misspelled and fill in the circle below it. If all the words are spelled correctly, fill in the fourth circle underneath *All correct*."

3 Assist students as needed while they read the sentences and complete the Test on their own.

1. After school our coach had us practice for three hours.
2. Mrs. Riley walked toward the building.
3. The strong man lifted the huge pumpkin above his head.
4. Fruit and shrimp were chosen for the reception meal.
5. The silky rope slipped out of Carrie's palm.
6. Mr. Logan was given a cruise as a retirement present.
7. The scratch on my toe has finally healed.
8. Mitch knew the rowboat was behind the shed.
9. The machine melted the chocolate in two minutes.
10. A Christian should choose to be truthful.
11. Carly is opening her Christmas gifts.
12. The second rock climber will slowly follow the leader.
13. A famous actor will throw the football during halftime.
14. The scientist kept the interesting mold in a container.
15. Miguel gulped, cleared his throat, and began his speech.
16. The squall calmed down as we neared the coast.
17. Paige bought black thread to sew her new uniform and suit.
18. Each cornstalk will be harvested from the fields tomorrow.
19. The skipper and crew guided the ship around the cove.
20. It is useful to read and understand the book of Psalms.

Words with Silent Letters

Lesson Materials

BLM SP3-13A
BLM SP3-13B
T-20
T-21
BLM SP3-13C
BLM SP3-13D
T-6
BLM SP3-01A
Whiteboards

Transportation

Lessons 13–17 utilize the theme of different kinds of vehicles. Lesson 13 begins with Cars. The first car was a steam car built in 1769 by a French Army officer named Captain Nicolas-Joseph Cugnot. Steam cars gave way to cars with internal-combustion engines. Today, new car technologies include hybrid cars and vehicles that have onboard navigation systems.

Day 1 Warm Up

Objective

The students will accurately spell and write **words with silent letters**. They will spell and write high-frequency words and challenge words.

Introduction

Before class, select Challenge Words for numbers 21 and 22 from a cross-curricular subject, words misspelled on previous assignments, or words that interest your students. The word *design* has the silent letter *g* before *n* and is suggested for number 21. Administer the Warm Up.

Directed Instruction

1 Say each word, use it in a sentence, and then repeat the word.

Pattern Words

1. whole	Henry bought a <u>whole</u> new set of tires.	whole
2. kneel	Sometimes I <u>kneel</u> when I pray to Jesus.	kneel
3. rack	Lucas placed his bicycle on the <u>rack</u>.	rack
4. wrist	Amber twisted her <u>wrist</u> when she fell.	wrist
5. whose	<u>Whose</u> car shall we use tonight?	whose
6. knock	Please <u>knock</u> loudly on the door.	knock
7. wrench	Jaye used a <u>wrench</u> to hold the bolt.	wrench
8. knotted	The ribbons were all <u>knotted</u> up.	knotted
9. wrecker	A <u>wrecker</u> came to the accident scene.	wrecker
10. slick	The roads were very <u>slick</u> after the storm.	slick
11. wrong	The <u>wrong</u> car part was ordered.	wrong
12. gnat	A <u>gnat</u> has two wings.	gnat
13. whom	<u>Whom</u> did you expect to see?	whom
14. sign	The highway <u>sign</u> posted the speed limit.	sign
15. writing	Rico is <u>writing</u> a poem for the contest.	writing
16. knife	The butcher sharpened his carving <u>knife</u>.	knife
17. checking	The mechanic is <u>checking</u> the engine.	checking
18. unknown	The <u>unknown</u> sound startled Karl.	unknown

High-Frequency Words

19. object	The broken <u>object</u> will be replaced.	object
20. directions	Alexis wrote down the <u>directions</u>.	directions

Challenge Words

21. _____

22. _____

2 Allow students to self-correct their pretest, using the following procedure:

a. Write each word on the board. Discuss the letter/sound relationships in each word. Point out that the lesson contains **words with silent letters**. The spelling patterns for these words consist of the following: *gn*, *kn*, *wr*, *ck*, and *wh* before *o*.

b. As a class, read, spell, and read each word again. Direct students to circle misspelled words with a colored pencil and rewrite them correctly.

3 Proof each student's Warm Up.

4 Add the Challenge Words and Test Dates before distributing a copy of **BLM SP3-13A Lessons 13–17 Spelling Lists** to each student for home study.

5 Homework suggestion: Use **BLM SP3-13B Cross Out** to review **words with silent letters**.

Day 2 Phonics

Objective

The students will sort **words with silent letters** and select a word with the same sound as a target word. They will pronounce and write **words with silent letters** and write high-frequency words.

Introduction

Display **T-20 Silent Letters** on the overhead to review the Pattern Words with silent letters in this lesson. Point to, say, and chorally spell each word. Chorally spell each word again and instruct students to place their pointer finger in front of their mouth when they say the silent letter in each word. As a visual guide, each silent letter is printed in orange. Invite a student to cross out the silent letter in the word. Repeat this process for all the words. Challenge students to find the two Pattern Words that contain two silent letter spelling patterns each. (**knock, wrecker**)

Directed Instruction

1 Display **T-21 Sounds** to practice selecting sounds that are the same in two words and to correctly say the pronunciation of a **word with silent letters**. In exercises 1–5, read each word carefully and have students identify which word has the same sound as the underlined letter. In exercises 6–12, remind students that entry words in a dictionary have their pronunciation after the word. Teach that the **words with silent letters** have a different spelling than their pronunciation because the **silent letter** is missing in the pronunciation. Say each pronunciation and allow students to spell the word. Write each word on the adjacent line to the pronunciation. Use **BLM SP3-13C T-21 Answer Key**.

2 Proceed to page 49. Say, spell, and say each Pattern and High-Frequency Word. Provide this week's Challenge Words and have students write them in the spaces provided. Read the generalization about **words with silent letters** at the top of the page. Have students chorally read the generalization. Allow students to complete the page.

(Proceed to page 49.)

Differentiated Instruction

- For students who spelled all the words correctly on the Warm Up, select and assign three Extra Challenge Words from the following list: hybrid, combustion, application, quiver, outrageous, Esther.

- For students who spelled less than half correctly, assign the following Pattern and High-Frequency Words: sign, knife, knock, whole, whose, wrong, writing, checking, object, directions. On the Wrap Up, evaluate these students on the ten words assigned; however, encourage them to attempt to spell all the list words to the best of their ability. They are also responsible for writing the dictated sentences.

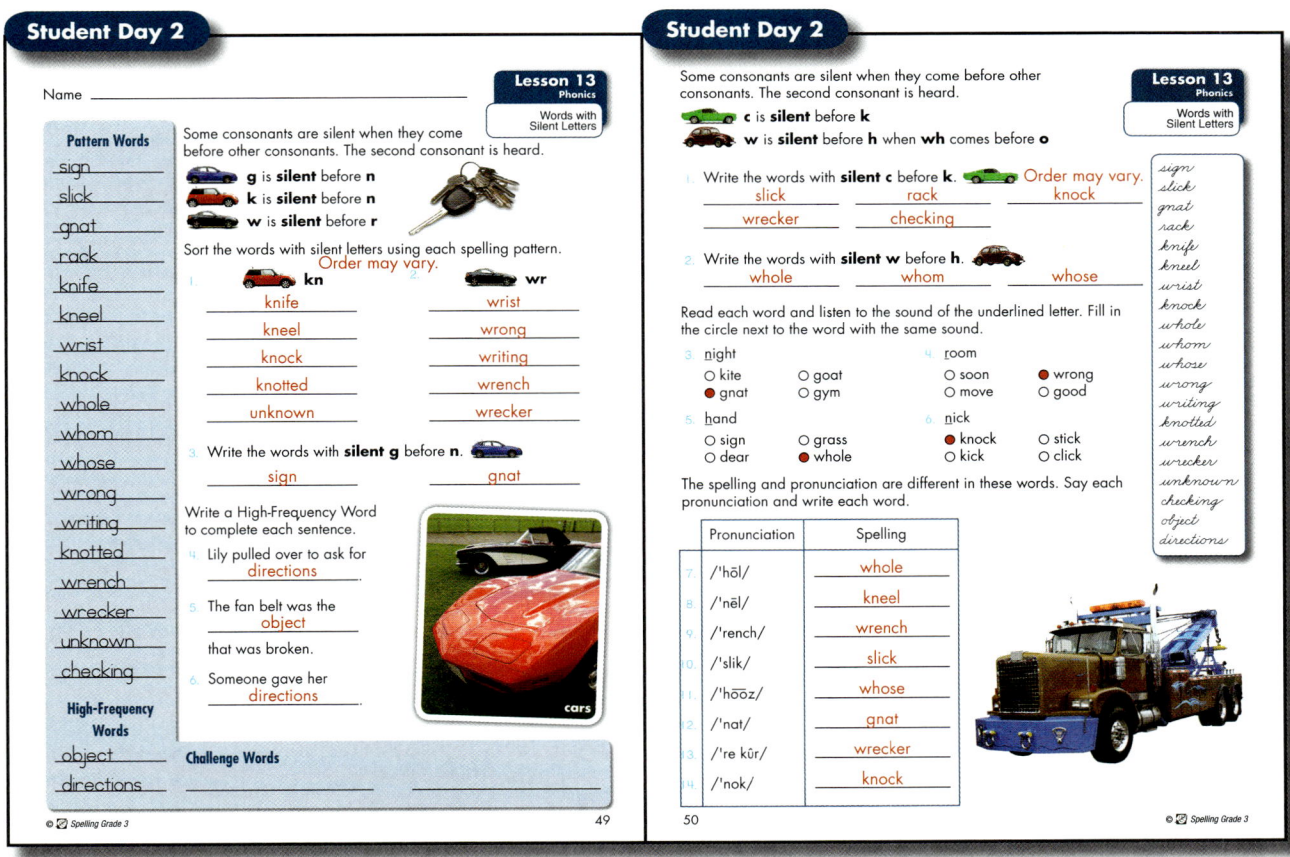

3 Proceed to page 50 and select a volunteer to repeat the generalization and read the examples. Students will complete the page independently.

4 Homework suggestion: Use **BLM SP3-13D Cars** to practice words from this lesson.

Day 3 Word Study

Objective

The students will utilize dictionary skills by answering questions about the different components of a dictionary entry. They will use definitions to determine which list words are nouns or verbs.

Introduction

Display **T-6 Dictionary Entry**—from Lesson 5—to review and remind students that a dictionary entry consists of the following five parts: entry word, pronunciation, part of speech, definition, sample sentence. Point out that an entry word may have more than one part of speech and more than one definition. Words with more than one definition may have more than one sample sentence. Words can also have multiple pronunciations. Invite students to identify and circle the five dictionary parts on the transparency.

Directed Instruction

1 Refer to the part of speech *n.* for the word *skyline*. Ask students to identify what *n.* stands for. (**noun**) Remind students that a noun is a person, place, or thing. Ask students to identify what an action word is called. (**verb**)

2 Write the following words on the board in random order:
- gnat, wrecker, wrench, wrist (**nouns**)
- checking, kneel, writing (**verbs**)
- knock (**both a noun and a verb**)

Use the Spelling Dictionary to assist with this exercise. Direct students to look up each word and identify which words are nouns, verbs, or both. Some words can have more than one part of speech, which may not be identified in the Spelling Dictionary. The part of speech for each word is based on its usage in this lesson.

3 Proceed to page 51. Encourage students to use their Spelling Dictionary to complete the exercises on their own. Utilizing dictionary skills is an essential study practice. Review the page as a class.

Day 4 Writing

Objective

The students will underline list words in an advertisement and complete graphic organizers. They will write a used car advertisement using ideas from lists.

Introduction

Remind students that a graphic organizer is a drawing that shows how words or ideas fit together. Draw the following word web on the board:

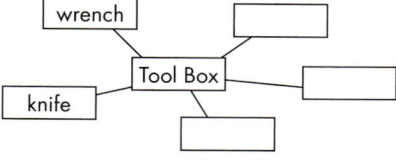

Invite students to assist in completing the word web for *tool box*. Some ideas are as follows: pliers, hammer, nails, wire, bolts, extra trays. Inform students that the words on the web will assist in writing an advertisement. Model writing a *for sale* advertisement on the board for the tool box.

Directed Instruction

1 Proceed to page 52 and point out the graphic organizer at the top of the page. Explain that the graphic organizer contains ideas that are found in the used car advertisement. Read the sentences about Wes, the graphic organizer, and the advertisement. Encourage students to listen for, identify, and underline the list words. (**slick, rack, whole**)

2 Read the directions toward the bottom of the page. Brainstorm ideas for each list and allow students to write phrases to complete each column. Students will write their own used car advertisement on another piece of paper.

3 Homework suggestion: Read the graphic organizer and advertisement on page 52 to an adult. Take a practice spelling test at home or use **BLM SP3-01A A Spelling Study Strategy** for additional practice.

Day 5 Wrap Up

Objective

The students will correctly write dictated spelling words and sentences.

Introduction

Provide a review, utilizing WHITEBOARDS or Student Spelling Support suggestions.

Directed Instruction

1 Dictate the list words by using the Warm Up sentences or developing original ones. Reserve *knife*, *whole*, and *writing* for the dictation sentences.

2 Follow this procedure for the dictation sentences: read the sentence, invite the class to say the sentence with you, then read the sentence again. Dictate the following sentences:
- They used a <u>knife</u> to cut the rope.
- Please wash the <u>whole</u> fruit.
- I am <u>writing</u> the address down.

3 If assigned, dictate Extra Challenge Words. Score the test.

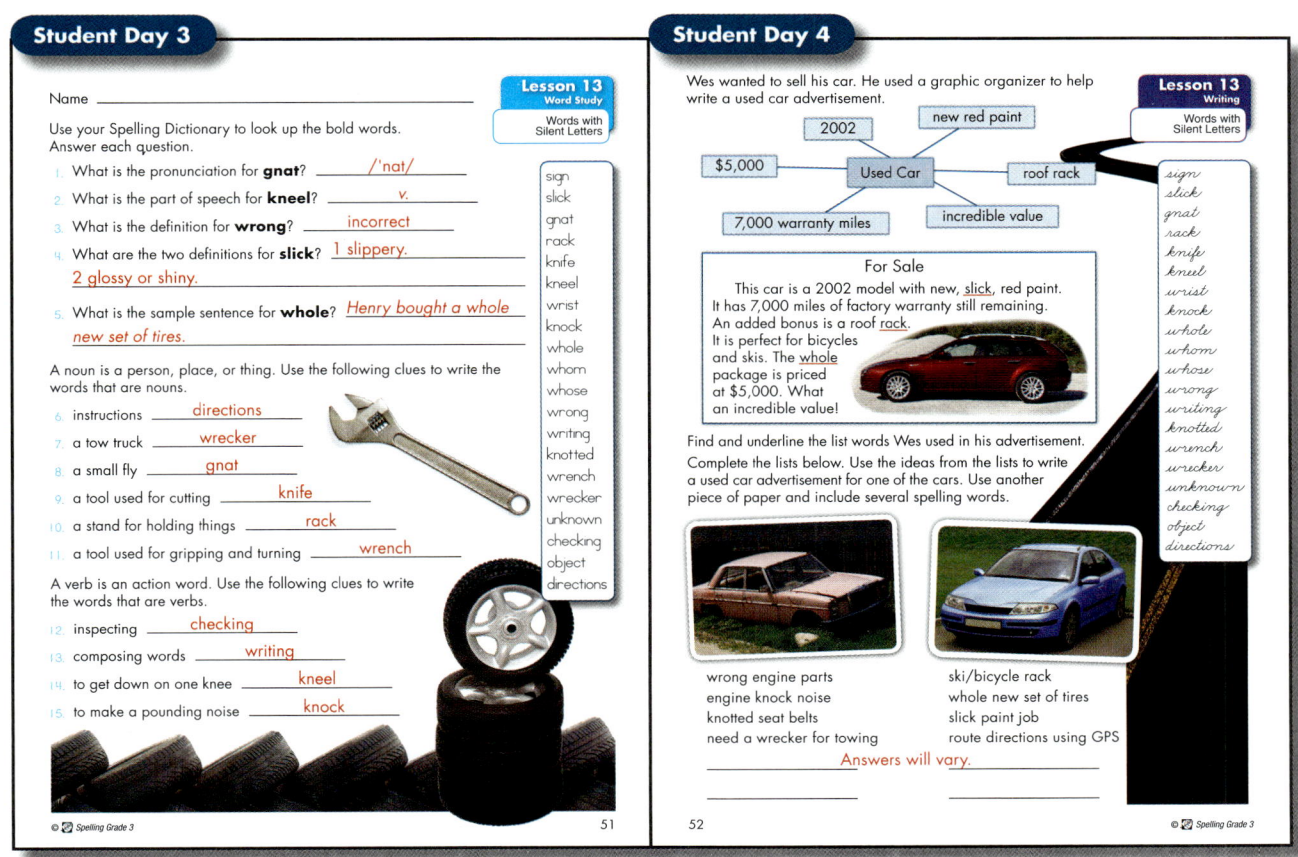

Student Pages

Pages 53–56

Lesson Materials

BLM SP3-14A
Black marker
Sentence strips
P-11
BLM SP3-14B
Envelope
BLM SP3-01A
Whiteboards

Transportation

The theme of this lesson is Recreational Vehicles and Campers. These vehicles offer vacationers the comforts of home while traveling on the road. Special parks for campers and recreational vehicles offer electrical and plumbing hookups as well as convenient places to spend the night. For these reasons, many families choose to vacation in recreational vehicles or campers.

Day 1 Warm Up

Objective

The students will accurately spell and write words with **consonant digraphs**. They will spell and write high-frequency words and challenge words.

Introduction

Before class, select Challenge Words for numbers 21 and 22 from a cross-curricular subject, words misspelled on previous assignments, or words that interest your students. The word *stretched* has **tch** and is suggested for number 21. Administer the Warm Up.

Directed Instruction

1 Say each word, use it in a sentence, and then repeat the word.

Pattern Words

1. then	We'll stop for lunch, <u>then</u> continue on.	then
2. which	<u>Which</u> way is the rest stop from here?	which
3. shelter	Let's eat lunch at the picnic <u>shelter</u>.	shelter
4. catcher	Ed played <u>catcher</u> on his baseball team.	catcher
5. whether	We're not sure <u>whether</u> or not we'll go.	whether
6. watched	Al <u>watched</u> his sister one afternoon.	watched
7. branches	There are <u>branches</u> of the military.	branches
8. telephone	Please answer the <u>telephone</u> politely.	telephone
9. photograph	Marcy took a <u>photograph</u> of the lake.	photograph
10. fifth	Tristin is in <u>fifth</u> grade.	fifth
11. than	Nathan is older <u>than</u> his brother.	than
12. wheel	The steering <u>wheel</u> became hot.	wheel
13. kitchen	Dad went to the <u>kitchen</u> to get a snack.	kitchen
14. children	People brought <u>children</u> to see Jesus.	children
15. weather	Will the <u>weather</u> be warm and sunny?	weather
16. matches	James' shirt <u>matches</u> his pants.	matches
17. sandwich	I like cheese on my <u>sandwich</u>.	sandwich
18. dashboard	Mom's sunglasses are on the <u>dashboard</u>.	dashboard

High-Frequency Words

19. subject	The next <u>subject</u> is math.	subject
20. recess	We will take a break at <u>recess</u>.	recess

Challenge Words

21. _____

22. _____

2 Allow students to self-correct their pretest, using the following procedure:

  a. Write each word on the board. Discuss the letter/sound relationships in each word. Point out the **consonant digraph(s)** in each word. The **consonant digraph th** has the following pronunciations: voiced in *then*, *than*, *weather*, and *whether* and unvoiced in *fifth*. *Then* and *than* are often confused. *Then* is used to tell the order of events. *Than* is used to compare two things. The words *weather* and *whether* are homophones.

  b. As a class, read, spell, and read each word again. Direct students to circle misspelled words with a colored pencil and rewrite them correctly.

3 Proof each student's Warm Up.

4 Homework suggestion: Use **BLM SP3-14A Going Camping** to practice the Pattern Words in this lesson.

©   *Spelling Grade 3*

Day 2 Phonics

Objective

The students will write words with **consonant digraphs**. They will write high-frequency words. They will divide words into syllables.

Introduction

Before class, use a BLACK MARKER to write the following words on SENTENCE STRIPS: shelter, subject, whether, weather, branches, catcher, dashboard. Attach the sentence strips to the board. Display **P-11 Syllables** to discuss the following syllabication generalizations:

- Divide after a consonant or consonant sound in a closed syllable (example number 1). Solicit volunteers to divide *shelter* and *subject* into syllables, using the black marker to make a vertical line between syllables. (**shel|ter, sub|ject—VC|CV pattern**) Explain that *weather* and *whether* have the **consonant diagraph th** after the short vowel sound in each word. **Consonant digraphs** stand for a single consonant sound, so these words are divided after **th**. Choose a student to divide *weather* and *whether*. (**weath|er, wheth|er—VC|V pattern**)

- Divide between a base word and a suffix (example number 7). Solicit a volunteer to divide the words *branches* and *catcher* into syllables after each base word. (**branch|es, catch|er**)

- Divide between two smaller words in a compound word (example number 3). Have a volunteer divide the word *dashboard* into syllables between the two smaller words. (**dash|board**)

Directed Instruction

1 Proceed to page 53. Say, spell, and say each Pattern and High-Frequency Word. Provide this week's Challenge Words and have students write them in the spaces provided. Clap out the syllables in each word. Ask volunteers to tell you which words have one, two, or three syllables.

2 Select a student to read the definition at the top of the page: a *consonant digraph* is two or more consonants together that stand for one sound. Remind students that the letters **tch** come after a short vowel in a word.

Differentiated Instruction

- For students who spelled all the words correctly on the Warm Up, select and assign three Extra Challenge Words from the following list: recreation, vacationing, certificate, acquire, adequate, Ecclesiastes.

- For students who spelled less than half correctly, assign the following Pattern and High-Frequency Words: then, than, whether, weather, matches, branches, telephone, photograph, recess, subject. On the Wrap Up, evaluate these students on the ten words assigned; however, encourage them to attempt to spell all the list words to the best of their ability. They are also responsible for writing the dictated sentences.

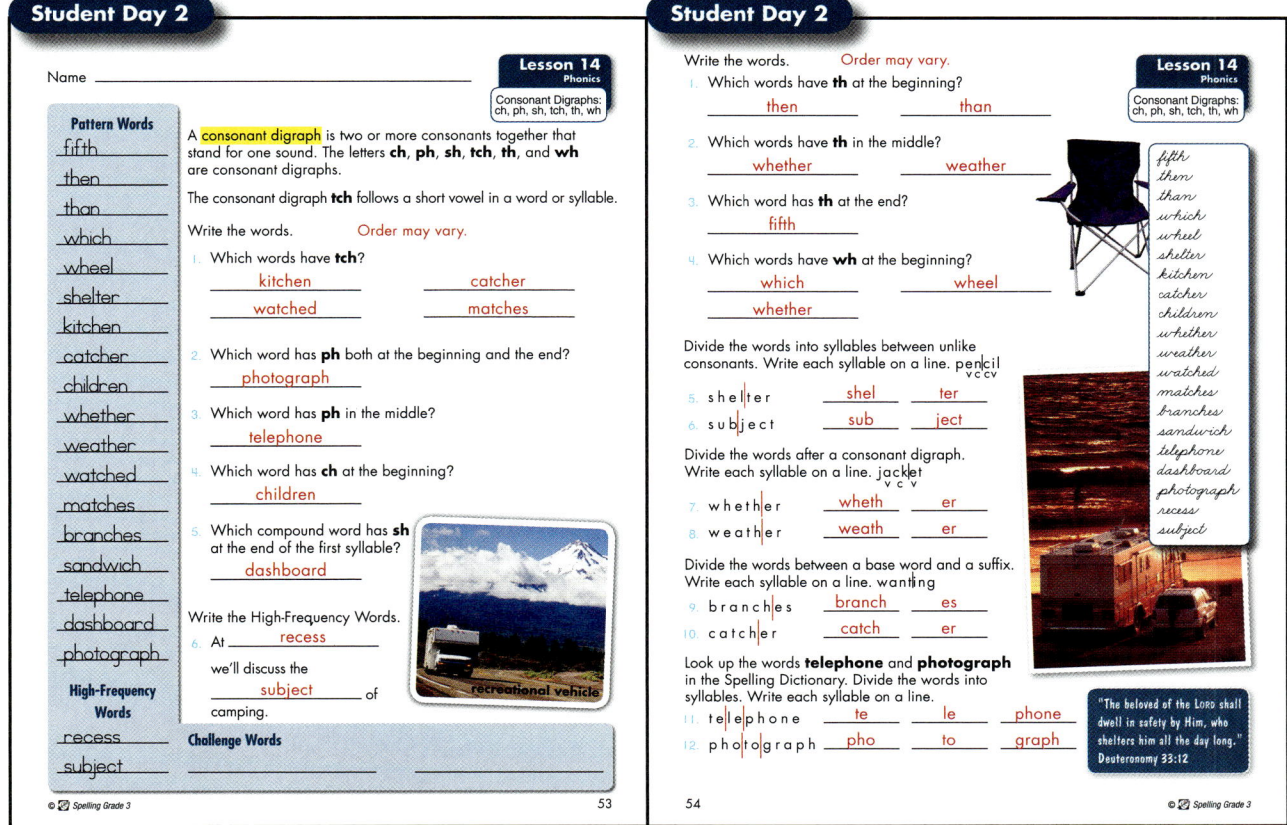

Student Spelling Support

1. Write this week's words categorized by patterns on a large piece of paper and attach to the Word Wall.
2. Duplicate **BLMs SP3-14C–D Lesson 14 Spelling Words I** and **II** on CARD STOCK for students to use as flash cards at school or at home.
3. Use **BLM SP3-01A A Spelling Study Strategy** in instructional groups to provide assistance with some or all of the words.
4. Assist students in writing the Challenge Words, numbers 21 and 22, in the section called My Words for Writing, in the back of their textbook.
5. For auditory learners, the **consonant digraphs sh** and **ch** may present difficulties since they are similar sounds. This is especially true for students whose first language is Spanish. To help students hear the difference, write **sh** on a 3" × 5" INDEX CARD and **ch** on another card. Provide a set of cards for each student. Pronounce each Pattern Word that has **sh** or **ch** very clearly so that the students can see your mouth as you speak. Tell them to listen for the crisp sound of **ch** and the gliding sound of **sh**. Have students repeat the word after you and hold up the appropriate card for the sound they hear.

Cont. on page 57

Ask students to tell you which short vowel sound comes before **tch** in *kitchen* (**short i**), *catcher* and *matches* (**short a**), and *watched* (**short o**).

3 Draw students' attention to the final syllable *wich* in *sandwich*. Point out the difference from the word *which*.

4 Continue to page 54. Students divide words into syllables following the generalizations provided. Draw attention to each spelling pattern.

5 Homework suggestion: Use **BLM SP3-14B Riddles** to practice the Pattern and High-Frequency Words.

Day 3 Word Study

Objective

The students will write frequently confused words and homophones to complete sentences. They will choose a sample sentence to match a given dictionary definition.

Introduction

Write *then* and *than* on the board along with the following incomplete sentences:
- We'll eat and ____ we'll rest. (**then**)   • Dad is older ____ Mom. (**than**)

Explain that *then* and *than* are often confused because they are similar. *Then* is used to tell the order of events and *than* is used for comparison. Have students complete the sentences.

Write *weather* and *whether* and the following incomplete sentences:
- The ____ today is cool and cloudy. (**weather**)
- I'm not sure ____ I'll go or not. (**whether**)

Explain that *weather* and *whether* are homophones—words that sound the same but have different meanings and spellings. *Weather* tells what the outside air is like, and *whether* indicates a choice between two things.

Directed Instruction

1 Write the following on the board:
- fly: a winged insect   • fly: to move through the air   • fly: to put up a flag

Explain that the word *fly* is an example of a dictionary entry word with more than one definition. Words with more than one definition also have more than one sample sentence. Each sample sentence fits the definition given. Brainstorm original sentences that fit each definition of *fly*. Write the suggested sentences below each entry word and its definition. Compare the sample sentences suggested to see if each one is a good match for the definition.

2 On page 55, students complete exercises 1–2 with the correct usage of *then*, *than*, *weather*, and *whether*. In exercises 3–6, students choose a sample sentence that matches the definition for each dictionary entry word. Remind students that although the sample sentences given use the entry words correctly, only one sentence listed fits the definition.

Day 4 Writing

Objective

The students will complete a cloze activity in the form of a letter. They will address an envelope.

Introduction

Display an ENVELOPE that you have received through the mail. Lead the class in a discussion about addressing letters. Explain that it is important for an envelope to be properly addressed so that the postal service can deliver it. Tell students that the mailing address is written on three lines and show the lines on the envelope. Demonstrate how the first line is for the name of the person receiving the letter, the second line is for the street address, and the third line is for the city, state, and zip code.

Directed Instruction

1 Draw a rectangle on the board to represent an envelope. Make three blank lines in the center of the rectangle for the address. Beneath the envelope, write your name and your school's mailing address. Review how to address an envelope Select volunteers to address the envelope to you at your school address.

2 Proceed to page 56. Remind students that letters include the date, greeting, body, and closing. Point out the comma in the date and after the greeting and closing before students complete the cloze activity.

3 Homework suggestion: Read the letter on page 56 to an adult. Take a practice spelling test at home or use **BLM SP3-01A A Spelling Study Strategy** for additional practice.

Day 5 Wrap Up

Objective

The students will correctly write dictated spelling words and sentences.

Introduction

Provide a review, utilizing WHITEBOARDS or Student Spelling Support suggestions.

Directed Instruction

1 Dictate the list words by using the Warm Up sentences or developing original ones. Reserve *than*, *photograph*, and *subject* for the dictation sentences.

2 Follow this procedure for the dictation sentences: read the sentence, invite the class to say the sentence with you, then read the sentence again. Dictate the following sentences:
- Tom is taller <u>than</u> Matt.
- I will take a <u>photograph</u> of the clouds.
- Our next <u>subject</u> in school is math.

3 If assigned, dictate Extra Challenge Words. Score the test.

Student Spelling Support

Cont. from page 56

6. Advanced learners may want to exchange letters with a student in another country. Your class can sponsor a child in a Christian school in another country through www.acsi.org/~sponsorship. Letters exchanged between your students and your sponsored student will provide exposure to another culture.

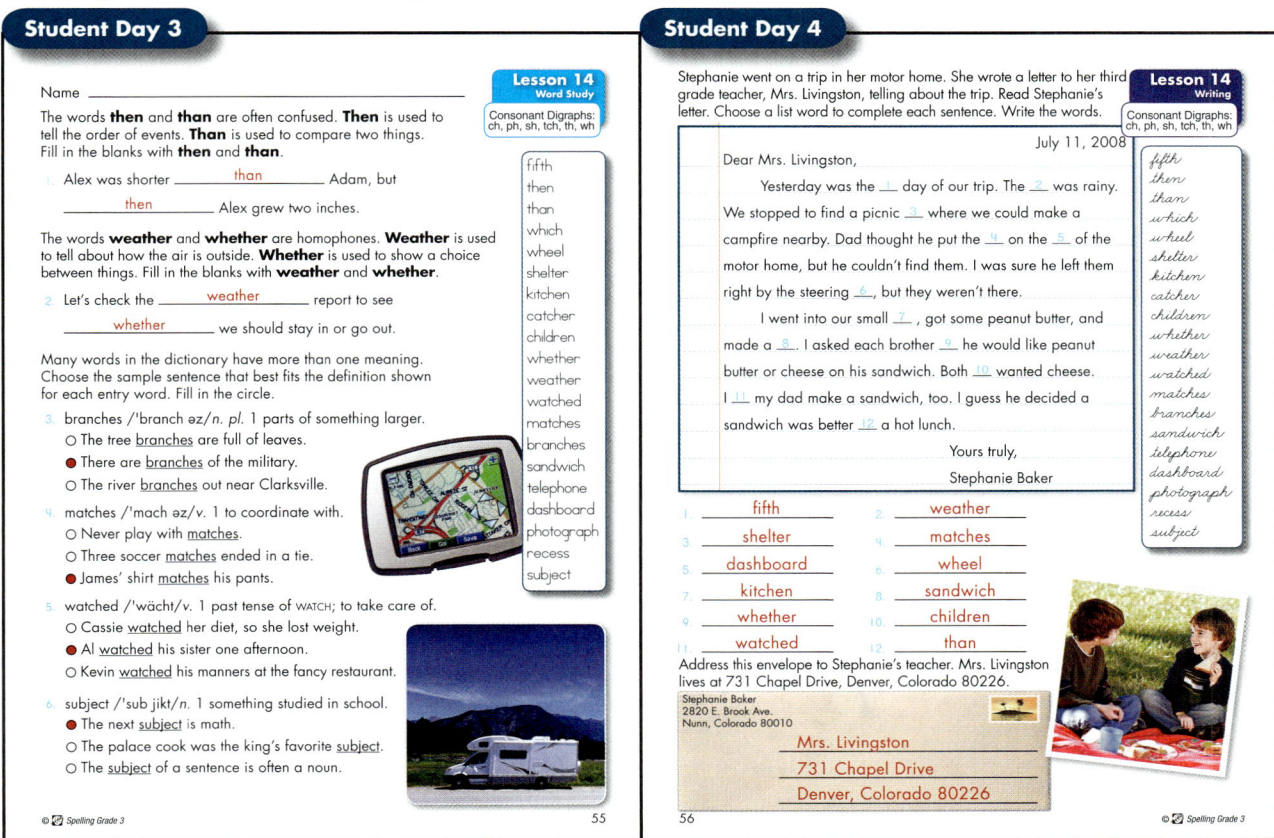

Student Pages

Pages 57–60

Lesson Materials

BLM SP3-15A
BLM SP3-15B
Road map
T-22
BLM SP3-15C
BLMs SP3-15D–E
BLM SP3-01A
Whiteboards

Transportation

The theme of this lesson is Trucks. The first pickup truck was built in Germany in 1896 by automotive pioneer, Gottlieb Daimler. It had a four-horsepower engine with two forward speeds and one reverse. As the highways expanded in the United States, so did the commercial trucking business. Long-haul trucking became practical for transporting goods and produce.

Day 1 Warm Up

Objective

The students will accurately spell and write words with **diphthongs**. They will spell and write high-frequency words and challenge words.

Introduction

Before class, select Challenge Words for numbers 21 and 22 from a cross-curricular subject, words misspelled on previous assignments, or words that interest your students. The word *employee* has **oy** and is suggested for number 21. Administer the Warm Up.

Directed Instruction

1 Say each word, use it in a sentence, and then repeat the word.

Pattern Words

1. rejoice	The Bible tells us to <u>rejoice</u> in the Lord.	rejoice
2. understood	Christy <u>understood</u> the rules of the game.	understood
3. voice	Mrs. Brown has a lovely singing <u>voice</u>.	voice
4. looked	Julianne <u>looked</u> for her lost coat.	looked
5. oily	The rain caused the road to be <u>oily</u>.	oily
6. enjoyed	Steven <u>enjoyed</u> eating the apple pie.	enjoyed
7. coins	Sue's piggy bank is full of <u>coins</u>.	coins
8. hood	The <u>hood</u> on the old truck is rusty.	hood
9. crooked	Freda straightened the <u>crooked</u> picture.	crooked
10. choice	We have a <u>choice</u> to do right or wrong.	choice
11. royal	The <u>royal</u> family lives in London.	royal
12. joining	Is anyone interested in <u>joining</u> the choir?	joining
13. destroy	An earthquake can <u>destroy</u> buildings.	destroy
14. spoiled	The rainy weather <u>spoiled</u> our trip.	spoiled
15. brook	Blake caught a fish in the <u>brook</u>.	brook
16. pointed	The top of the church steeple is <u>pointed</u>.	pointed
17. annoy	Talking out in class will <u>annoy</u> teachers.	annoy
18. loyal	A dog is <u>loyal</u> to its master.	loyal

High-Frequency Words

19. divided	The teacher <u>divided</u> the class into teams.	divided
20. exercise	Robert will <u>exercise</u> for twenty minutes.	exercise

Challenge Words

21. _____

22. _____

2 Allow students to self-correct their pretest, using the following procedure:

   a. Write each word on the board. Discuss the letter/sound relationships in each word. Point out that the letters **oi**, **oo**, and **oy** are called **diphthongs**. Teach that a *diphthong* is <u>two or more vowels gliding together to make one vowel sound in a syllable</u>. The letter *y* is considered a vowel in **oy**. Call attention to the location of **oi** and **oy** in the words. In this lesson, **oo** is a short sound, heard in *hood*; not its long sound, heard in *root*.

   b. As a class, read, spell, and read each word again. Direct students to circle misspelled words with a colored pencil and rewrite them correctly.

3 Proof each student's Warm Up.

4 Homework suggestion: Use **BLM SP3-15A Mud Puddles** to review Pattern Words with **diphthongs oi**, **oo**, and **oy** and High-Frequency Words.

Day 2 Phonics

Objective

The students will correctly sort words by **diphthongs**. They will write words with two and three syllables, circle words that rhyme, and sort words ending with the suffix -ed using the correct ending sound.

Introduction

On one area of the board, write each list word. On another area, write the column headings shown below. Invite students to come to the board, select, and write a list word.

<u>oi</u>		<u>oy</u>	<u>oo</u>	<u>no diphthongs</u>
oily	voice	loyal	hood	divided
coins	joining	royal	brook	exercise
choice	rejoice	annoy	looked	
spoiled	pointed	destroy	crooked	
		enjoyed	understood	

Directed Instruction

1 Chorally read each column. Ask, "Which words have three syllables? (**understood, divided, exercise**) How many syllables does *voice* have? (**one**) Which **oy** words rhyme?" (**loyal, royal; annoy, destroy**)

2 Point out the words ending with the suffix -ed. Ask if each word ending with -ed has the same ending sound. Discuss the three sounds of -ed— /ed/, /t/, and /d/. Point out that /ed/ usually follows t or d (for example, poin<u>ted</u> and divi<u>ded</u>); the word *crooked* is an exception.

3 Proceed to page 57. Say, spell, and say each Pattern and High-Frequency Word. Provide this week's Challenge Words and have students write them in the spaces provided. Read the sentences and the directions at the top of the page. Instruct students to complete the page independently.

4 Continue to page 58. Select a volunteer to read the directions. Answer any questions before allowing the students to complete the page.

Proceed to page 57. Continue to page 58.

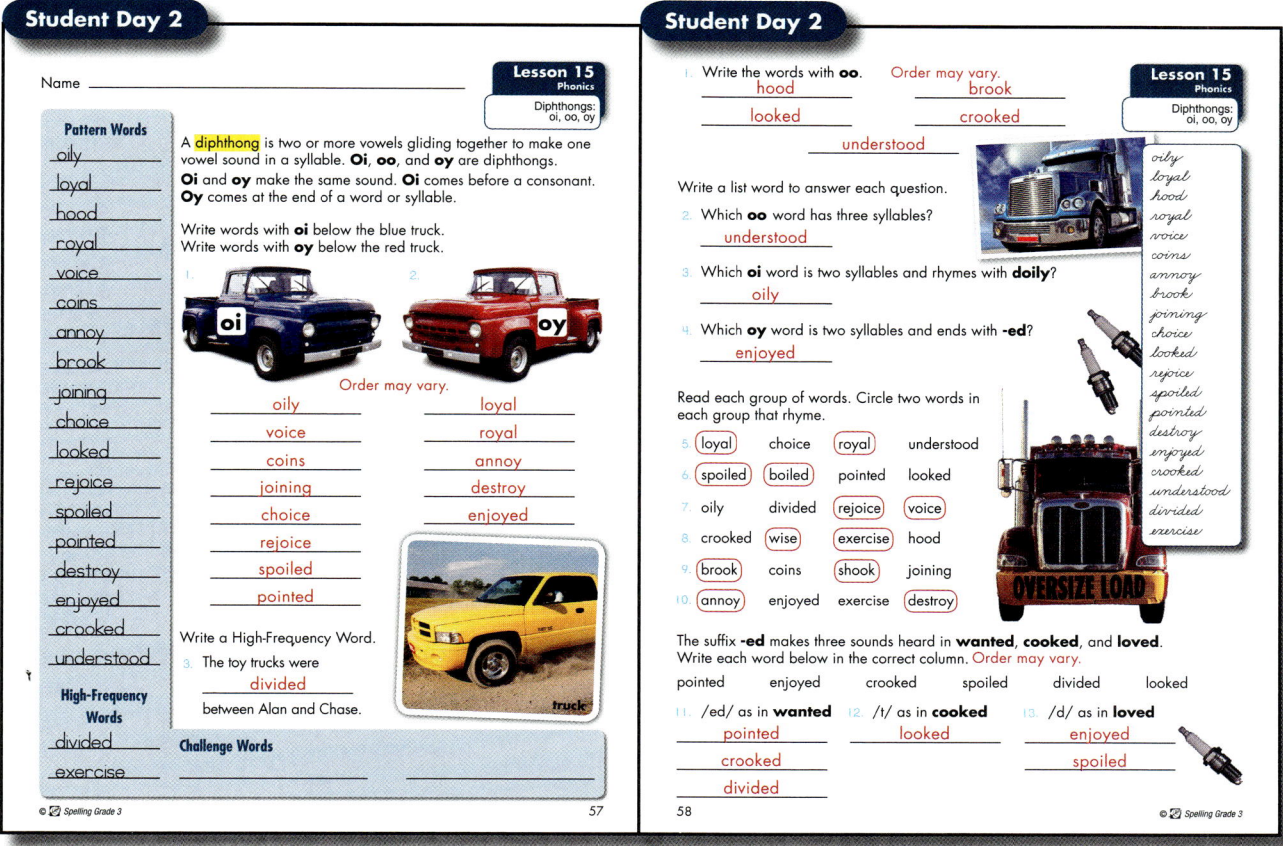

Student Day 2

Name _____

Lesson 15
Phonics
Diphthongs: oi, oo, oy

Pattern Words
oily
loyal
hood
royal
voice
coins
annoy
brook
joining
choice
looked
rejoice
spoiled
pointed
destroy
enjoyed
crooked
understood

High-Frequency Words
divided
exercise

A **diphthong** is two or more vowels gliding together to make one vowel sound in a syllable. **Oi**, **oo**, and **oy** are diphthongs.
Oi and **oy** make the same sound. **Oi** comes before a consonant. **Oy** comes at the end of a word or syllable.

Write words with **oi** below the blue truck.
Write words with **oy** below the red truck.

Order may vary.

oi	oy
oily	loyal
voice	royal
coins	annoy
joining	destroy
choice	enjoyed
rejoice	
spoiled	
pointed	

Write a High-Frequency Word.
3. The toy trucks were divided between Alan and Chase.

Challenge Words
_____

© *Spelling Grade 3* 57

Student Day 2

1. Write the words with **oo**. *Order may vary.*
hood   brook
looked   crooked
understood

Lesson 15
Phonics
Diphthongs: oi, oo, oy

Write a list word to answer each question.
2. Which **oo** word has three syllables?
understood
3. Which **oi** word is two syllables and rhymes with **doily**?
oily
4. Which **oy** word is two syllables and ends with **-ed**?
enjoyed

Read each group of words. Circle two words in each group that rhyme.
5. (loyal) choice (royal) understood
6. (spoiled) (boiled) pointed looked
7. oily divided (rejoice) (voice)
8. crooked (wise) (exercise) hood
9. (brook) coins (shook) joining
10. (annoy) enjoyed exercise (destroy)

The suffix **-ed** makes three sounds heard in **wanted**, **cooked**, and **loved**. Write each word below in the correct column. *Order may vary.*

pointed   enjoyed   crooked   spoiled   divided   looked

11. /ed/ as in **wanted**	12. /t/ as in **cooked**	13. /d/ as in **loved**
pointed	looked	enjoyed
crooked		spoiled
divided		

oily
loyal
hood
royal
voice
coins
annoy
brook
joining
choice
looked
rejoice
spoiled
pointed
destroy
enjoyed
crooked
understood
divided
exercise

58   © *Spelling Grade 3*

Student Spelling Support

1. Write this week's words categorized by patterns on a large piece of paper and attach to the Word Wall.
2. Duplicate **BLMs SP3-15F–G Lesson 15 Spelling Words I** and **II** on CARD STOCK for students to use as flash cards at school or at home.
3. Use **BLM SP3-01A A Spelling Study Strategy** in instructional groups to provide assistance with some or all of the words.
4. Assist students in writing the Challenge Words, numbers 21 and 22, in the section called My Words for Writing, in the back of their textbook.
5. For auditory learners, read the following silly sentences that will aid in discerning the spelling patterns in this week's list words:
   - **oi**: Mom began to **rejoice** with her **voice** when she found the **coins**.
   - **oi**: The **pointed** pencil had a **choice** of **joining** the **oily** red or the **spoiled** blue team.
   - **oo**: I **understood** when I **looked** into the **crooked brook** and saw my **hood**.
   - **oy**: It did not **annoy** the **royal** family who **enjoyed** watching the **loyal** workers **destroy** the old castle.

Cont. on page 61

5 Homework suggestion: Use **BLM SP3-15B Jumbled Freight** to review list words for this lesson.

Day 3 Word Study

Objective

The students will use their Spelling Dictionary to find multiple meanings of list words.

Introduction

Write the following sentences, with underlined words, on the board:
- Prime rib is a <u>choice</u> piece of meat. (**definition number two**)
- We have a <u>choice</u> to do right or wrong. (**definition number one**)
- The train was <u>pointed</u> in the wrong direction. (**definition number two**)
- The top of the church steeple is <u>pointed</u>. (**definition number one**)

Guide students to use their Spelling Dictionary in the back of their textbook to locate *choice* and *pointed*. Select students to read the definitions and tell the number of the definition that matches the way the word was used in the sentence on the board.

Directed Instruction

1 Write the following groups of words on the board and select a student to orally read each group of words:
- ruin, wreck, shatter (**destroy**)
- peeked, glanced, saw (**looked**)
- pick, option, selection (**choice**)
- liked, pleased, delighted (**enjoyed**)

Dictate the Pattern Words from the lesson and have students raise their hand when they hear a word that belongs in each group and explain why they think so.

2 Proceed to page 59 and encourage students to use their Spelling Dictionary as they complete the page independently.

Day 4 Writing

Objective

The students will use proofreading marks to identify mistakes in a list of directions. They will correctly write misspelled words.

Introduction

Display a ROAD MAP. Point to the compass rose on the map or draw a compass rose on the board and explain that it shows direction—N for north, S for south, E for east, and W for west. Ask students if they or their parents have ever needed directions to get somewhere. Share about a time when you needed directions to get to an unfamiliar place.

Directed Instruction

1 Display **T-22 Proofreading Directions**. Inform students there are errors that need to be corrected in the list of directions. Point to the proofreading box and explain that the "add something" mark has been added. The "add something" mark is often referred to as a *caret*. It is used when a word has been left out of a sentence or when a comma, question mark, or exclamation point is needed. Solicit volunteers to identify the mistakes and use proofreading marks to make the corrections. Refer to **BLM SP3-15C T-22 Answer Key**.

Proofreading Marks
- Circle misspellings.
- Make a capital letter.
- Add a period.
- Delete.
- Add something.

2 Proceed to page 60. Select a volunteer to read the directions at the top of the page. Assist students as needed to proofread directions to Zacky's Grocery Store, making sure that all errors are corrected. (**9 misspellings; 3 capital letters needed; 3 periods needed; 1 delete; 1 add something**—*the*) Distribute a copy of **BLM SP3-15D Proofreading Marks** for each student to use as a self check. Distribute a copy of **BLM SP3-15E Corrected Driving Directions** for each student to observe the page written correctly. Chorally read the page.

3 Homework suggestion: Read the list of directions on page 60 to an adult. Take a practice spelling test at home or use **BLM SP3-01A A Spelling Study Strategy** for additional practice.

Day 5 Wrap Up

Objective
The students will correctly write dictated spelling words and sentences.

Introduction
Provide a review, utilizing WHITEBOARDS or Student Spelling Support suggestions.

Directed Instruction
1 Dictate the list words by using the Warm Up sentences or developing original ones. Reserve *choice*, *looked*, and *enjoyed* for the dictation sentences.

2 Follow this procedure for the dictation sentences: read the sentence, invite the class to say the sentence with you, then read the sentence again. Dictate the following sentences:
- God wants us to make the <u>choice</u> to follow Him.
- The lady <u>looked</u> both ways before crossing the street.
- My friends and I <u>enjoyed</u> the birthday party.

3 If assigned, dictate Extra Challenge Words. Score the test.

Student Spelling Support

Cont. from page 60

6. For a biblical connection read Psalm 9:2: "I will be glad and **rejoice** in You; I will sing praise to Your name, O Most High." Discuss with the students ways in which they can be glad and rejoice in the Lord. Impress upon the students that even in difficult times, they can still **rejoice** in the Lord.

7. Point out how people affect one another's lives. The invention of the truck has been a great asset to our lives. Tell how members of the body of Christ may bless one another.

8. Challenge advanced learners to write complete sentences describing ways in which they can rejoice in the Lord. For example, I can rejoice because Jesus died on the cross for me.

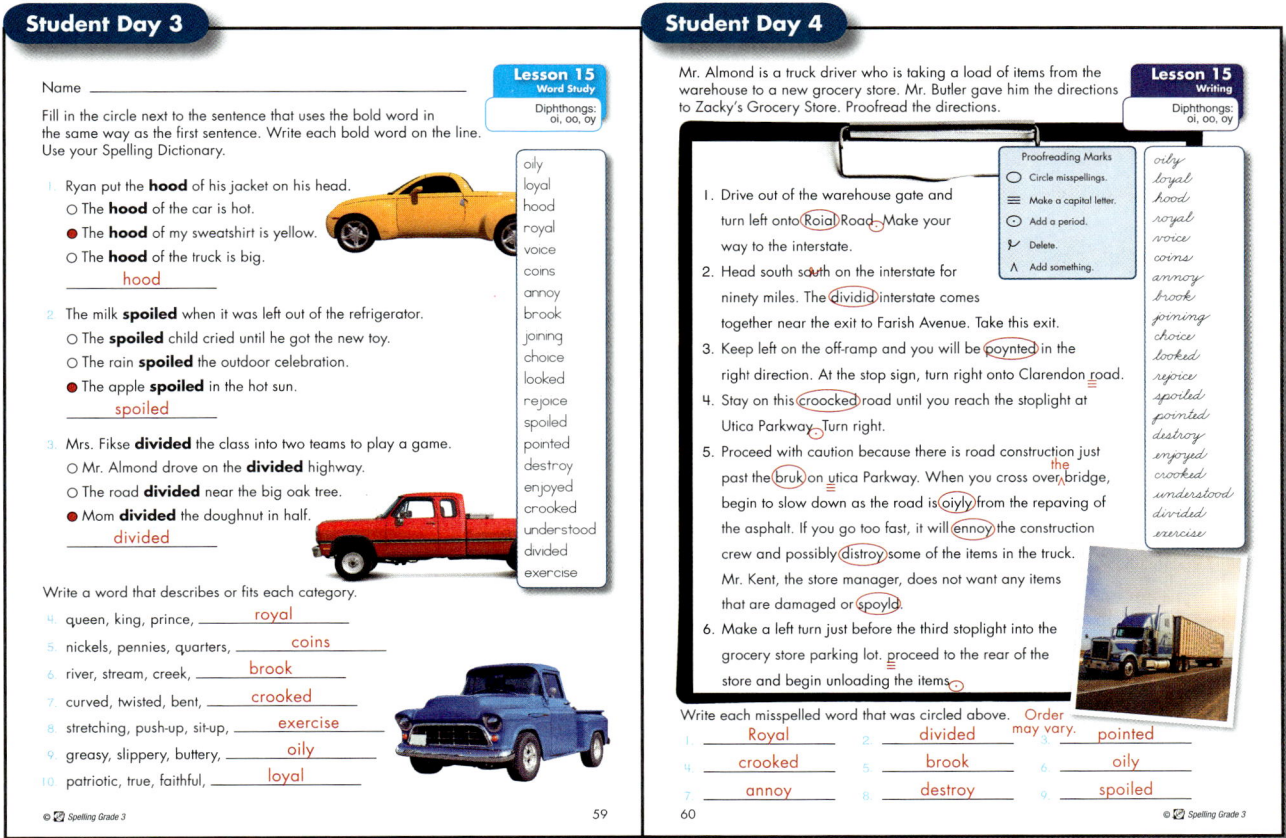

Words with the /ou/ Sound

Student Pages

Pages 61–64

Lesson Materials

BLM SP3-16A
BLMs SP3-16B–C
BLM SP3-16D
BLM SP3-16E
Card stock
BLM SP3-01A
Whiteboards

Transportation

The theme of this lesson is Emergency Vehicles. An emergency vehicle is any authorized vehicle, such as a police car, fire engine, or an ambulance, that responds to an emergency. Most emergency vehicles have sirens and flashing lights to help them navigate through traffic and to provide some protection at the scene of the emergency.

Day 1 Warm Up

Objective

The students will accurately spell and write **words with the /ou/ sound**. They will spell and write high-frequency words and challenge words.

Introduction

Before class, select Challenge Words for numbers 21 and 22 from a cross-curricular subject, words misspelled on previous assignments, or words that interest your students. The word *rebound* has the **/ou/** sound, spelled *ou*, and is suggested for number 21. Administer the Warm Up.

Directed Instruction

1 Say each word, use it in a sentence, and then repeat the word.

Pattern Words

1.	towels	Torrey folded the <u>towels</u> neatly.	towels
2.	browse	Annette will <u>browse</u> through the books.	browse
3.	surround	The policemen will <u>surround</u> the area.	surround
4.	cloudy	Yesterday was a <u>cloudy</u> day.	cloudy
5.	sounded	The school bell <u>sounded</u> every hour.	sounded
6.	count	How many police cars did you <u>count</u>?	count
7.	louder	Please speak <u>louder</u> so I can hear you.	louder
8.	crowd	There was a <u>crowd</u> in front of the door.	crowd
9.	power	Jesus has the <u>power</u> to do all things.	power
10.	frown	The odd situation caused Ava to <u>frown</u>.	frown
11.	pounds	How many <u>pounds</u> does a car weigh?	pounds
12.	downtown	Ivan drove <u>downtown</u> to work.	downtown
13.	playground	The <u>playground</u> was full of toys.	playground
14.	drown	The music will <u>drown</u> out the city noise.	drown
15.	outstanding	Hank did an <u>outstanding</u> job today.	outstanding
16.	outdoors	Megan ate her lunch <u>outdoors</u>.	outdoors
17.	household	Jason has five members in his <u>household</u>.	household
18.	however	I slept well, <u>however</u>, I am still tired.	however

High-Frequency Words

19.	different	A siren can make many <u>different</u> sounds.	different
20.	probably	Melissa will <u>probably</u> win the race.	probably

Challenge Words

21. _____

22. _____

2 Allow students to self-correct their pretest, using the following procedure:

a. Write each word on the board. Discuss the letter/sound relationships in each word. Point out that the letters *ou* and *ow* are called diphthongs and make the sound **/ou/**. Remind students that a diphthong is two or more vowels gliding together to make one vowel sound in a syllable.

b. As a class, read, spell, and read each word again. Direct students to circle misspelled words with a colored pencil and rewrite them correctly.

3 Proof each student's Warm Up.

4 Homework suggestion: Use **BLM SP3-16A Emergency** to review words in this lesson.

Day 2 Phonics

Objective

The students will correctly sort words by diphthongs and the number of syllables in words. They will write missing syllables and divide words into syllables. They will write high-frequency words.

Introduction

Before class, duplicate one copy of **BLMs SP3-16B–C Lesson 16 Spelling Words I** and **II**. Cut the cards apart and distribute the Pattern Words to students. Write the following column headings on the board: one-syllable **/ou/** words, two-syllable **/ou/** words, three-syllable **/ou/** words. Invite students to read each word card, come to the board, and place each word card under the appropriate heading. After all cards have been placed, read each card and correct any cards that have been misplaced. Write each word under the correct heading.

one-syllable /ou/ words	two-syllable /ou/ words		three-syllable /ou/ words
count	louder	cloudy	however
frown	towels	power	outstanding
drown	sounded	outdoors	
crowd	surround	household	
pounds	downtown	playground	
browse			

Chorally read and clap out the number of syllables in each word.

Directed Instruction

1 Proceed to page 61. Say, spell, and say each Pattern and High-Frequency Word. Provide this week's Challenge Words and have students write them in the spaces provided. Point out the answer blanks found inside the cross while explaining that a red cross is a symbol used by medical personnel. Students complete the page independently.

Proceed to page 61.

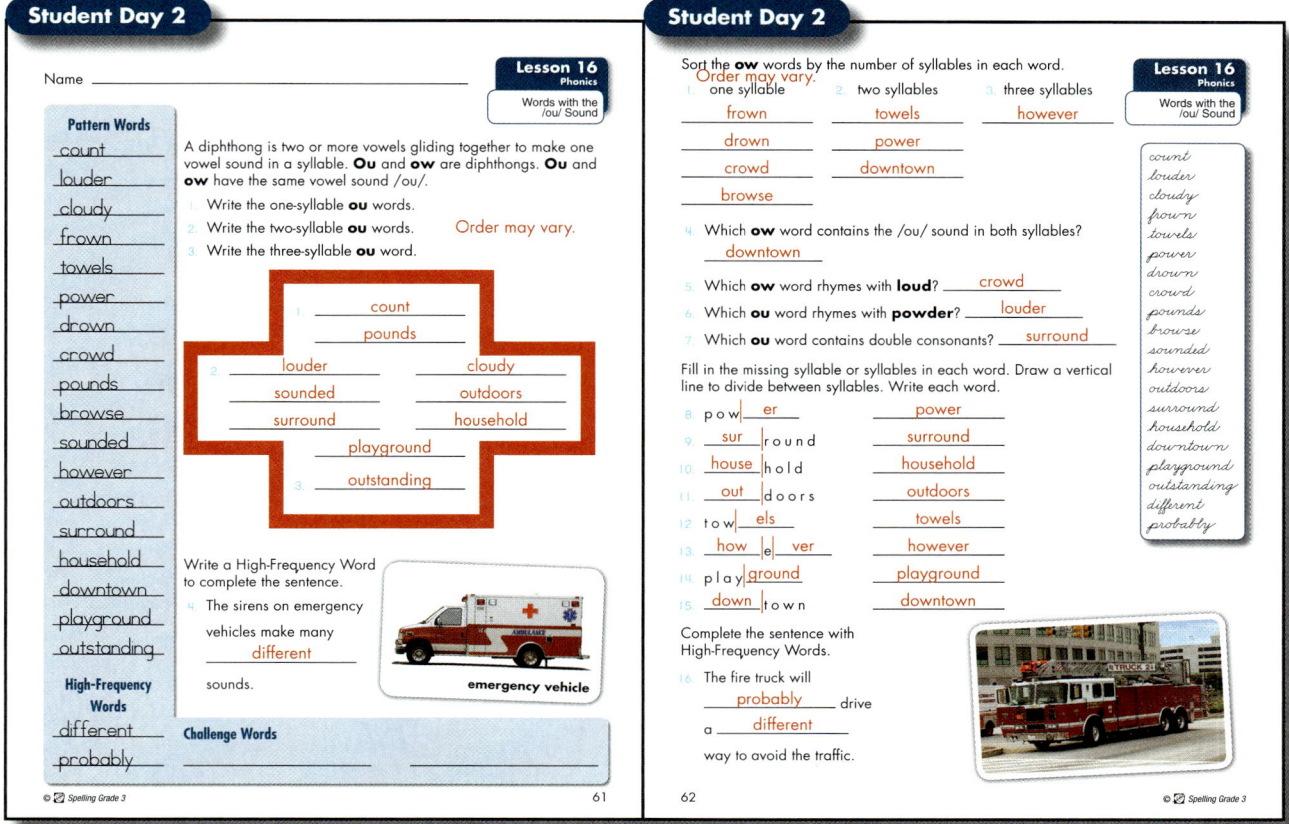

Differentiated Instruction

- For students who spelled all the words correctly on the Warm Up, select and assign three Extra Challenge Words from the following list: authorized, emergency, portrait, elaborate, ridiculous, Jeremiah.

- For students who spelled less than half correctly, assign the following Pattern and High-Frequency Words: count, louder, towels, crowd, browse, however, surround, playground, different, probably. On the Wrap Up, evaluate these students on the ten words assigned; however, encourage them to attempt to spell all the list words to the best of their ability. They are also responsible for writing the dictated sentences.

Student Spelling Support Materials

BLMs SP3-16B–C
Card stock
BLM SP3-01A
Sentence strips
Letter tiles
BLMs SP3-16F–G
File folder
Envelope

Student Spelling Support

1. Write this week's words categorized by patterns on a large piece of paper and attach to the Word Wall.
2. Duplicate **BLMs SP3-16B–C Lesson 16 Spelling Words I** and **II** on CARD STOCK for students to use as flash cards at school or at home.
3. Use **BLM SP3-01A A Spelling Study Strategy** in instructional groups to provide assistance with some or all of the words.
4. Assist students in writing the Challenge Words, numbers 21 and 22, in the section called My Words for Writing, in the back of their textbook.
5. For visual learners, write each Pattern Word on a SENTENCE STRIP, omitting the *ou* and *ow*. Direct students to use LETTER TILES to complete each word.
6. For a small group activity, play Emergency Hopscotch. You will need **BLMs SP3-16F–G Emergency Hopscotch I** and **II**, a FILE FOLDER, CARD STOCK, and an ENVELOPE. Follow the assembly instructions on the blackline master.

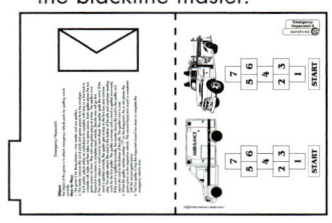

2 Proceed to page 62. Allow students to complete exercises 1–7 on their own. Read the directions for exercises 8–15 together as a class. Complete exercises 8–9 together to check for understanding.

3 Homework suggestion: Use **BLM SP3-16D Words with ou and ow** to review words in this lesson.

Day 3 Word Study

Objective
The students will identify declarative, interrogative, and exclamatory sentences. They will fill in the missing list words and apply the appropriate ending punctuation to sentences.

Introduction
Before class, duplicate **BLM SP3-16E Punctuation Marks** on CARD STOCK for each student. Separate the cards. Make an additional set of cards for demonstration. Show each card and tell students the name of each punctuation mark. Explain that the students are to listen to sentences and respond to the type of punctuation that is needed at the end of each sentence by holding up the appropriate card. Explain that if they hear a sentence that just states something, they are to hold up the card with a period. If a sentence asks a question, they should hold up the question mark. If the sentence is exciting or shows a strong feeling, they should hold up the exclamation point. Read the following, using the tone of your voice to indicate the punctuation needed:

- I folded the towels (**.**)
- Will you help me (**?**)
- Wow, the day was hot (**!**)
- Great, I'm glad you can come (**!**)
- Today is a cloudy day (**.**)
- How heavy is the box (**?**)

Directed Instruction
1 Write the words *declarative*, *interrogative*, and *exclamatory* on the board. Next to each word, write the type of ending punctuation implied. Define each type of sentence: declarative—a statement; interrogative—a question; exclamatory—an expression of strong feeling. Explain that in the lesson Introduction, all three types of sentences were practiced. Invite students to generate original sentences and specify each type of sentence. Record these on the board and draw students' attention to the ending punctuation.

2 Proceed to page 63. Read the definitions and note the examples given. Read the directions and allow students to complete the page.

Day 4 Writing

Objective
The students will complete a poem using **words with the /ou/ sound**.

Introduction
Write the following lines of poetry on the board, leaving out the list words indicated:

The p_____ was full of chatter. (**playground**)
Mandi was picked to be the new batter.
She swung, she hit, and the ball flew away.
She did an o_____ job that day! (**outstanding**)

Read the incomplete poem aloud. Write the following word choices on the board: power, pounds, outdoors, probably, playground, outstanding. Explain that the word choices begin with the same letters as the missing words in the poem. Allow students to select the correct word for the missing lines. Write in the correct words and chorally read the poem.

Directed Instruction
1 Proceed to page 64. Read the poem together. Reread the poem, pausing to allow students to write each missing word. Remind students

to use the first letter on the blank as a clue to find the missing word. Invite students to discover the pairs of rhyming words in each stanza. Read the poem chorally.

2 Invite students to brainstorm ideas about the importance of emergency vehicles. For discussion starters ask, "What would happen if emergency crews did not have emergency vehicles?" and "How do the vehicles help the crews do their jobs?" Record students' ideas on the board and ask students to write a paragraph about an emergency vehicle on another piece of paper.

3 Homework suggestion: Read the poem on page 64 to an adult. Take a practice spelling test at home or use **BLM SP3-01A A Spelling Study Strategy** for additional practice.

Day 5 Wrap Up

Objective
The students will correctly write dictated spelling words and sentences.

Introduction
Provide a review, utilizing WHITEBOARDS or Student Spelling Support suggestions.

Directed Instruction

1 Dictate the list words by using the Warm Up sentences or developing original ones. Reserve *louder, crowd,* and *playground* for the dictation sentences.

2 Follow this procedure for the dictation sentences: read the sentence, invite the class to say the sentence with you, then read the sentence again. Dictate the following sentences:
- Please speak a little <u>louder</u>.
- A <u>crowd</u> stood by the building.
- The school <u>playground</u> was full of children.

3 If assigned, dictate Extra Challenge Words. Score the test.

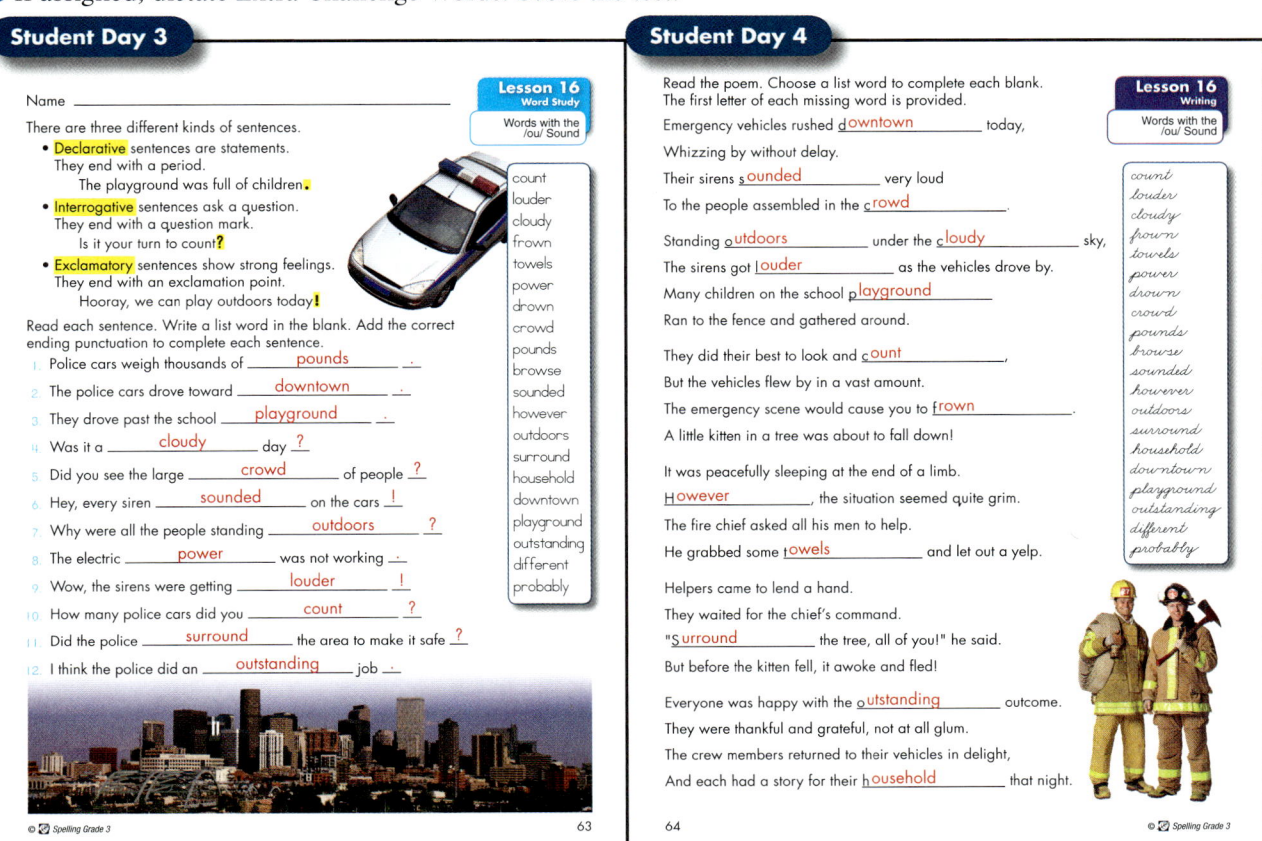

Lesson 17

Words with the /ȯ/ Sound

Lesson Materials

BLM SP3-17A
BLMs SP3-17B–C
Card stock
BLM SP3-17D
BLM SP3-01A
Whiteboards

Transportation

The theme of this lesson is Motorcycles. There are many different kinds of motorcycles. Each is designed for a different type of riding. Street motorcycles are designed to be used on paved roads. Motocross and racing motorcycles are designed for off-road use. Police officers use cruisers to patrol streets and highways.

Day 1 Warm Up

Objective

The students will accurately spell and write **words with the /ȯ/ sound**. They will spell and write high-frequency words and challenge words.

Introduction

Before class, select Challenge Words for numbers 21 and 22 from a cross-curricular subject, words misspelled on previous assignments, or words that interest your students. The word *autumn* has **au** and is suggested for number 21. Administer the Warm Up.

Directed Instruction

1 Say each word, use it in a sentence, and then repeat the word.

Pattern Words

1. thoughtful	Her <u>thoughtful</u> gift made me smile.	thoughtful
2. daughter	Mary's <u>daughter</u> gave her a card.	daughter
3. naughty	The <u>naughty</u> dog was covered in mud.	naughty
4. lawyer	Ellen's dad is a <u>lawyer</u>.	lawyer
5. caught	The fisherman <u>caught</u> a large fish.	caught
6. almost	I <u>almost</u> forgot your birthday!	almost
7. often	Jesus <u>often</u> prayed for others.	often
8. haul	Will the tow truck <u>haul</u> the wreck?	haul
9. also	I like salt, but I <u>also</u> like pepper.	also
10. loss	The <u>loss</u> of his money made him sad.	loss
11. stall	The parking <u>stall</u> was very narrow.	stall
12. fault	He was at <u>fault</u> in the accident.	fault
13. rainfall	Seattle receives a lot of <u>rainfall</u>.	rainfall
14. always	God is <u>always</u> with us.	always
15. bought	Pat <u>bought</u> a new motorcycle.	bought
16. authors	That book has two <u>authors</u>.	authors
17. yawned	The sleepy baby <u>yawned</u>.	yawned
18. awesome	God's power is <u>awesome</u>!	awesome

High-Frequency Words

19. distance	He rode his bike a long <u>distance</u>.	distance
20. beside	My Bible is <u>beside</u> my bed.	beside

Challenge Words

21. _____

22. _____

2 Allow students to self-correct their pretest, using the following procedure:

    a. Write each word on the board. Discuss the letter/sound relationships in each word. Point out the following ways to spell the **/ȯ/** sound: o, ough, augh, au, aw. In *ough* and *augh*, the *gh* is silent. The letter *a* may also spell the **/ȯ/** sound in *all* and *al*.

    b. As a class, read, spell, and read each word again. Direct students to circle misspelled words with a colored pencil and rewrite them correctly.

3 Proof each student's Warm Up.

4 Homework suggestion: Use **BLM SP3-17A Motocross** to practice words from this lesson.

Day 2 Phonics

Objective

The students will sort **words with the /ȯ/ sound**. They will cross out silent letters in each word, divide words into syllables, and change letters in words to make new words. They will write rhyming words and high-frequency words.

Introduction

Teacher Note: The common sound of **/ȯ/** is heard in the words with **o**, **au**, **aw**, **augh**, and **ough**. The spellings **o**, **augh**, and **ough** may denote other sounds; however, the focus of this lesson is the **/ȯ/** sound. Regional pronunciations of this sound vary, especially in the pronunciation of *lawyer*.

Before class, duplicate **BLMs SP3-17B–C Lesson 17 Spelling Words I** and **II** on CARD STOCK to provide each student with a set of flash cards. Cut the cards apart. The High-Frequency Words and the Challenge Words are not needed for this activity. Write the list words and each of the following spellings across the board: o, ough, augh, au, aw, al, all. Explain that the **/ȯ/** sound may be spelled different ways. Begin sorting by asking a volunteer to suggest a word with an **o** spelling for **/ȯ/**. Write the word under the **o** heading. Write several list words under the proper headings before allowing students to sort their flashcards on their desktop. Check for correct sorting.

o	ough	augh	au	aw	al	all
loss	bought	caught	haul	lawyer	also	stall
often	thoughtful	naughty	fault	yawned	almost	rainfall
		daughter	authors	awesome	always	

Directed Instruction

1 Proceed to page 65. Say, spell, and say each Pattern and High-Frequency Word. Provide this week's Challenge Words and have students write them in the spaces provided.

2 Write the following words on the board: also, almost, always, although,

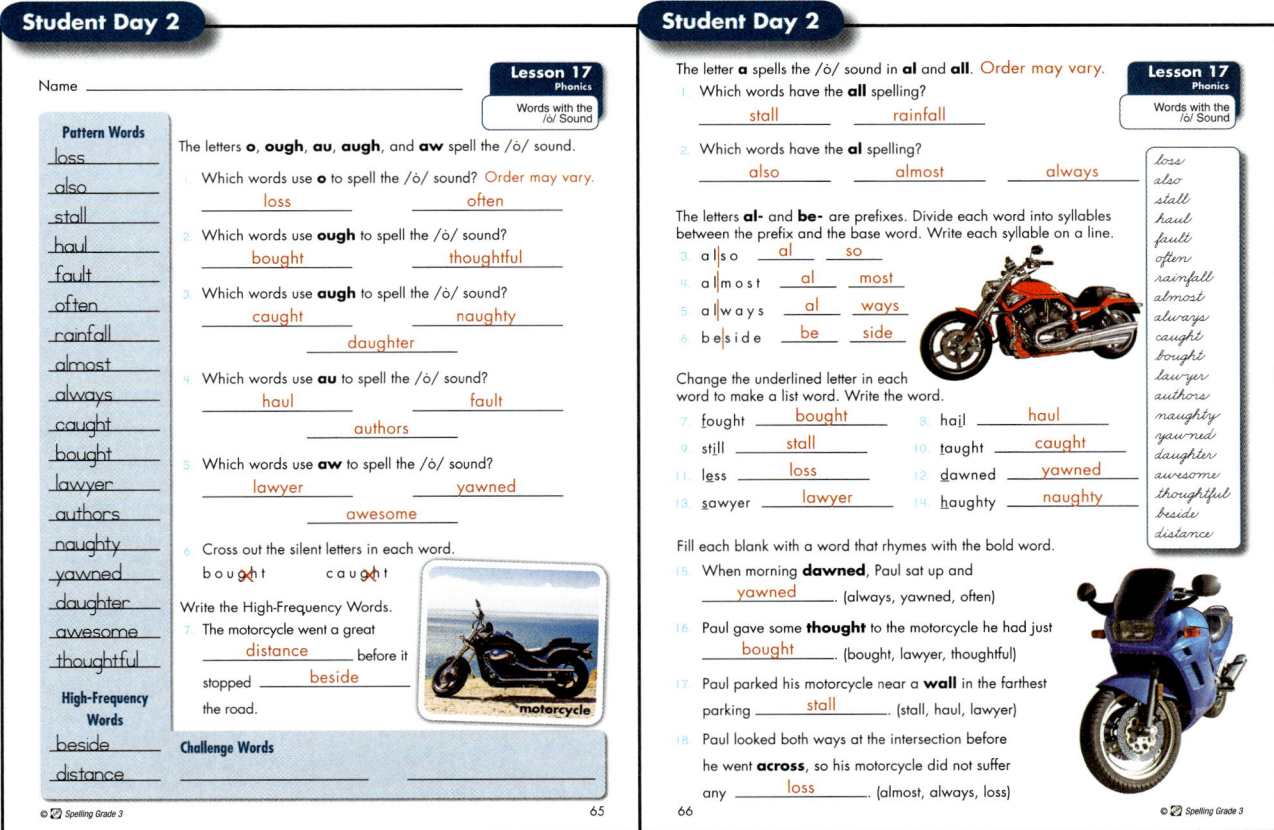

beside, belong, become. Remind students that, in these words, the letters *al* and *be* are prefixes—word parts that are added to the beginning of a base word.

3 Proceed to page 66. Invite volunteers to make a vertical line between each prefix and base word to divide the words into syllables. (**al|so, al|most, al|ways, al|though, be|side, be|long, be|come**)

4 Homework suggestion: Use **BLM SP3-17D Motorcycles** to practice the Pattern and High-Frequency Words in this lesson.

Day 3 Word Study

Objective
The students will complete analogies, match definitions to list words, and select list words with the same meaning as the bold words in a sentence.

Introduction
Before class, write the following incomplete analogies on the board:
- <u>On</u> is to <u>off</u> as <u>open</u> is to ____. (**closed**)
- <u>Artist</u> is to <u>painting</u> as <u>chef</u> is to ____. (**meal**)
- <u>Sport</u> is to <u>coach</u> as <u>lesson</u> is to ____. (**teacher**)
- <u>Drive</u> is to <u>drove</u> as <u>come</u> is to ____. (**came**)

In another area of the board, write the following words: meal, closed, came, teacher. Explain that in order to complete an analogy, it is necessary to understand the relationship between the first two words and to apply that relationship to the second pair of words. Read the first two words in the first analogy. Ask students to indentify how the words are related. (**They are antonyms.**) Apply the same relationship to *open*. Choose a volunteer to complete the analogy and write the word *closed* on the line.

Directed Instruction
1 Proceed to page 67. In exercises 1–7, students complete analogies. In exercises 8–13, students look up words in their Spelling Dictionary to match the definition to the entry word.

2 In exercises 14–16, students use the context of the sentence to select a synonym for the targeted word(s) in each sentence.

Day 4 Writing

Objective
The students will complete a cloze activity within the context of a graphic organizer. They will answer questions in complete sentences.

Introduction
Draw four boxes with arrows on the board in a column as shown. Leave enough room in each box to write a sentence. Explain to the students that this graphic organizer is called a flow chart. A flow chart is used to organize a chain of events. Inside each box in the flow chart, write one of the following incomplete sentences:
- Before I got my motorcycle, I learned ____ I could about motorcycles. (**all**)
- When I was ready, I ____ a motorcycle at the dealership. (**bought**)
- I ____ bought a helmet and gloves. (**also**)
- With this equipment, I would ____ ride safely. (**always**)

Read the incomplete sentences aloud. On another area of the board, write the following word choices: also, all, bought, always. Ask students to identify the missing word in each sentence. Write in each missing word to complete each sentence. When completed, read the sentences and point out to students that the chain of events is in a logical sequence.

Directed Instruction
1 Review the following requirements for a complete sentence:
- It expresses a complete thought.
- It has a subject—someone or something that acts in the sentence.

- It has a verb—the action done by the subject.
- It begins with a capital letter and ends with the appropriate punctuation. Solicit volunteers to give examples of subjects and verbs that each subject might do, such as *dogs can bark*. Write suggestions on the board. Have students tell if the suggestions are complete sentences. Add necessary information if they are incomplete.

2 Proceed to page 68. Allow students to complete the cloze activity independently. Invite students to answer the questions in exercise 12 in complete sentences.

3 Homework suggestion: Read the paragraphs on page 68 to an adult. Take a practice spelling test at home or use **BLM SP3-01A A Spelling Study Strategy** for additional practice.

Day 5 Wrap Up

Objective
The students will correctly write dictated spelling words and sentences.

Introduction
Provide a review, utilizing WHITEBOARDS or Student Spelling Support suggestions.

Directed Instruction

1 Dictate the list words by using the Warm Up sentences or developing original ones. Reserve *almost*, *beside*, and *distance* for the dictation sentences.

2 Follow this procedure for the dictation sentences: read the sentence, invite the class to say the sentence with you, then read the sentence again. Dictate the following sentences:
- I <u>almost</u> fell on the playground today.
- The driver had to stop the car <u>beside</u> the road.
- The <u>distance</u> was too far for us to walk.

3 If assigned, dictate Extra Challenge Words. Score the test.

Notes

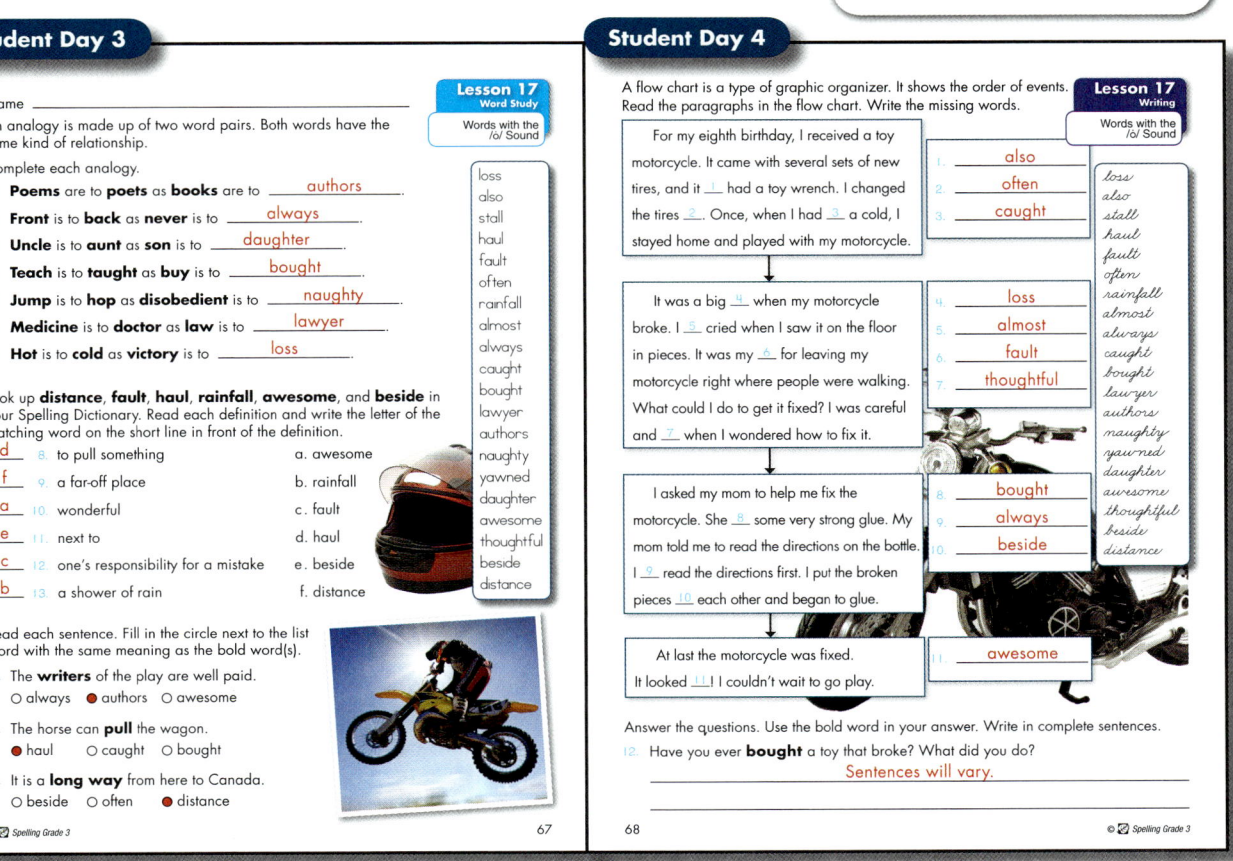

Student Day 3

Name _____

An analogy is made up of two word pairs. Both words have the same kind of relationship.

Complete each analogy.

1. **Poems** are to **poets** as **books** are to ___authors___.
2. **Front** is to **back** as **never** is to ___always___.
3. **Uncle** is to **aunt** as **son** is to ___daughter___.
4. **Teach** is to **taught** as **buy** is to ___bought___.
5. **Jump** is to **hop** as **disobedient** is to ___naughty___.
6. **Medicine** is to **doctor** as **law** is to ___lawyer___.
7. **Hot** is to **cold** as **victory** is to ___loss___.

Look up **distance**, **fault**, **haul**, **rainfall**, **awesome**, and **beside** in your Spelling Dictionary. Read each definition and write the letter of the matching word on the short line in front of the definition.

___d___ 8. to pull something   a. awesome
___f___ 9. a far-off place   b. rainfall
___a___ 10. wonderful   c. fault
___e___ 11. next to   d. haul
___c___ 12. one's responsibility for a mistake   e. beside
___b___ 13. a shower of rain   f. distance

Read each sentence. Fill in the circle next to the list word with the same meaning as the bold word(s).

14. The **writers** of the play are well paid.
○ always ● authors ○ awesome
15. The horse can **pull** the wagon.
● haul ○ caught ○ bought
16. It is a **long way** from here to Canada.
○ beside ○ often ● distance

© *Spelling Grade 3*

Lesson 17
Word Study
Words with the /ó/ Sound

loss
also
stall
haul
fault
often
rainfall
almost
always
caught
bought
lawyer
authors
naughty
yawned
daughter
awesome
thoughtful
beside
distance

67

Student Day 4

A flow chart is a type of graphic organizer. It shows the order of events. Read the paragraphs in the flow chart. Write the missing words.

For my eighth birthday, I received a toy motorcycle. It came with several sets of new tires, and it _1_ had a toy wrench. I changed the tires _2_. Once, when I had _3_ a cold, I stayed home and played with my motorcycle.

1. ___also___
2. ___often___
3. ___caught___

It was a big _4_ when my motorcycle broke. I _5_ cried when I saw it on the floor in pieces. It was my _6_ for leaving my motorcycle right where people were walking. What could I do to get it fixed? I was careful and _7_ when I wondered how to fix it.

4. ___loss___
5. ___almost___
6. ___fault___
7. ___thoughtful___

I asked my mom to help me fix the motorcycle. She _8_ some very strong glue. My mom told me to read the directions on the bottle. I _9_ read the directions first. I put the broken pieces _10_ each other and began to glue.

8. ___bought___
9. ___always___
10. ___beside___

At last the motorcycle was fixed. It looked _11_! I couldn't wait to go play.

11. ___awesome___

Answer the questions. Use the bold word in your answer. Write in complete sentences.

12. Have you ever **bought** a toy that broke? What did you do?
___Sentences will vary.___

68

Lesson 17
Writing
Words with the /ó/ Sound

loss
also
stall
haul
fault
often
rainfall
almost
always
caught
bought
lawyer
authors
naughty
yawned
daughter
awesome
thoughtful
beside
distance

© *Spelling Grade 3*

Student Pages
Pages 69–72

Lesson Materials
T-23
BLM SP3-18A
BLM SP3-18B
T-24
Bookmarks
BLM SP3-18C
BLM SP3-18D
BLMs SP3-18E–F
3" × 5" Index cards

Day 1 Words with Silent Letters

Objective
The students will identify and circle **words with silent letters**. They will write words that contain silent letters.

Introduction
Teacher Note: This week's lesson incorporates the Pattern and High-Frequency Words taught in Lessons 13–17 using a variety of activities such as a word search, crossword puzzle, shape boxes, and book titles.

Review **words with silent letters** by writing the Pattern Words from Lesson 13 on the board. Select volunteers to circle the silent letter or letters in each word. Review that when the following combinations of letters appear together in a word, one of the letters is silent: *g* is silent in *gn*, *k* is silent in *kn*, *w* is silent in *wr*, *c* is silent in *ck*, and *w* is silent in *wh* only when *wh* precedes the letter *o*. When *wh* precedes other vowels as in *whale*, *why*, and *when*, the *wh* glides together to make one sound, a consonant digraph. Check for accuracy of the students' work on the board and correct any errors.

Directed Instruction
1 Ask the students what the words *knock* and *wrecker* have in common. (**They each have two silent letters: *k* and *c* in knock; *w* and *c* in wrecker.**)

2 Display **T-23 Lessons 13–17 Study Sheet** on the overhead to review Lesson 13 words in unison, using the say-spell-say technique.

3 Proceed to page 69. Explain that the box contains all the Pattern and High-Frequency Words in Lessons 13–17. This list is the same list of words that was previously displayed on the overhead. Encourage students to use this list as a review tool.

4 Distribute one copy of **BLM SP3-18A Lessons 13–17 Study Sheet** to each student to take home for study.

5 Homework suggestion: Duplicate one copy of **BLM SP3-18B Pairs of Letters** for each student to practice **words with silent letters** and **consonant digraphs**.

Day 2 Consonant Digraphs: ch, ph, sh, tch, th, wh

Objective
The students will find and circle words with **consonant digraphs** in a word search. They will write the remaining letters to find a riddle and its answer.

Introduction
Display **T-23 Lessons 13–17 Study Sheet** to review Pattern Words with **consonant digraphs** from Lesson 14. Say-spell-say each word then ask students to identify the following:

- words with the **consonant digraph ch** (**which, children, branches, sandwich**)
- words with the **consonant digraph ph** (**telephone, photograph**)
- words with the **consonant digraph sh** (**shelter, dashboard**)
- words with the **consonant digraph tch** (**kitchen, catcher, watched, matches**)

- words with the **consonant digraph th** (**fifth, then, than, whether, weather**)
- words with the **consonant digraph wh** (**which, wheel, whether**)
- words with more than one **consonant digraph** (**which, whether**)

Directed Instruction

1 Display **T-24 Word Search…with a Secret!** Select students to find the following words from Lesson 14: fifth, than, then, wheel, which.

2 Explain that the leftover letters, when written in order from the top left and going across each consecutive row, form a sentence. Write each letter beginning with *s*. When complete, the sentence should read *Spelling is fun!* Remind students that all sentences begin with a capital letter. The letter *s* in *spelling* must be written as a capital.

3 Proceed to page 70. Explain that after all the words are found in the word search, the students are to write each leftover letter on the lines below. They must begin at the top left-hand side (letter *h*) and continue going across. To assist students who may have difficulty tracking the unused letters, have them place a BOOKMARK under each row. As each row is completed, students can slide the bookmark to the next row.

4 Homework suggestion: Distribute a copy of **BLM SP3-18C Unscramble and Match** to each student to practice words with **diphthongs oi**, **oo**, **and oy** and **words with the /ou/ sound**.

Day 3 Diphthongs: oi, oo, oy and Words with the /ou/ Sound

Objective

The students will spell and write words with **diphthongs oi**, **oo**, and **oy** in a crossword puzzle. They will find and circle misspelled words that make the **/ou/** sound and correctly write them.

Introduction

Write the following words on the board, some of which are misspelled: rejoyce, downtown, poynted, voice, brouk, owever, drown, destroy, crookid, browse. Read the list of words and select volunteers to circle each misspelled word. On another area of the board, allow students to correctly write the misspelled words.

Directed Instruction

1 Display **T-23 Lessons 13–17 Study Sheet** to review Lessons 15–16 words in unison, using the say-spell-say technique.

2 Announce a spelling guessing game. Begin by slowly spelling a Pattern Word from Lessons 15–16 one letter at a time. Ask students to raise their hand as soon as they know which word you are spelling. Allow students to share their guess and spell the word for the class. Choose volunteers who

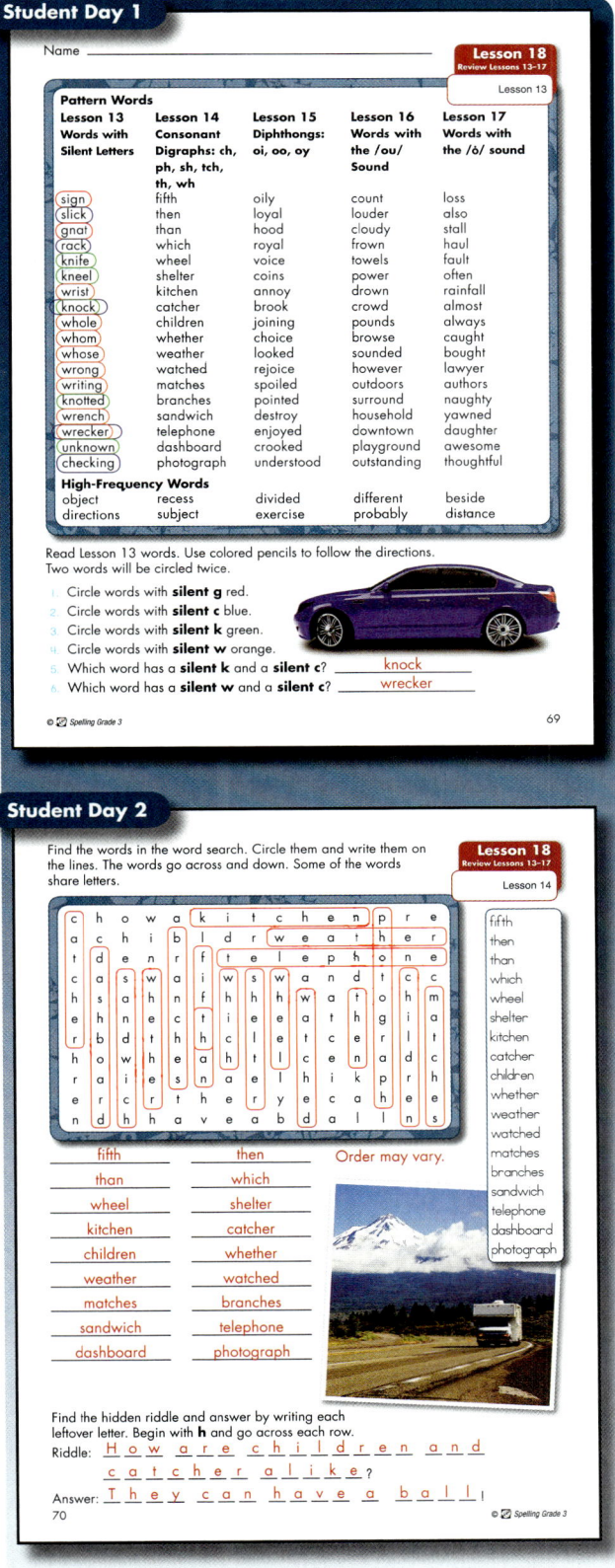

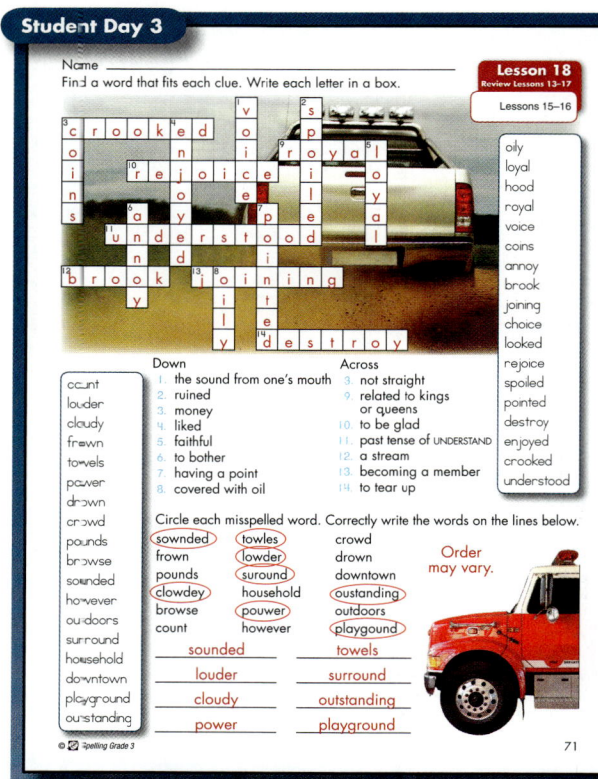

Name _____

Find a word that fits each clue. Write each letter in a box.

Lesson 18
Review Lessons 13–17
Lessons 15–16

oily
loyal
hood
royal
voice
coins
annoy
brook
joining
choice
looked
rejoice
spoiled
pointed
destroy
enjoyed
crooked
understood

Down
1. the sound from one's mouth
2. ruined
3. money
4. liked
5. faithful
6. to bother
7. having a point
8. covered with oil

Across
3. not straight
9. related to kings or queens
10. to be glad
11. past tense of UNDERSTAND
12. a stream
13. becoming a member
14. to tear up

Circle each misspelled word. Correctly write the words on the lines below.

sownded   towles   crowd
frown   lowder   drown   Order
pounds   suround   downtown   may vary.
clowdey   household oustanding
browse   pouwer   outdoors
count   however   playground

sounded   towels
louder   surround
cloudy   outstanding
power   playground

© Spelling Grade 3   71

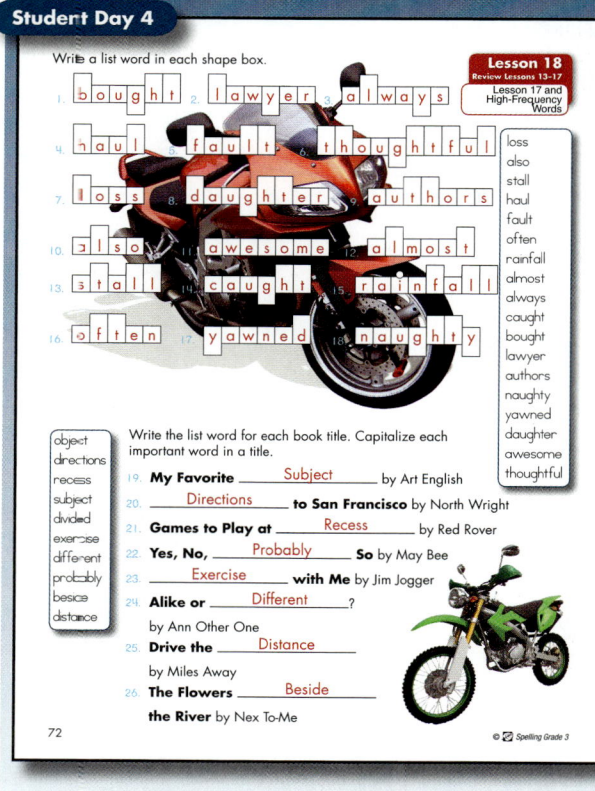

Write a list word in each shape box.

Lesson 18
Review Lessons 13–17
Lesson 17 and High-Frequency Words

1. bought 2. lawyer 3. always
4. haul 5. fault 6. thoughtful
7. loss 8. daughter 9. authors
10. also 11. awesome 12. almost
13. stall 14. caught 15. rainfall
16. often 17. yawned 18. naughty

loss
also
stall
haul
fault
often
rainfall
almost
always
caught
bought
lawyer
authors
naughty
yawned
daughter
awesome
thoughtful

Write the list word for each book title. Capitalize each important word in a title.

object
directions
recess
subject
divided
exercise
different
probably
beside
distance

19. **My Favorite** _____Subject_____ by Art English
20. _____Directions_____ **to San Francisco** by North Wright
21. **Games to Play at** _____Recess_____ by Red Rover
22. **Yes, No,** _____Probably_____ **So** by May Bee
23. _____Exercise_____ **with Me** by Jim Jogger
24. **Alike or** _____Different_____ **?**
    by Ann Other One
25. **Drive the** _____Distance_____
    by Miles Away
26. **The Flowers** _____Beside_____
    the River by Nex To-Me

72   © Spelling Grade 3

---

answered correctly to continue the game with other Pattern Words.

3 Proceed to page 71. Select a student to read the directions aloud. Allow students to complete the page independently.

Day 4 Words with the /ȯ/ Sound and High-Frequency Words

Objective

The students will spell and write words with the /ȯ/ sound in shape boxes. They will write high-frequency words in funny book titles.

Introduction

Write the following words on the board: also, thoughtful, rainfall, awesome, naughty. To strengthen visual memory, ask which word has the most tall letters (**thoughtful**), which word has the most tail letters (**naughty**), which word does not have any tall or tail letters (**awesome**), which word has the fewest letters (**also**), and which word has an *i* as well as two tall letters standing side-by-side (**rainfall**).

Teacher Note: The first word of a book title is always capitalized. All other words are capitalized except for articles, conjunctions, and prepositions with four or fewer letters.

Directed Instruction

1 Ask the students if they have ever read a book in a car, especially on a long trip, or while on vacation in their camper or RV. Instill that reading is fun and can be done anywhere, not just at school or at home.

2 Write the following nonsense book titles on the board:
- I've Been _____ by Mat H. Problem (**Divided**)
- This _____ Is Mine by Givit Back (**Object**)
- The _____ Between Us by Uann Mee (**Distance**)

On another area of the board, write the following answer choices: object, distance, divided. Select volunteers to read the book titles and choose a word from the board that best fits each blank. Inform the students that the other words, as well as the author's name, both give clues to the missing word. Point out that in a book title, each important word must have a capital letter, not just the first word.

3 Display **T-23 Lessons 13–17 Study Sheet** to review Lesson 17 and High-Frequency Words in unison, using the say-spell-say technique.

4 Proceed to page 72. Allow students to read the directions and complete the page independently.

5 Homework suggestion: Duplicate one copy of **BLM SP3-18D Motorcycle Races** for each student to practice **words with the /ȯ/ sound** and High-Frequency Words. Prepare for the Assessment by studying the words on **BLM SP3-18A Lessons 13–17 Study Sheet** that was sent home on Day 1.

Day 5 Assessment

Objective
The students will accurately select the appropriate answer circle within the context of a sentence and fill it in.

Introduction
Teacher Note: The Test makes provision for Differentiated Instruction. The first ten sentences include the words assigned to students with shortened lists. Encourage these students to try all the sentences, but only grade the first ten sentences. The Sample will be dictated and the sentences are provided below for reference. The Test is found on two blackline masters.

Prior to distributing the Test, read through the sentences and select words that may be confusing or challenging for students. Inform students that the Test will not be a teacher-dictated test, but that you will be reviewing some difficult words that are in sentences on the test. Write the words on the board and sound them out with students before the Test.

Directed Instruction

1 Distribute a copy of **BLMs SP3-18E–F Lessons 13–17 Test I** and **II** to each student and a 3" × 5" INDEX CARD to be used as a marker. Remind students to fill in each answer circle completely and to erase completely if they wish to change an answer.

2 Lead students to correctly place their marker below the Sample, listen to the following dictation, and find the correct answer choice:
Sample
    Mom is <u>probably</u> <u>checking</u> the <u>wheather</u> on the news. <u>All correct</u>

Say, "The circle below the third underlined word has been filled in to show that it is the misspelled word. You will continue the test now on your own. Move your marker below each sentence and read each sentence. Choose the word that you think is misspelled and fill in the circle below it. If all the words are spelled correctly, fill in the fourth circle underneath *All correct.*"

3 Assist students as needed while they read the sentences and complete the Test on their own.
1. Dad will haul away the branches that surround the house.
2. Mom pointed to the wrong sign.
3. Mia enjoyed joining the team at recess.
4. I answered the telephone and then began writing a message.
5. José began to count his coins before he bought a new toy.
6. The photograph of the mountains looked awesome.
7. We always carry our towels and lay them beside the pool.
8. Dad drove the whole distance without needing directions.
9. Julie's favorite subject is different than Mark's.
10. The twins often yell louder on the playground.
11. As the catcher began to kneel, he yawned.
12. I wanted to browse, however, there was a big crowd.
13. There was a loss of electric power downtown.
14. The naughty children were caught.
15. Which wheel is too oily?
16. Luke put his wrench on the dashboard before eating a sandwich.
17. I watched an unknown object fly through the air.
18. The cat sounded frightened and found shelter in the kitchen.
19. The spoiled royal prince would not play outdoors.
20. My daughter is thoughtful and also kind.

R-Controlled Vowels: ar, are, or, ore, our

Student Pages

Pages 73–76

Lesson Materials

BLM SP3-19A
BLM SP3-19B
BLM SP3-19C
P-11
Weather report
BLM SP3-01A
Whiteboards

Transportation

Lessons 19–23 utilize the theme of modes of transportation by rail. Lesson 19 begins with Commuter Trains. Commuter rail transit uses the same technology as freight trains, including diesel or electric locomotives. Some commuter rail lines only operate during peak hours to transport commuters from the suburbs to downtown areas and back home again.

Day 1 Warm Up
Objective
The students will accurately spell and write words with **ar**, **are**, **or**, **ore**, and **our**. They will spell and write high-frequency words and challenge words.

Introduction
Before class, select Challenge Words for numbers 21 and 22 from a cross-curricular subject, words misspelled on previous assignments, or words that interest your students. The word *morning* has **or** and is suggested for number 21. Administer the Warm Up.

Directed Instruction
1 Say each word, use it in a sentence, and then repeat the word.

Pattern Words

1. forgotten	I had <u>forgotten</u> to send her birthday card.	forgotten
2. shortest	December 21st is the <u>shortest</u> day of the year.	shortest
3. market	We buy our fresh vegetables at the <u>market</u>.	market
4. careful	Be <u>careful</u> when riding your bike on the road.	careful
5. depart	The train will <u>depart</u> on time.	depart
6. corner	Lin lives in the house on the <u>corner</u>.	corner
7. course	Dr. Gordon teaches a Bible <u>course</u>.	course
8. worry	Jesus told the people not to <u>worry</u>.	worry
9. share	Will you <u>share</u> your snack with me?	share
10. yours	Are those mittens <u>yours</u>?	yours
11. warm	Mom will <u>warm</u> the cinnamon rolls.	warm
12. fourth	My friend is in <u>fourth</u> grade.	fourth
13. report	His book <u>report</u> is on *Charlotte's Web*.	report
14. before	We will practice our song <u>before</u> chapel.	before
15. storms	Strong <u>storms</u> can damage crops.	storms
16. worker	The highway <u>worker</u> wore a hard hat.	worker
17. warning	A blue jay will call a <u>warning</u> to other birds.	warning
18. seashore	The <u>seashore</u> is a wonderful place to play.	seashore

High-Frequency Words

19. mountain	Eric plans to climb a tall <u>mountain</u>.	mountain
20. noisy	That crow is very <u>noisy</u>!	noisy

Challenge Words

21. _____
22. _____

2 Allow students to self-correct their pretest, following this procedure:
  a. Write each word on the board. Discuss the letter/sound relationships in each word. <u>Vowels that come before *r* are called *r-controlled vowels*</u>. The letter *r* affects the sound of the vowel(s) and gives the vowel(s) a special sound. Point out each **r-controlled vowel** spelling and pronounce the vowel sound in each word. Have students repeat after you.
  b. As a class, read, spell, and read each word again. Direct students to circle misspelled words with a colored pencil and rewrite them correctly.

3 Proof each student's Warm Up.

4 Add the Challenge Words and Test Dates before distributing a copy of **BLM SP3-19A Lessons 19–23 Spelling Lists** to each student for home study.

5 Homework suggestion: Use **BLM SP3-19B Commuter Trains** to provide practice with this week's words.

Day 2 Phonics

Objective
The students will correctly sort words by vowel sounds. They will match words that have the same vowel sounds and complete a poem. They will write high-frequency words.

Introduction
Write the following on the board: /ôr/ as in **for**. Tell students to listen for the /ôr/ sound as you slowly pronounce each Pattern Word. Direct students to raise their hand when they hear an /ôr/ word. List each word. Draw the diagram to the right on the board. Teach that the /ôr/ sound can be spelled different ways. Select volunteers to complete the diagram by writing the /ôr/ words in the appropriate boxes.

our	**ore**
yours	before
fourth	seashore
course	

(w)ar	**or**
warm	report
warning	corner
	storms
	shortest
	forgotten

Write the following generalizations on the board to teach additional **r-controlled vowel** sounds and spellings:
- The spelling pattern **wor** makes the initial consonant and vowel sound heard in *worry* and *worker*.
- The spelling pattern **are** makes the vowel sound heard in *share* and *careful*.
- The spelling pattern **ar** makes the vowel sound heard in *depart* and *market*.

Underline each spelling as it is discussed.

Directed Instruction

1 Proceed to page 73. Say, spell, and say each Pattern and High-Frequency Word. Provide this week's Challenge Words and have students write them in the spaces provided.

2 Select students to read the generalization at the top of the page to reinforce the /ôr/ spellings presented in the lesson. Complete the page.

Differentiated Instruction

- For students who spelled all the words correctly on the Warm Up, select and assign three Extra Challenge Words from the following list: commuter, transit, avocado, sever, camouflaged, Ezekiel.
- For students who spelled less than half correctly, assign the following Pattern and High-Frequency Words: yours, share, worry, fourth, report, before, depart, careful, noisy, mountain. On the Wrap Up, evaluate these students on the ten words assigned; however, encourage them to attempt to spell all the list words to the best of their ability. They are also responsible for writing the dictated sentences.

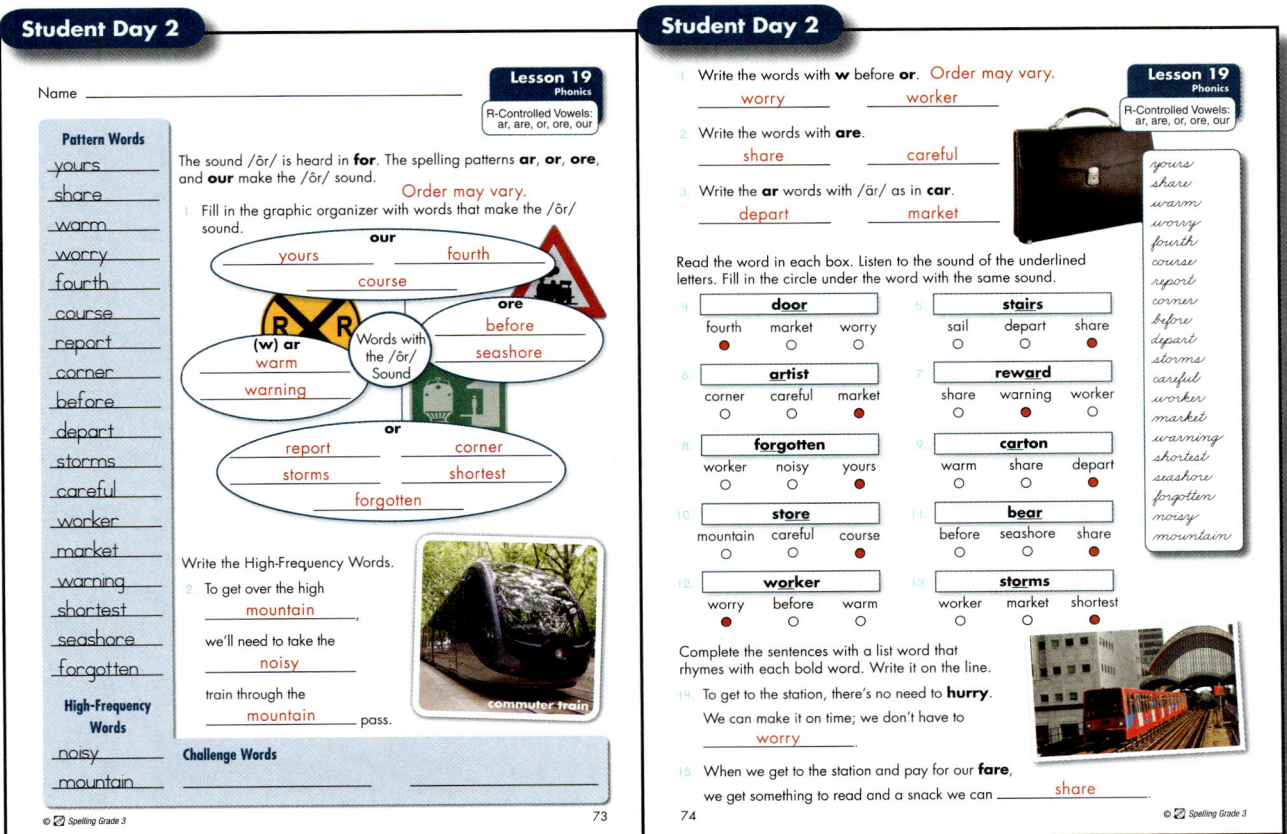

© Spelling Grade 3

Cont. on page 77

3 Proceed to page 74. Remind students to use the generalizations written on the board in the lesson Introduction to complete exercises 1–3. Encourage students to listen carefully to the sound made by the underlined letters in each word before choosing another word with the same sound in exercises 4–13. After students complete the sentences, review the rhyming words.

4 Homework suggestion: Use **BLM SP3-19C Train Trip** to review the **r-controlled vowel** spellings in this lesson.

Day 3 Word Study

Objective

The students will identify and capitalize proper nouns. They will divide words into syllables between base words and prefixes or suffixes.

Introduction

Write the following sentences on the board. Capitalize the first word of each sentence, but do not capitalize any other words.

• Jack and jill went up the hill.   • My friends are greg and nan.

Ask students to tell you which words need to be capitalized and why. (**Jill, Greg, and Nan need to be capitalized because they are proper names.**) Explain that names are proper nouns. A *proper noun* is <u>a noun that names a specific person, place, or thing</u>. Proper nouns are always capitalized, no matter where they come in the sentence. Write the following sentences on the board, capitalizing only the first word:

• Carl goes to church.   • Carl goes to southwest christian church.
• Will you come to my church? • Will you come to mayfair church?

Have students read and identify the noun that is the same in each sentence. (**church**) Ask them to tell you in which sentences a specific church is named. Select a volunteer to capitalize the name of each church. (**Southwest Christian Church, Mayfair Church**) Remind students that the noun *church* is not capitalized when it does not name a specific church.

Directed Instruction

1 Refer to **P-11 Syllables** to review the following syllabication generalizations: Divide between a prefix and a base word (example number 4). Divide between a base word and a suffix (example number 7). The prefixes used are *de-*, *re-*, and *be-*. The suffixes are *-est*, *-ing*, and *-ful*. The suffix *-est* may be new to some students; teach that *-est* is used to compare.

2 Proceed to page 75. Students read each sentence to determine if the word beneath each blank is used as a proper noun in the sentence. Instruct students to capitalize the word if it is used as a proper noun. Remind students to draw a vertical line between syllables when dividing words into syllables. Allow students to complete the page independently.

Day 4 Writing

Objective

The students will read and complete a brief weather report. They will write the list words used in the report.

Introduction

Display a WEATHER REPORT from the newspaper. Talk about how weather reports may be useful when planning the day's activities. Discuss various types of weather, such as rainy, windy, or snowy, and how the weather may change when a weather front comes through your area.

Directed Instruction

1 Proceed to page 76. Have students read the weather report and complete it with original sentences. Their sentences should include list words. They may use words that were previously used in the weather report. Instruct students to write the bold words on the numbered lines below.

2 Homework suggestion: Read the weather report on page 76 to an adult. Take a practice spelling test at home or use **BLM SP3-01A A Spelling Study Strategy** for additional practice.

Day 5 Wrap Up

Objective
The students will correctly write dictated spelling words and sentences.

Introduction
Provide a review, utilizing WHITEBOARDS or Student Spelling Support suggestions.

Directed Instruction

1 Dictate the list words by using the Warm Up sentences or developing original ones. Reserve *yours*, *careful*, and *mountain* for the dictation sentences.

2 Follow this procedure for the dictation sentences: read the sentence, invite the class to say the sentence with you, then read the sentence again. Dictate the following sentences:
- Is that telephone <u>yours</u>?
- Please be <u>careful</u> when you skateboard.
- The weather is cold on the snowy <u>mountain</u>.

3 If assigned, dictate Extra Challenge Words. Score the test.

Student Spelling Support
Cont. from page 76

7. For a small group activity, play All Aboard! You will need a FILE FOLDER, an ENVELOPE, CARD STOCK, **BLMs SP3-19D–E Lesson 19 Spelling Words I** and **II** and **BLMs SP3-19F–G All Aboard! I** and **II**. Follow the assembly instructions given on the blackline master.

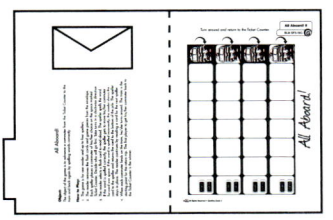

Student Day 3

Lesson 19
Word Study
R-Controlled Vowels: ar, are, or, ore, our

Name _____

A <mark>proper noun</mark> is a noun that names a specific person, place, or thing. Proper nouns are capitalized.

Read each pair of sentences and the word below the blank. Capitalize the word if it is to be used as a proper noun. Write the words.

1. We got off the train at the ___fourth___ stop.
   fourth
2. We got off the train at ___Fourth___ Street.
   fourth
3. Mom went to Best Food ___Market___.
   market
4. Mom went to buy groceries at the ___market___.
   market
5. Mark wants to climb a tall ___mountain___.
   mountain
6. Mark wants to climb Copper ___Mountain___.
   mountain
7. Let's eat lunch at the Cozy ___Corner___ Café.
   corner
8. Let's eat lunch at the café on the ___corner___.
   corner

Word list:
yours
share
warm
worry
fourth
course
report
corner
before
depart
storms
careful
worker
market
warning
shortest
seashore
forgotten
noisy
mountain

Divide the words into syllables between the prefix and the base word. Write each syllable on a line.

9. d e|p a r t   de   part
10. r e|p o r t   re   port
11. b e|f o r e   be   fore

Divide the words into syllables between the base word and the suffix. Write each syllable on a line.

12. s h o r t|e s t   short   est
13. w a r n|i n g   warn   ing
14. c a r e|f u l   care   ful

© Spelling Grade 3   75

Student Day 4

Lesson 19
Writing
R-Controlled Vowels: ar, are, or, ore, our

Marco and his family are going to take the train to visit his cousins. He read the weather report online. Complete the report. Use some list words.

Weather **Report** for Tuesday, March 3, 2008

The morning will be mostly foggy. The **shortest** period of fog will be from 6 A.M. to 8 A.M. Be **careful** when driving to work. The heaviest fog will be near the **seashore**. Later in the day, the fog will disappear and the temperature should be quite **warm**. Don't **worry** about showers just yet. Clouds won't be seen **before** sunset. Tonight you can expect **storms** in the **mountain** areas with **noisy** thunder claps. Tomorrow _____

___Sentences will vary.___
_____
_____
_____
_____

Word list:
yours
share
warm
worry
fourth
course
report
corner
before
depart
storms
careful
worker
market
warning
shortest
seashore
forgotten
noisy
mountain

Write the bold list words that were used in the weather report. Order may vary.

1. Report
2. shortest
3. careful
4. seashore
5. warm
6. worry
7. before
8. storms
9. mountain
10. noisy

76   © Spelling Grade 3

R-Controlled Vowels: air, ear, er, ir

Student Pages
Pages 77–80

Lesson Materials

BLM SP3-20A
BLM SP3-20B
Favorite book
BLMs SP3-20C–D
BLM SP3-01A
Whiteboards

Transportation

The theme of this lesson is Bullet Trains. Japan, having designed the original high-speed train in 1964, is the first country to use a bullet train. Today, bullet trains are widely used in Japan as well as in countries throughout Europe and the United States.

Day 1 Warm Up

Objective

The students will accurately spell and write words with **air**, **ear**, **er**, and **ir**. They will spell and write high-frequency words and challenge words.

Introduction

Before class, select Challenge Words for numbers 21 and 22 from a cross-curricular subject, words misspelled on previous assignments, or words that interest your students. The word *thirsty* has **ir** and is suggested for number 21. Administer the Warm Up.

Directed Instruction

1 Say each word, use it in a sentence, and then repeat the word.

Pattern Words

1. airport	Our plane landed safely at the <u>airport</u>.	airport
2. skirts	Mom bought three new <u>skirts</u> for me.	skirts
3. chair	You should never lean back in your <u>chair</u>.	chair
4. early	Mr. Fikse gets up <u>early</u> every morning.	early
5. answer	What is the <u>answer</u> to five times eight?	answer
6. upstairs	Rebecca walked <u>upstairs</u> to her room.	upstairs
7. heard	Have you <u>heard</u> the story of Ruth and Boaz?	heard
8. fearful	Many people are <u>fearful</u> of spiders.	fearful
9. thirteen	A *baker's dozen* means <u>thirteen</u>.	thirteen
10. shepherd	A <u>shepherd</u> takes care of his sheep.	shepherd
11. nearly	Robert is <u>nearly</u> as tall as Tyler.	nearly
12. together	Our class recites Bible verses <u>together</u>.	together
13. stir	Jean began to <u>stir</u> the pancake mix.	stir
14. silver	The beautiful ring was made from <u>silver</u>.	silver
15. first	Alex raised his hand <u>first</u>.	first
16. learn	Conner likes to <u>learn</u> about the planets.	learn
17. stairs	Cindy took the <u>stairs</u>, not the elevator.	stairs
18. covered	Rachel likes chocolate-<u>covered</u> strawberries.	covered

High-Frequency Words

19. engine	The <u>engine</u> on the train is loud.	engine
20. symbol	The flag is a <u>symbol</u> of the United States.	symbol

Challenge Words

21. _____

22. _____

2 Allow students to self-correct their pretest, following this procedure:

  a. Write each word on the board. Discuss the letter/sound relationships in each word. Remind students that vowels that come before *r* are called *r*-controlled vowels. The letter *r* affects the sound of the vowel(s) and gives the vowel(s) a special sound. Point out that this week's list contains words with more **r-controlled vowels**. The spelling pattern **ear** has two pronunciations in this lesson—/ûr/ in *learn* and /îr/ in *nearly*.

  b. As a class, read, spell, and read each word again. Direct students to circle misspelled words with a colored pencil and rewrite them correctly.

3 Proof each student's Warm Up.

4 Homework suggestion: Use **BLM SP3-20A Bullet Trains** to provide practice with this week's list.

Day 2 Phonics

Objective

The students will correctly sort pattern words by vowel sounds and identify misspelled words. They will identify words with two and three syllables and change a letter in a word to make a list word. They will write high-frequency words.

Introduction

Write the Pattern Words in one area of the board. In another area, write the column headings shown below. Invite students to come to the board, select, and write a list word with the appropriate spelling pattern under the correct heading.

<u>air</u>	<u>ear</u>		<u>er</u>	<u>ir</u>
chair	learn	nearly	silver	stir
stairs	early	fearful	answer	first
airport	heard		covered	skirts
upstairs			together	thirteen
			shepherd	

Directed Instruction

1 Chorally read each column and clap out the syllables. Select students to name the words with one, two, and three syllables.

2 Point to each of the four spelling patterns and explain that these patterns make three different r-controlled vowel sounds in this week's list. Demonstrate, using the list words, that **air** makes one sound, **ear** makes two sounds, and **er** and **ir** make the same sound.

3 Draw students' attention to the **ear** spelling pattern in the second column. Explain that the /ûr/ sound is heard in *learn*, *early*, and *heard*. Teach that the /îr/ sound is heard in *nearly* and *fearful*. Invite a volunteer to circle the **ear** words with the /ûr/ sound and box the **ear** words the /îr/ sound.

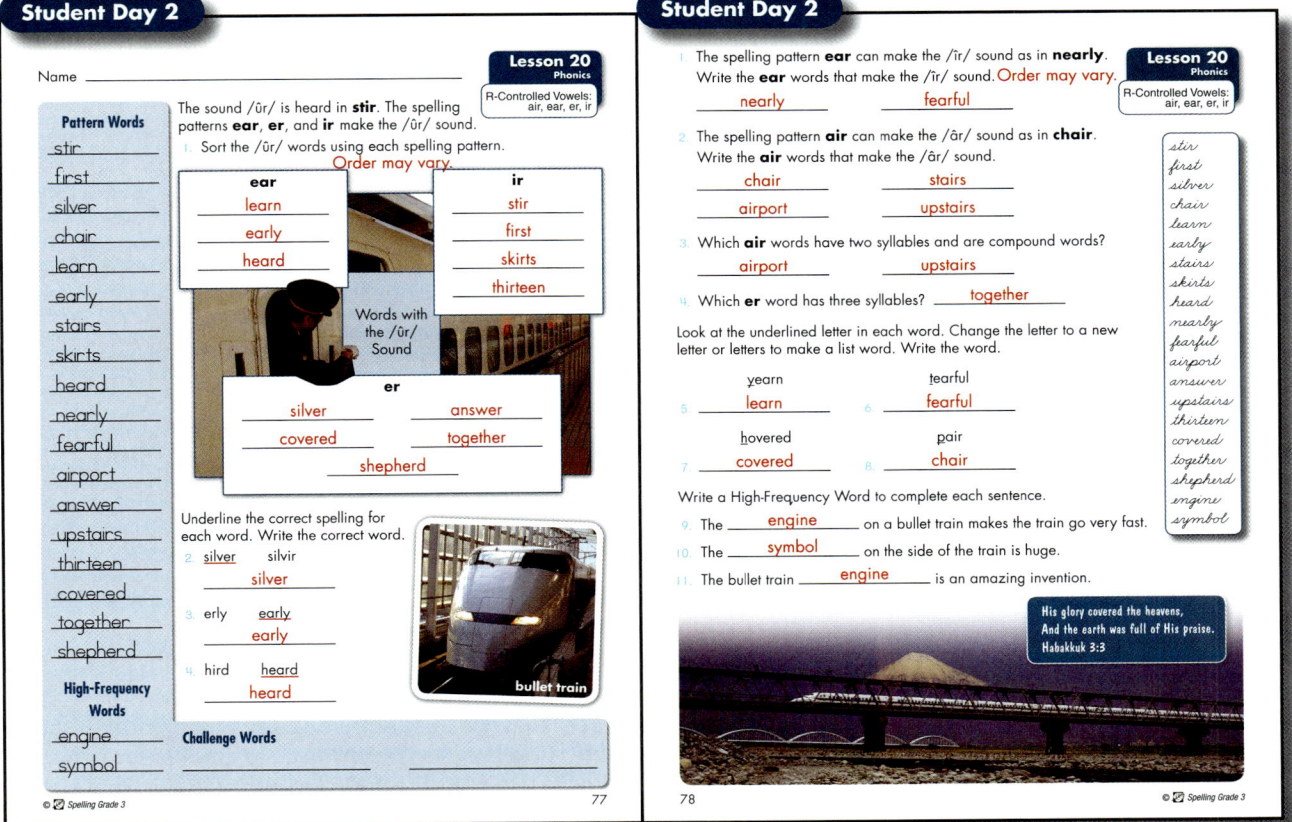

Cont. on page 81

4 Proceed to page 77. Say, spell, and say each Pattern and High-Frequency Word. Provide this week's Challenge Words and have students write them in the spaces provided. Read the sentences and the directions at the top of the page. Instruct students to complete the page independently.

5 Continue to page 78. Select a volunteer to read the directions. Answer any questions before allowing the students to complete the page. Have a student read Habakkuk 3:3. Comment that we can praise the Lord for His majestic creation anytime and anywhere.

6 Homework suggestion: Use **BLM SP3-20B Train Stations** to review words with **r-controlled vowels** and High-Frequency Words.

Day 3 Word Study

Objective
The students will write antonyms, classify words, and answer questions in complete sentences.

Introduction
Write the following words on the board:
- shortest (**longest**)
- warm (**cool**)
- forward (**backward**)
- before (**after**)

Review the definition of antonym—a word that means the opposite of another word. Invite volunteers to come forward and write an antonym for each word.

Directed Instruction

1 Write the following groups of words on the board:
- boots, sandals, slippers (**shoes, etc.**)
- morning, noon, night (**day, etc.**)
- water, sand, waves (**beach, etc.**)
- leaves, branches, trunk (**tree, etc.**)

Select volunteers to write a word that fits each group.

2 Ask the students what the words *rain*, *hail*, and *snow* have in common. (**They are different kinds of weather conditions.**) Remind students to write complete sentences when answering questions.

3 Proceed to page 79. Answer any questions before allowing students to complete the page independently.

Day 4 Writing

Objective
The students will use proofreading marks to identify mistakes in a book report. They will correctly write misspelled words.

Introduction
Display a FAVORITE BOOK and give a short oral book report. Invite students to share the title of their favorite book.

Directed Instruction

1 On the board, draw the Proofreading Marks box and write the following sentences with errors:
- a bullet train travels through tunnels over bridges (**A bullet train travels through tunnels and over bridges.**)
- Many trains are Painted sliver. (**Many trains are painted silver.**)
- the New bullet train is is number thritene (**The new bullet train is number thirteen.**)

2 Point to the new mark "make a small letter" in the Proofreading Marks box. Explain that this is used when a word has a capital letter but should have a lowercase letter. A line is drawn through the capital letter to indicate the error.

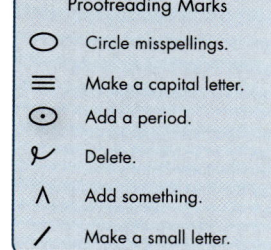

Proofreading Marks
- ⬭ Circle misspellings.
- ≡ Make a capital letter.
- ⊙ Add a period.
- ⏧ Delete.
- ∧ Add something.
- / Make a small letter.

3 Select volunteers to come to the board and make the appropriate corrections.

4 Proceed to page 80. Select a volunteer to read the sentences at the top of the page. Assist students as needed to make sure that all errors are corrected. (**6 misspellings; 4 capital letters needed; 2 periods needed; 2 deletes; 2 add something—*is* and *a*; 2 small letters needed**) Utilize **BLMs SP3-20C–D Proofreading Marks Box** and **Corrected Book Report Form** for students to self-check page 80 and then read a corrected version.

5 Homework suggestion: Read the book report on page 80 to an adult. Take a practice spelling test at home or use **BLM SP3-01A A Spelling Study Strategy** for additional practice.

Day 5 Wrap Up

Objective
The students will correctly write dictated spelling words and sentences.

Introduction
Provide a review, utilizing WHITEBOARDS or Student Spelling Support suggestions.

Directed Instruction
1 Dictate the list words by using the Warm Up sentences or developing original ones. Reserve *first*, *stairs*, and *together* for the dictation sentences.

2 Follow this procedure for the dictation sentences: read the sentence, invite the class to say the sentence with you, then read the sentence again. Dictate the following sentences:
- Who was <u>first</u> in the race?
- Be careful to not fall down the <u>stairs</u>.
- It is fun to play a game <u>together</u>.

3 If assigned, dictate Extra Challenge Words. Score the test.

Student Spelling Support

Cont. from page 80

7. Read Psalm 23:1: "The LORD is my **shepherd**; I shall not want." Discuss with the class that the Lord protects us and cares for us because He loves us so much. When we are in need, He provides for us. Often when hearing this verse, students are under the impression that people do not want or need Jesus. Explain that the context of *want* in this verse pertains to the need of food, clothing, and shelter. If time permits, read and discuss the remaining verses in the chapter.

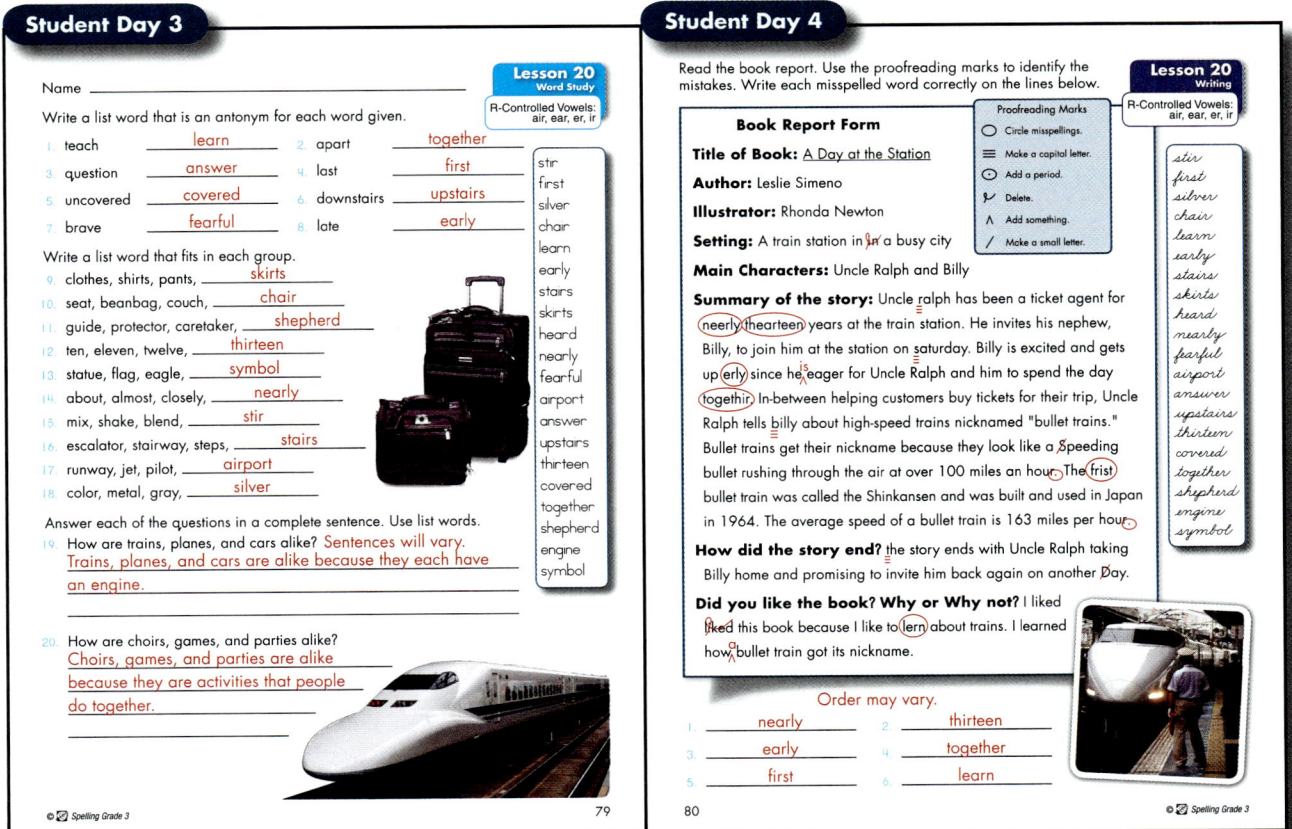

Student Pages

Pages 81–84

Lesson Materials

BLM SP3-21A
BLMs SP3-21B–C
BLM SP3-21D
T-6
BLM SP3-01A
Whiteboards

Transportation

The theme of this lesson is Cable Cars and Trolleys. A cable car is a type of streetcar that is pulled along a track by a cable running under the street. A trolley is a streetcar that is electrically powered and runs on steel tracks. Overhead wires are attached to trolleys.

Day 1 Warm Up

Objective

The students will accurately spell and write words with **eer**, **err**, **ur**, and **ure**. They will spell and write high-frequency words and challenge words.

Introduction

Before class, select Challenge Words for numbers 21 and 22 from a cross-curricular subject, words misspelled on previous assignments, or words that interest your students. The word *turquoise* has **ur** and is suggested for number 21. Administer the Warm Up.

Directed Instruction

1 Say each word, use it in a sentence, and then repeat the word.

Pattern Words

1.	nurse	The <u>nurse</u> rode a cable car to work.	nurse
2.	hurry	Do not <u>hurry</u> me while I'm driving.	hurry
3.	cheerful	Jesus wants us to have <u>cheerful</u> hearts.	cheerful
4.	curve	The <u>curve</u> in the road was very wide.	curve
5.	turns	A cable car <u>turns</u> around on a turntable.	turns
6.	deer	A young <u>deer</u> walked along the stream.	deer
7.	nature	God created all we see in <u>nature</u>.	nature
8.	steer	The driver does not <u>steer</u> a cable car.	steer
9.	error	Isaac made an <u>error</u> on his paper.	error
10.	merry	Mandi was having a <u>merry</u> day.	merry
11.	purpose	What is the <u>purpose</u> of your trip?	purpose
12.	pasture	The cows were grazing in the <u>pasture</u>.	pasture
13.	surprised	Ben <u>surprised</u> his mom with a gift.	surprised
14.	errand	Anya went on an <u>errand</u> to the store.	errand
15.	adventure	My <u>adventure</u> began on the seashore.	adventure
16.	picture	Which <u>picture</u> is your favorite?	picture
17.	purse	Jasmine bought a yellow <u>purse</u>.	purse
18.	fracture	There was a <u>fracture</u> in the cable line.	fracture

High-Frequency Words

19.	bottom	We drove toward the <u>bottom</u> of the hill.	bottom
20.	straight	The road was very <u>straight</u> and narrow.	straight

Challenge Words

21. ⎯⎯⎯⎯⎯⎯⎯⎯⎯⎯⎯⎯⎯⎯⎯⎯⎯⎯⎯⎯

22. ⎯⎯⎯⎯⎯⎯⎯⎯⎯⎯⎯⎯⎯⎯⎯⎯⎯⎯⎯⎯

2 Allow students to self-correct their pretest, following this procedure:

a. Write each word on the board. Discuss the letter/sound relationships in each word. Remind students that vowels that come before *r* are called *r*-controlled vowels. The letter *r* affects the sound of the vowel(s) and gives the vowel(s) a special sound. Point to each **r-controlled vowel** spelling and have students pronounce the vowel sound in each word. Point out the noun *deer*. *Deer* is both a singular and plural noun.

b. As a class, read, spell, and read each word again. Direct students to circle misspelled words with a colored pencil and rewrite them correctly.

3 Proof each student's Warm Up.

4 Homework suggestion: Use **BLM SP3-21A Cable Cars** to review words with **r-controlled vowels** in this lesson.

Day 2 Phonics

Objective

The students will correctly sort words by vowel sounds and spelling patterns. They will answer questions and write high-frequency words.

Introduction

Before class, duplicate one copy each of **BLMs SP3-21B–C Lesson 21 Spelling Words I** and **II**. Use only the Pattern Words for this activity. Cut the cards apart and distribute them to students. Write **eer**, **err**, **ur**, and **ure** as column headings on the board. Allow students to come to the board and place the word cards in a pile below the appropriate column heading. If any student seems unsure about the placement of a card, provide assistance. After all the cards have been placed, invite four students to each remove a set of cards and write the words under each indicated column heading.

eer	err	ur		ure	
deer	error	turns	purse	nature	picture
steer	merry	hurry	nurse	pasture	fracture
cheerful	errand	curve	purpose	adventure	
		surprised			

Directed Instruction

1 Chorally read and clap out the syllables in each word. Select volunteers to come to the board, read a word, and circle the **r-controlled vowel** spelling pattern.

2 Remind students of the following definitions:
- A consonant blend is a group of two or three consonants together in a word or syllable. Each consonant sound is heard in a blend.
- A consonant digraph is two or more consonants together that stand for one sound.

Point to the **eer** column words and ask students to identify which word contains a consonant blend (**steer**) and which word contains a consonant digraph (**cheerful**).

Differentiated Instruction

- For students who spelled all the words correctly on the Warm Up, select and assign three Extra Challenge Words from the following list: electrically, attached, pamphlet, demolish, convex, Titus.
- For students who spelled less than half correctly, assign the following Pattern and High-Frequency Words: steer, error, hurry, merry, picture, cheerful, surprised, adventure, bottom, straight. On the Wrap Up, evaluate these students on the ten words assigned; however, encourage them to attempt to spell all the list words to the best of their ability. They are also responsible for writing the dictated sentences.

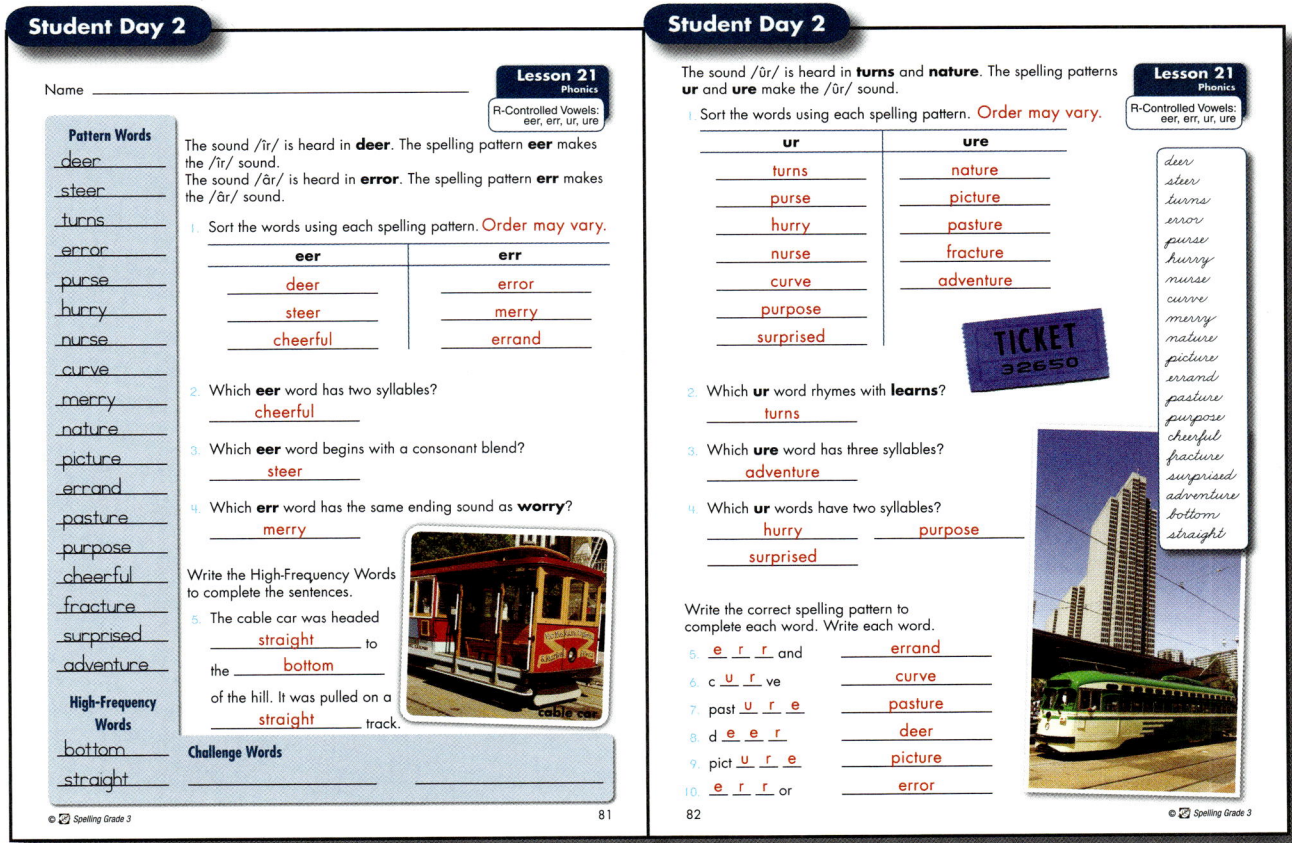

Student Spelling Support

1. Write this week's words categorized by patterns on a large piece of paper and attach to the Word Wall.

2. Duplicate **BLMs SP3-21B–C Lesson 21 Spelling Words I** and **II** on CARD STOCK for students to use as flash cards at school or at home.

3. Use **BLM SP3-01A A Spelling Study Strategy** in instructional groups to provide assistance with some or all of the words.

4. Assist students in writing the Challenge Words, numbers 21 and 22, in the section called My Words for Writing, in the back of their textbook.

5. For auditory and visual learners, play Stand Up, Sit Down. Duplicate enough copies of **BLMs SP3-21B–C Lesson 21 Spelling Words I** and **II** so that each student receives three Pattern Word cards. Say an **r-controlled vowel** sound, presented in this lesson, and have students stand up when a card they have contains the appropriate sound and spelling pattern. Pronounce the words to verify whether or not they should be standing. Students remain standing until the next sound is heard. When the next sound is presented, students will remain standing or sit down if the cards they have do not contain the next sound.

Cont. on page 85

---

3 Point to each column heading and say the appropriate sound for each of the following spelling patterns: /îr/ for the **eer** column, /âr/ for the **err** column, /ûr/ for the **ur** and **ure** columns. Point out that the sound /ûr/ has two spelling patterns in this lesson. Note that the **ure** spelling for /ûr/ follows *t* in this lesson and the *ture* syllable sounds like /chûr/.

4 Proceed to page 81. Say, spell, and say each Pattern and High-Frequency Word. Provide this week's Challenge Words and have students write them in the spaces provided. Choose volunteers to read the directions for each section of the page. Students may complete the page independently.

5 Proceed to page 82. Read the directions and assist students as they complete the page.

6 Homework suggestion: Use **BLM SP3-21D Curves** to practice words from this lesson.

Day 3 Word Study

Objective

The students will utilize dictionary skills by answering questions about the different components of a dictionary entry. They will write spelling words to match definitions.

Introduction

Display **T-6 Dictionary Entry**—from Lesson 5—to review and remind students that a dictionary entry consists of the following five parts: entry word, pronunciation, part of speech, definition, sample sentence. Point out that an entry word may have more than one part of speech and more than one definition. Words with more than one definition may have more than one sample sentence. Words can also have multiple pronunciations.

Directed Instruction

1 Have students look up *nurse* in their Spelling Dictionary. Select a volunteer to identify the two parts of speech for *nurse* in this lesson. (***noun* and *verb***) Have students chorally read each definition and sample sentence.

2 Proceed to page 83. Encourage students to use their Spelling Dictionary to complete the exercises on their own. Review the page, as a class, when complete.

Day 4 Writing

Objective

The students will write spelling words to complete a journal entry written in a cloze format. They will answer a question with a complete sentence.

Introduction

Write the following word choices on the board: picture, nurse, purse, surprised, hurry, fracture. Write the following incomplete sentences on the board:

- Mom was in a ____ and left her ____ at home. (**hurry/purse**)
- The ____ told me that I had a ____ in my bone. (**nurse/fracture**)
- Dad was ____ when I gave him the framed ____. (**surprised/picture**)

Inform students that each sentence needs to be completed with two words. Read the incomplete sentences aloud and have students identify the words that complete each sentence. Write in the missing words.

Directed Instruction

1 Proceed to page 84 and select a volunteer to read the sentences at the top of the page. Read the journal entry aloud while pausing at each missing word. Encourage students to silently reread the journal entry and to write the missing words on the lines below the entry.

2 Read the directions and the question at the bottom of the page. Remind students to answer the question with a complete sentence. Have volunteers share their answers.

3 Homework suggestion: Read the journal entry on page 84 to an adult. Take a practice spelling test at home or use **BLM SP3-01A A Spelling Study Strategy** for additional practice.

Day 5 Wrap Up

Objective
The students will correctly write dictated spelling words and sentences.

Introduction
Provide a review, utilizing WHITEBOARDS or Student Spelling Support suggestions.

Directed Instruction

1 Dictate the list words by using the Warm Up sentences or developing original ones. Reserve *hurry*, *picture*, and *cheerful* for the dictation sentences.

2 Follow this procedure for the dictation sentences: read the sentence, invite the class to say the sentence with you, then read the sentence again. Dictate the following sentences:
- Do not <u>hurry</u> up the stairs.
- The <u>picture</u> was on the chair.
- I am a <u>cheerful</u> worker.

3 If assigned, dictate Extra Challenge Words. Score the test.

Student Spelling Support
Cont. from page 84

6. Read Proverbs 15:13: "A **merry** heart makes a **cheerful** countenance." Define *countenance* as *face* or *expression*. Discuss with students how our heart feelings can be reflected on the outside. We should have **merry** hearts and be **cheerful** because Jesus loves us!

7. For advanced learners, assign a writing extension activity. Have students research and compare and contrast cable cars and trolleys.

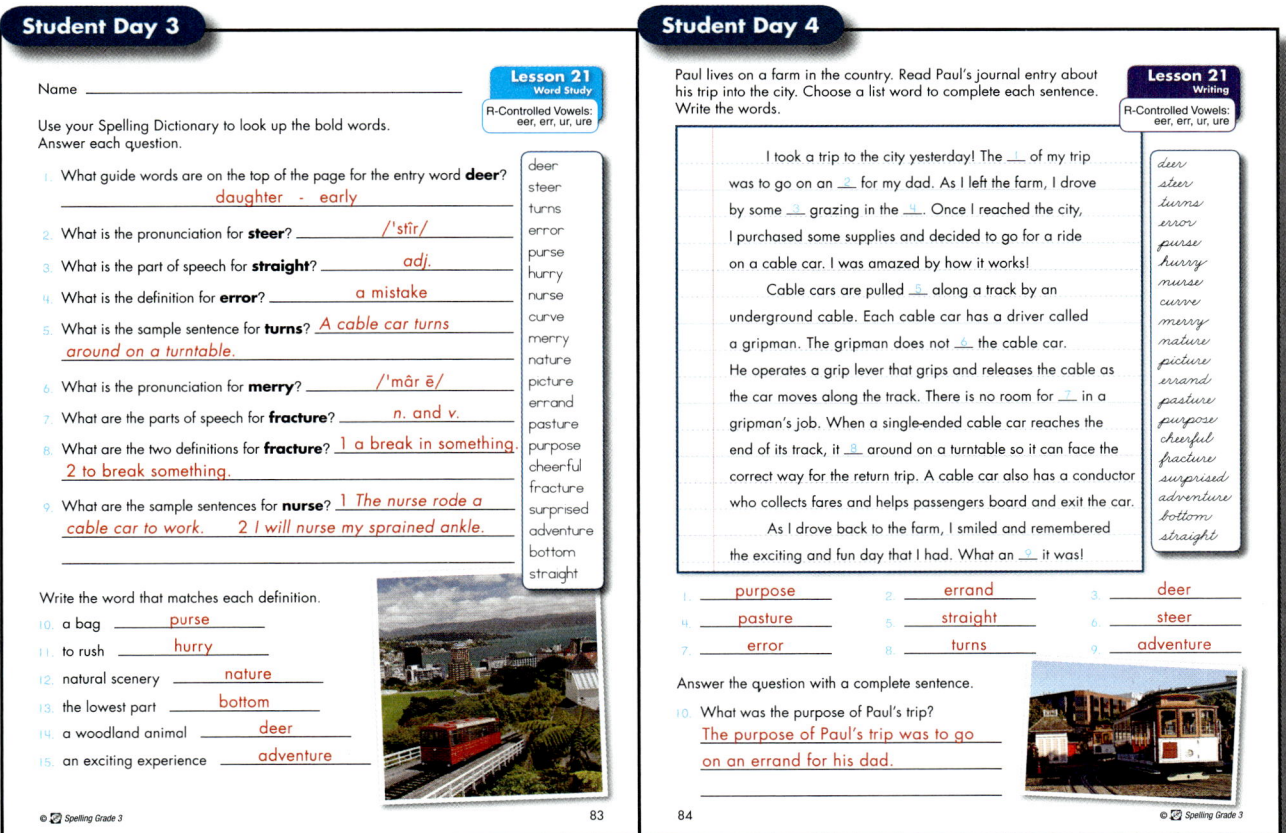

Lesson Materials

BLM SP3-22A
BLM SP3-22B
Sentence strips
Black marker
BLM SP3-01A
Whiteboards

Transportation

The theme of this lesson is Freight Trains. Freight trains deliver goods to cities all over the world. Freight trains can have as many as 200 cars attached to several diesel locomotives. Boxcars, gondolas, flatcars, hopper cars, tank cars, and auto rack cars are the various types of railroad cars used to transport freight.

Day 1 Warm Up

Objective

The students will accurately spell and write words that are **contractions**. They will spell and write high-frequency words and challenge words.

Introduction

Before class, select Challenge Words for numbers 21 and 22 from a cross-curricular subject, words misspelled on previous assignments, or words that interest your students. The word *doesn't* is a **contraction** and is suggested for number 21. Administer the Warm Up.

Directed Instruction

1 Say each word, use it in a sentence, and then repeat the word.

Pattern Words

1.	aren't	My brother and I <u>aren't</u> twins.	aren't
2.	they'll	Tom and Diana said <u>they'll</u> come home.	they'll
3.	shouldn't	Children <u>shouldn't</u> disobey their parents.	shouldn't
4.	that's	The ball <u>that's</u> red belongs to Everett.	that's
5.	I'm	<u>I'm</u> going to draw a picture.	I'm
6.	you'd	I knew <u>you'd</u> do just fine on the test.	you'd
7.	it's	<u>It's</u> Zachary's birthday this week.	it's
8.	weren't	Doug and Lisa <u>weren't</u> able to come.	weren't
9.	they'd	<u>They'd</u> have gone if it had started earlier.	they'd
10.	wouldn't	Annie <u>wouldn't</u> tell a lie.	wouldn't
11.	we'll	<u>We'll</u> leave for church in five minutes.	we'll
12.	let's	<u>Let's</u> sing praises to the Lord.	let's
13.	couldn't	Mom <u>couldn't</u> open the jar of pickles.	couldn't
14.	there's	"<u>There's</u> a bee on me!" screamed Ruth.	there's
15.	they've	<u>They've</u> traveled a long way.	they've
16.	we're	<u>We're</u> going on a field trip next week.	we're
17.	you're	<u>You're</u> a precious child of God.	you're
18.	might've	He <u>might've</u> come if he had not been sick.	might've

High-Frequency Words

19.	direct	Can you <u>direct</u> me to the office?	direct
20.	captain	The <u>captain</u> sailed the ship across the ocean.	captain

Challenge Words

21. _____

22. _____

2 Allow students to self-correct their pretest, following this procedure:

  a. Write each word on the board. Discuss the letter/sound relationships in each word. Teach students that a *contraction* is a way of <u>combining two words into one word</u>. <u>One or more letters are left out</u>. An *apostrophe* shows <u>where the letter or letters used to be</u>. Point out that *I'm* is capitalized because the word *I* is always capitalized.

  b. As a class, read, spell, and read each word again. Direct students to circle misspelled words with a colored pencil and rewrite them correctly.

3 Proof each student's Warm Up.

4 Homework suggestion: Use **BLM SP3-22A Freight Trains** to provide practice with **contractions**.

Day 2 Phonics

Objective
The students will write word pairs as **contractions** and list the letters left out. They will write high-frequency words.

Introduction
Draw a large apostrophe on the board and put a happy face on the top curved area as shown to the right. Tell the students that this is Herbie. Herbie is a very helpful apostrophe. He likes to put word pairs together to make a shorter word and stay in the area where the letter or letters are left out. As an example, write *we'll* on the board, point to the apostrophe, and explain that this is Herbie in action. He is taking the place of the letters *wi* in *will*. *We'll* is a contraction of *we will*.

Directed Instruction

1 Write the following bold column headings on the board:

not=n't	**am='m**	**are='re**	**is='s**	**had='d**	**have='ve**	**will='ll**
aren't	I'm	we're	us='s	would='d	they've	we'll
couldn't		you're	has='s	you'd	might've	they'll
weren't			it's	they'd		
wouldn't			let's			
shouldn't			that's			
			there's			

2 Explain that a letter or letters are usually left out of the second word in a **contraction**. Point to *not*, *am*, *are*, *is*, and *us*; select volunteers to name the missing letters written in contractions that use those words. Solicit a volunteer to name the missing letters in *had*, *have*, *has*, and *will* when used in **contractions**. Point to the word *would* and ask a volunteer to specify the name and number of letters that are left out.

3 Point out that *'s* is used for *is*, *us*, and *has*; *'d* is used for *had* and *would*.

4 Call out the word pair for each **contraction**. Select students to write them below the appropriate heading. Chorally read the list words.

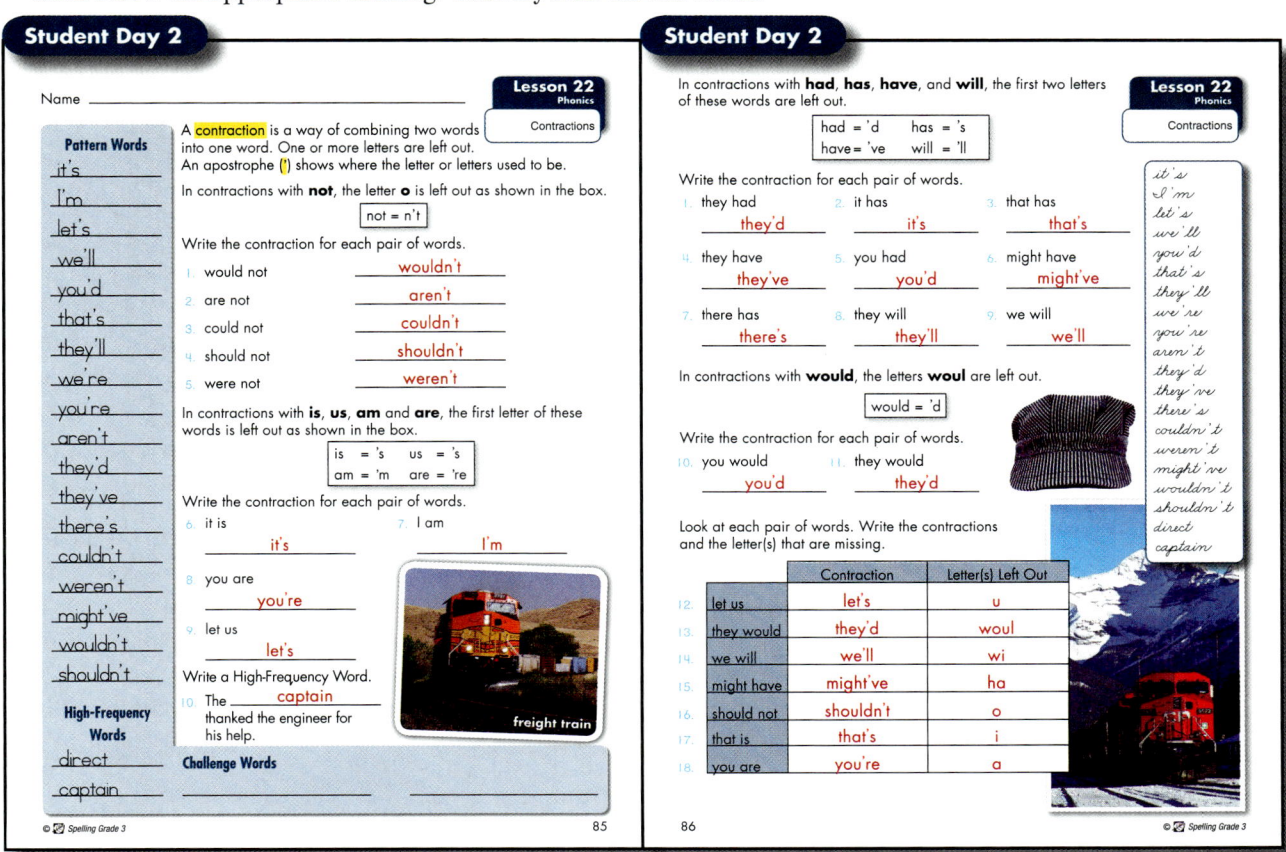

5 Proceed to page 85. Say, spell, and say each Pattern and High-Frequency Word. Provide this week's Challenge Words and have students write them in the spaces provided. Have students complete the page.

6 Continue to page 86. Select a volunteer to read the directions. Answer any questions before allowing the students to complete the page.

7 Homework suggestion: Use **BLM SP3-22B Train Stations** to review **contractions** and High-Frequency Words.

Day 3 Word Study

Objective

The students will circle **contractions** that complete sentences. They will add and subtract words and letters to write **contractions**.

Introduction

Before class, cut two SENTENCE STRIPS that are each 11½ inches long. Follow the diagram to make two folding cards for the following: it is/it's, it has/it's. Use a BLACK MARKER for printing each word pair/contraction on a card. Write the following sentences on the board, leaving a blank where indicated.

- _____ been a fun day. (**It has/It's**)
- _____ going to be sunny and warm today. (**It is/It's**)

Read the first sentence aloud, omitting the correct word in the blank. Hold up an incorrect card, showing the word pair but not the **contraction** and read the sentence again. For example, "*It is been a fun day.*" As you read each word pair, have the students put their thumb down if the sentence reads incorrectly and put their thumb up if the sentence reads correctly. When the word pair makes sense in the sentence, fold the flap on the card to show the **contraction**. Explain that when the word pair makes sense in a sentence, so does the **contraction**. Point out that *it's* has two different word pairs—*it is* and *it has*.

Directed Instruction

1 Remind students that an apostrophe is placed in a **contraction** where the missing letter or letters used to be. A mistake students often make is to always place an apostrophe in between the two smaller words. This strategy applies to **contractions** such as *I'm* and *there's*, but not to *weren't* and *aren't*.

2 Write the following word math problems on the board:
- let + us = _____ (**let's**)
- you + would = _____ (**you'd**)
- were + not = _____ (**weren't**)
- they + will = _____ (**they'll**)

Select volunteers to come to the board, follow the math signs, and write the **contraction**. When complete, chorally read the words.

3 Proceed to page 87. Demonstrate reading each answer choice in the sentence in exercise 1 to determine which one makes sense. Allow students to complete the page independently.

Day 4 Writing

Objective

The students will read a story with word pairs and replace the word pairs with **contractions**.

Introduction

Select volunteers to come to the board and write the **contraction** for the following word pairs:
- they would (**they'd**)
- might have (**might've**)
- we will (**we'll**)

© Spelling Grade 3

Directed Instruction

1 Write the following sentences on the board:
- Since <u>it is</u> cold outside, <u>I am</u> putting on my coat. (**it's, I'm**)
- <u>Let us</u> see if <u>they will</u> come over. (**Let's, they'll**)
- "Today <u>you are</u> going to the dentist," said Mom. (**you're**)

Read each sentence and select volunteers to come to the board, erase the underlined word pair, and write the correct **contraction**.

2 Proceed to page 88. Ask the students to share any information they've read or learned about freight trains. Have students complete the page.

3 Homework suggestion: Read the story on page 88 to an adult. Take a practice spelling test at home or use **BLM SP3-01A A Spelling Study Strategy** for additional practice.

Day 5 Wrap Up

Objective
The students will correctly write dictated spelling words and sentences.

Introduction
Provide a review, utilizing WHITEBOARDS or Student Spelling Support suggestions.

Directed Instruction

1 Dictate the list words by using the Warm Up sentences or developing original ones. Reserve *I'm*, *we'll*, and *you're* for the dictation sentences.

2 Follow this procedure for the dictation sentences: read the sentence, invite the class to say the sentence with you, then read the sentence again. Dictate the following sentences:
- <u>I'm</u> going to the market to buy eggs.
- <u>We'll</u> go to the seashore together.
- Be careful when <u>you're</u> crossing a street.

3 If assigned, dictate Extra Challenge Words. Score the test.

Student Spelling Support

Cont. from page 88

Include the word pairs/contractions that were used in the lesson Introduction on Day 3 so that students can practice all eighteen Pattern Words.

6. Read *Seymour Simon's Book of Trains* by Seymour Simon (New York: HarperCollins Children's Books, 2004). This book details the freight train and the various types of railroad cars and their purpose.

7. Encourage advanced learners to write their own "Freight Car Adventure."

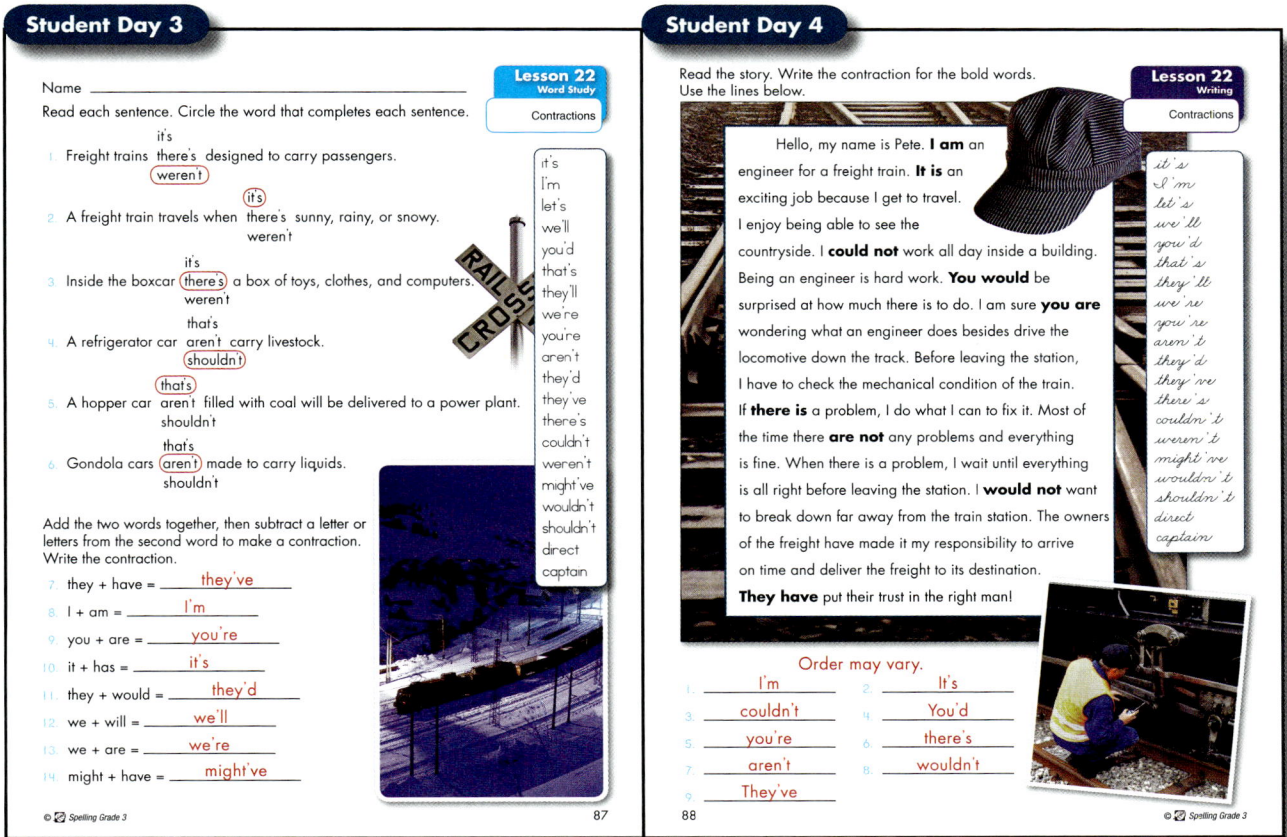

Student Pages
Pages 89–92

Lesson Materials

BLM SP3-23A
BLMs SP3-23B–D
BLM SP3-23E
P-11
BLM SP3-01A
Whiteboards

Transportation

The theme of this lesson is Subways. Subways are often called *mass transit* or *rapid transit railway systems* because of the ability to move a large number of people with frequency. These transit systems also must be independent of other city traffic. Millions of people use subways for their daily travel in many countries.

Day 1 Warm Up

Objective

The students will accurately spell and write **compound words**. They will spell and write high-frequency words and challenge words.

Introduction

Before class, select Challenge Words for numbers 21 and 22 from a cross-curricular subject, words misspelled on previous assignments, or words that interest your students. The word *windshield* is a **compound word** and is suggested for number 21. Administer the Warm Up.

Directed Instruction

1 Say each word, use it in a sentence, and then repeat the word.

Pattern Words

1.	without	Denny left home <u>without</u> his lunch.	without
2.	afternoon	It rained yesterday <u>afternoon</u>.	afternoon
3.	watercolors	Diana used the <u>watercolors</u>.	watercolors
4.	anybody	Can <u>anybody</u> help me fix the chair?	anybody
5.	underground	The <u>underground</u> tunnel was long.	underground
6.	anywhere	Fernando can fall asleep <u>anywhere</u>!	anywhere
7.	throughout	The tunnel runs <u>throughout</u> the city.	throughout
8.	cannot	Jenna <u>cannot</u> come to the movie.	cannot
9.	suitcase	Edward's <u>suitcase</u> is red and black.	suitcase
10.	downstairs	The <u>downstairs</u> has windows.	downstairs
11.	something	I would like <u>something</u> to eat.	something
12.	everyone	<u>Everyone</u> is invited to the party.	everyone
13.	roadblock	The <u>roadblock</u> made us an hour late.	roadblock
14.	herself	Shirley made the gift all by <u>herself</u>.	herself
15.	proofread	Mrs. Lim will <u>proofread</u> my paper.	proofread
16.	himself	Jesus <u>Himself</u> died for our sins.	himself
17.	northwest	The subway train headed <u>northwest</u>.	northwest
18.	landmark	The White House is a <u>landmark</u>.	landmark

High-Frequency Words

19.	electric	Subways run off of <u>electric</u> power.	electric
20.	business	The <u>business</u> opened on time today.	business

Challenge Words

21. _____
22. _____

2 Allow students to self-correct their pretest, following this procedure:

a. Write each word on the board. Discuss the letter/sound relationships in each word. Point out the two smaller words in each **compound word**. Inform students that a *compound word* is <u>made of two smaller words</u>.

b. As a class, read, spell, and read each word again. Direct students to circle misspelled words with a colored pencil and rewrite them correctly.

3 Proof each student's Warm Up.

4 Homework suggestion: Use **BLM SP3-23A Word Parts** to review **compound words** and High-Frequency Words.

Day 2 Phonics

Objective
The students will combine two smaller words to write **compound words** and separate **compound words** into smaller words. They will sort **compound words** according to the number of syllables and write high-frequency words.

Introduction
Duplicate **BLMs SP3-23B–D Smaller Words I**, **II**, and **III**. Cut the cards apart and distribute them to students. Some students may receive more than one word card if necessary. Inform students that you will be reading a **compound word** from the lesson aloud and that they are to listen very carefully. If the student is holding a card that makes up part of the **compound word**, he or she is to bring the card up to the board. Some of the Pattern Words are made up of common words such as *self*, *out*, and *any*. Inform students of this so they are aware that another person may have the same word card as their own. If their word has already been used by another person, they should keep listening for a **compound word** that contains the smaller word on their card. After two word cards are brought up to the board, have the students say each word aloud and face the class so that the two words make a **compound word**. Write the two smaller words and the complete **compound word** on the board as reflected in the following examples:

• can + not = cannot   • him + self = himself

Repeat the above process for all the Pattern Words. Chorally read the **compound words** while clapping out each syllable.

Directed Instruction

1 Write the following sentences on the board:
  • Vince went <u>out</u> <u>through</u> the main entrance. (**throughout**)
  • Liz ran up the <u>road</u> and around the <u>block</u>. (**roadblock**)
Select a volunteer to read each sentence aloud. Inform students that

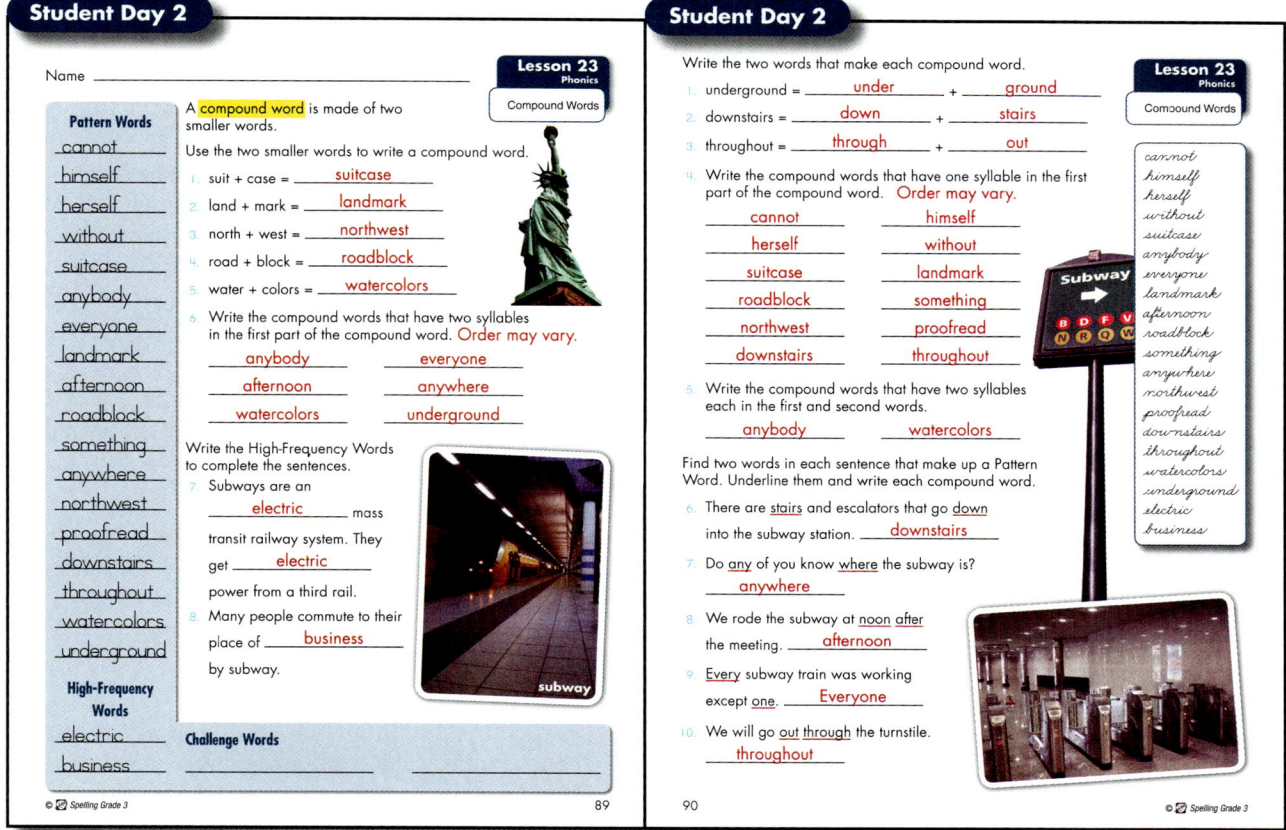

Student Day 2

Name _____

Lesson 23
Phonics
Compound Words

Pattern Words

cannot
himself
herself
without
suitcase
anybody
everyone
landmark
afternoon
roadblock
something
anywhere
northwest
proofread
downstairs
throughout
watercolors
underground

High-Frequency Words
electric
business

A **compound word** is made of two smaller words.

Use the two smaller words to write a compound word.

1. suit + case = __suitcase__
2. land + mark = __landmark__
3. north + west = __northwest__
4. road + block = __roadblock__
5. water + colors = __watercolors__
6. Write the compound words that have two syllables in the first part of the compound word. Order may vary.

__anybody__   __everyone__
__afternoon__   __anywhere__
__watercolors__   __underground__

Write the High-Frequency Words to complete the sentences.

7. Subways are an __electric__ mass transit railway system. They get __electric__ power from a third rail.

8. Many people commute to their place of __business__ by subway.

subway

Challenge Words
_____
_____

© Spelling Grade 3   89

Student Day 2

Write the two words that make each compound word.

1. underground = ___under___ + ___ground___
2. downstairs = ___down___ + ___stairs___
3. throughout = ___through___ + ___out___

4. Write the compound words that have one syllable in the first part of the compound word. Order may vary.

___cannot___   ___himself___
___herself___   ___without___
___suitcase___   ___landmark___
___roadblock___   ___something___
___northwest___   ___proofread___
___downstairs___   ___throughout___

5. Write the compound words that have two syllables each in the first and second words.

___anybody___   ___watercolors___

Find two words in each sentence that make up a Pattern Word. Underline them and write each compound word.

6. There are <u>stairs</u> and escalators that go <u>down</u> into the subway station. ___downstairs___

7. Do <u>any</u> of you know <u>where</u> the subway is? ___anywhere___

8. We rode the subway at <u>noon</u> <u>after</u> the meeting. ___afternoon___

9. <u>Every</u> subway train was working except <u>one</u>. ___Everyone___

10. We will go <u>out</u> <u>through</u> the turnstile. ___throughout___

Lesson 23
Phonics
Compound Words

cannot
himself
herself
without
suitcase
anybody
everyone
landmark
afternoon
roadblock
something
anywhere
northwest
proofread
downstairs
throughout
watercolors
underground
electric
business

Subway
→

90   © Spelling Grade 3

Student Spelling Support Materials

BLMs SP3-23F–G
Card stock
BLM SP3-01A

Student Spelling Support

1. Write this week's words categorized by patterns on a large piece of paper and attach to the Word Wall.

2. Duplicate **BLMs SP3-23F–G Lesson 23 Spelling Words I** and **II** on CARD STOCK for students to use as flash cards at school or at home.

3. Use **BLM SP3-01A A Spelling Study Strategy** in instructional groups to provide assistance with some or all of the words.

4. Assist students in writing the Challenge Words, numbers 21 and 22, in the section called My Words for Writing, in the back of their textbook.

5. Have auditory learners pair up to identify and spell the two smaller words in each **compound word**. Use word cards from **BLMs SP3-23F–G Lesson 23 Spelling Words I** and **II**. Encourage one student to read a list word while the other student identifies and spells the smaller words. Students alternate turns with spelling and reading.

6. Invite students to write about how subways work and why they are such an efficient mode of transportation for millions of people.

7. Read 1 Thessalonians 5:16–17: "Rejoice always, pray **without** ceasing." Discuss with students how our Christian walk should reflect a behavior of being thankful and prayerful in all situations.

Cont. on page 93

there are two words in each sentence that make up a **compound word** from the lesson. Allow students to refer to the list of words on the board to find and select two words that make up a **compound word**. Underline the two words and write the **compound word**.

2 Proceed to page 89. Say, spell, and say each Pattern and High-Frequency Word. Provide this week's Challenge Words and have students write them in the spaces provided. Encourage students to clap out the syllables in each **compound word** as they complete the page.

3 Proceed to page 90 and have students complete the page. When complete, ask students to restate the definition of a **compound word**.

4 Homework suggestion: Use **BLM SP3-23E Boxes** to review words from this lesson.

Day 3 Word Study
Objective
The students will complete sentences with **compound words** and divide each **compound word** into syllables. They will write **compound words** to match definitions.

Introduction
Before class, write the following incomplete sentences on the board:
• My teacher will _____ my paper. (**proofread**)
• Bree walked to school by _____. (**herself**)
• The rabbit's burrow is _____. (**underground**)
Write the following **compound words** on the board: herself, proofread, underground. Read the incomplete sentences aloud and invite students to identify which **compound word** will complete each sentence. Write the words in the blanks to complete the sentences.

Directed Instruction
1 Refer to **P-11 Syllables** to review the following example: Divide between two smaller words in a compound word (example number 3).

2 Invite volunteers to come to the board and divide each **compound word** into two smaller words with a vertical line. (**proof|read; her|self; under|ground**)

3 Ask students if any of the smaller words contain more than one syllable. (**Yes.**) Invite a student to come up and divide one of the smaller words into syllables. (**un|der|ground**)

4 Proceed to page 91 and read the directions at the top of the page. Encourage students to read each incomplete sentence and choose the best list word to complete each sentence. For help with syllable division, have students use their Spelling Dictionary. Students may use the pronunciation for each word to check for syllabication breaks.

Day 4 Writing
Objective
The students will underline **compound words** in a nonfiction story and write **compound words**.

Introduction
Have students relate their experiences with subways. For students who have not experienced the subway, ask them how they think it would feel to ride a subway train. Share the following informative facts about subways:
• Subways are often called *mass transit railway systems* because of the ability to move large numbers of people with frequency in highly populated areas.
• A subway train is usually made up of multiple cars and generally runs on rails underground. Some subways do run partly above ground.
• The trains run on a pair of rails and are usually powered by electricity from a third rail. Trains can reach speeds of up to 80 miles per hour.

• Most subway trains have drivers, but some are remotely controlled.

Directed Instruction

1 Proceed to page 92 and read the directions. Inform students that a *nonfiction story* is <u>a story that contains true facts</u>. The story on page 92 has true facts about the subway system in New York City. Encourage students to listen to the story as you read it aloud.

2 Have students reread the story independently and look for list words. Students underline list words and write the words.

3 Homework suggestion: Read the New York City Subway story on page 92 to an adult. Take a practice spelling test at home or use **BLM SP3-01A A Spelling Study Strategy** for additional practice.

Day 5 Wrap Up

Objective

The students will correctly write dictated spelling words and sentences.

Introduction

Provide a review, utilizing WHITEBOARDS or Student Spelling Support suggestions.

Directed Instruction

1 Dictate the list words by using the Warm Up sentences or developing original ones. Reserve *cannot*, *afternoon*, and *proofread* for the dictation sentences.

2 Follow this procedure for the dictation sentences: read the sentence, invite the class to say the sentence with you, then read the sentence again. Dictate the following sentences:

• I <u>cannot</u> go on the errand.
• They'll come in the <u>afternoon</u>.
• Be careful when you <u>proofread</u>.

3 If assigned, dictate Extra Challenge Words. Score the test.

Student Spelling Support

Cont. from page 92

8. Invite students to imagine themselves lost on a subway system. Ask them to write a story entitled "Lost in New York City" and base several of their adventures on New York City landmarks. Students should incorporate spelling words in their adventures.

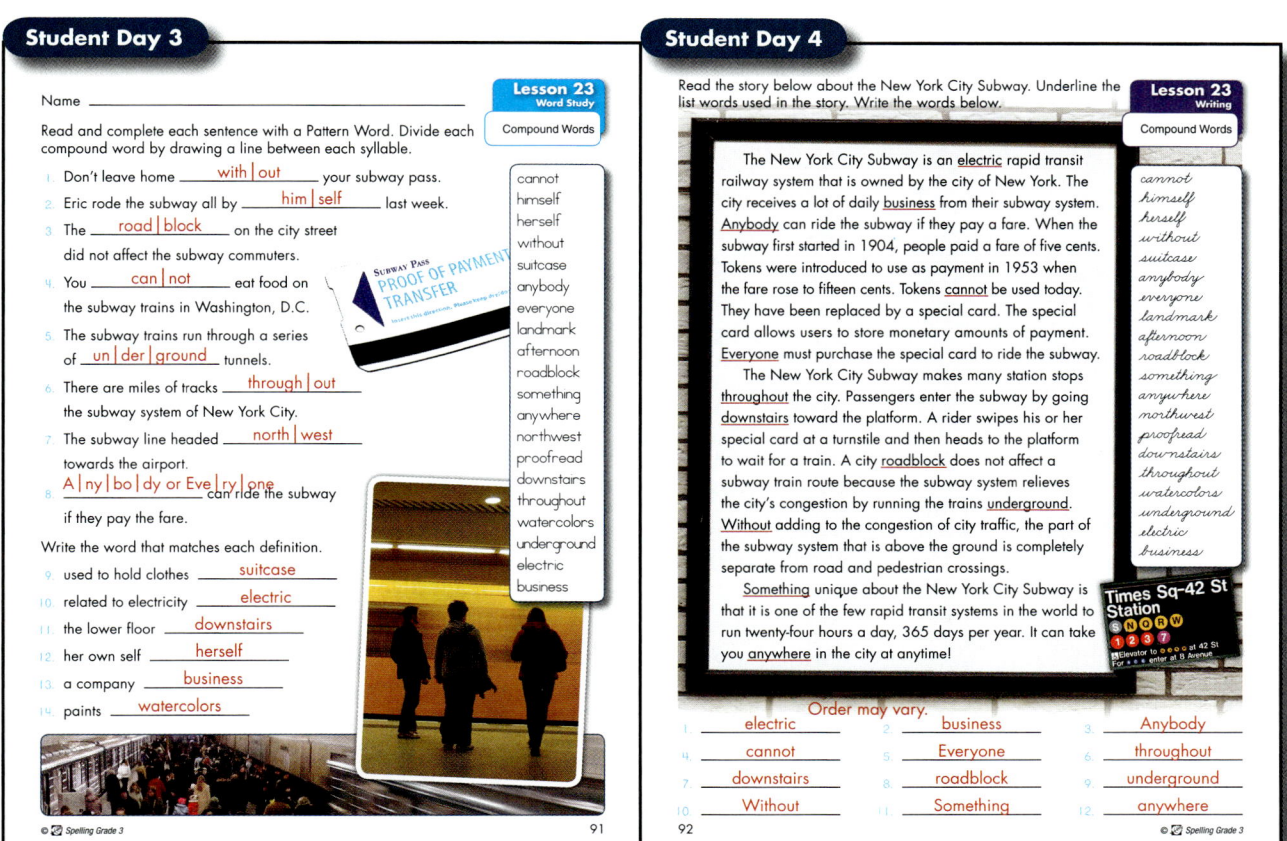

Student Pages
Pages 93–96

Lesson Materials

T-25
BLM SP3-24A
BLM SP3-24B
Transparency pens
BLM SP3-24C
BLM SP3-24D
BLMs SP3-24E–F
3" × 5" Index cards

Day 1 R-Controlled Vowels: ar, are, or, ore, our

Objective
The students will identify and circle words with the following **r-controlled vowels: ar, are, or, ore, our.**

Introduction
Teacher Note: This week's lesson incorporates the Pattern and High-Frequency Words taught in Lessons 19–23 using a variety of activities such as a word search, crossword puzzle, shape boxes, and decoding.

Review the **r-controlled vowels: ar, are, or, ore,** and **our** by writing the Pattern Words from Lesson 19 on the board. Select volunteers to circle the **r-controlled vowel** spelling in each word, and pronounce the sound made by each spelling. Review that when *w* comes before *ar*, the /ôr/ sound is heard, and when *w* comes before *or*, the /ûr/ sound is heard. Check students' work on the board and correct any errors.

Directed Instruction

1 Ask the students to state the common sound heard in *yours, warm, shortest,* and *seashore.* (**They each have the /ôr/ sound.**) Have the students count the number of different spellings for this sound. (**There are four spellings—our, (w)ar, or, and ore.**) Write each spelling on the board.

2 Display **T-25 Lessons 19–23 Study Sheet** on the overhead to review Lesson 19 words in unison, using the say-spell-say technique.

3 Proceed to page 93. Explain that the box contains all the Pattern and High-Frequency Words in Lessons 19–23. This list is the same list of words that was previously displayed on the overhead. Encourage students to use this list as a review tool. Complete the page.

4 Distribute one copy of **BLM SP3-24A Lessons 19–23 Study Sheet** to each student to take home for study.

5 Homework suggestion: Duplicate one copy of **BLM SP3-24B Train Derailed!** for each student to practice the **r-controlled vowels** in this lesson and the High-Frequency Words.

Day 2 R-Controlled Vowels: air, ear, er, ir and R-Controlled Vowels: eer, err, ur, ure

Objective
The students will unscramble words with **air, ear, er,** and **ir**. They will read the clues for a crossword puzzle and complete the puzzle using words with the following **r-controlled vowels: eer, err, ur,** and **ure**.

Introduction
Display **T-25 Lessons 19–23 Study Sheet** to review Pattern Words with **r-controlled vowels** from Lesson 20. Using a different color of TRANSPARENCY PEN for each r-controlled vowel sound, have volunteers circle the spelling pattern that makes each sound in the words. Three different colors are needed. Say-spell-say each word, then ask students to identify the following:

• words with the /âr/ sound spelled **air** (**chair, stairs, airport, upstairs**)

- words with the /îr/ sound spelled **ear** (**nearly, fearful**)
- words with the /ûr/ sound spelled **er** (**silver, answer, covered, together, shepherd**); words with the /ûr/ sound spelled **ir** (**stir, first, skirts, thirteen**); words with the /ûr/ sound spelled **ear** (**learn, early, heard**)

Directed Instruction

1 Use **T-25 Lessons 19–23 Study Sheet** to review Pattern Words with **r-controlled vowels** from Lesson 21. Write the following scrambled letters on the board and select volunteers to unscramble the letters to form words: h r u y r (**hurry**), s e n u r (**nurse**), c v e u r (**curve**).

2 Proceed to page 94. Explain that the scrambled letters spell the Pattern Words in Lesson 20 when they are correctly unscrambled.

3 Direct students to use the clues given to solve the crossword puzzle containing Lesson 21 words. Students may refer to their Spelling Dictionary for help.

4 Homework suggestion: Distribute a copy of **BLM SP3-24C Speedy Bullet Trains** to each student to practice words with **r-controlled vowels**.

Day 3 Contractions

Objective

The students will decode and write **contractions** in a decoding activity.

Introduction

Write the following words on the board, some of which are misspelled: it's, we'l, youd, you'r, arent, could'nt, were'nt, might've. Read the list of words and select volunteers to circle each misspelled word. In another area of the board, allow students to correctly write the misspelled words. Conclude the Introduction by asking each student to explain what made the misspelled words incorrect. (**Some words do not have enough letters; other words have a missing or misplaced apostrophe.**)

Directed Instruction

1 Display **T-25 Lessons 19–23 Study Sheet** to review Lesson 22 words in unison, using the say-spell-say technique.

2 Announce a **contraction** riddle game. Begin saying two words that are used to form a **contraction** in Lesson 22, such as *I am*. Ask students to raise their hand as soon as they know which **contraction** can be formed by the words you mentioned. Allow students to share their guess and spell the **contraction** for the class. Continue with the following word pairs: it is/it has, let us, we will, you had/you would, that is/that has, they will, we are, you are, are not, they would/they had, they have, there is/there has, could not, were not, might have, would not, should not.

3 Proceed to page 95. Direct students' attention to the code box at the top of the page. Each image represents a different word ending for a **contraction**. Allow students to complete the page independently.

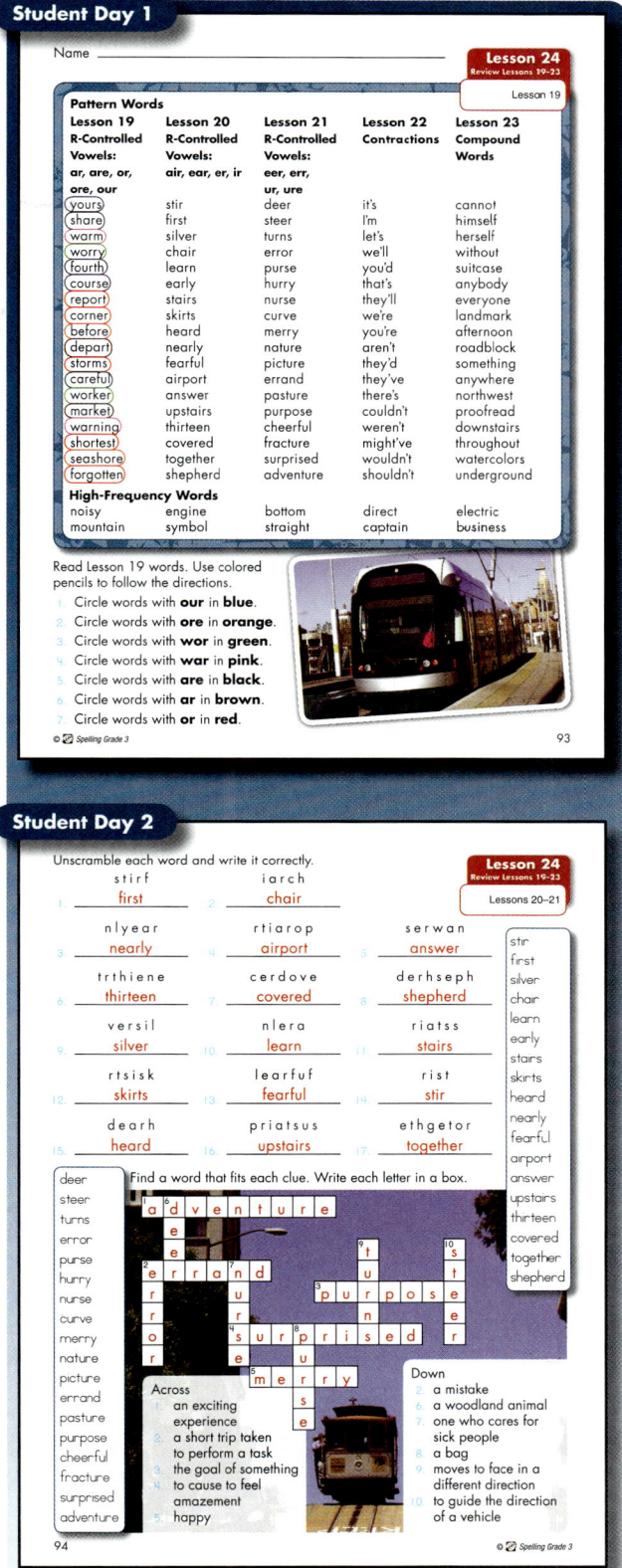

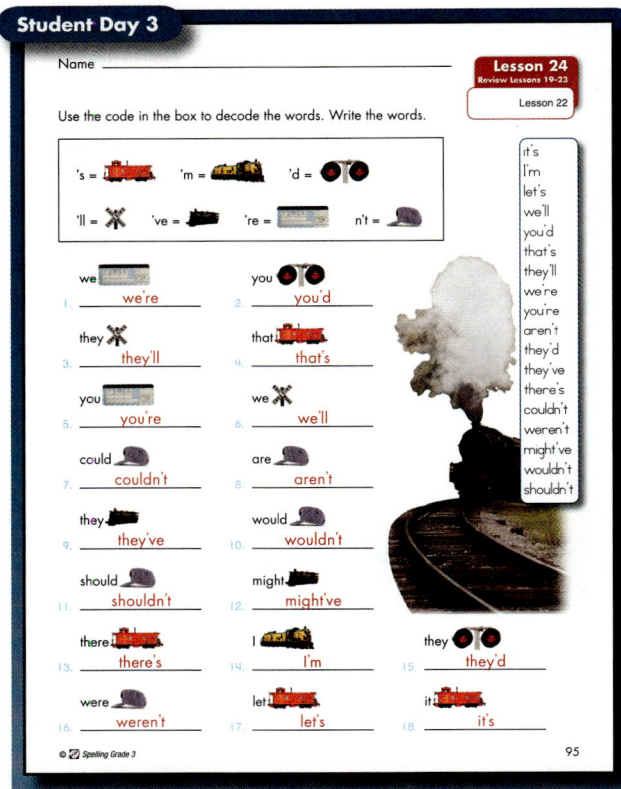

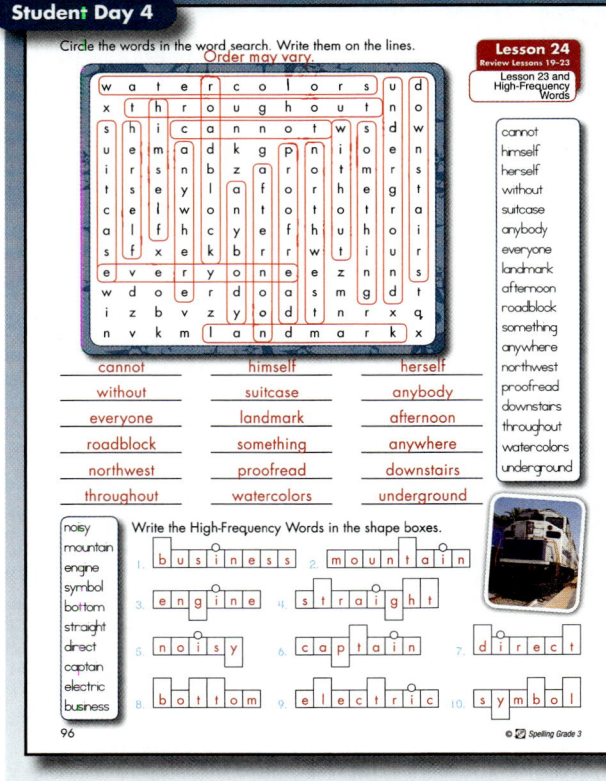

Day 4 Compound Words and High-Frequency Words

Objective

The students will find and write **compound words** hidden in a word search. They will write high-frequency words in shape boxes.

Introduction

Write the following words on the board: noisy, bottom, business, symbol. To strengthen visual memory, ask which word has the most tall letters (**bottom**), which word does not have any tail letters (**bottom or business**), which word is the shortest (**noisy**), and which word has a tail letter in the first syllable (**symbol**).

Directed Instruction

1 Ask the students to define a compound word. (**A compound word is made of two smaller words.**)

2 Play a brief game to identify **compound words**. Read the following list of words and phrases, and have students raise their hand if they hear a compound word: himself, salt and pepper, roadblock, downstairs, up and down, watercolors, water fountain, anywhere, throughout, in and out, underground, ground level. Correct any errors by reinforcing the definition of a **compound word**.

3 Display **T-25 Lessons 19–23 Study Sheet** to review Lesson 23 and High-Frequency Words in unison, using the say-spell-say technique.

4 Proceed to page 96. Allow students to read the directions. Since a **compound word** consists of two smaller words, students may try to circle each smaller word. Circle one or two **compound words** together. Invite students to complete the page independently.

5 Homework suggestion: Duplicate one copy of **BLM SP3-24D Train Time** for each student to practice **contractions** and **compound words**. Prepare for the Assessment by studying the words on **BLM SP3-24A Lessons 19–23 Study Sheet** that was sent home on Day 1.

Day 5 Assessment

Objective

The students will accurately select the appropriate answer circle within the context of a sentence and fill it in.

Introduction

Teacher Note: The Test makes provision for Differentiated Instruction. The first ten sentences include the words assigned to students with shortened lists. Encourage these students to try all the sentences, but only grade the first ten sentences. The Sample will be dictated and the sentences are provided below for reference. The Test is found on two blackline masters.

Prior to distributing the Test, read through the

sentences and select words that may be confusing or challenging for students. Inform students that the Test will not be a teacher-dictated test, but that you will be reviewing some difficult words that are in sentences on the test. Write the words on the board and sound them out with students before the Test.

Directed Instruction

1 Distribute a copy of **BLMs SP3-24E–F Lessons 19–23 Test I** and **II** to each student and a 3" × 5" INDEX CARD to be used as a marker. Remind students to fill in each answer circle completely and to erase completely if they wish to change an answer.

2 Lead students to correctly place their marker below the Sample, listen to the following dictation, and find the correct answer choice:

Sample

Can you <u>direct</u> me to the <u>fourth</u> floor of your <u>buziness</u>? <u>All correct</u>
        Ⓐ   Ⓑ   ●   Ⓓ

Say, "The circle below the third underlined word has been filled in to show that it is the misspelled word. You will continue the test now on your own. Move your marker below each sentence and read each sentence. Choose the word that you think is misspelled and fill in the circle below it. If all the words are spelled correctly, fill in the fourth circle underneath *All correct*."

3 Assist students as needed while they read the sentences and complete the Test on their own.

  1. Something just reminded me of our cheerful time together.
  2. Be careful to check your ticket before you depart.
  3. Will anybody be going downstairs this afternoon?
  4. The hikers had their first adventure on the mountain today.
  5. You cannot share your dessert without asking your mom.
  6. The symbol on the engine told us that it was an electric train.
  7. I will leave early and hurry straight home.
  8. Everyone can learn to make a fine picture with oil paint.
  9. I'm pleased by your good work when I proofread your report.
10. Jack heard a noisy creaking sound on the stairs.
11. The shepherd had forgotten the sheep in the pasture.
12. Let's take Grover Street because it turns by the market.
13. They'd run their errand in the shortest possible time.
14. They'll take a flight course at the airport.
15. Erin's leg had a bad fracture when she was nearly thirteen.
16. The fearful deer wouldn't let us take its picture.
17. We'll heed the warning of storms at the seashore.
18. There's a silver covered casserole dish on the counter.
19. The worker will answer us about the purpose of the delay.
20. Wayne headed northwest with his watercolors to paint nature.

Hard and Soft c

Student Pages
Pages 97–100

Lesson Materials
BLM SP3-25A
BLM SP3-25B
BLM SP3-25C
BLMs SP3-25D–E
3" × 5" Index cards
BLM SP3-01A
Whiteboards

Transportation

Lessons 25–29 utilize the theme of different aircraft. Lesson 25 begins with Airplanes. The Wright brothers pioneered the skies in 1904, and ten years later, in 1914, the first regular commercial route in the world began. It took passengers between St. Petersburg and Tampa, Florida. The era of large commercial propeller airplanes ended in the 1950s due to the development of jet engine technology during WWII.

Day 1 Warm Up

Objective

The students will accurately spell and write words with **hard and soft c**. They will spell and write high-frequency words and challenge words.

Introduction

Before class, select Challenge Words for numbers 21 and 22 from a cross-curricular subject, words misspelled on previous assignments, or words that interest your students. The word *discipline* has **soft c** and is suggested for number 21. Administer the Warm Up.

Directed Instruction

1 Say each word, use it in a sentence, and then repeat the word.

Pattern Words

1. service	The project was done as a <u>service</u> to a family.	service
2. advice	The doctor gave the patient helpful <u>advice</u>.	advice
3. score	The final <u>score</u> was Chargers 41, Broncos 24.	score
4. clothes	I packed my <u>clothes</u> in the suitcase.	clothes
5. scale	The fish weighed twelve pounds on the <u>scale</u>.	scale
6. colorful	The <u>colorful</u> sunset was beautiful.	colorful
7. notice	"Did you <u>notice</u> my clean room?" asked Avery.	notice
8. place	We should always <u>place</u> our trust in Jesus.	place
9. balance	Mom will <u>balance</u> the checkbook.	balance
10. cities	Airplanes land in many <u>cities</u>.	cities
11. circle	Coins are in the shape of a <u>circle</u>.	circle
12. close	"Please <u>close</u> the door," said the pilot.	close
13. cabin	The passengers took their seats in the <u>cabin</u>.	cabin
14. pencil	Bree used a <u>pencil</u> to complete her homework.	pencil
15. cycle	Evaporation is part of the water <u>cycle</u>.	cycle
16. ascend	Airplanes <u>ascend</u> into the air after takeoff.	ascend
17. descend	Airplanes <u>descend</u> when beginning to land.	descend
18. icicle	Jim broke off an <u>icicle</u> from the eave.	icicle

High-Frequency Words

19. airplane	The <u>airplane</u> landed safely at the airport.	airplane
20. modern	<u>Modern</u> cars look different from older ones.	modern

Challenge Words

21. _____

22. _____

2 Allow students to self-correct their pretest, following this procedure:

　a. Write each word on the board. Discuss the letter/sound relationships in each word. Point out that the letter *c* says its soft sound /s/ before the letters *e*, *i*, and *y*. The letter *c* says its hard sound /k/ before all other letters. Teach that the word *close* is pronounced /ˈklōz/ in this lesson.

　b. As a class, read, spell, and read each word again. Direct students to circle misspelled words with a colored pencil and rewrite them correctly.

3 Proof each student's Warm Up.

4 Add the Challenge Words and Test Dates before distributing a copy of **BLM SP3-25A Lessons 25–29 Spelling Lists** to each student for home study.

5 Homework suggestion: Use **BLM SP3-25B Sorting Sounds of c** to practice words with **hard and soft c**.

Day 2 Phonics

Objective
The students will sort words that contain **hard and soft c** and write list words that rhyme with a given word. They will write high-frequency words.

Introduction
Write the Pattern Words in one area of the board. In another area, write the column headings shown below. Invite students to come to the board, select, and write a list word under the correct heading.

soft c /s/			hard c /k/		soft and hard c /s/ and /k/
cities	place	pencil	close	scale	icicle
notice	advice	service	cabin	score	cycle
ascend	balance	descend	clothes	colorful	circle

Directed Instruction

1 Chorally read each column and clap for each syllable.

2 Teach students the generalization for soft c, "C says /s/ before e, i, and y." Select volunteers to circle the letter c and underline e, i, or y in the soft c column. For hard c, teach students the generalization, "C says /k/ before any other letter." Select volunteers to circle the letter c and underline the letter that follows it in the hard c column. Have students chant both generalizations consecutively.

3 Call out the following words and have students name a list word that rhymes:
- nose (**close/clothes**) • store (**score**) • pretend (**descend**)

4 Remind students that the word *close* is a homograph because it has two pronunciations and meanings. When pronounced /'klōz/, it means *to shut* and when pronounced /'klōs/, it means *to be near*. Explain that when *close* is pronounced /'klōz/, it is a homophone with *clothes*

Differentiated Instruction

- For students who spelled all the words correctly on the Warm Up, select and assign three Extra Challenge Words from the following list: development, technology, transmitter, refract, hazardous, Obadiah.

- For students who spelled less than half correctly, assign the following Pattern and High-Frequency Words: cycle, close, place, circle, pencil, score, clothes, colorful, airplane, modern. On the Wrap Up, evaluate these students on the ten words assigned; however, encourage them to attempt to spell all the list words to the best of their ability. They are also responsible for writing the dictated sentences.

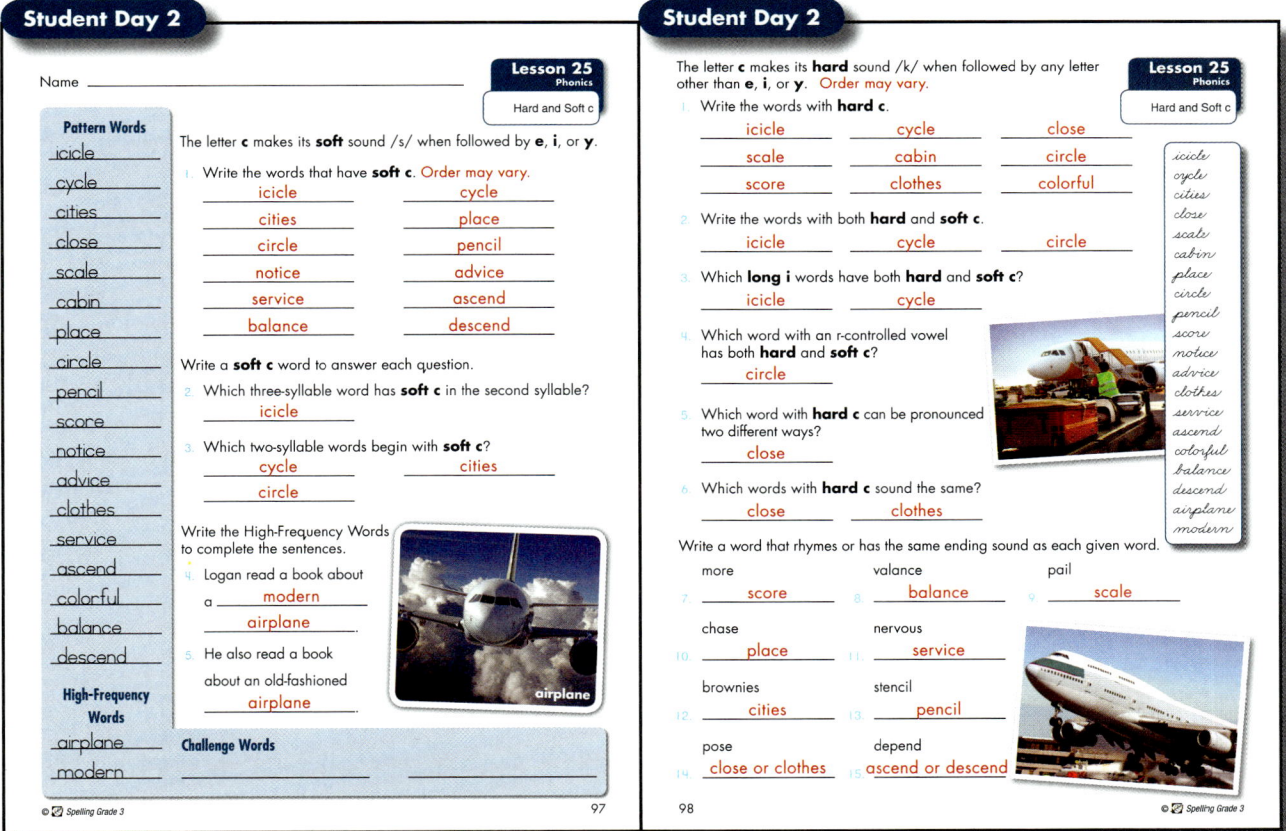

Student Day 2

Name _____

Lesson 25 Phonics
Hard and Soft c

Pattern Words
icicle
cycle
cities
close
scale
cabin
place
circle
pencil
score
notice
advice
clothes
service
ascend
colorful
balance
descend

High-Frequency Words
airplane
modern

Challenge Words
_____

The letter **c** makes its **soft** sound /s/ when followed by **e**, **i**, or **y**.

1. Write the words that have **soft c**. Order may vary.

icicle	cycle
cities	place
circle	pencil
notice	advice
service	ascend
balance	descend

Write a **soft c** word to answer each question.

2. Which three-syllable word has **soft c** in the second syllable?
icicle

3. Which two-syllable words begin with **soft c**?
cycle   cities
circle

Write the High-Frequency Words to complete the sentences.

4. Logan read a book about a modern airplane.

5. He also read a book about an old-fashioned airplane.

airplane

97

Student Day 2

The letter **c** makes its **hard** sound /k/ when followed by any letter other than **e**, **i**, or **y**. Order may vary.

1. Write the words with **hard c**.

icicle	cycle	close
scale	cabin	circle
score	clothes	colorful

2. Write the words with both **hard** and **soft c**.
icicle   cycle   circle

3. Which **long i** words have both **hard** and **soft c**?
icicle   cycle

4. Which word with an r-controlled vowel has both **hard** and **soft c**?
circle

5. Which word with **hard c** can be pronounced two different ways?
close

6. Which words with **hard c** sound the same?
close   clothes

Write a word that rhymes or has the same ending sound as each given word.

more	valance	pail
7. score	8. balance	9. scale
chase	nervous	
10. place	11. service	
brownies	stencil	
12. cities	13. pencil	
pose	depend	
14. close or clothes	15. ascend or descend	

icicle
cycle
cities
close
scale
cabin
place
circle
pencil
score
notice
advice
clothes
service
ascend
colorful
balance
descend
airplane
modern

Lesson 25 Phonics
Hard and Soft c

98

© Spelling Grade 3

Student Spelling Support Materials

BLMs SP3-25F–G
Card stock
BLM SP3-01A
File folder
Envelope
Paper clip
Paper fastener
Tape
BLMs SP3-25H–I

Student Spelling Support

1. Write this week's words categorized by patterns on a large piece of paper and attach to the Word Wall.
2. Duplicate **BLMs SP3-25F–G Lesson 25 Spelling Words I** and **II** on CARD STOCK for students to use as flash cards at school or at home.
3. Use **BLM SP3-01A A Spelling Study Strategy** in instructional groups to provide assistance with some or all of the words.
4. Assist students in writing the Challenge Words, numbers 21 and 22, in the section called My Words for Writing, in the back of their textbook.
5. For auditory learners, pronounce and spell each word twice. Students are invited to spell the word with the teacher the second time they hear it. This activity can be done in a small group or as a whole class.
6. For a biblical connection, read Ephesians 6:7: "With good will doing **service**, as to the Lord, and not to men." Discuss that in all we do, we should please the Lord. Our actions should not be self-seeking.

Cont. on page 101

because the words sound the same but have different meanings.

5 Proceed to page 97. Say, spell, and say each Pattern and High-Frequency Word. Provide this week's Challenge Words and have students write them in the spaces provided. Select a volunteer to read the generalization about soft *c* words at the top of the page and the directions before allowing them to complete the page.

6 Proceed to page 98. Select a student to read the generalization about hard *c* words at the top of the page. Have students complete the page.

7 Homework suggestion: Use **BLM SP3-25C Hard and Soft c** to practice the Pattern and High-Frequency Words in this lesson.

Day 3 Word Study

Objective

The students will write words with **hard and soft c** as antonyms, synonyms, and homophones. They will write words in alphabetical order.

Introduction

Review the following terms:

- An antonym is a word that means the opposite of another word.
- A synonym is a word that means the same or almost the same as another word.
- Homophones are words that sound the same but have different meanings and spellings.
- Homographs are words that are spelled the same but have different meanings.

Before class, write the Pattern Words on the board for students to reference. Select a student to spell a list word that is an antonym for *descend*. (**ascend**) Write *put* on the board. Select a volunteer to spell a synonym for *put*. (**place**) Write *close* on the board. Select a student to name a homophone for *close* (**clothes**) and a homograph (**close, pronounced /'klōs/**).

Directed Instruction

1 Before class, duplicate one copy each of **BLMs SP3-25D–E Practice Cards I** and **II** and cut apart. Write the column headings on the board that are shown below. Distribute the cards. Instruct students to read his/her card, decide the relationship of the two words, and attach the card in the correct column. As a class, read each column.

Antonyms	Synonyms	Homophones	Homographs
awake-asleep	fix-repair	be-bee	tear-tear (/'tîr/, /'târ/)
hard-soft	parts-pieces	buy-bye	close-close (/'klōz/, /'klōs/)
stand-sit	naughty-bad	cents-sense	dove-dove (/'dōv/, /'duv/)
work-play	correct-right	flea-flee	wind-wind (/'wīnd/, /'wind/)

2 Prepare the following words printed on 3" × 5" INDEX CARDS: service, pencil, score, place, scale. Select five volunteers to come forward and hold the cards. Select an additional volunteer to arrange the students and cards in the following alphabetical order: pencil, place, scale, score, service. Review with students how to place words in ABC order to the fourth letter, using *close* and *clothes*.

3 Proceed to page 99. Allow students to complete the page independently.

Day 4 Writing

Objective

The students will read questions and write answers in complete sentences.

Introduction

Share with the students about a time when you took a trip, perhaps on an airplane. Tell about items you packed in a suitcase, where you went, how you got there, and how long you were away from home.

Directed Instruction

1 Write three questions on the board related to your trip that the students will be able to answer in a complete sentence. Use the following questions and answers as a model:
- Where did Mrs. Fikse take a trip? Mrs. Fikse took a trip to Hawaii.
- How did Mrs. Fikse get to her destination? Mrs. Fikse flew on an airplane.
- How long was Mrs. Fikse on vacation? Mrs. Fikse was on vacation for ten days.

2 Proceed to page 100. Have students complete the page independently.

3 Homework suggestion: Read the questions and answers on page 100 to an adult. Take a practice spelling test at home or use **BLM SP3-01A A Spelling Study Strategy** for additional practice.

Day 5 Wrap Up

Objective
The students will correctly write dictated spelling words and sentences.

Introduction
Provide a review, utilizing WHITEBOARDS or Student Spelling Support suggestions.

Directed Instruction

1 Dictate the list words by using the Warm Up sentences or developing original ones. Reserve *cycle*, *close*, and *place* for the dictation sentences.

2 Follow this procedure for the dictation sentences: read the sentence, invite the class to say the sentence with you, then read the sentence again. Dictate the following sentences:
- The water cycle never stops.
- The suitcase wouldn't close because it was too full.
- Please place the fruit on the table.

3 If assigned, dictate Extra Challenge Words. Score the test.

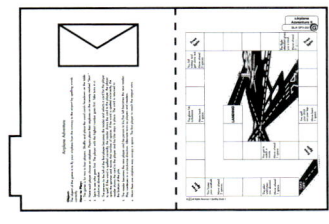

Student Spelling Support
Cont. from page 100

7. For a small group activity, play Airplane Adventure. You will need a FILE FOLDER, an ENVELOPE, a PAPER CLIP, a PAPER FASTENER, TAPE, CARD STOCK, **BLMs SP3-25F–G Lesson 25 Spelling Words I and II**, and **BLMs SP3-25H–I Airplane Adventure I and II**. Follow the assembly instructions given on the blackline master.

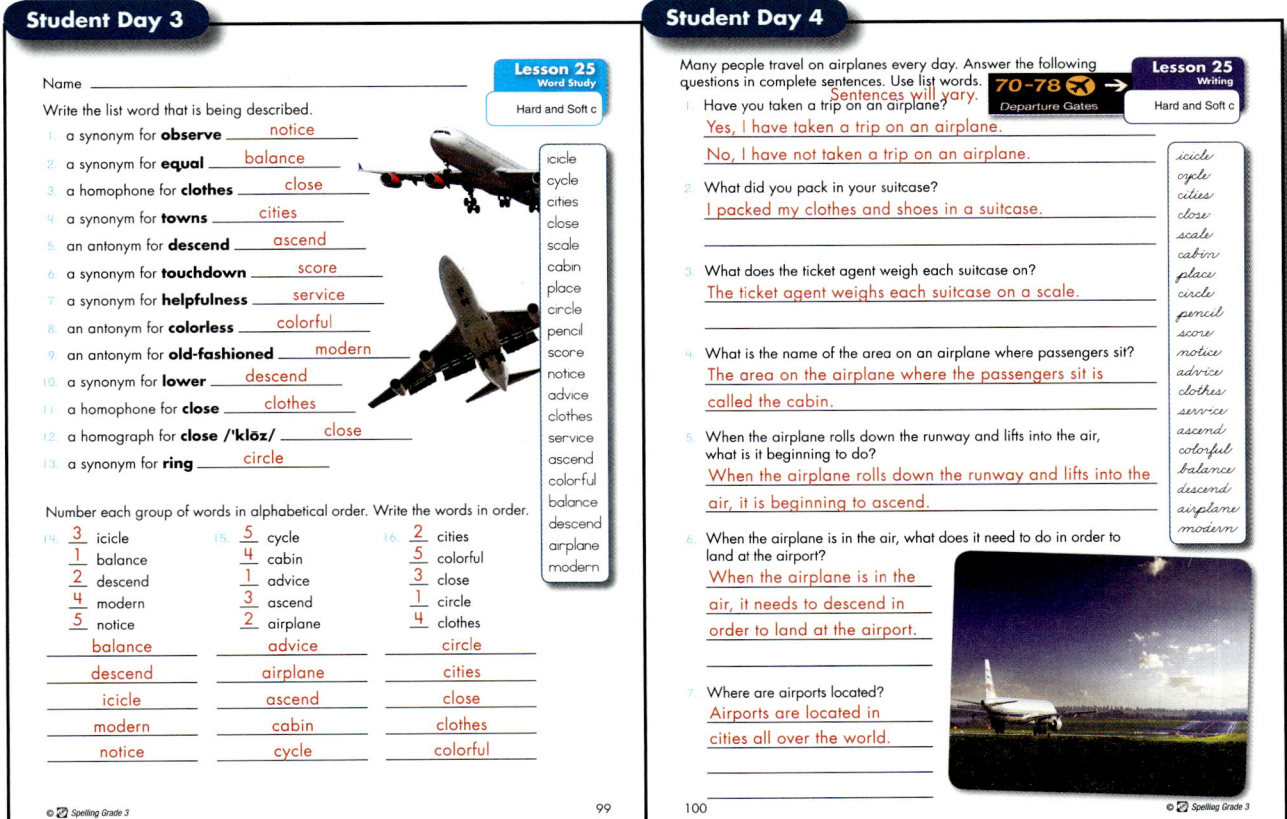

Student Day 3

Name _____

Write the list word that is being described.

Lesson 25 Word Study
Hard and Soft c

1. a synonym for **observe** — notice
2. a synonym for **equal** — balance
3. a homophone for **clothes** — close
4. a synonym for **towns** — cities
5. an antonym for **descend** — ascend
6. a synonym for **touchdown** — score
7. a synonym for **helpfulness** — service
8. an antonym for **colorless** — colorful
9. an antonym for **old-fashioned** — modern
10. a synonym for **lower** — descend
11. a homophone for **close** — clothes
12. a homograph for **close /'klōz/** — close
13. a synonym for **ring** — circle

icicle, cycle, cities, close, scale, cabin, place, circle, pencil, score, notice, advice, clothes, service, ascend, colorful, balance, descend, airplane, modern

Number each group of words in alphabetical order. Write the words in order.

14.
3 icicle
1 balance
2 descend
4 modern
5 notice

balance
descend
icicle
modern
notice

15.
5 cycle
4 cabin
1 advice
3 ascend
2 airplane

advice
airplane
ascend
cabin
cycle

16.
2 cities
5 colorful
3 close
1 circle
4 clothes

circle
cities
close
clothes
colorful

© Spelling Grade 3   99

Student Day 4

Many people travel on airplanes every day. Answer the following questions in complete sentences. Use list words. Sentences will vary.

70–78 ✈ → Departure Gates

Lesson 25 Writing
Hard and Soft c

1. Have you taken a trip on an airplane?
Yes, I have taken a trip on an airplane.
No, I have not taken a trip on an airplane.

2. What did you pack in your suitcase?
I packed my clothes and shoes in a suitcase.

3. What does the ticket agent weigh each suitcase on?
The ticket agent weighs each suitcase on a scale.

4. What is the name of the area on an airplane where passengers sit?
The area on the airplane where the passengers sit is called the cabin.

5. When the airplane rolls down the runway and lifts into the air, what is it beginning to do?
When the airplane rolls down the runway and lifts into the air, it is beginning to ascend.

6. When the airplane is in the air, what does it need to do in order to land at the airport?
When the airplane is in the air, it needs to descend in order to land at the airport.

7. Where are airports located?
Airports are located in cities all over the world.

icicle, cycle, cities, close, scale, cabin, place, circle, pencil, score, notice, advice, clothes, service, ascend, colorful, balance, descend, airplane, modern

100   © Spelling Grade 3

Transportation

The theme of this lesson is Fighter Jets. Fighter jets are combat aircraft and can reach speeds of at least twice the speed of sound. They are small military planes that are flown from land bases and aircraft carriers. Their speed and size give the pilot easy maneuverability. Fighter jets are heavily armed and can carry guns, missiles, and bombs.

Day 1 Warm Up

Objective
The students will accurately spell and write words with **hard and soft g**. They will spell and write high-frequency words and challenge words.

Introduction
Before class, select Challenge Words for numbers 21 and 22 from a cross-curricular subject, words misspelled on previous assignments, or words that interest your students. The word *gauge* has both **hard and soft g** and is suggested for number 21. Administer the Warm Up.

Directed Instruction

1 Say each word, use it in a sentence, and then repeat the word.

Pattern Words

1.	guide	Jesus will <u>guide</u> you in all that you do.	guide
2.	angle	Joe will <u>angle</u> his jet sharply.	angle
3.	courage	A fighter pilot needs to have <u>courage</u>.	courage
4.	edge	The jet was at the <u>edge</u> of the runway.	edge
5.	gather	Chris will <u>gather</u> his flight gear.	gather
6.	hangar	David's jet is parked in the <u>hangar</u>.	hangar
7.	guard	Fighter jets protect and <u>guard</u> our country.	guard
8.	badge	A pilot's <u>badge</u> has wings on it.	badge
9.	danger	A fighter pilot's job is full of <u>danger</u>.	danger
10.	guest	Paige was a <u>guest</u> at the Air Force base.	guest
11.	garage	Rosa parked her car in the <u>garage</u>.	garage
12.	dodge	Jeremy will <u>dodge</u> his jet quickly.	dodge
13.	cages	There were five <u>cages</u> for sale.	cages
14.	guess	Can you <u>guess</u> how much it cost?	guess
15.	giant	A jet does not have a <u>giant</u> fuel tank.	giant
16.	gasoline	Jeff put <u>gasoline</u> into the car's tank.	gasoline
17.	village	The tiny <u>village</u> was on the mountain.	village
18.	judge	The pilot will need to <u>judge</u> his landing.	judge

High-Frequency Words

19.	listen	You should always <u>listen</u> to directions.	listen
20.	scared	The loud noise <u>scared</u> the baby.	scared

Challenge Words

21. _____

22. _____

2 Allow students to self-correct their pretest, following this procedure:

a. Write each word on the board. Discuss the letter/sound relationships in each word. Point out that the letter *g* usually says its soft sound /j/ when followed by *e, i,* or *y.* The letter *g* says its hard sound /g/ when followed by any other letter. Teach that in words with *dge,* the *d* is silent. *Dge* follows a short vowel and is pronounced with the soft *g* sound /j/. Discuss the word *hangar* so it is not confused with *hanger.*

b. As a class, read, spell, and read each word again. Direct students to circle misspelled words with a colored pencil and rewrite them correctly.

3 Proof each student's Warm Up.

4 Homework suggestion: Use **BLM SP3-26A Jets** to review **hard and soft g** words.

Day 2 Phonics

Objective

The students will correctly sort **hard and soft g** words. They will answer questions and write high-frequency words.

Introduction

Before class, write the following generalization on the board:

- The letter *g* usually makes its soft sound /j/ when followed by *e, i,* or *y,* and its hard sound /g/ when followed by any other letter.

Read the generalization and ask the following:

- "What sound does the letter *g* usually make when followed by *e, i,* or *y*? (**/j/**) Is this soft or hard *g*? (**soft g**) What is the hard sound of *g*? (**/g/**) When does *g* make this sound?" (**when it is followed by any other letter than e, i, or y**)

Directed Instruction

1 Write the Pattern Words from Lesson 26 on the board. On a separate area of the board, write the following column headings:

soft g /j/			hard g /g/		
giant	edge	judge	angle	guide	guest
cages	village	badge	guess	guard	gather
dodge	danger	garage	hangar	garage	gasoline
courage					

Select volunteers to come to the board, read a word, and circle each *g* in the word. Have them identify whether the letter *g* produces the hard or soft *g* sound, and write the word in the appropriate column.

2 Read the words in each column and have a volunteer read the generalization for **hard and soft g** aloud. Allow students to come to the board and circle the letters following each *g*. Make sure that each column contains the correct words based on the generalization for **hard and soft g**.

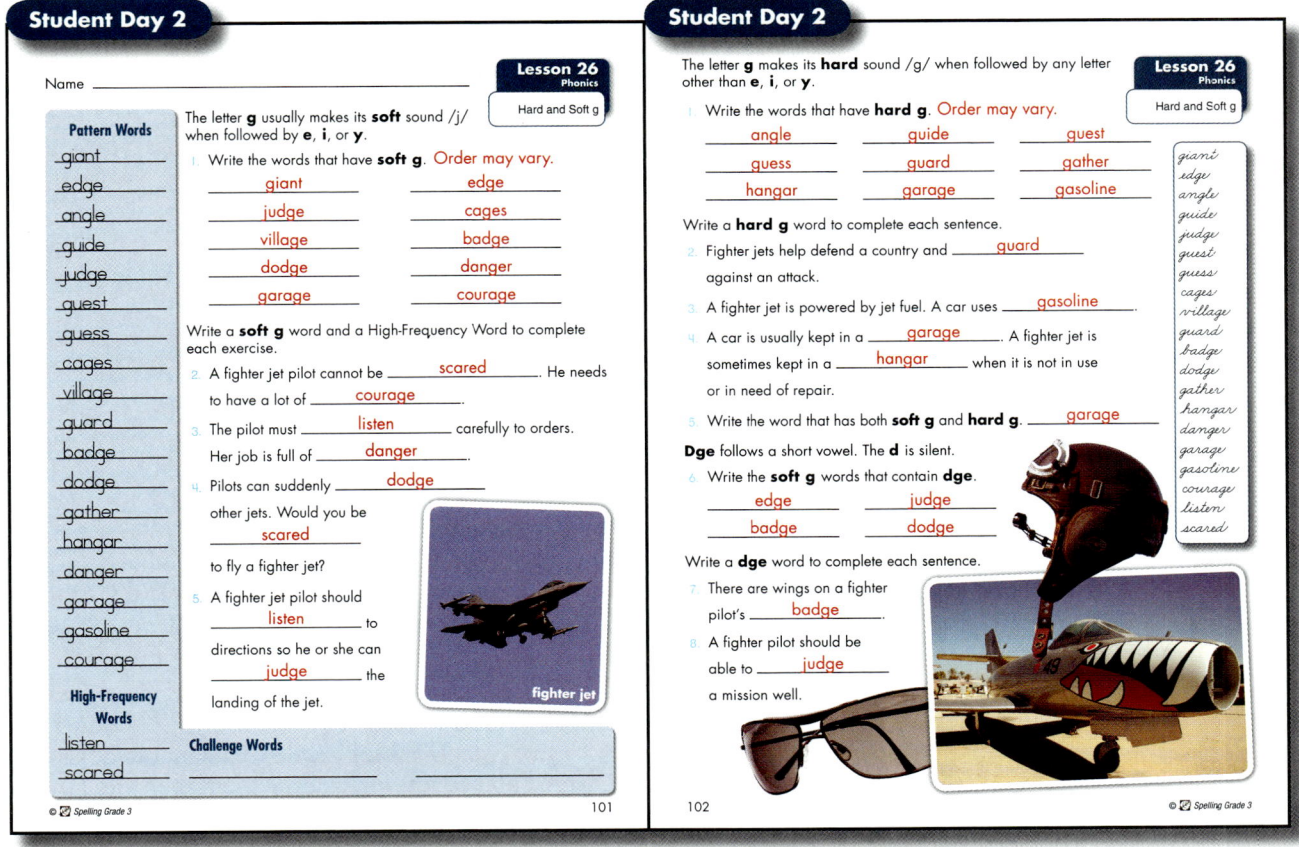

Student Day 2

Name _____

Lesson 26
Phonics

Hard and Soft g

Pattern Words
- giant
- edge
- angle
- guide
- judge
- guest
- guess
- cages
- village
- guard
- badge
- dodge
- gather
- hangar
- danger
- garage
- gasoline
- courage

High-Frequency Words
- listen
- scared

The letter **g** usually makes its **soft** sound /j/ when followed by **e, i,** or **y**.

1. Write the words that have **soft g**. Order may vary.

giant / edge
judge / cages
village / badge
dodge / danger
garage / courage

Write a **soft g** word and a High-Frequency Word to complete each exercise.

2. A fighter jet pilot cannot be _____scared_____. He needs to have a lot of _____courage_____.

3. The pilot must _____listen_____ carefully to orders. Her job is full of _____danger_____.

4. Pilots can suddenly _____dodge_____ other jets. Would you be _____scared_____ to fly a fighter jet?

5. A fighter jet pilot should _____listen_____ to directions so he or she can _____judge_____ the landing of the jet.

Challenge Words

fighter jet

101

Student Day 2

The letter **g** makes its **hard** sound /g/ when followed by any letter other than **e, i,** or **y**.

Lesson 26
Phonics

Hard and Soft g

1. Write the words that have **hard g**. Order may vary.

angle / guide / guest
guess / guard / gather
hangar / garage / gasoline

Write a **hard g** word to complete each sentence.

2. Fighter jets help defend a country and _____guard_____ against an attack.

3. A fighter jet is powered by jet fuel. A car uses _____gasoline_____.

4. A car is usually kept in a _____garage_____. A fighter jet is sometimes kept in a _____hangar_____ when it is not in use or in need of repair.

5. Write the word that has both **soft g** and **hard g**. _____garage_____

Dge follows a short vowel. The **d** is silent.

6. Write the **soft g** words that contain **dge**.

edge / judge
badge / dodge

Write a **dge** word to complete each sentence.

7. There are wings on a fighter pilot's _____badge_____.

8. A fighter pilot should be able to _____judge_____ a mission well.

giant
edge
angle
guide
judge
guest
guess
cages
village
guard
badge
dodge
gather
hangar
danger
garage
gasoline
courage
listen
scared

102

Student Spelling
Support Materials

BLMs SP3-26C–D
Card stock
BLM SP3-01A
Letter tiles

Student Spelling Support

1. Write this week's words categorized by patterns on a large piece of paper and attach to the Word Wall.

2. Duplicate **BLMs SP3-26C–D Lesson 26 Spelling Words I and II** on CARD STOCK for students to use as flash cards at school or at home.

3. Use **BLM SP3-01A A Spelling Study Strategy** in instructional groups to provide assistance with some or all of the words.

4. Assist students in writing the Challenge Words, numbers 21 and 22, in the section called My Words for Writing, in the back of their textbook.

5. For auditory learners, verbalize sentences with multiple Pattern Words from this lesson. Challenge students to listen and count how many words contain **soft g** and how many contain **hard g**.

- The pilots will **guard** our country and face **danger** with **courage**. (**hard g; soft g; soft g**)

- The **giant gasoline** station is on the **edge** of the **village**. (**soft g; hard g; soft g; soft g**)

- Each **guest** will need a **badge** before they **gather** inside the **hangar**. (**hard g; soft g; hard g; hard g**)

Cont. on page 105

---

3 Have students identify the word that has both **hard and soft g**. (**garage**)

4 Remind students that the *d* is silent in the words with *dge*.

5 Proceed to page 101. Say, spell, and say each Pattern and High-Frequency Word. Provide this week's Challenge Words and have students write them in the spaces provided. Select a volunteer to read the directions.

6 Proceed to page 102. Read the directions at the top of the page. Check for understanding as students complete the page independently.

7 Homework suggestion: Use **BLM SP3-26B Jet Streams** to review words in this lesson.

Day 3 Word Study

Objective

The students will distinguish the difference between *guest* and *guess*. They will write **hard and soft g** words to complete analogies and match definitions to **hard and soft g** words.

Introduction

Write the following jingle on the board: You don't have to guess who the guest will be; just drop the *s* and add a *t*! Chorally read the jingle aloud. Invite volunteers to point out the words that contain a hard *g*. (**guess and guest**) Underline the words and point out the difference between the two. (*Guess* has an *s* at the end and *guest* has a *t*.) Invite students to use their Spelling Dictionary to look up the definition for each word. Read the definitions aloud. (**guess—to suppose something; guest—a visitor to whom hospitality is given**)

Directed Instruction

1 Write the following analogies on the board:
- <u>Fearless</u> is to <u>brave</u> as <u>fearful</u> is to _____. (**scared**)
- <u>To not hear</u> is to <u>ignore</u> as _____ is to <u>pay attention</u>. (**listen**)
- <u>Circle</u> is to <u>curve</u> as <u>triangle</u> is to _____. (**angle**)

Remind students that an analogy is made up of two word pairs. Both pairs of words have the same kind of relationship. Write the following word choices on the board: listen, angle, scared. Read the analogies and have students identify the correct answer. Complete each analogy.

2 Proceed to page 103 and encourage students to use their Spelling Dictionary. Select a student to read Deuteronomy 31:6.

Day 4 Writing

Objective

The students will use proofreading marks to identify mistakes in a story featuring a fighter jet pilot. They will correctly write misspelled words.

Introduction

Draw the Proofreading Marks box on the board. Explain that the "make a new paragraph" mark is used when a line of text contains a new idea and needs to be set apart from the previous paragraph. A paragraph begins with a main point and contains sentences about a particular idea. When a new idea is introduced, another paragraph begins. The beginning of a paragraph is usually indented—set aside from the margin.

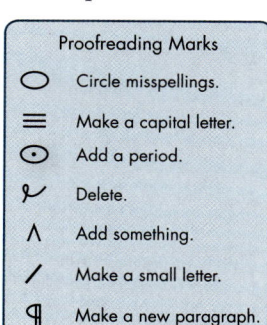

Proofreading Marks

◯ Circle misspellings.

≡ Make a capital letter.

⊙ Add a period.

␡ Delete.

∧ Add something.

／ Make a small letter.

¶ Make a new paragraph.

Directed Instruction

1 Display **T-26 Fighter Jet Pilots** on the overhead and introduce students to Captain David Paulus (/ˈpȯl əs/) and Major Joe Lortie (/ˈlȯr dē/) by reading the brief descriptive paragraphs for each pilot. Point out how each new paragraph is indented and begins a new idea about the main point. All of the pilots in this lesson trust God as they fly in the face of danger.

2 Proceed to page 104. This is a brief biography of a fighter jet pilot named Major Chris Reifel (/ˈrī fəl/). Read the page aloud. Reread the story and use **T-27 Proofreading a Descriptive Story** to complete the proofreading exercise with students. Make sure all errors are corrected. (**12 misspellings; 5 capital letters needed; 2 periods needed; 2 deletes; 1 add something—*the*; 1 small letter needed; 3 new paragraphs**)

3 When complete, display **T-28 Corrected Descriptive Story** for students to see the story in its correct layout.

4 Homework suggestion: Read the fighter pilot story on page 104 to an adult. Take a practice spelling test at home or use **BLM SP3-01A A Spelling Study Strategy** for additional practice.

Day 5 Wrap Up

Objective
The students will correctly write dictated spelling words and sentences.

Introduction
Provide a review, utilizing WHITEBOARDS or Student Spelling Support suggestions.

Directed Instruction

1 Dictate the list words by using the Warm Up sentences or developing original ones. Reserve *angle*, *guest*, and *garage* for the dictation sentences.

2 Follow this procedure for the dictation sentences: read the sentence, invite the class to say the sentence with you, then read the sentence again. Dictate the following sentences:
- Hold the pencil at an <u>angle</u>.
- I was a <u>guest</u> on the airplane.
- Let's park the car in the <u>garage</u>.

3 If assigned, dictate Extra Challenge Words. Score the test.

Student Spelling Support
Cont. from page 104

6. Use LETTER TILES to build **hard and soft g** words.

7. Read Deuteronomy 31:6: "Be strong and of good **courage**." Discuss with students how the Lord is always with us and that we should not be afraid when trials come upon us.

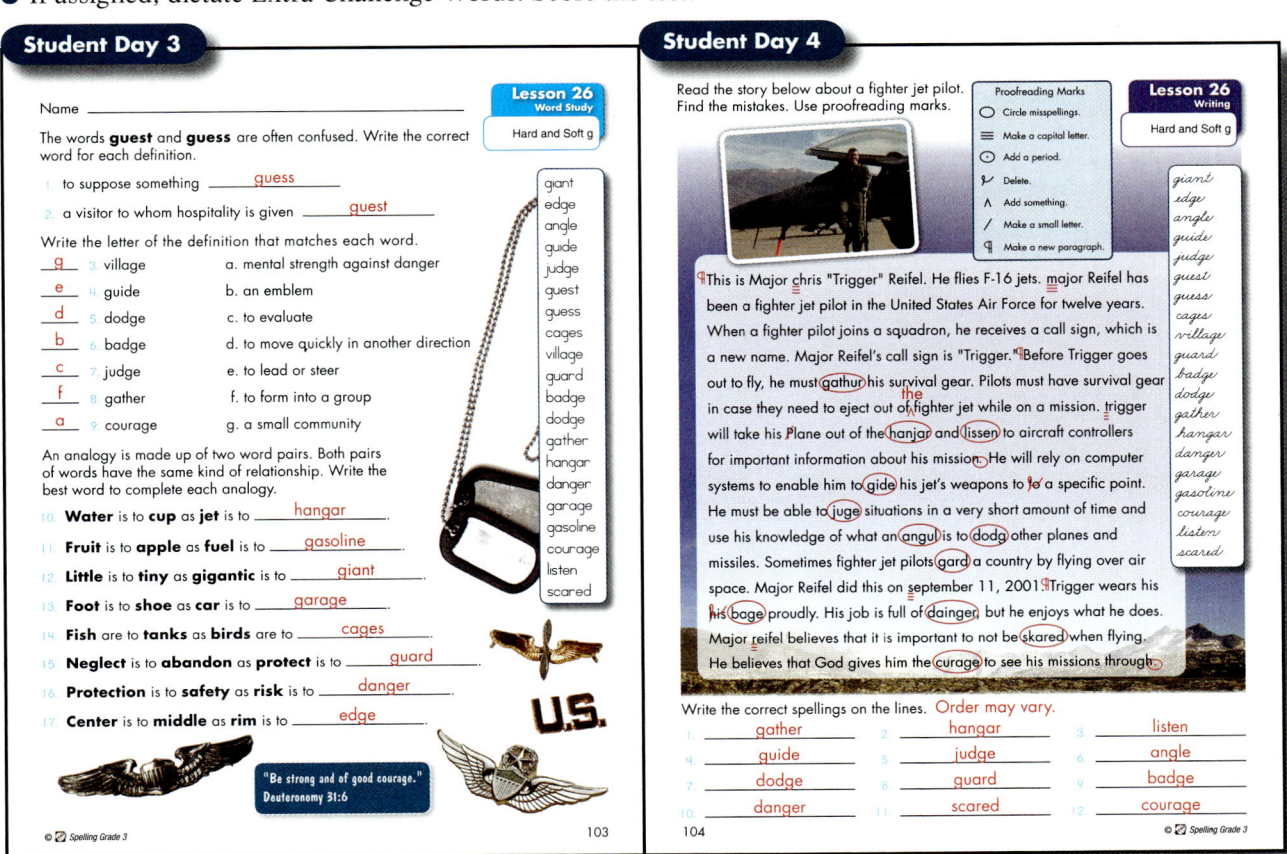

Lesson 27

Prefixes: a-, in-, pre-, re-, un-

Student Pages
Pages 105–108

Lesson Materials
BLM SP3-27A
BLMs SP3-27B–C
Card stock
P-11
BLM SP3-27D
T-29
BLM SP3-01A
Whiteboards

Transportation
The theme of this lesson is Hot-Air Balloons. Manned hot-air balloon flights were first successfully completed in 1783. Since that time hot-air balloons have been used for military purposes and for pleasure. Today many cities have hot-air balloon festivals including the cities of Albuquerque, New Mexico and Colorado Springs, Colorado.

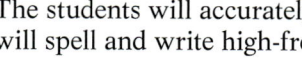

Day 1 Warm Up

Objective
The students will accurately spell and write words with **prefixes**. They will spell and write high-frequency words and challenge words.

Introduction
Before class, select Challenge Words for numbers 21 and 22 from a cross-curricular subject, words misspelled on previous assignments, or words that interest your students. The word *afloat* has the **prefix a-** and is suggested for number 21. Administer the Warm Up.

Directed Instruction

1 Say each word, use it in a sentence, and then repeat the word.

Pattern Words
1.	unthinkable	For Jim to tell a lie was <u>unthinkable</u>.	unthinkable
2.	unable	Max is <u>unable</u> to climb a large tree.	unable
3.	removed	Andrew <u>removed</u> the dead tree limbs.	removed
4.	rebuilt	The students <u>rebuilt</u> the block tower.	rebuilt
5.	preschool	Tessa just finished <u>preschool</u>.	preschool
6.	preview	The movie <u>preview</u> seems interesting.	preview
7.	incomplete	The math problems were <u>incomplete</u>.	incomplete
8.	invisible	God is <u>invisible</u>, but He's always here.	invisible
9.	aglow	The candle was <u>aglow</u> in the darkness.	aglow
10.	unspoken	God hears <u>unspoken</u> prayers.	unspoken
11.	aloft	The hot-air balloons went <u>aloft</u>.	aloft
12.	inactive	Bears are <u>inactive</u> during the winter.	inactive
13.	incorrect	The answer was <u>incorrect</u>.	incorrect
14.	prepay	We will <u>prepay</u> for the field trip.	prepay
15.	prewrite	I'll use an outline to <u>prewrite</u> my story.	prewrite
16.	return	One day Jesus will <u>return</u> again.	return
17.	rewrote	Jackson <u>rewrote</u> his book report.	rewrote
18.	unfair	It is <u>unfair</u> to refuse to take turns.	unfair

High-Frequency Words
19.	earth	God made the heavens and the <u>earth</u>.	earth
20.	tied	The hot-air balloon was <u>tied</u> down.	tied

Challenge Words
21. _____
22. _____

2 Allow students to self-correct their pretest, following this procedure:

a. Write each word on the board. Discuss the letter/sound relationships in each word. Remind students that a *base word* is <u>a word to which a letter or letters may be added to make new words</u>. A *prefix* is <u>a word part added to the beginning of a base word</u>. Point out each prefix by circling it. Underline each base word.

b. As a class, read, spell, and read each word again. Direct students to circle misspelled words with a colored pencil and rewrite them correctly.

3 Proof each student's Warm Up.

4 Homework suggestion: Use **BLM SP3-27A Balloons Away** to practice the words in this week's lesson.

Day 2 Phonics

Objective

The students will write words that contain **prefixes**. They will write pattern words by combining **prefixes** and base words, change **prefixes** to make list words, and divide words into syllables between the prefix and base word. They will write high-frequency words.

Introduction

Before class, duplicate **BLMs SP3-27B–C Prefixes and Base Words I** and **II** on CARD STOCK. Cut the cards apart. Attach them randomly to the board in two columns with the **prefixes** to the left of the base word cards. Set the plus and equal signs aside for use by student volunteers. Write the Pattern Words in a column to one side of the board. Inform students that the prefixes and the base words shown on the cards will make the Pattern Words listed. Select a volunteer to choose a prefix and a base word that form a Pattern Word, separate those cards with the plus sign, and place the equal sign after the base word. The student then writes the Pattern Word at the end. [a-] + [loft] = aloft Reuse the plus and equal signs for each Pattern Word.

Directed Instruction

1 Proceed to page 105. Say, spell, and say each Pattern and High-Frequency Word. Provide this week's Challenge Words and have students write them in the spaces provided.

2 Allow students to identify each prefix and sort the words accordingly. Complete the page.

3 At the top of page 106, students supply a prefix, base word, or Pattern Word as needed to make each statement correct.

4 In the middle section, have students identify the prefix in each word, then change the prefix to make a Pattern Word.

Proceed to page 105. ... At the top of page 106,

Differentiated Instruction

- For students who spelled all the words correctly on the Warm Up, select and assign three Extra Challenge Words from the following list: festivals, pleasure, musician, lavish, unconscious, Philemon.

- For students who spelled less than half correctly, assign the following Pattern and High-Frequency Words: aloft, inactive, prepay, preview, return, removed, unfair, unable, tied, earth. On the Wrap Up, evaluate these students on the ten words assigned; however, encourage them to attempt to spell all the list words to the best of their ability. They are also responsible for writing the dictated sentences.

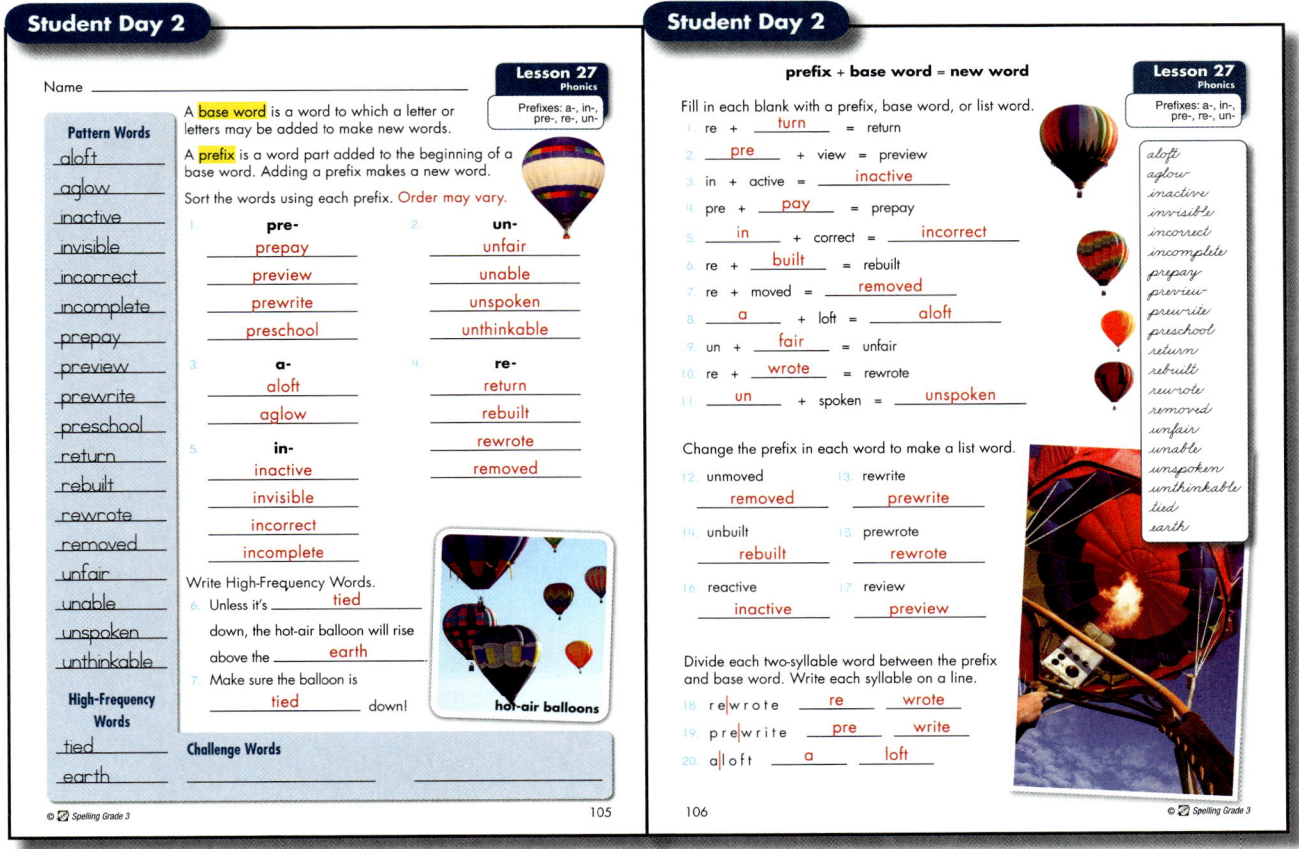

5 Remind students to refer to **P-11 Syllables** to reinforce the following generalization: Divide between a prefix and a base word (example number 4). Direct students to make a vertical line to divide the words at the bottom of the page into syllables.

6 Homework suggestion: Use **BLM SP3-27D Prefixes** to practice the Pattern Words in the lesson.

Day 3 Word Study

Objective

The students will match words that contain **prefixes** to the correct definition. They will write words with **prefixes** to correctly complete sentences.

Introduction

Before class, write the following word choices on the board: preview, rebuilt, unfair. Write the following incomplete sentence pairs on the board:

• Brian <u>built</u> a tower with blocks yesterday.

  He _____ the tower today. (**rebuilt**)

• Kylie's rules are quite <u>fair</u>.

  She doesn't care for _____ play. (**unfair**)

• Martin will <u>view</u> the movie later today.

  He saw a _____ of that movie yesterday. (**preview**)

Read the sentences and inform students that the underlined word in the first sentence is the base word for the missing word in the second sentence. Allow volunteers to choose the correct word that completes the second sentence. Write the missing word and read the completed sentence pair.

Directed Instruction

1 Write the **prefixes a-, in-, pre-, re-,** and **un-** with their meanings on the board as shown to the right. Write the following Pattern Words on the board: unable, rewrote, incorrect, preview, aglow. Have the students use the meaning of each prefix to define the following words:

a-	in a state of being
in-	not
pre-	before; ahead of time
re-	again
un-	not

• unable (**not able**)   • rewrote (**wrote again**)
• incorrect (**not correct**)   • preview (**view ahead of time**)
• aglow (**in a state of glowing**)

2 Proceed to page 107 and read the **prefixes** and their definitions at the top of the page. Encourage students to use the meanings given for each prefix as a clue to help match the Pattern Words to their definitions.

3 Complete exercises 11–17. Ask students to read their completed sentences.

Day 4 Writing

Objective

The students will identify list words in haiku poetry. They will write a haiku verse of their own.

Introduction

Place **T-29 Haiku** on the overhead. Explain that the paragraphs on this transparency are haiku verses. Haiku is a kind of unrhymed poetry that originated in Japan. It always has three lines and is often about nature. The first line has five syllables, the second has seven syllables, and the third has five syllables. Use the transparency to assist the students in counting the number of syllables in each line and in reviewing the bold list words. At the bottom of the transparency are lines for the class to compose and write a haiku poem.

Directed Instruction

1 Proceed to page 108. Select a volunteer to read each haiku verse. Have

students hold up one finger for each syllable they hear in each line.

2 Instruct students to write each list word on the lines provided. Direct students to reread the haiku verses before writing their own poem at the bottom of the page using list words. Words already used in the poems printed on the page may be repeated in the students' work.

3 Have each student read his/her haiku verse to another student. The other student may check to see if each line contains the correct number of syllables.

4 Homework suggestion: Read the haiku poetry on page 108 to an adult. Take a practice spelling test at home or use **BLM SP3-01A A Spelling Study Strategy** for additional practice.

Day 5 Wrap Up

Objective
The students will correctly write dictated spelling words and sentences.

Introduction
Provide a review, utilizing WHITEBOARDS or Student Spelling Support suggestions.

Directed Instruction

1 Dictate the list words by using the Warm Up sentences or developing original ones. Reserve *preview*, *return*, and *unfair* for the dictation sentences.

2 Follow this procedure for the dictation sentences: read the sentence, invite the class to say the sentence with you, then read the sentence again. Dictate the following sentences:
- Let's <u>preview</u> the show before we go to see it.
- Jesus will <u>return</u> to take us with Him.
- Taking someone's place in line is <u>unfair</u>.

3 If assigned, dictate Extra Challenge Words. Score the test.

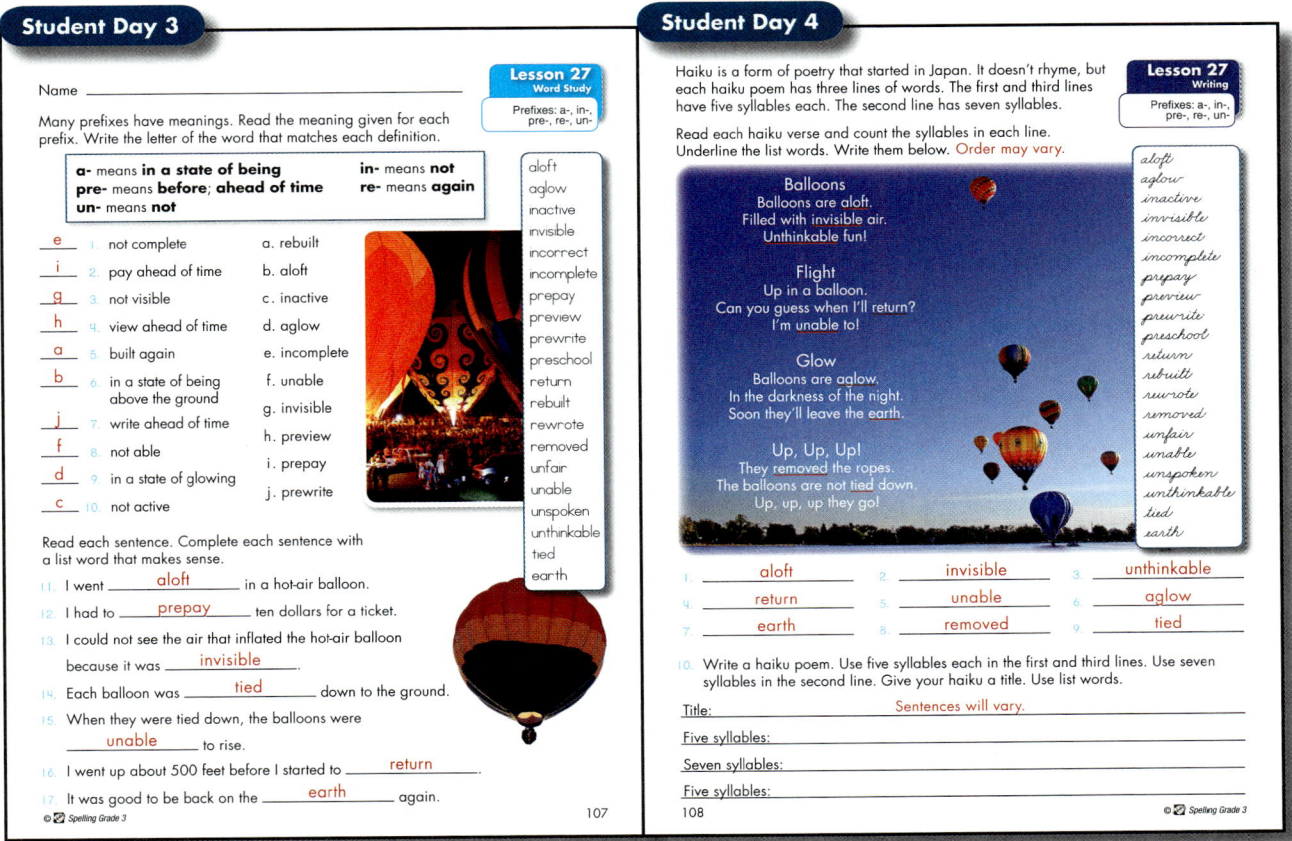

Transportation

The theme of this lesson is Blimps. Blimps are one of three types of airships which also include zeppelins and semirigid airships. These are essentially very large, but controllable, hot-air balloons. Blimps are powered by engines and steered via rudders and elevator flaps. Passengers ride in an attached gondola.

Day 1 Warm Up

Objective

The students will accurately spell and write words with the **suffixes -ed, -er, -est,** and **-ing**. They will spell and write high-frequency words and challenge words.

Introduction

Before class, select Challenge Words for numbers 21 and 22 from a cross-curricular subject, words misspelled on previous assignments, or words that interest your students. The word *shinier* has the **suffix -er**, and is suggested for number 21. Administer the Warm Up.

Directed Instruction

1 Say each word, use it in a sentence, and then repeat the word.

Pattern Words

1.	grabbing	We were <u>grabbing</u> treats from a piñata.	grabbing
2.	hopping	Lee was <u>hopping</u> in the hopscotch game.	hopping
3.	biggest	A blimp is the <u>biggest</u> thing I've seen.	biggest
4.	gliding	The skaters were <u>gliding</u> on the ice.	gliding
5.	happiest	JoAnn is <u>happiest</u> of all the girls.	happiest
6.	hoping	I am <u>hoping</u> to receive a birthday gift.	hoping
7.	largest	The <u>largest</u> state is Alaska.	largest
8.	stopping	The highway worker was <u>stopping</u> cars.	stopping
9.	tiniest	Even the <u>tiniest</u> child is precious to Jesus.	tiniest
10.	bigger	Goliath was <u>bigger</u>, but David won!	bigger
11.	glided	The sailboat <u>glided</u> over the lake.	glided
12.	grabbed	Mom <u>grabbed</u> her purse before leaving.	grabbed
13.	happier	His words made me <u>happier</u> than ever!	happier
14.	hoped	Teresa <u>hoped</u> to win a prize.	hoped
15.	hopped	My rabbit <u>hopped</u> all over the lawn.	hopped
16.	larger	California is <u>larger</u> than Hawaii.	larger
17.	stopped	It <u>stopped</u> raining just as I left.	stopped
18.	tinier	From up high, many things seem <u>tinier</u>.	tinier

High-Frequency Words

19.	underneath	My cat sleeps <u>underneath</u> my bed.	underneath
20.	great	A <u>great</u> crowd came to see Jesus.	great

Challenge Words

21. _____

22. _____

2 Allow students to self-correct their pretest, following this procedure:

a. Write each word on the board. Discuss the letter/sound relationships in each word. Define a *suffix* as <u>a word part added to the end of a base word</u>. Point out the **suffixes -ed, -er, -est,** and **-ing** and tell how each base word was changed with the addition of the suffix. Guide students to see that the final consonant was doubled, the final **y** was changed to **i**, or the **silent e** was dropped before the addition of each suffix.

b. As a class, read, spell, and read each word again. Direct students to circle misspelled words with a colored pencil and rewrite them correctly.

3 Proof each student's Warm Up.

4 Homework suggestion: Use **BLM SP3-28A Airships** to practice the Pattern Words in this lesson.

Day 2 Phonics

Objective

The students will add **suffixes** to base words. They will complete a graphic organizer and build words by adding and subtracting letters. They will write misspelled words correctly, and write high-frequency and challenge words.

Introduction

Before class, cut six SENTENCE STRIPS 11½ inches long and four, one-inch pieces from another sentence strip. Use a BLACK MARKER for printing words and suffixes on the strips. Tape the one-inch pieces to the sentence strips. Follow the diagram to make the folding display cards for the following words: hoped, hoping, bigger, biggest, happier, happiest. To teach the suffix rules, use the following steps:

Fold over. Cover **silent e.**

hope~~d~~ ed

Write **g** on the back.

big er

Write **i** on the back. Flip down over **y.**

happy er

- Show the base word *hope* by unfolding the card with *hoped*. Explain that in words that end in **silent e**, the **silent e** is dropped before adding a suffix that begins with a vowel. Use a black marker to cross out the **silent e** in the base word *hope*. Fold over the suffix. Repeat this procedure with the word *hoping*. Spell the new words aloud.

- Show the base word *big* by unfolding the card with *bigger*. Ask students to tell the sound of the vowel in the base word. Explain that since the vowel is *short i*, the final consonant must be doubled before adding **-er**. Fold down the second consonant *g*. Fold over the suffix. Have students spell the new word. Repeat the procedure with the word *biggest*.

- Show the base word *happy* by unfolding the card with *happier*. Explain that in words ending in **y**, the **y** must be changed to **i** before adding a

Differentiated Instruction

- For students who spelled all the words correctly on the Warm Up, select and assign three Extra Challenge Words from the following list: blimps, zeppelin, stationery, terminate, galore, Nahum.

- For students who spelled less than half correctly, assign the following Pattern and High-Frequency Words: bigger, glided, happier, hoped, hopped, largest, stopping, tinier, great, underneath. On the Wrap Up, evaluate these students on the ten words assigned; however, encourage them to attempt to spell all the list words to the best of their ability. They are also responsible for writing the dictated sentences.

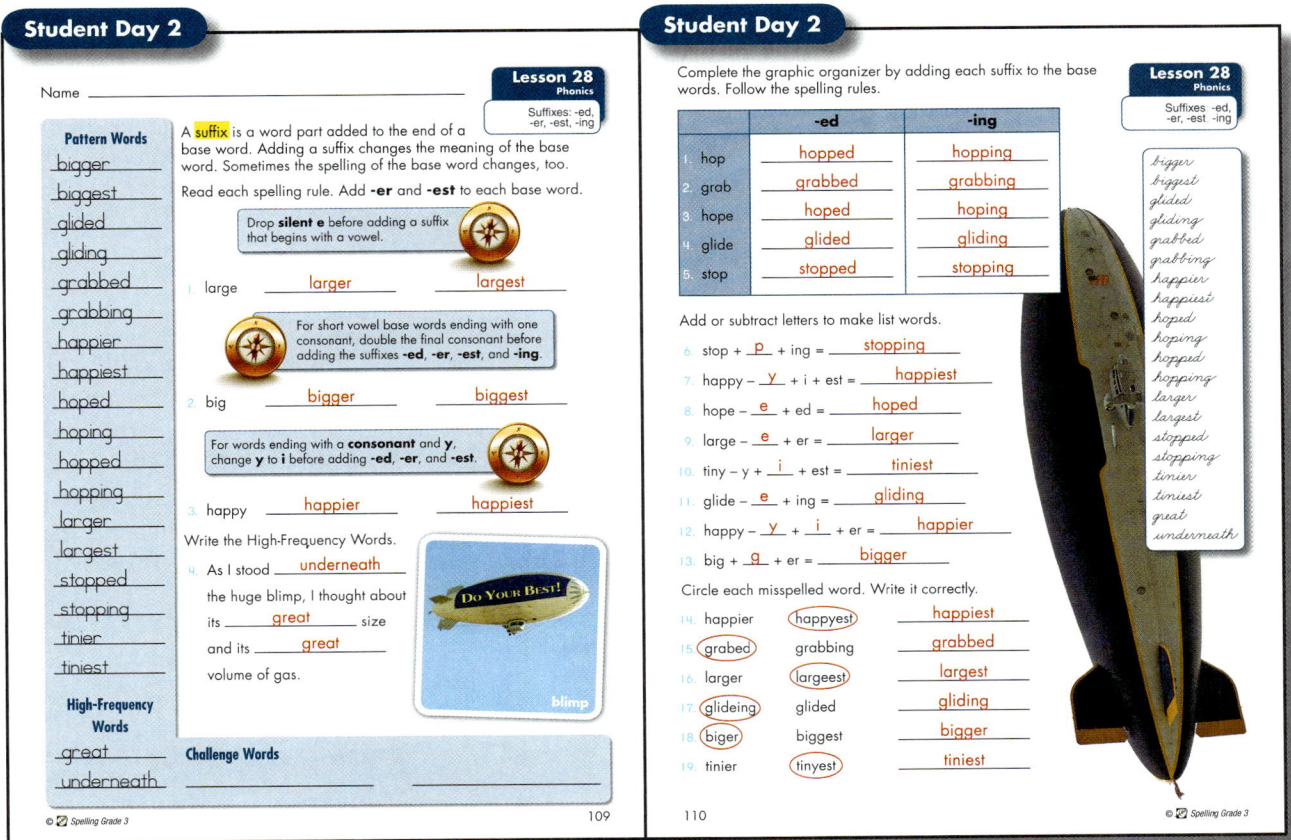

Student Day 2

Name _____

Lesson 28 Phonics
Suffixes: -ed, -er, -est, -ing

Pattern Words
bigger
biggest
glided
gliding
grabbed
grabbing
happier
happiest
hoped
hoping
hopped
hopping
larger
largest
stopped
stopping
tinier
tiniest

High-Frequency Words
great
underneath

A suffix is a word part added to the end of a base word. Adding a suffix changes the meaning of the base word. Sometimes the spelling of the base word changes, too.

Read each spelling rule. Add **-er** and **-est** to each base word.

Drop **silent e** before adding a suffix that begins with a vowel.

1. large   larger   largest

For short vowel base words ending with one consonant, double the final consonant before adding the suffixes **-ed, -er, -est,** and **-ing.**

2. big   bigger   biggest

For words ending with a **consonant** and **y,** change **y** to **i** before adding **-ed, -er,** and **-est.**

3. happy   happier   happiest

Write the High-Frequency Words.

4. As I stood __underneath__ the huge blimp, I thought about its __great__ size and its __great__ volume of gas.

DO YOUR BEST!
blimp

Challenge Words

© Spelling Grade 3   109

Student Day 2

Complete the graphic organizer by adding each suffix to the base words. Follow the spelling rules.

Lesson 28 Phonics
Suffixes -ed, -er, -est -ing

	-ed	-ing
1. hop	hopped	hopping
2. grab	grabbed	grabbing
3. hope	hoped	hoping
4. glide	glided	gliding
5. stop	stopped	stopping

Add or subtract letters to make list words.

6. stop + _p_ + ing = __stopping__
7. happy – _y_ + i + est = __happiest__
8. hope – _e_ + ed = __hoped__
9. large – _e_ + er = __larger__
10. tiny – y + _i_ + est = __tiniest__
11. glide – _e_ + ing = __gliding__
12. happy – _y_ + _i_ + er = __happier__
13. big + _g_ + er = __bigger__

Circle each misspelled word. Write it correctly.

14. happier   (happyest)   __happiest__
15. (grabed)   grabbing   __grabbed__
16. larger   (largeest)   __largest__
17. (glideing)   glided   __gliding__
18. (biger)   biggest   __bigger__
19. tinier   (tinyest)   __tiniest__

bigger
biggest
glided
gliding
grabbed
grabbing
happier
happiest
hoped
hoping
hopped
hopping
larger
largest
stopped
stopping
tinier
tiniest
great
underneath

110   © Spelling Grade 3

suffix that begins with *e*. Fold down the letter *i* so that the *y* is covered. Fold over the suffix. Have students spell the new word. Repeat the procedure with the word *happiest*.

Directed Instruction

1 Display **P-6** and **P-7 Spelling Rules** to teach the following rules: Drop **silent e** before adding a suffix that begins with a vowel (rule number 6). Some examples are *hoped* and *hoping*. For short vowel base words ending with one consonant, double the final consonant before adding the suffixes **-ed**, **-er**, **-est**, and **-ing** (rule number 7). Some examples are *bigger* and *biggest*. For words ending with a **consonant** and **y**, change **y** to **i** before adding **-ed**, **-er**, and **-est** (rule number 8). Some examples are *happier* and *happiest*.

2 Proceed to page 109. Say, spell, and say each Pattern and High-Frequency Word. Provide this week's Challenge Words and have students write them in the spaces provided.

3 Review the definition of a suffix at the top of the page. The rules below the definition are the same as those presented on the posters.

4 On page 110, students complete a graphic organizer by adding **suffixes** to the base words given. They add and subtract letters to base words.

5 Homework suggestion: Use **BLM SP3-28B David and Goliath** to practice words with **suffixes** and High-Frequency Words.

Day 3 Word Study
Objective

The students will add **suffixes** to base words to form comparative and superlative adjectives. Students will add **-ed** or **-ing** to verbs.

Introduction

Before class, write the following incomplete sentences on the board.

- A blue whale is the _____ mammal on earth. (**biggest**)
- A blue whale is even _____ than an elephant. (**bigger**)
- The bumblebee bat is the _____ mammal on earth. (**tiniest**)
- The bumblebee bat is _____ than a hamster. (**tinier**)

Write the following words with **suffixes** on the board: bigger, biggest, tinier, tiniest. Explain that the word choices are all adjectives. *Adjectives* are words that describe or compare things. Adjectives ending in **-er** compare two things or groups of things. The word *than* is used in sentences after adjectives ending in **-er**. Adjectives ending in **-est** compare more than two things. Read each sentence to decide how many things are being compared.

Directed Instruction

1 Write the following incomplete sentences on the board:

- Today the ice skater is (glide) _____ over the ice. (**gliding**)
- Yesterday the ice skater (glide) _____ over the ice. (**glided**)

Explain that the base word *glide* is a verb. Review that verbs are action words. Adding a **suffix** to a verb changes the tense of the verb. Present tense verbs may end in **-ing**. Past tense verbs may end in **-ed**.

2 Display **P-6** and **P-7 Spelling Rules** as a reference before proceeding to page 111. Read the definition at the top of the page. Remind students to read each sentence carefully and to follow the spelling rules. Select a volunteer to read Psalm 48:1.

Day 4 Writing
Objective

The students will underline and write list words found in a cartoon. They will complete the cartoon with list words and words of their choice.

Introduction

Display a CARTOON from a newspaper that features a conversation between two characters. Explain that a *cartoon* is <u>a series of humorous drawings that often show a conversation between characters</u>. Read the cartoon to the class. Ask students to add further conversation between the characters. Consider the setting, characters, and humorous aspects.

Directed Instruction

1 On page 112, select volunteers to read the part of each character in the cartoon. Discuss what might be said in the final panel. Direct students to complete the activities on the page.

2 Homework suggestion: Read the cartoon on page 112 to an adult. Take a practice spelling test at home or use **BLM SP3-01A A Spelling Study Strategy** for additional practice.

Day 5 Wrap Up

Objective

The students will correctly write dictated spelling words and sentences.

Introduction

Provide a review, utilizing WHITEBOARDS or Student Spelling Support suggestions.

Directed Instruction

1 Dictate the list words by using the Warm Up sentences or developing original ones. Reserve *bigger*, *hoped*, and *underneath* for the dictation sentences.

2 Follow this procedure for the dictation sentences: read the sentence, invite the class to say the sentence with you, then read the sentence again. Dictate the following sentences:
- The cabin was <u>bigger</u> than the small garage.
- Mark <u>hoped</u> to win a prize in the contest.
- We stood <u>underneath</u> the large tree.

3 If assigned, dictate Extra Challenge Words. Score the test.

Notes

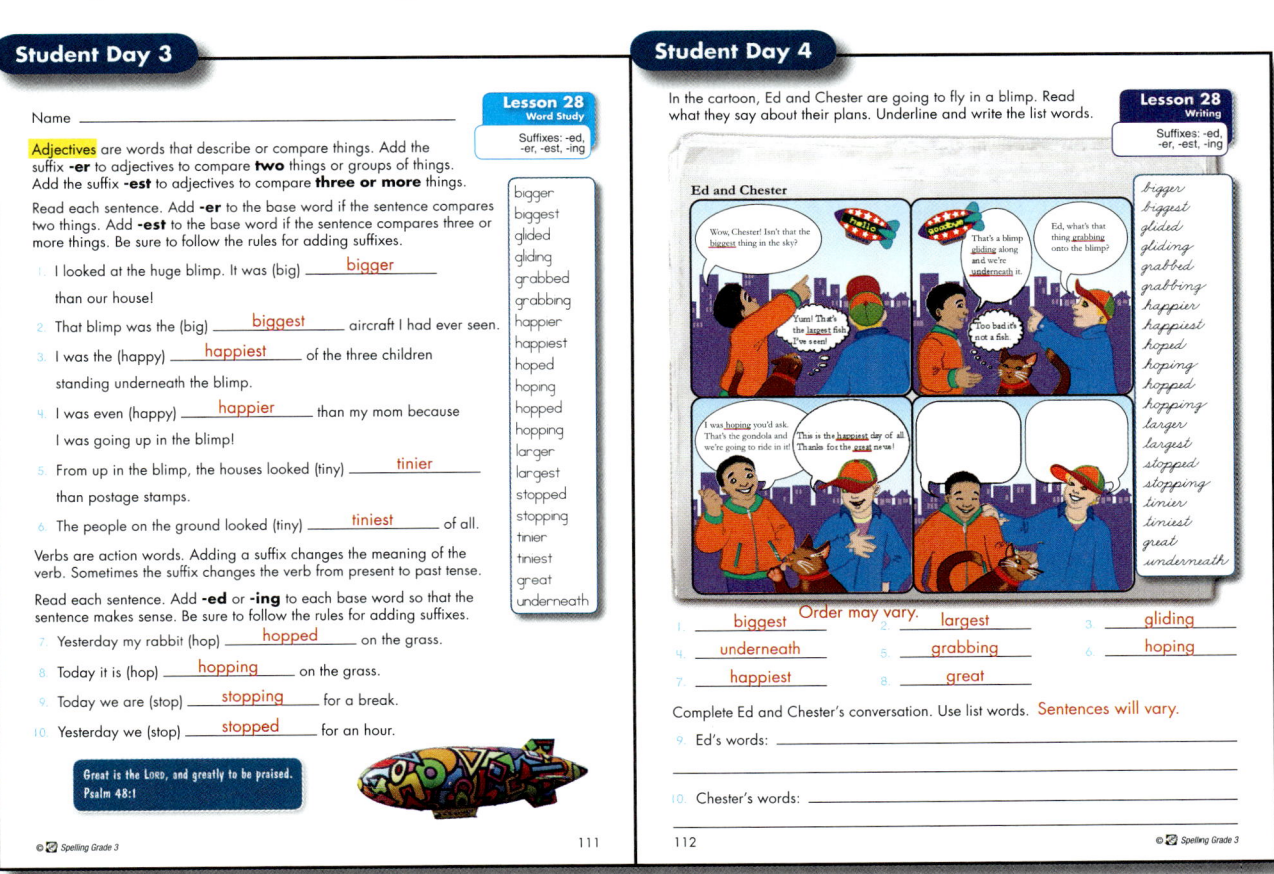

Suffixes: -ful, -less, -ly, -ness, -y

Transportation

The theme of this lesson is Helicopters. The inspiration for the helicopter came from a Chinese top since it moved upward when spun rapidly. Leonardo da Vinci was one of the earliest inventors of the helicopter, having sketched his design in 1490. However, it was not until 1936 that the first successful helicopter flight occurred.

Day 1 Warm Up

Objective

The students will accurately spell and write words with the **suffixes -ful**, **-less**, **-ly**, **-ness**, and **-y**. They will spell and write high-frequency words and challenge words.

Introduction

Before class, select Challenge Words for numbers 21 and 22 from a cross-curricular subject, words misspelled on previous assignments, or words that interest your students. The word *amazingly* has the **suffix -ly** and is suggested for number 21. Administer the Warm Up.

Directed Instruction

1 Say each word, use it in a sentence, and then repeat the word.

Pattern Words

1.	mostly	We eat <u>mostly</u> cereal for breakfast.	mostly
2.	penniless	The <u>penniless</u> child earned money.	penniless
3.	beautiful	Al saw the <u>beautiful</u> sunset.	beautiful
4.	happiness	Jesus fills our lives with <u>happiness</u>.	happiness
5.	wavy	Chloe's hair is <u>wavy</u>, not straight.	wavy
6.	shaky	The <u>shaky</u> straw house collapsed.	shaky
7.	fearlessness	The fireman showed <u>fearlessness</u>.	fearlessness
8.	quickly	The fire spread <u>quickly</u>.	quickly
9.	spotless	The clean floor was <u>spotless</u>.	spotless
10.	darkness	The helicopter flew in the <u>darkness</u>.	darkness
11.	forgetful	The <u>forgetful</u> child did not have a lunch.	forgetful
12.	suddenly	The helicopter <u>suddenly</u> swerved left.	suddenly
13.	windy	On Saturday it was very <u>windy</u>.	windy
14.	lazily	The cow <u>lazily</u> swatted at the flies.	lazily
15.	careless	The builders did a <u>careless</u> job.	careless
16.	graceful	Katie is a <u>graceful</u> skater.	graceful
17.	friendly	Mrs. Rideout is a <u>friendly</u> lady.	friendly
18.	peaceful	Sophie fell asleep in the <u>peaceful</u> room.	peaceful

High-Frequency Words

19.	away	My family went <u>away</u> on vacation.	away
20.	soldiers	The <u>soldiers</u> camped in the desert.	soldiers

Challenge Words

21. _____
22. _____

2 Allow students to self-correct their pretest, following this procedure:

a. Write each word on the board. Discuss the letter/sound relationships in each word. Remind students that a suffix is a word part added to the end of a base word. Point out the **suffixes -ful**, **-less**, **-ly**, **-ness**, and **-y** and explain that some of the base words are changed with the addition of the suffix. The letter **y** changes to **i**; for example, *penny* changes to *penniless*. **Silent e** changes to **y**; for example, *wave* changes to *wavy*. Inform students that the **silent e** remains in *careless*, *graceful*, and *peaceful*. Point to the word *fearlessness*, explaining that this word has two suffixes added to the base word *fear*.

b. As a class, read, spell, and read each word again. Direct students to circle misspelled words with a colored pencil and rewrite them correctly.

3 Proof each student's Warm Up.

4 Homework suggestion: Use **BLM SP3-29A Heliports** to practice the Pattern and High Frequency Words in this lesson.

Day 2 Phonics

Objective
The students will add suffixes to base words by adding and/or subtracting letters. They will sort pattern words by the suffix and select the correct suffix to make a word. They will write high-frequency words.

Introduction
Before class, cut six SENTENCE STRIPS 11½ inches long and four one-inch pieces from another sentence strip. Follow the directions to complete the folding display cards that were given in Lesson 28. Using the diagrams to the right as a guide, complete the display cards for the following words: wavy, shaky, lazily, beautiful, penniless, happiness.

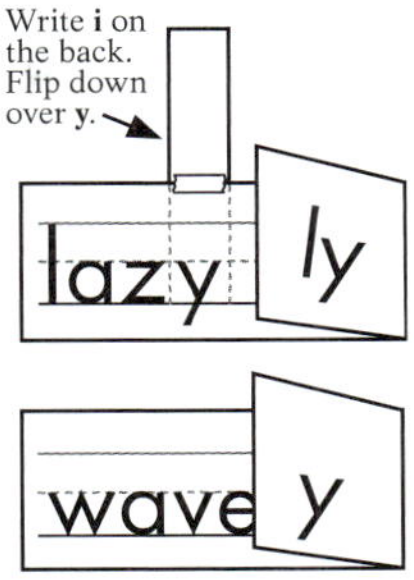

Write **i** on the back. Flip down over **y**.

lazy | ly

wave | y

To teach the suffix rules, use the following steps:
- Show the base word *lazy* by unfolding the card with *lazily*. Explain that in base words that end with **y**, the **y** must be changed to **i** before adding the suffix **-ly**. Fold down the letter **i** so that the **y** is covered. Fold over the suffix **-ly**. Have students spell the new word. Teach that the process of changing **y** to **i** also applies before adding suffixes **-ful**, **-less**, and **-ness**. Follow the same procedure above for *beautiful*, *penniless*, and *happiness*.
- Show the base word *wave* by unfolding the card with *wavy*. Explain that when a word ends with **silent e**, the **silent e** is dropped before adding the suffix **-y**. Use a BLACK MARKER to cross out the **silent e** in the base word *wave*. Fold over the suffix **-y**. Repeat this procedure with the word *shaky*. Spell the new words aloud.

Directed Instruction
1 Display **P-8 Spelling Rules** to teach the following rules: For words

---

Student Day 2

Name _____

Lesson 29 Phonics
Suffixes: -ful, -less, -ly, -ness, -y

Pattern Words
wavy
shaky
windy
lazily
quickly
mostly
friendly
suddenly
spotless
careless
penniless
beautiful
graceful
peaceful
forgetful
darkness
happiness
fearlessness

High-Frequency Words
away
soldiers

A suffix is a word part added to the end of a base word. Adding a suffix changes the meaning of the base word. Sometimes the spelling of the base word changes, too.

For words ending with a **consonant** and **y**, change **y** to **i** before adding **-ly**, **-ful**, **-less**, and **-ness**.

Subtract and add letters to complete each word. 
1. penny – y + i + less = **penniless**
2. happy – y + i + ness = **happiness**
3. lazy – y + i + ly = **lazily**
4. beauty – y + i + ful = **beautiful**

Drop **silent e** before adding the suffix **-y**.

Subtract and add letters to complete each word.
5. shake – e + y = **shaky**
6. wave – e + y = **wavy**

Sometimes when adding suffix **-y** to a base word, nothing is changed.
Add suffix **-y** to complete the word.
7. wind + y = **windy**

helicopter

Challenge Words

© Spelling Grade 3   113

Student Day 2

Sort the Pattern Words according to each suffix. One word is used twice. Order may vary.

Lesson 29 Phonics
Suffixes: -ful, -less, -ly, -ness, -y

1. **-ness**	2. **-less**
darkness	spotless
happiness	careless
fearlessness	penniless
	fearlessness

3. **-ly**	4. **-ful**
lazily	beautiful
quickly	graceful
mostly	peaceful
friendly	forgetful
suddenly	

5. Which three-syllable word has two suffixes?
fearlessness

Read each base word. Fill in the circle next to the suffix that can be added to make a new word. Write the new word.

6. grace ○ ness ● ful — **graceful**
7. care ○ ness ● less — **careless**
8. quick ○ less ● ly — **quickly**
9. friend ● ly ○ y — **friendly**
10. spot ● less ○ ful — **spotless**
11. sudden ○ y ● ly — **suddenly**
12. forget ● ful ○ y — **forgetful**

Write the High-Frequency Words to complete the sentences.
13. Two **soldiers** flew a helicopter.
14. The **soldiers** walked **away** from the helicopter after it landed.

(side list, cursive):
wavy
shaky
windy
lazily
quickly
mostly
friendly
suddenly
spotless
careless
penniless
beautiful
graceful
peaceful
forgetful
darkness
happiness
fearlessness
away
soldiers

114   © Spelling Grade 3

Student Spelling Support Materials

BLMs SP3-29D–E
Card stock
BLM SP3-01A
Sentence strips
Book: *Helicopters*
Pictures of various types of helicopters

Student Spelling Support

1. Write this week's words categorized by patterns on a large piece of paper and attach to the Word Wall.

2. Duplicate **BLMs SP3-29D–E Lesson 29 Spelling Words I** and **II** on CARD STOCK for students to use as flash cards at school or at home.

3. Use **BLM SP3-01A A Spelling Study Strategy** in instructional groups to provide assistance with some or all of the words.

4. Assist students in writing the Challenge Words, numbers 21 and 22, in the section called My Words for Writing, in the back of their textbook.

5. For visual learners, provide the folding sentence strips used in Day 2 of this lesson. Make additional cards using SENTENCE STRIPS for the remaining Pattern Words. Invite students to begin with the folded strip. Encourage students to spell the base word, then unfold the strip as a self-check. Allow students to use the cards as an independent activity.

6. For a literature connection, read *Helicopters* by Darlene R. Stille (Minneapolis, MN: Compass Pointe Books, 2004). Students will enjoy learning facts about various types of helicopters and their uses.

Cont. on page 117

ending with a **consonant** and **y**, change **y** to **i** before adding **-ly**, **-ful**, **-less**, and **-ness** (rule number 9). Some examples are *penniless* and *beautiful*. Drop **silent e** before adding the suffix **-y** (rule number 10). Some examples are *wavy* and *shaky*.

2 Explain that some base words do not need to be changed before adding a suffix. On the board, write the following words in a column: friend, grace, dark, spot, wind. On another area, write the following suffixes in a column: **-ful**, **-ness**, **-y**, **-ly**, **-less**. Solicit volunteers to match a base word to its suffix, then say and spell the new list word.

3 Proceed to page 113. Say, spell, and say each Pattern and High-Frequency Word. Provide this week's Challenge Words and have students write them in the spaces provided.

4 Review the definition of a suffix at the top of the page. Remind students to use the rule boxes to assist in completing the page.

5 Proceed to page 114. Answer any questions before allowing students to complete the page independently.

6 Homework suggestion: Use **BLM SP3-29B Suffix Practice** to practice words in this lesson.

Day 3 Word Study
Objective

The students will read definitions and write appropriate pattern words.

Introduction

Before class, duplicate **BLM SP3-29C Suffix Definitions and Words** on CARD STOCK. Cut the cards apart and keep the definitions and words in two separate piles. Distribute the cards to ten volunteers. Relate that one set of cards has definitions and the other set has words. The object is for each volunteer to find a partner so that there are five groups, each having a definition and its matching word. When each group has been formed, have the volunteers read their cards, beginning with the definition and followed by the matching word.

Directed Instruction

1 Teach the following meanings for the **suffixes -ful, -less, -ly, -ness**, and **-y**:
  • **-ful** means full of
  • **-less** means without
  • **-ly** tells how something is done
  • **-ness** and **-y** tell the condition of something
  Explain that when *full* is used as a suffix, only one *l* is written.

2 Before class, write each Pattern Word on the board for students to reference. Give a definition and have a student respond with the correct Pattern Word. For example, say *"without a penny"* and ask which word is being defined. (**penniless**) Reverse the process by calling out a Pattern Word and asking for the definition. For the word *fearlessness*, ask the students to name the Pattern Word that means *the condition of being without fear.*

3 Proceed to page 115. Allow students to complete the page independently.

Day 4 Writing
Objective

The students will complete a description in the context of a cloze activity using pattern and high-frequency words.

Introduction

Have the students pretend that they are on a helicopter ride. Ask them to describe the things they might see, hear, touch, and smell. If you have ridden in a helicopter, share your experience.

Directed Instruction

1 Proceed to page 116. Instruct students to quietly read through the description first to familiarize themselves with it. Then, have them read through it a second time writing the appropriate words that best complete the sentences with the blanks. Explain that the title of each tour is also used in its description.

2 Homework suggestion: Read the description on page 116 to an adult. Take a practice spelling test at home or use **BLM SP3-01A A Spelling Study Strategy** for additional practice.

Day 5 Wrap Up

Objective

The students will correctly write dictated spelling words and sentences.

Introduction

Provide a review, utilizing WHITEBOARDS or Student Spelling Support suggestions.

Directed Instruction

1 Dictate the list words by using the Warm Up sentences or developing original ones. Reserve *mostly*, *careless*, and *forgetful* for the dictation sentences.

2 Follow this procedure for the dictation sentences: read the sentence, invite the class to say the sentence with you, then read the sentence again. Dictate the following sentences:
- Children eat <u>mostly</u> sandwiches for lunch.
- The queen was <u>careless</u> and lost her keys.
- People can be <u>forgetful</u> when they're busy.

3 If assigned, dictate Extra Challenge Words. Score the test.

Student Spelling Support

Cont. from page 116

7. As a biblical connection, read Mark 12:41–44. Tell how the widow became **penniless** after giving all she had. The widow put her faith in God, not money, to provide for her needs.

8. For a social studies connection, provide PICTURES OF VARIOUS TYPES OF HELICOPTERS and explain their purpose. For example, medical helicopters take injured people to the hospital. Police helicopters clock speeding cars and help find runaway criminals. News helicopters report events as they are happening and also provide current traffic conditions.

9. Challenge advanced learners to research how a helicopter flies and write a one-page report. Have students illustrate their report.

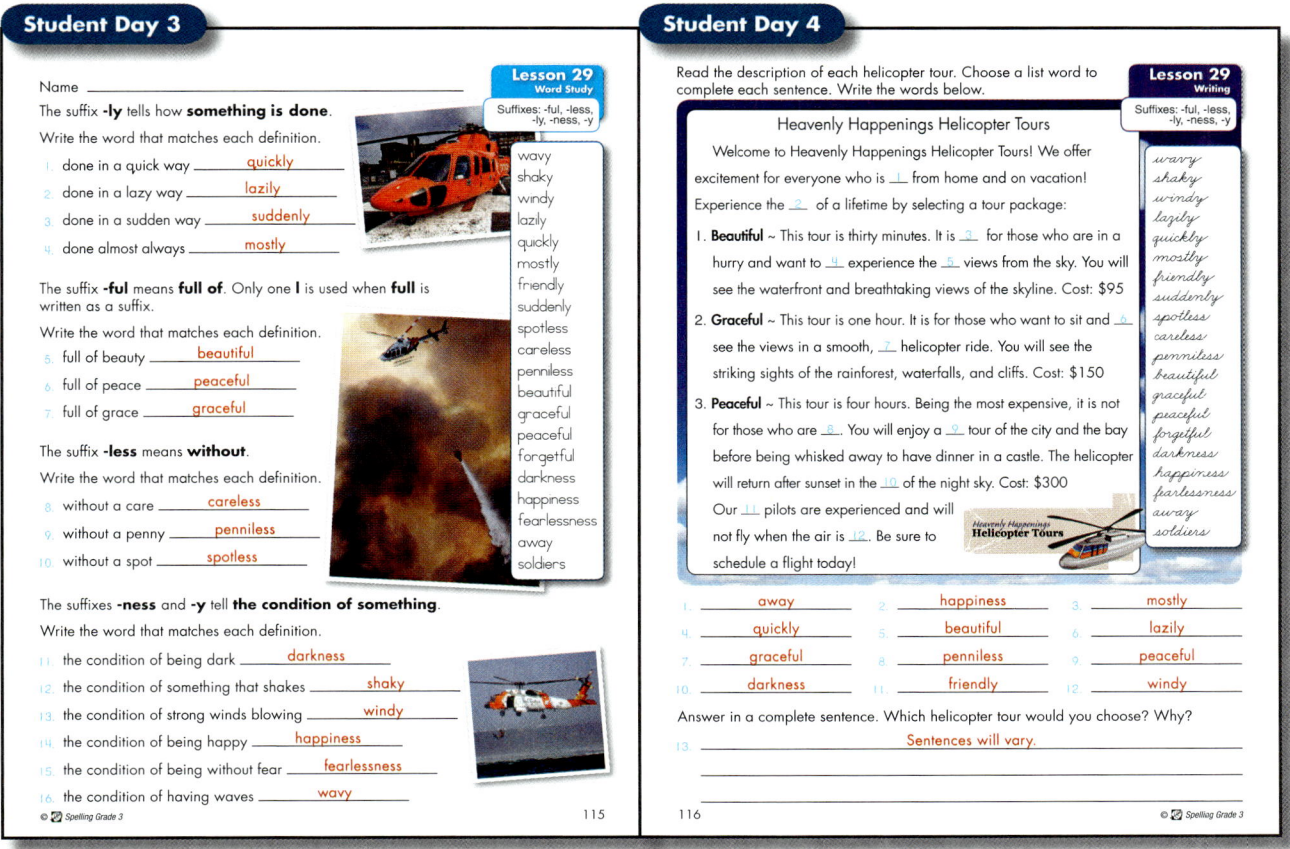

Review Lessons 25–29

Student Pages
Pages 117–120

Lesson Materials

T-30
BLM SP3-30A
BLM SP3-30B
P-11
BLM SP3-30C
P-6
P-7
BLM SP3-30D
BLMs SP3-30E–F
3" × 5" Index cards

Day 1 Hard and Soft c

Objective
The students will spell, identify, circle, and write words with **hard and soft c**.

Introduction
Teacher Note: This week's lesson incorporates the Pattern and High-Frequency Words taught in Lessons 25–29 using a variety of activities such as sorting, a crossword puzzle, decoding words, a word search, scrambled words, and shape boxes.

Review words with **hard and soft c** by writing the Pattern Words from Lesson 25 on the board. Remind students of the following: The letter *c* says its soft sound /s/ before the letters *e*, *i*, and *y*. The letter *c* says its hard sound /k/ before all other letters.

Directed Instruction

1 Display **T-30 Lessons 25–29 Study Sheet** on the overhead to review Lesson 25 words in unison, using the say-spell-say technique.

2 Ask students to identify Lesson 25 words that contain hard *c*, soft *c*, and both **hard and soft c**.

3 Proceed to page 117. Explain that the box contains all the Pattern and High-Frequency Words in Lessons 25–29. This list is the same list of words that was previously displayed on the overhead. Encourage students to use this list as a review tool. Allow students to complete the page independently.

4 Distribute one copy of **BLM SP3-30A Lessons 25–29 Study Sheet** to each student to take home for study.

5 Homework suggestion: Duplicate one copy of **BLM SP3-30B Flying** for each student to practice words with **hard and soft c** and **hard and soft g**.

Day 2 Hard and Soft g and Prefixes: a-, in-, pre-, re-, un-

Objective
The students will spell and write words with **hard and soft g** in a crossword puzzle. They will use a code to spell and write words with the **prefixes a-, in-, pre-, re-,** and **un-**.

Introduction
Remind students of the following: The letter *g* usually says its soft sound /j/ when followed by *e*, *i*, or *y*. The letter *g* says its hard sound /g/ when followed by any other letter. Write the following words from Lesson 26 on the board: edge, guide, danger, garage. Read the following definitions and invite students to select a word from the board to identify which word is being defined:

• a repair shop (**garage**)
• a border (**edge**)

• harm or risk (**danger**)
• to lead or steer (**guide**)

Directed Instruction

1 Review the following definitions for base word and **prefix**: A base word is a word to which letters may be added to make new words. A prefix is a word part added to the beginning of a base word.

Refer to **P-11 Syllables** to review the following generalization: Divide between a prefix and a base word (example number 4).

2 Write the following words from Lesson 27 on the board and invite volunteers to divide each word by drawing a vertical line between the **prefix** and base word:
- preview (**pre|view**)
- removed (**re|moved**)
- unspoken (**un|spoken**)
- invisible (**in|visible**)

3 Display **T-30 Lessons 25–29 Study Sheet** to review Lessons 26–27 words in unison, using the say-spell-say technique.

4 Proceed to page 118. Allow students to complete the page independently. Encourage them to use their Spelling Dictionary if needed.

5 Homework suggestion: Distribute a copy of **BLM SP3-30C Prefixes and Suffixes** to each student to practice words with the **prefixes a-**, **in-**, **pre-**, **re-**, and **un-**, suffixes **-ed**, **-er**, **-est**, and **-ing**, and rules from **P-6** and **P-7 Spelling Rules**.

Day 3 Suffixes: -ed, -er, -est, -ing

Objective
The students will find and circle words with the **suffixes -ed**, **-er**, **-est**, and **-ing** in a word search and write them.

Introduction
Display **P-6** and **P-7 Spelling Rules**. Write the Pattern Words from Lesson 28 on the board. Ask students to identify words that apply to the following rules:

- Drop **silent e** before adding a suffix that begins with a vowel (rule number 6). (**glided, gliding, hoped, hoping, larger, largest**)
- For short vowel base words ending with one consonant, double the final consonant before adding the suffixes **-ed**, **-er**, **-est**, and **-ing** (rule number 7). (**bigger, biggest, grabbed, grabbing, hopped, hopping, stopped, stopping**)
- For words ending with a **consonant** and **y**, change **y** to **i** before adding **-ed**, **-er**, and **-est** (rule number 8). (**happier, happiest, tinier, tiniest**)

Directed Instruction

1 Display **T-30 Lessons 25–29 Study Sheet** to review Lesson 28 words in unison, using the say-spell-say technique.

2 Select a few Pattern Words from Lesson 28 to design a mini word search on the board. Choose words with similar letters so the words can intersect one another.

3 Proceed to page 119 and allow students to independently read the directions and complete the page.

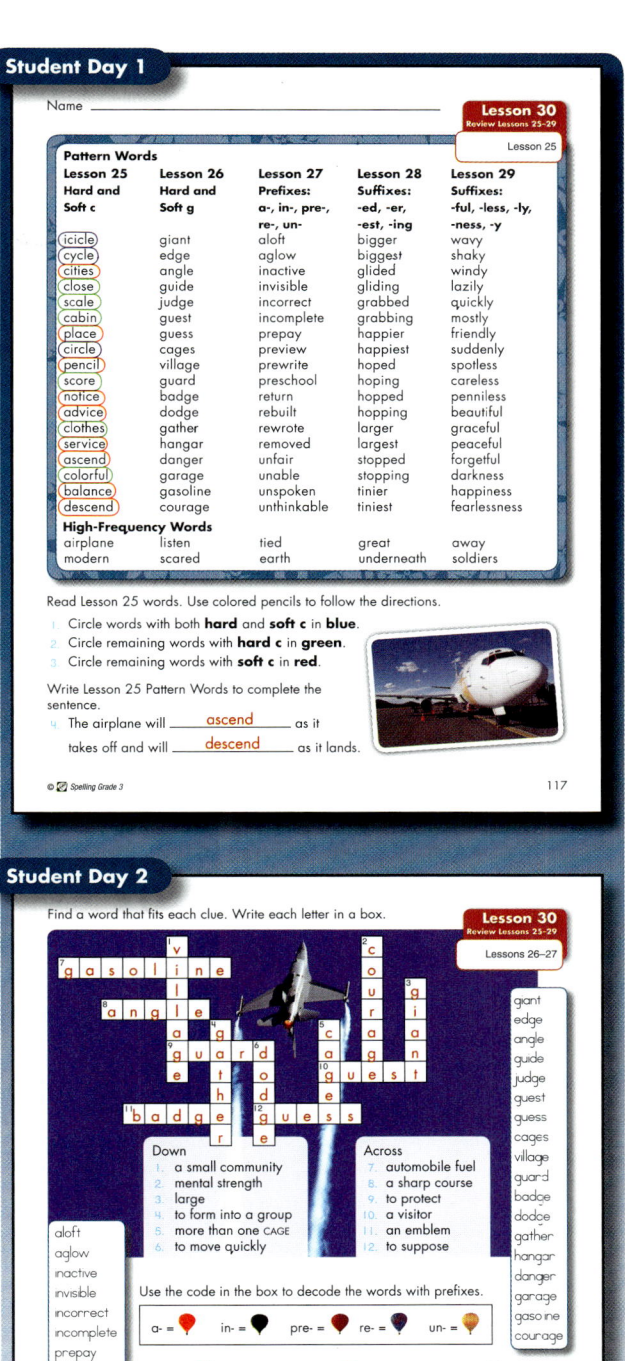

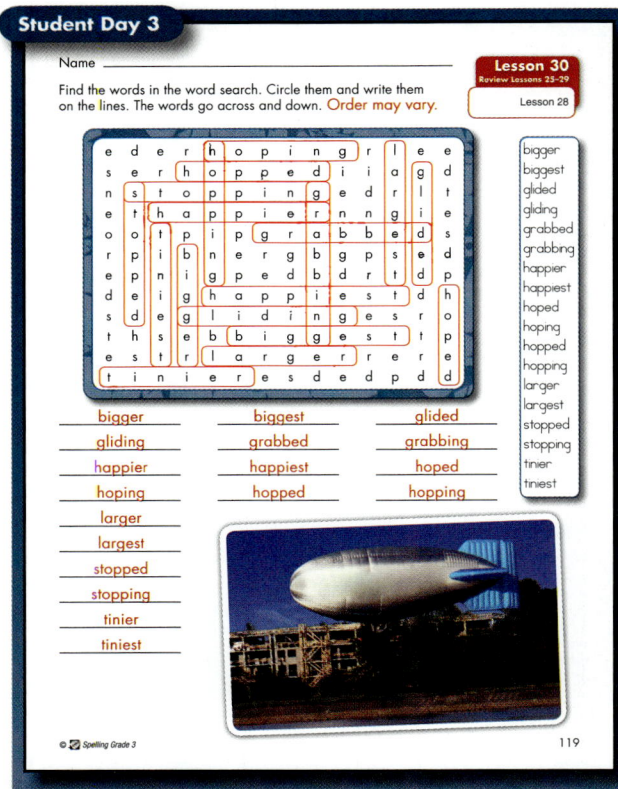

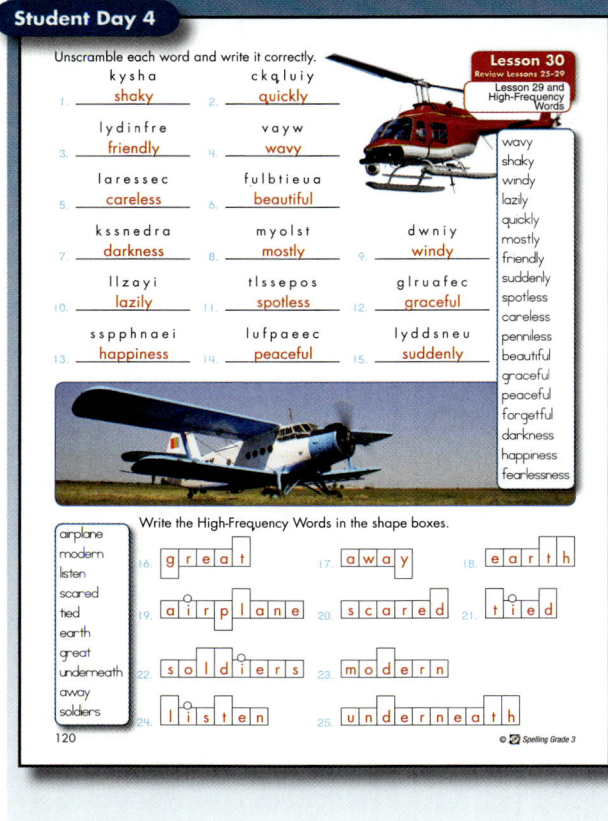

Day 4 Suffixes: -ful, -less, -ly, -ness, -y and High-Frequency Words

Objective

The students will unscramble words with the **suffixes -ful**, **-less**, **-ly**, **-ness**, and **-y**. They will write high-frequency words in shape boxes.

Introduction

Display **T-30 Lessons 25–29 Study Sheet** to review Lesson 29 words. Write the following scrambled words from Lesson 29 on the board:

- f f t g l u o e r (**forgetful**)
- s s n n p l i e e (**penniless**)
- d i w n y (**windy**)
- o m t s y l (**mostly**)
- e e a e s s f s s n r l (**fearlessness**)

Encourage students to refer to the transparency to find a word that contains the same letters as the scrambled word on the board. Remind students that Lesson 29 words contain the **suffixes -ful**, **-less**, **-ly**, **-ness**, and **-y**. Select students to unscramble the letters and write each word on the board.

Directed Instruction

1 Refer to **T-30 Lessons 25–29 Study Sheet** to review Lesson 29 and High-Frequency Words in unison, using the say-spell-say technique.

2 Challenge students to count and identify how many letters are in each High-Frequency Word. Have them identify how many words contain the vowel *i*.

3 Proceed to page 120. Allow students to complete the page independently.

4 Homework suggestion: Duplicate one copy of **BLM SP3-30D Scripture** for each student to practice words with the **suffixes** and High-Frequency Words. Prepare for the Assessment by studying the words on **BLM SP3-30A Lessons 25–29 Study Sheet** that was sent home on Day 1.

Day 5 Assessment

Objective

The students will accurately select the appropriate answer circle within the context of a sentence and fill it in.

Introduction

Teacher Note: The Test makes provision for Differentiated Instruction. The first ten sentences include the words assigned to students with shortened lists. Encourage these students to try all the sentences, but only grade the first ten sentences. The Sample will be dictated and the sentences are provided below for reference. The Test is found on two blackline masters.

Prior to handing out the Test, read through the sentences and select words that may be confusing or challenging for students. Inform students that the

Test will not be a teacher-dictated test, but that you will be reviewing some difficult words that are in sentences on the test. Write the words on the board and sound them out with students before the Test.

Directed Instruction

1 Distribute a copy of **BLMs SP3-30E–F Lessons 25–29 Test I** and **II** to each student and a 3" × 5" INDEX CARD to be used as a marker. Remind students to fill in each answer circle completely and to erase completely if they wish to change an answer.

2 Lead students to correctly place their marker below the Sample, listen to the following dictation, and find the correct answer choice:

Sample

The <u>soljers</u> will <u>guard</u> the president's <u>airplane</u>. <u>All correct</u>
    ●   Ⓑ   Ⓒ   Ⓓ

Say, "The circle below the first underlined word has been filled in to show that it is the misspelled word. You will continue the test now on your own. Move your marker below each sentence and read each sentence. Choose the word that you think is misspelled and fill in the circle below it. If all the words are spelled correctly, fill in the fourth circle underneath *All correct*."

3 Assist students as needed while they read the sentences and complete the Test on their own.

1. Use your pencil to draw a bigger circle.
2. A scared rabbit hopped underneath the bush.
3. The forgetful guest left the garage door open.
4. Al was unable to guess the score of the game.
5. Vicky hoped to preview the movie about the earth.
6. Brice will place the badge into a beautiful case.
7. Please close the door after putting your clothes away.
8. The colorful balloon went aloft and glided across the sky.
9. Pilots can use an angle to move their modern jets quickly.
10. A great number of pilots have courage in times of danger.
11. Did you notice the graceful swan at the edge of the lake?
12. The peaceful townspeople will gather in the village.
13. The cat lazily grabbed at the tied shoelace.
14. The giant icicle suddenly fell from the roof.
15. The friendly preschool teacher gave me some advice.
16. Before driving to the cabin, we stopped to get gasoline.
17. A pilot will judge his speed to guide and dodge his jet.
18. The tiniest cages were removed from the pet shop.
19. Mr. Colburn rebuilt the plane in the spotless hangar.
20. Grace was hoping to prewrite her report on cities today.

Student Pages

Pages 121–124

Lesson Materials

BLM SP3-31A
BLM SP3-31B
Pennies
Clear container
P-9
P-10
BLM SP3-31C
Quarters
Dimes
Nickels
Paintbrushes
Clear drinking glasses
T-31
Transparency pen
BLM SP3-31D
T-32
T-33
BLM SP3-01A
Whiteboards

Transportation

Lessons 31–35 utilize the theme of different modes of space transportation. Lesson 31 begins with Rockets. The Saturn V rockets were used to launch the Apollo Program spacecraft into Earth's orbit and on toward the moon. The Apollo Program was designed to successfully land astronauts on the lunar surface.

Day 1 Warm Up

Objective

The students will accurately spell and write **plural nouns**. They will spell and write high-frequency words and challenge words.

Introduction

Before class, select Challenge Words for numbers 21 and 22 from a cross-curricular subject, words misspelled on previous assignments, or words that interest your students. The word *asteroids* is a **plural noun** and is suggested for number 21. Administer the Warm Up.

Directed Instruction

1 Say each word, use it in a sentence, and then repeat the word.

Pattern Words

1.	rockets	Special <u>rockets</u> are used as launch vehicles.	rockets
2.	galaxies	<u>Galaxies</u> are classified by their shapes.	galaxies
3.	heroes	David and Samson are <u>heroes</u> in the Bible.	heroes
4.	glasses	Gwen filled the <u>glasses</u> with apple juice.	glasses
5.	brushes	Astronauts use <u>brushes</u> to clean lenses.	brushes
6.	switches	The <u>switches</u> are on the control panel.	switches
7.	sheep	The group of <u>sheep</u> followed the shepherd.	sheep
8.	telescopes	Miss Choi brought two <u>telescopes</u> to class.	telescopes
9.	pennies	There are one hundred <u>pennies</u> in a dollar.	pennies
10.	mice	The <u>mice</u> were brown and white.	mice
11.	women	Are there any <u>women</u> who are astronauts?	women
12.	potatoes	Ila put butter on her sweet <u>potatoes</u>.	potatoes
13.	waltzes	<u>Waltzes</u> are danced in many ballets.	waltzes
14.	geese	A flock of <u>geese</u> flew overhead.	geese
15.	shelves	Tiffany and Sara built the wooden <u>shelves</u>.	shelves
16.	knives	Judd sharpened the kitchen <u>knives</u> today.	knives
17.	moose	<u>Moose</u> wandered into the clearing.	moose
18.	indexes	The <u>indexes</u> listed the correct information.	indexes

High-Frequency Words

19.	chapel	Tad went to the <u>chapel</u> and prayed to Jesus.	chapel
20.	famous	Many astronauts are <u>famous</u> and respected.	famous

Challenge Words

21. _____

22. _____

2 Allow students to self-correct their pretest, following this procedure:

a. Write each word on the board. Discuss the letter/sound relationships in each word. Note that some **plural nouns** are the same as their singular form—*sheep* and *moose*. Some **plural nouns** are also formed in unusual ways from their singular form—*mice*, *geese*, and *women*.

b. As a class, read, spell, and read each word again. Direct students to circle misspelled words with a colored pencil and rewrite them correctly.

3 Proof each student's Warm Up.

4 Add the Challenge Words and Test Dates before distributing a copy of **BLM SP3-31A Lessons 31–35 Spelling Lists** to each student for home study.

5 Homework suggestion: Use **BLM SP3-31B Space** to review **plural nouns** and High-Frequency Words. When reviewing this page with the class, prompt students for an answer to the question at the bottom of the blackline. The names of two famous telescopes are the *Hubble* and the *Spitzer*.

Day 2 Phonics

Objective

The students will sort and write **plural nouns**. They will write high-frequency words and challenge words.

Introduction

Give each student a PENNY. Ask one volunteer to identify what they are holding. (**a penny**) Invite the students to come up and return each penny to a CLEAR CONTAINER. Once all pennies have been collected, ask students to name the items inside the container. (**pennies**) Ask, "Why are they called *pennies* when they are all together?" (**because there is more than one penny**) Review singular and plural noun concepts.

Directed Instruction

1 Remind students that a *noun* is a person, place, or thing. Write the following definition on the board: *Plural* means more than one. A *plural noun* identifies more than one. Say each Pattern Word aloud as you write it on the board. Remind students that this week's words are all **plural nouns**.

2 Display **P-9 Spelling Rules** to teach the following rules: For most nouns, add **-s** to make them plural (rule number 11). Have students identify and circle the words that follow this rule. (**rockets, telescopes**) For nouns that end with *ch, sh, s, x, o,* or *z,* add **-es** to make them plural (rule number 12). Invite volunteers to identify and underline the words that follow this rule. (**heroes, glasses, indexes, waltzes, brushes, switches, potatoes**)

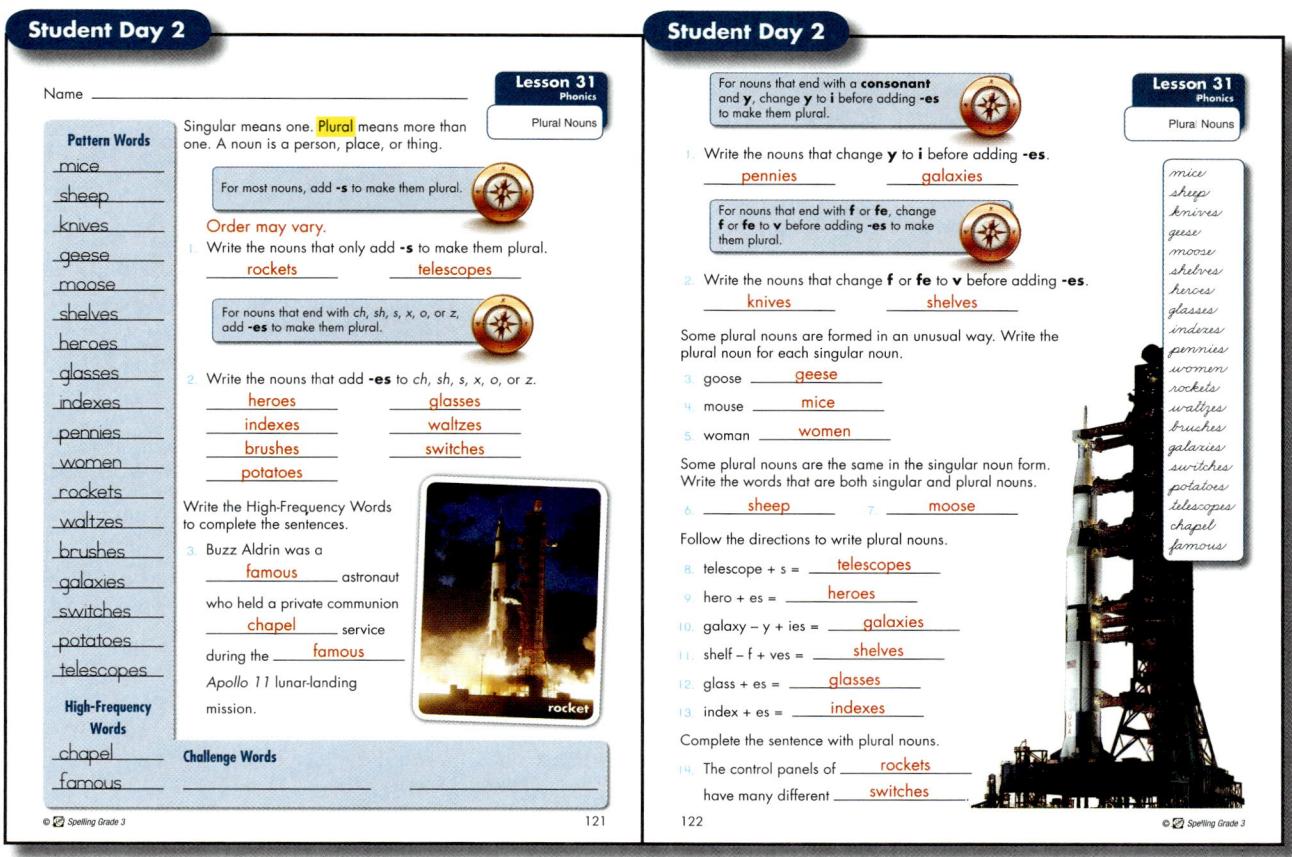

Student Spelling Support Materials

BLMs SP3-31E–F
Card stock
BLM SP3-01A
Letter tiles
Book: *Reaching for the Moon*
File folder
Envelope
BLMs SP3-31G–I

Student Spelling Support

1. Write this week's words categorized by patterns on a large piece of paper and attach to the Word Wall.

2. Duplicate **BLMs SP3-31E–F Lesson 31 Spelling Words I** and **II** on CARD STOCK for students to use as flash cards at school or at home.

3. Use **BLM SP3-01A A Spelling Study Strategy** in instructional groups to provide assistance with some or all of the words.

4. Assist students in writing the Challenge Words, numbers 21 and 22, in the section called My Words for Writing, in the back of their textbook.

5. For auditory and visual learners, dictate the **plural nouns** from this lesson and invite students to build the words with LETTER TILES. As an extra challenge, dictate the singular noun form of each word and challenge students to build the correct plural noun form of each word.

6. Read *Reaching for the Moon* by Buzz Aldrin (New York: HarperCollins Children's Books, 2005). Buzz Aldrin recounts his journey to the Moon—from his childhood days to the famous *Apollo 11* mission. Aldrin shares many personal experiences and insights in this book, which contains paintings by Wendell Minor.

7. Challenge advanced learners to research the Apollo Program missions to
Cont. on page 125

3 Display **P-10 Spelling Rules** to teach the following rules: For nouns that end with a **consonant** and **y**, change **y** to **i** before adding **-es** to make them plural (rule number 13). Invite students to point out and box in the words that follow this rule. (**pennies, galaxies**) For nouns that end with **f** or **fe**, change **f** or **fe** to **v** before adding **-es** to make them plural (rule number 14). Have volunteers place a star by the words that follow this rule. (**knives, shelves**)

4 Erase all the words that have been associated with the rules on the posters. Inform students that some **plural nouns** are unique and formed in an unusual way. Circle *mice, geese,* and *women*. These **plural nouns** are formed from the singular nouns *mouse, goose,* and *woman*, respectively. Remind students that *singular* means <u>one</u>. Erase the circled **plural nouns**.

5 Point to the last **plural nouns** on the board—*sheep* and *moose*. Remind students that these two **plural nouns** are the same as their singular form.

6 Proceed to page 121. Say, spell, and say each Pattern and High-Frequency Word. Provide this week's Challenge Words and have students write them in the spaces provided.

7 Proceed to page 122 and assist students as they complete the page.

8 Homework suggestion: Use **BLM SP3-31C Rockets** to review words.

Day 3 Word Study
Objective
The students will categorize **plural nouns** and complete sentences with **plural nouns**.

Introduction
Display some QUARTERS, DIMES, and NICKELS. Have students identify each group of items. Display some PAINTBRUSHES, CLEAR DRINKING GLASSES, and PENNIES. Ask students to identify the displayed items. Have students select the group of items that match the items in the previous group. Write the words on the board. (**quarters, dimes, nickels, pennies**) Explain that *pennies* was the answer because it fit with the other **plural nouns** in the category of *coins*.

Directed Instruction

1 Proceed to page 123 and allow students to complete exercises 1–3 independently.

2 Read the directions and sentences for exercises 4–8 and complete them together. When complete, read each sentence pair aloud.

3 Conclude the lesson by reviewing the definition of **plural nouns**.

Day 4 Writing
Objective
The students will use proofreading marks to identify mistakes in several paragraphs about the Apollo Program. They will correctly write misspelled words.

Introduction
Display **T-31 Chapel Service on the Moon!** on the overhead. Cover up the text on the bottom portion of the transparency. Read the text on the upper portion aloud. Select students to reread each sentence aloud and to point out errors. Use proofreading marks to mark the errors with a TRANSPARENCY PEN. Use **BLM SP3-31D T-31 Answer Key** as a guide. Uncover the bottom portion of the transparency to chorally read the corrected text. Read John 15:5.

Directed Instruction

1 Proceed to page 124. The paragraphs relate information about Apollo missions and contain a problem and a solution. Direct students to read all the paragraphs, then reread to complete the proofreading exercise independently. When complete, use **T-32 Proofreading a Problem/Solution** to correct the exercise with students. Make sure all errors are corrected. (**9 misspellings, 5 capital letters needed, 2 periods needed, 1 delete, 2 add something—*a* and question mark, 2 small letters needed, 1 new paragraph**)

2 Display **T-33 Corrected Problem/Solution** for students to see the paragraphs written correctly.

3 Homework suggestion: Read the paragraphs about the Apollo missions on page 124 to an adult. Take a practice spelling test at home or use **BLM SP3-01A A Spelling Study Strategy** for additional practice.

Day 5 Wrap Up

Objective
The students will correctly write dictated spelling words and sentences.

Introduction
Provide a review, utilizing WHITEBOARDS or Student Spelling Support suggestions.

Directed Instruction

1 Dictate the list words by using the Warm Up sentences or developing original ones. Reserve *heroes*, *rockets*, and *galaxies* for the dictation sentences.

2 Follow this procedure for the dictation sentences: read the sentence, invite the class to say the sentence with you, then read the sentence again. Dictate the following sentences:
- Many <u>heroes</u> have gone into space.
- <u>Rockets</u> were used to go into space.
- There are many <u>galaxies</u> in space.

3 If assigned, dictate Extra Challenge Words. Score the test.

Student Spelling Support

Cont. from page 124

the moon. Encourage students to find out interesting details of the missions, such as the following: development of the Saturn V rocket, astronaut training rigors, samples collected from the moon, items that have been left on the moon. Students write and illustrate their report.

8. For a small group activity, play Space Suits. You will need a FILE FOLDER, an ENVELOPE, CARD STOCK, **BLMs SP3-31E–F Lesson 31 Spelling Words I** and **II**, and **BLMs SP3-31G–I Space Suits I**, **II**, and **III**. Follow the assembly instructions on the blackline master.

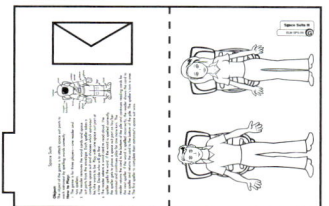

Student Day 3

Name _____

Lesson 31
Word Study
Plural Nouns

Write a list word that fits each group.

1. carrots, onions, peas, ___**potatoes**___
2. chopsticks, forks, spoons, ___**knives**___
3. sanctuary, temple, church, ___**chapel**___

Read each sentence. Write the correct plural form of the bold singular nouns to complete each sentence.

4. The vehicle used to launch the Apollo Program missions to the moon was the Saturn V **rocket**.

___**Rockets**___ are able to accelerate in space by using exhaust gases to push and propel the rocket.

5. Neil Armstrong is admired as a **hero** because of his historical first steps on the moon.

Neil Armstrong, Buzz Aldrin, and Michael Collins are ___**heroes**___ of the *Apollo 11* Program.

6. A **woman** was never an astronaut on any of the Apollo missions.

Since then, many ___**women**___ astronauts have been a part of space exploration missions.

7. A **telescope** is an instrument that is used to observe faraway objects by making them appear larger and closer.

The *Hubble* and the *Spitzer* are names of two ___**telescopes**___ that NASA has launched into orbit.

8. The Milky Way is the **galaxy** that we live in.

Gravity pulls stars, gases, and dust clouds together to form ___**galaxies**___.

Word box: mice, sheep, knives, geese, moose, shelves, heroes, glasses, indexes, pennies, women, rockets, waltzes, brushes, galaxies, switches, potatoes, telescopes, chapel, famous

© Spelling Grade 3   123

Student Day 4

Read the paragraphs about Apollo missions. Find the mistakes. Use proofreading marks.

Lesson 31
Writing
Plural Nouns

Proofreading Marks
- ◯ Circle misspellings.
- ≡ Make a capital letter.
- ⊙ Add a period.
- ✗ Delete.
- ∧ Add something.
- / Make a small letter.
- ¶ Make a new paragraph.

The Apollo Program was an American manned lunar-space program for the National Aeronautics and Space Administration (NASA). nASA successfully landed astronauts on the moon in the missions of *Apollo 11–12* and *14–17*. However, one mission ran into a problem

Apollo 13 was launched on April 11, 1970, atop a Saturn V rocket. saturn V rockets were used to launch the spacecraft that were sent on lunar missions. The crew faced dangerous Problem when an oxygen tank exploded two days after launch. NASA experts on the ground assisted the crew in figuring out a solution to the problem. They told them to to turn off systems and switches in the main spacecraft to save power. the crew returned safely to Earth on April 17, 1970. The apollo 13 astronauts are heros because of their brave efforts during the famus crisis in space.

all manned Apollo missions had a crew of three men They needed to consume healthy Foods while in space. Since items tend to float in space, the astronauts could not store their food on shelfs or drink from glases. Food packets were attached to cabinets and astronauts drank from plastic packets. ¶The technology from the Apollo Program paved the way for future NASA missions that have included wumen astronauts, sending rovers to Mars, and launching giant telescops into orbit. These telescopes can take pictures of faraway galaxys. Isn't it amazing how far space exploration has come

Word box: mice, sheep, knives, geese, moose, shelves, heroes, glasses, indexes, women, rockets, waltzes, brushes, galaxies, switches, potatoes, telescopes, chapel, famous

Write the correct spellings on the lines below.   Order may vary.

1. rockets
2. switches
3. heroes
4. famous
5. shelves
6. glasses
7. women
8. telescopes
9. galaxies

124   © Spelling Grade 3

Schwa Before n Syllables

Lesson Materials

BLM SP3-32A
Black marker
T-36
P-11
BLM SP3-32B
BLMs SP3-32C–D
Card stock
BLM SP3-01A
Whiteboards

Transportation

The theme of this lesson is Lunar Rovers. Lunar Rovers were used by the crews of *Apollo 15, 16,* and *17* in the early 1970s. The lunar rover was nicknamed the "Moon Buggy" and was used to explore the moon and pick up rocks and dust. The lunar rover could only travel up to nine miles per hour!

Day 1 Warm Up

Objective

The students will accurately spell and write words ending with **schwa before n syllables**. They will spell and write high-frequency words and challenge words.

Introduction

Before class, select Challenge Words for numbers 21 and 22 from a cross-curricular subject, words misspelled on previous assignments, or words that interest your students. The word *comparison* has a **schwa before n syllable** and is suggested for number 21. Administer the Warm Up.

Directed Instruction

1 Say each word, use it in a sentence, and then repeat the word.

Pattern Words

1.	taken	Have you <u>taken</u> your vitamins today?	taken
2.	broken	The old chair has a <u>broken</u> leg.	broken
3.	cousin	My <u>cousin</u> lives in Mobile, Alabama.	cousin
4.	open	Who left the door <u>open</u>?	open
5.	lessons	Mrs. Powell teaches piano <u>lessons</u>.	lessons
6.	bacon	Doug likes to eat <u>bacon</u> and eggs for breakfast.	bacon
7.	buttons	Have you pushed the <u>buttons</u> on an elevator?	buttons
8.	gallons	Mom bought two <u>gallons</u> of milk at the store.	gallons
9.	eleven	Conner found <u>eleven</u> tadpoles in the pond.	eleven
10.	robin	The <u>robin</u> caught a worm.	robin
11.	human	Each <u>human</u> is created by God.	human
12.	common	It has become <u>common</u> to own a computer.	common
13.	glisten	The clean window began to <u>glisten</u>.	glisten
14.	sunken	The craters on the moon are <u>sunken</u>.	sunken
15.	heavens	The <u>heavens</u> were created by God.	heavens
16.	frozen	The pizzas were <u>frozen</u> in the freezer.	frozen
17.	person	Jesus is the only <u>person</u> who has not sinned.	person
18.	happens	Do you know what <u>happens</u> when the sun sets?	happens

High-Frequency Words

19.	sight	A full moon is a pretty <u>sight</u>.	sight
20.	expect	Do you <u>expect</u> to see the moon tonight?	expect

Challenge Words

21. _____

22. _____

2 Allow students to self-correct their pretest, following this procedure:

  a. Write each word on the board. Discuss the letter/sound relationships in each word. Point out the schwa before *n* in each word. Teach that a *schwa* is <u>a vowel sound heard in an unstressed syllable. The symbol ə represents a schwa. It makes the short *u* sound heard in *sun*.</u> The letters *ea* in the word *heavens* make the short *e* sound heard in *pet*.

  b. As a class, read, spell, and read each word again. Direct students to circle misspelled words with a colored pencil and rewrite them correctly.

3 Proof each student's Warm Up.

4 Homework suggestion: Use **BLM SP3-32A Lunar Sort** to review words with **schwa before n syllables** in this lesson and High-Frequency Words.

Day 2 Phonics

Objective

The students will correctly sort words with **schwa before n syllables** by their spelling pattern, divide words with open syllables, and complete words with missing syllables. They will write high-frequency words.

Introduction

Write the letter *e* on a sheet of paper with a BLACK MARKER. Ask students to name the letter they see. (**lowercase e**) Turn the paper around so that the letter *e* is upside down. State that now it is no longer a lowercase *e* but a symbol for *schwa*. Teach students that ə is only shown in the dictionary or other texts that provide the pronunciations of words; ə isn't used in regular English text. Write *human*, *open*, *cousin*, and *bacon* on the board. Review that a schwa says the short *u* sound heard in *sun* and can be spelled with *a* as in *human*, *e* as in *open*, *i* as in *cousin*, or *o* as in *bacon*. Solicit a volunteer to underline the vowels that have the schwa sound before the letter *n*.

Directed Instruction

1 Display **T-36 Lessons 31–35 Study Sheet** on the overhead. Look at the list of words for Lesson 32. Say each word and clap for each syllable. Have a student name the three-syllable list word (**eleven**) and the one-syllable list word (**sight**).

2 Display **P-11 Syllables** to review the following rules:
• Divide between double consonants (example number 2).
• Divide after a long vowel in an open syllable (example number 6). Write the following words on the board: open, taken, bacon, frozen, human, broken, gallons, lessons, buttons, happens, common. Invite volunteers to divide the words into syllables using examples 2 and 6. (**example number 2: gal|lons, les|sons, but|tons, hap|pens, com|mon; example number 6: o|pen, ta|ken, ba|con, fro|zen, hu|man, bro|ken**)

3 On another area of the board, write the following words: sunken,

Differentiated Instruction

• For students who spelled all the words correctly on the Warm Up, select and assign three Extra Challenge Words from the following list: lunar, nicknamed, symphony, disguise, delightful, Hebrews.

• For students who spelled less than half correctly, assign the following Pattern and High-Frequency Words: open, robin, taken, human, person, broken, happens, common, sight, expect. On the Wrap Up, evaluate these students on the ten words assigned; however, encourage them to attempt to spell all the list words to the best of their ability. They are also responsible for writing the dictated sentences.

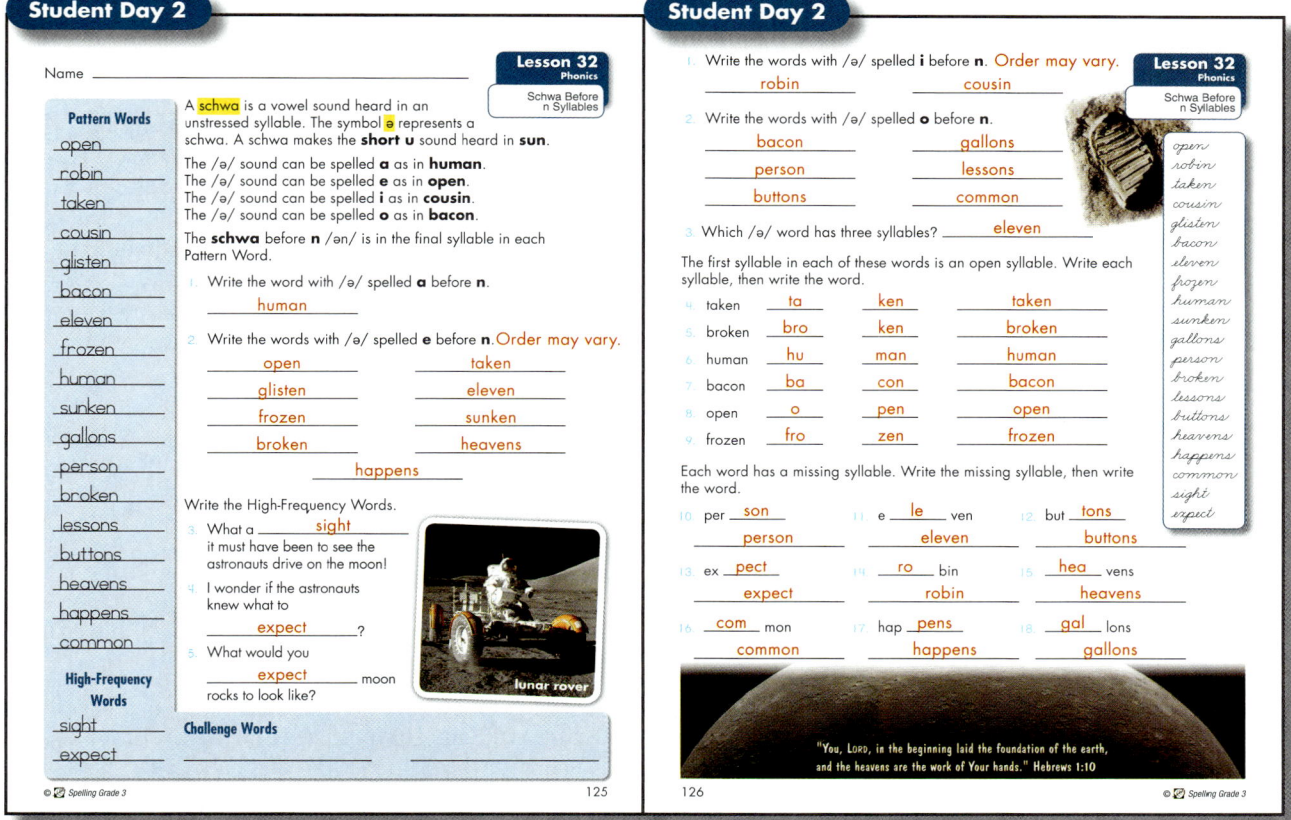

Student Day 2

Name _____

Lesson 32 Phonics — Schwa Before n Syllables

Pattern Words
open, robin, taken, cousin, glisten, bacon, eleven, frozen, human, sunken, gallons, person, broken, lessons, buttons, heavens, happens, common

High-Frequency Words
sight, expect

A **schwa** is a vowel sound heard in an unstressed syllable. The symbol ə represents a schwa. A schwa makes the **short u** sound heard in **sun**.

The /ə/ sound can be spelled **a** as in **human**.
The /ə/ sound can be spelled **e** as in **open**.
The /ə/ sound can be spelled **i** as in **cousin**.
The /ə/ sound can be spelled **o** as in **bacon**.

The **schwa** before **n** /ən/ is in the final syllable in each Pattern Word.

1. Write the word with /ə/ spelled **a** before **n**.
   human

2. Write the words with /ə/ spelled **e** before **n**. Order may vary.
   open   taken
   glisten   eleven
   frozen   sunken
   broken   heavens
        happens

Write the High-Frequency Words.
3. What a ___sight___ it must have been to see the astronauts drive on the moon!
4. I wonder if the astronauts knew what to ___expect___?
5. What would you ___expect___ moon rocks to look like?

lunar rover

Challenge Words
_____

© Spelling Grade 3   125

Student Day 2

1. Write the words with /ə/ spelled **i** before **n**. Order may vary.
   robin   cousin

2. Write the words with /ə/ spelled **o** before **n**.
   bacon   gallons
   person   lessons
   buttons   common

3. Which /ə/ word has three syllables? ___eleven___

The first syllable in each of these words is an open syllable. Write each syllable, then write the word.

4. taken   ta   ken   taken
5. broken   bro   ken   broken
6. human   hu   man   human
7. bacon   ba   con   bacon
8. open   o   pen   open
9. frozen   fro   zen   frozen

Each word has a missing syllable. Write the missing syllable, then write the word.

10. per ___son___   11. e ___le___ ven   12. but ___tons___
    person   eleven   buttons

13. ex ___pect___   14. ___ro___ bin   15. ___hea___ vens
    expect   robin   heavens

16. ___com___ mon   17. hap ___pens___   18. ___gal___ lons
    common   happens   gallons

Lesson 32 Phonics — Schwa Before n Syllables

Pattern Words list: open, robin, taken, cousin, glisten, bacon, eleven, frozen, human, sunken, gallons, person, broken, lessons, buttons, heavens, happens, common, sight, expect

"You, LORD, in the beginning laid the foundation of the earth, and the heavens are the work of Your hands." Hebrews 1:10

126   © Spelling Grade 3

Student Spelling Support

1. Write this week's words categorized by patterns on a large piece of paper and attach to the Word Wall.

2. Duplicate **BLMs SP3-32E–F Lesson 32 Spelling Words I** and **II** on CARD STOCK for students to use as flash cards at school or at home.

3. Use **BLM SP3-01A A Spelling Study Strategy** in instructional groups to provide assistance with some or all of the words.

4. Assist students in writing the Challenge Words, numbers 21 and 22, in the section called My Words for Writing, in the back of their textbook.

5. For kinesthetic learners, write each Pattern Word on a SENTENCE STRIP, omitting the schwa before *n*. Provide LETTER TILES. Have students read a word on the sentence strip, decide which vowel says /ə/, place the correct letter tile on the sentence strip, and self-check the word using a spelling list.

6. Read Psalm 19:1: "The **heavens** declare the glory of God; and the firmament shows His handiwork." Explain that *firmament* is the sky. Hold a discussion about God's handiwork and all that He has created. Invite students to write and illustrate a prayer to God, thanking him for the sun, moon, stars, and galaxies. Post on the bulletin board.

Cont. on page 129

person, expect. Explain that these words can be divided between unlike consonants before volunteers divide the words. (**sun|ken, per|son, ex|pect**)

4 On another area of the board, write the following words: robin, cousin, glisten, eleven, heavens. Explain that these words are unique because they each have a short vowel sound and are divided after the short vowel sound. Select volunteers to divide these words into syllables. (**ro|bin, cou|sin, gli|sten, e|le|ven, hea|vens**)

5 Ask the students if they see a pattern in each of the final syllables of the schwa before *n* words. (**The schwa before *n* is preceded by a consonant. In *glisten*, there are two consonants, but only one is heard.**)

6 Proceed to page 125. Say, spell, and say each Pattern and High-Frequency Word. Provide this week's Challenge Words and have students write them in the spaces provided. Choose volunteers to read the sentences at the top of the page. Students may complete the page independently.

7 Proceed to page 126. Select a student to read Hebrews 1:10 at the bottom of the page. Read the directions and assist students as needed.

8 Homework suggestion: Use **BLM SP3-32B Syllable Chart** to practice words from this lesson.

Day 3 Word Study

Objective

The students will correctly write pattern words in singular possessive phrases and number and write list words in alphabetical order.

Introduction

Before class, duplicate one copy of **BLMs SP3-32C–D Possessives I** and **II** on CARD STOCK and cut apart the cards. Write the word *possessive* on the board. Teach students that a *possessive* form of a word shows that something belongs to a person, place, thing, or animal. An *apostrophe* and *s* ('*s*) are placed at the end of a singular noun to show that it is possessive.

Directed Instruction

1 On the board, write the following phrases: the hat of Steve, the principal of the school, the tire of the bike, the paw of the cat. Read the first phrase on the board and ask who is the owner (**Steve**) and what belongs to him (**hat**). Distribute the card with the word *Steve* to a volunteer and have him/her stand facing the class. Explain that *Steve* is a singular noun. In order to make it possessive, an '*s* must be added. Select another volunteer to hold the card with '*s* next to the card with *Steve*. Select a third volunteer to hold the card with *hat* next to *Steve's*. Explain that *Steve's* is not plural, but singular possessive to show that the hat belongs to him. Tell the students that an easier way to say the *hat of Steve* is *Steve's hat*. Repeat the process with the remaining cards and phrases.

2 Proceed to page 127. Read the definition of *possessive* and complete exercises 1–5 as a class. Before completing exercises 6–8, remind students that when the first letter of each word is the same, look at the second letter. If the second letter is the same, look at the third letter, and so on. Allow students to complete the page independently.

Day 4 Writing

Objective

The students will write words to complete a make-believe story in a cloze format. They will write their own ending to the make-believe story.

Introduction

Hold a discussion and have students share their knowledge of the moon and the lunar rover. Share with the students the facts about the lunar rover in the *Transportation* theme box on the first page of this lesson.

Then share the following additional facts about the moon:
- The moon is about 2,160 miles in diameter.
- The moon is about 238,900 miles from earth.
- It takes about three days to get to the moon in a spacecraft.

Directed Instruction

1 Proceed to page 128. Select a volunteer to read the directions and allow students to complete the page independently. Select volunteers to read their stories.

2 Homework suggestion: Read the story on page 128 to an adult. Take a practice spelling test at home or use **BLM SP3-01A A Spelling Study Strategy** for additional practice.

Day 5 Wrap Up

Objective
The students will correctly write dictated spelling words and sentences.

Introduction
Provide a review, utilizing WHITEBOARDS or Student Spelling Support suggestions.

Directed Instruction

1 Dictate the list words by using the Warm Up sentences or developing original ones. Reserve *taken*, *person*, and *expect* for the dictation sentences.

2 Follow this procedure for the dictation sentences: read the sentence, invite the class to say the sentence with you, then read the sentence again. Dictate the following sentences:
- Tom has <u>taken</u> the glasses to the kitchen.
- Mr. Smith is a friendly <u>person</u>.
- Did you <u>expect</u> this roadblock?

3 If assigned, dictate Extra Challenge Words. Score the test.

Student Spelling Support
Cont. from page 128

7. Challenge advanced learners to make a list of words in which the schwa sound is heard in any syllable. For example, *canoe* has a schwa for the letter *a* in the first syllable. Provide a DICTIONARY for students to check if the words on their list indeed contain a schwa.

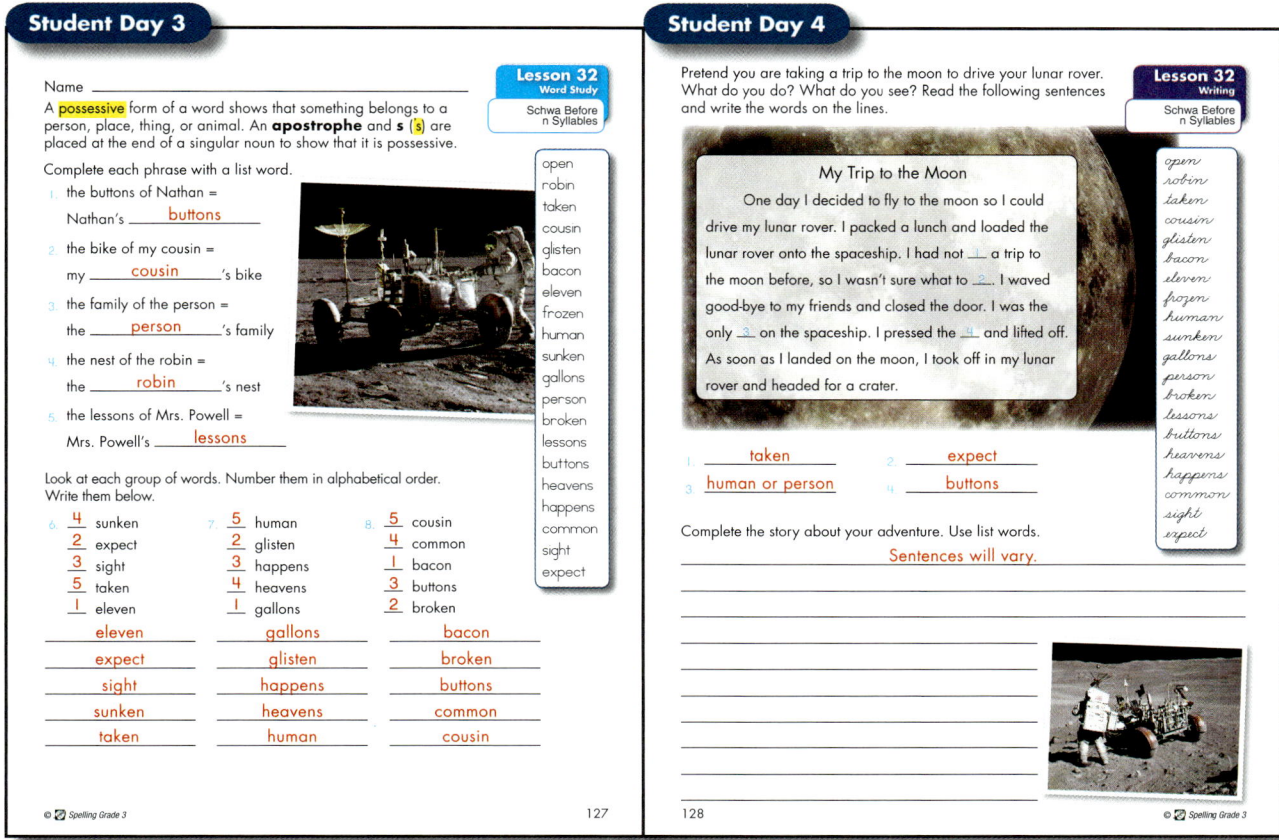

Student Pages

Pages 129–132

Lesson Materials

BLM SP3-33A
Sentence strips
Black marker
P-11
BLM SP3-33B
T-6
BLM SP3-01A
Whiteboards

Transportation

The theme of this lesson is the Space Shuttle. It was designed in the 1970s as a way to transport people and cargo into orbit. The space shuttle is a rocket with a reusable orbiter about the size of a jet airplane. The orbiter may launch satellites and aid in experiments. *Atlantis, Discovery,* and *Endeavour* are some of the orbiters.

Day 1 Warm Up

Objective

The students will accurately spell and write words that have **final syllables with -le**. They will spell and write high-frequency words and challenge words.

Introduction

Before class, select Challenge Words for numbers 21 and 22 from a cross-curricular subject, words misspelled on previous assignments, or words that interest your students. The word *adorable* has a **final syllable with -le** and is suggested for number 21. Administer the Warm Up.

Directed Instruction

1 Say each word, use it in a sentence, and then repeat the word.

Pattern Words

1. title	The <u>title</u> of the book is *The Borrowers*.	title
2. riddle	Jackie told me a funny <u>riddle</u>.	riddle
3. jungle	Kipling wrote stories about the <u>jungle</u>.	jungle
4. buckle	Don't forget to <u>buckle</u> your seatbelt.	buckle
5. people	Many <u>people</u> brought children to see Jesus.	people
6. temple	Jesus went to the <u>temple</u> with His disciples.	temple
7. rumble	The rocket lifted off with a <u>rumble</u>.	rumble
8. trouble	Chris didn't expect any <u>trouble</u> with the car.	trouble
9. capable	Third graders are <u>capable</u> of spelling well!	capable
10. able	Are you <u>able</u> to attend the concert?	able
11. settle	They'll soon <u>settle</u> on a name for their team.	settle
12. handle	Our secretary can <u>handle</u> the book orders.	handle
13. double	Mom will <u>double</u> the cookie recipe.	double
14. shuttle	The orbiter is part of the space <u>shuttle</u>.	shuttle
15. whistle	Manuel likes to <u>whistle</u> while he works.	whistle
16. sample	A free <u>sample</u> of soap came in the mail.	sample
17. sparkle	Diamonds <u>sparkle</u> in the sunlight.	sparkle
18. vegetable	Aunt Sophie's <u>vegetable</u> soup tastes great!	vegetable

High-Frequency Words

19. planets	Our solar system has several <u>planets</u>.	planets
20. history	The Bible records the <u>history</u> of Israel.	history

Challenge Words

21. _____

22. _____

2 Allow students to self-correct their pretest, following this procedure:

  a. Write each word on the board. Discuss the letter/sound relationships in each word. Point out the final syllable in each list word. Inform students that the letters **-le** in the final syllable make the sound /əl/ as heard in *rumble*. The letter *t* is silent in *-stle* as in *whistle*.

  b. As a class, read, spell, and read each word again. Direct students to circle misspelled words with a colored pencil and rewrite them correctly.

3 Proof each student's Warm Up.

4 Homework suggestion: Use **BLM SP3-33A Launch Countdown** to review words that contain **final syllables with -le** and High-Frequency Words.

Day 2 Phonics

Objective

The students will sort words that contain **final syllables with -le**, divide words into syllables, write rhyming words, and high-frequency words.

Introduction

Before class, write the following Pattern Words on 11½ inch SENTENCE STRIPS, using a BLACK MARKER: title, riddle, handle. Attach the sentence strips to the board. Inform students that they will be dividing the words into syllables. Refer to **P-11 Syllables** to review the following example: Divide after a long vowel in an open syllable (example number 6). Invite a volunteer to come to the board, remove the word with a long vowel in an open syllable, and divide the word by cutting the sentence strip into two pieces between syllables. (**ti|tle**) Review the following example: Divide between double consonants (example number 2). Choose another volunteer to remove the word with double consonants and cut the word between syllables. (**rid|dle**) Continue with the following example: Divide after a consonant or consonant sound in a closed syllable (example number 1). Select a volunteer to cut the last word into syllables between consonants. (**han|dle**) Reattach the syllables to the board in random order and invite volunteers to reassemble the words by matching the correct syllables. Read and spell all the words.

Directed Instruction

1 Teach students that each Pattern Word in this week's list contains a schwa /ə/ sound before the letter *l* in the final syllable. A frequent misspelling for /əl/ is *el*. Remind students that each Pattern Word ends with **-le**. Read each Pattern Word and have students chant the letters *l-e* after you read each word. Point out that *whistle* has a silent *t* before **-le**.

2 Proceed to page 129. Say, spell, and say each Pattern and High-Frequency Word. Provide this week's Challenge Words and have students write them in the spaces provided. Read the information at the top of the page before allowing students to work independently.

Differentiated Instruction

- For students who spelled all the words correctly on the Warm Up, select and assign three Extra Challenge Words from the following list: orbiter, launch, papaya, substitute, tenacious, Haggai.

- For students who spelled less than half correctly, assign the following Pattern and High-Frequency Words: title, able, settle, handle, double, people, shuttle, sample, history, planets. On the Wrap Up, evaluate these students on the ten words assigned; however, encourage them to attempt to spell all the list words to the best of their ability. They are also responsible for writing the dictated sentences.

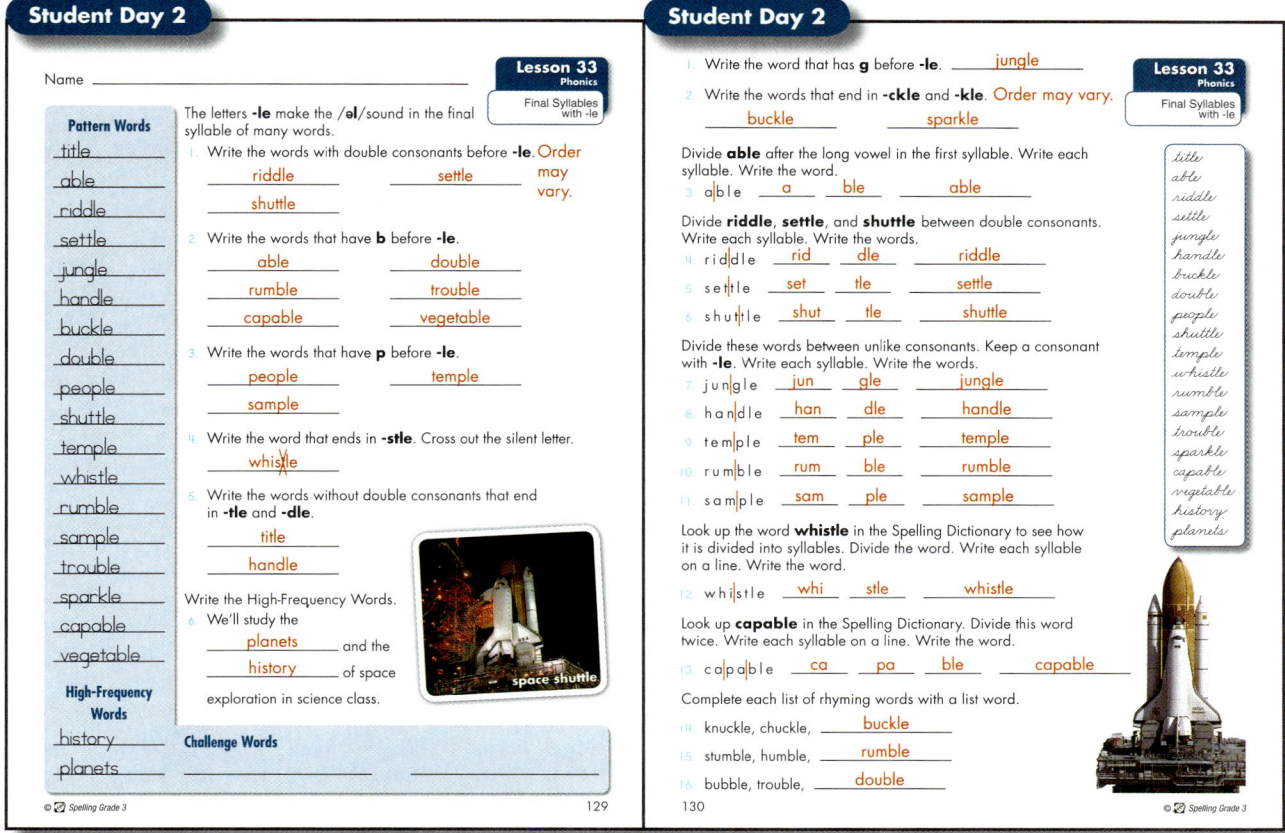

---

3 Proceed to page 130. Assist students as they complete the page. When complete, ask students to find the two list words that rhyme. (**double and trouble**)

4 Homework suggestion: Use **BLM SP3-33B Up in Space** to review the Pattern Words from this lesson.

Day 3 Word Study

Objective

The students will complete idioms with list words. They will place accent marks in front of stressed syllables.

Introduction

Before class, write the bulleted incomplete sentences on the board and read them aloud. On another area of the board, write the following phrases: eyes in the back of his/her head, no spring chicken, old hat.

- Great-grandmother isn't young anymore; she's ___. (**no spring chicken**)
- My teacher never misses anything; he/she must have ___. (**eyes in the back of his/her head**)
- That story has been told so many times; it's ___. (**old hat**)

Define the phrases used to complete each sentence as idioms. *Idioms* are <u>fun ways to talk about everyday things</u>. Read and discuss the idioms, including how the literal meanings differ from the meanings implied. Guide the students to see how silly each sentence would be if it were taken literally.

Directed Instruction

1 Place **T-6 Dictionary Entry** on the overhead. Draw students' attention to the pronunciation of the word *skyline*. Explain that an *accent mark* (') is <u>a short line placed at the beginning of the stressed syllable</u>. Pronounce the word *skyline*, using your voice to emphasize the stress placed on the first syllable.

2 Write the following words and their pronunciations on the board, allowing a space for an accent mark: temple / tem pəl/ (**'tem pəl**), trouble / tru bəl/ (**'tru bəl**), sparkle / spär kəl/ (**'spär kəl**). Pronounce each word slowly, using your voice to indicate the stressed syllable. Help students to understand that, in any word, the stressed syllable is the loudest syllable. Invite volunteers to come to the board, read each word and place an accent mark in front of each stressed syllable. Have students clap out each syllable; make sure the stressed syllable receives the louder clap.

3 Proceed to page 131. Invite students to read Psalm 8:3–4. Share that even though God created the entire universe, He still cares deeply for each one of us. Assist students as needed in completing the exercises. To end the lesson, guide students to conclude that the **final syllables with -le** are unstressed syllables.

Day 4 Writing

Objective

The students will read a schedule for the launch of a space shuttle and write list words. Students will write their own daily schedule.

Introduction

Ask students if they have ever seen a space shuttle liftoff. Discuss that there is a lot of planning by many people before a shuttle can be successfully launched. Inform students that much of the work is done according to a schedule. Schedules are used in many different ways. Solicit suggestions for various ways schedules are used in students' lives and write their suggestions on the board.

Directed Instruction

1 Proceed to page 132 and read the directions. Inform students that the schedule below the directions is a shortened version of an actual NASA launch schedule. Students write the bold words on the lines below the schedule.

2 Invite students to write their own daily schedules. Encourage students to list times and activities, using as many list words as possible.

3 Homework suggestion: Read the launch schedule on page 132 to an adult. Take a practice spelling test at home or use **BLM SP3-01A A Spelling Study Strategy** for additional practice.

Day 5 Wrap Up

Objective

The students will correctly write dictated spelling words and sentences.

Introduction

Provide a review, utilizing WHITEBOARDS or Student Spelling Support suggestions.

Directed Instruction

1 Dictate the list words by using the Warm Up sentences or developing original ones. Reserve *title*, *shuttle*, and *history* for the dictation sentences.

2 Follow this procedure for the dictation sentences: read the sentence, invite the class to say the sentence with you, then read the sentence again. Dictate the following sentences:
- Sam began his book report by reading the title.
- The space shuttle returned to the earth.
- We can read all about sunken ships in history books.

3 If assigned, dictate Extra Challenge Words. Score the test.

Notes

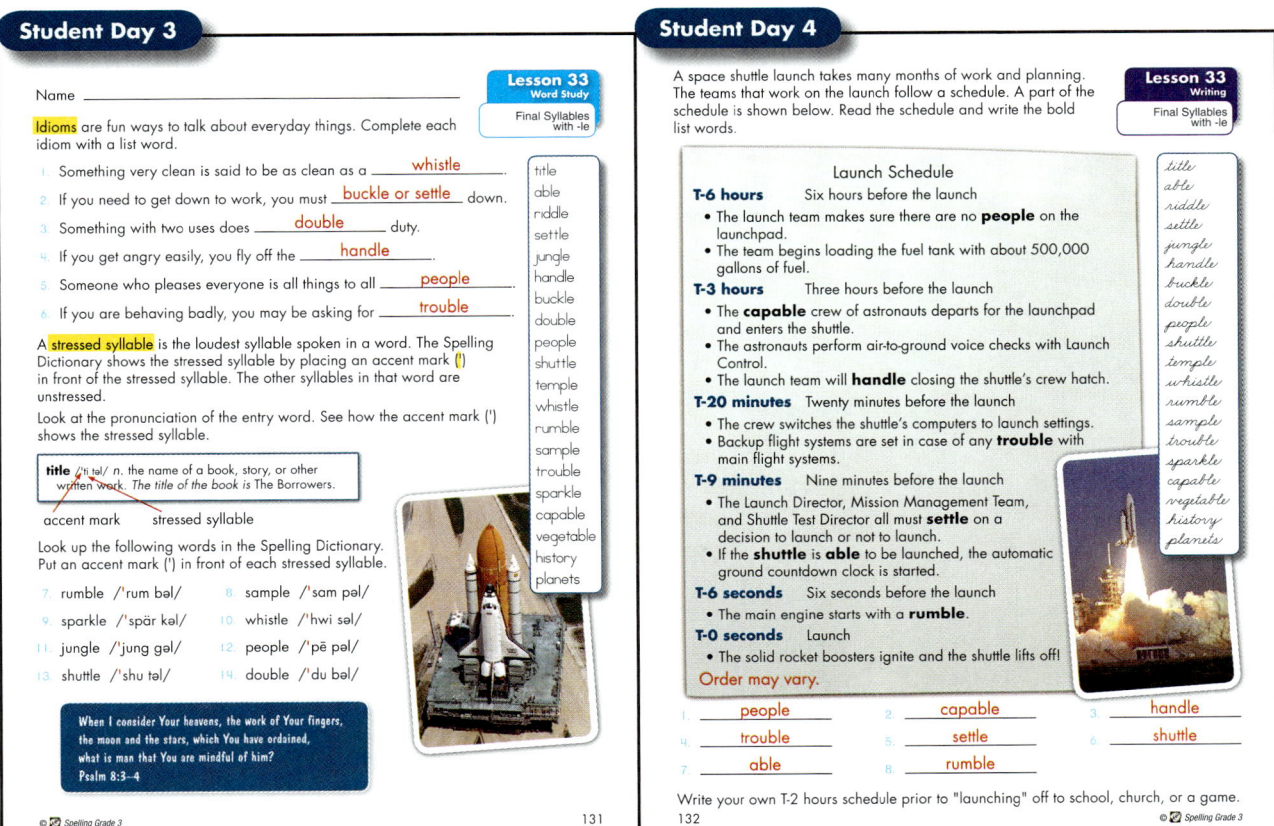

Student Pages

Pages 133–136

Lesson Materials

BLM SP3-34A
BLMs SP3-34B–C
BLM SP3-34D
T-6
T-34
BLM SP3-34E
BLM SP3-01A
Whiteboards

Transportation

The theme of this lesson is the *International Space Station (ISS)* and how crew members move about in space. Astronauts conduct space walks outside the *ISS* to repair, maintain, and build the station. During a space walk, astronauts can be maneuvered by a robotic space arm or tethered to a line while they float in space.

Day 1 Warm Up

Objective

The students will accurately spell and write **homophones**. They will spell and write high-frequency words and challenge words.

Introduction

Before class, select Challenge Words for numbers 21 and 22 from a cross-curricular subject, words misspelled on previous assignments, or words that interest your students. The word *allowed* is a **homophone** and is suggested for number 21. Administer the Warm Up.

Directed Instruction

1 Say each word, use it in a sentence, and then repeat the word.

Pattern Words

1. where	<u>Where</u> will this mission take us?	where
2. cents	How many <u>cents</u> make one dollar?	cents
3. weight	Astronauts feel no <u>weight</u> while in space.	weight
4. peace	Jesus gives us <u>peace</u> when we pray.	peace
5. wear	The astronauts <u>wear</u> special space suits.	wear
6. piece	Steven will repair the <u>piece</u> of equipment.	piece
7. wait	We had to <u>wait</u> for permission to launch.	wait
8. road	The truck drove down a long <u>road</u>.	road
9. two	<u>Two</u> astronauts performed a space walk.	two
10. rode	Christa <u>rode</u> in a van to the launchpad.	rode
11. too	The mission in space was not <u>too</u> long.	too
12. rowed	The disciples <u>rowed</u> a boat toward land.	rowed
13. to	Seven astronauts headed <u>to</u> the spacecraft.	to
14. their	The astronauts wore <u>their</u> space suits.	their
15. sense	They felt no <u>sense</u> of heaviness in space.	sense
16. there	<u>There</u> are many parts to a space station.	there
17. scents	Sweet and spicy <u>scents</u> smell good!	scents
18. they're	<u>They're</u> going to perform a space walk.	they're

High-Frequency Words

19. once	<u>Once</u> the mission is complete, we will rest.	once
20. entire	The <u>entire</u> space station is very large.	entire

Challenge Words

21. _____

22. _____

2 Allow students to self-correct their pretest, following this procedure:

a. Write each word on the board. Discuss the letter/sound relationships in each word. Point out that the lesson contains **homophones**. *Homophones* are <u>words that sound the same but have different meanings and spellings</u>.

b. As a class, read, spell, and read each word again. Direct students to circle misspelled words with a colored pencil and rewrite them correctly.

3 Proof each student's Warm Up.

4 Homework suggestion: Use **BLM SP3-34A Solar Arrays** to review **homophones** and High-Frequency Words.

Day 2 Phonics

Objective

The students will sort **homophones** by pairs and trios. They will write high-frequency words and sort **homophones** according to vowel sounds, rhymes, and pronunciations.

Introduction

Before class, duplicate **BLMs SP3-34B–C Homophones I** and **II**. Make enough copies so that each student receives one homophone card. Write the following on the board: Homophones are words that sound the same but have different meanings and spellings. Chorally read the definition together. Distribute the homophone cards to students. Select one student to come to the front of the room and read his or her homophone card aloud, while keeping the card's spelling from the view of the class. Invite the students who have the same pronounced word to come forward. Have each student show the class his/her homophone card so that the different spellings can be seen. Depending on class size, there may be duplicate **homophones**. Assist students in correctly using their **homophones** in sentences. Repeat this process for each pair or trio of **homophones** until all cards have been used.

Directed Instruction

1 Proceed to page 133. Say, spell, and say each Pattern and High-Frequency Word. Provide this week's Challenge Words and have students write them in the spaces provided. Allow students to complete the page independently.

2 Continue to page 134 and assist students by reading questions 1–6 aloud and completing the answers as a class. Allow students to complete exercises 7–10 independently.

3 Homework suggestion: Use **BLM SP3-34D Homophone Sentences** to review words in this lesson.

Proceed to page 133. / Continue to page 134

Differentiated Instruction

- For students who spelled all the words correctly on the Warm Up, select and assign three Extra Challenge Words from the following list: tethered, maneuverable, scorpion, acknowledge, illustrative, Malachi.

- For students who spelled less than half correctly, assign the following Pattern and High-Frequency Words: to, too, two, piece, peace, their, there, they're, once, entire. On the Wrap Up, evaluate these students on the ten words assigned; however, encourage them to attempt to spell all the list words to the best of their ability. They are also responsible for writing the dictated sentences.

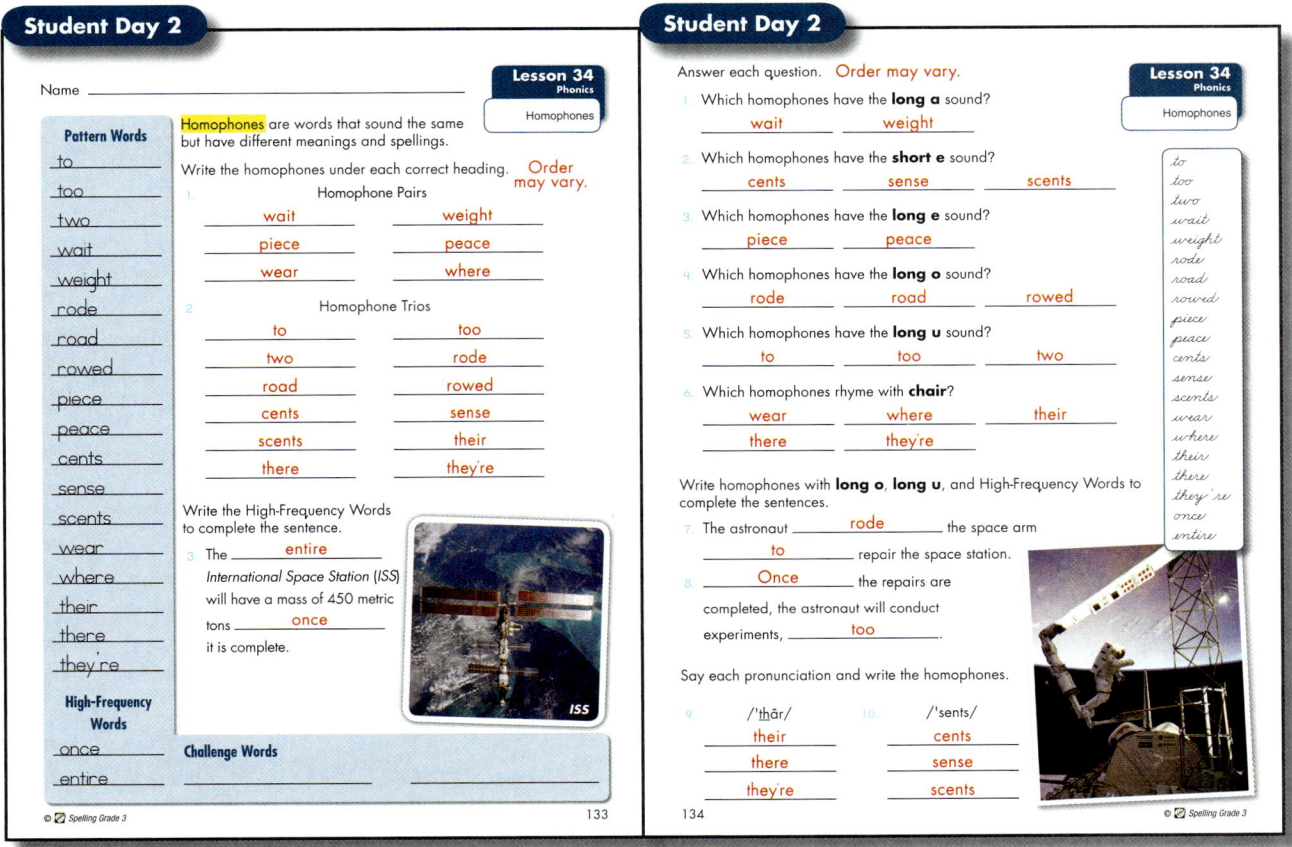

Student Day 2

Name _____

Lesson 34 Phonics
Homophones

Pattern Words

to
too
two
wait
weight
rode
road
rowed
piece
peace
cents
sense
scents
wear
where
their
there
they're

High-Frequency Words

once
entire

Challenge Words

Homophones are words that sound the same but have different meanings and spellings.

Write the homophones under each correct heading.   Order may vary.

1. Homophone Pairs

wait   weight
piece   peace
wear   where

2. Homophone Trios

to   too
two   rode
road   rowed
cents   sense
scents   their
there   they're

Write the High-Frequency Words to complete the sentence.

3. The _entire_ International Space Station (ISS) will have a mass of 450 metric tons _once_ it is complete.

© Spelling Grade 3   133

Student Day 2

Answer each question.   Order may vary.

Lesson 34 Phonics
Homophones

1. Which homophones have the **long a** sound?
   wait   weight

2. Which homophones have the **short e** sound?
   cents   sense   scents

3. Which homophones have the **long e** sound?
   piece   peace

4. Which homophones have the **long o** sound?
   rode   road   rowed

5. Which homophones have the **long u** sound?
   to   too   two

6. Which homophones rhyme with **chair**?
   wear   where   their
   there   they're

Write homophones with **long o**, **long u**, and High-Frequency Words to complete the sentences.

7. The astronaut _rode_ the space arm _to_ repair the space station.

8. _Once_ the repairs are completed, the astronaut will conduct experiments, _too_.

Say each pronunciation and write the homophones.

9. /ˈthâr/   10. /ˈsents/
   their   cents
   there   sense
   they're   scents

to
too
two
wait
weight
rode
road
rowed
piece
peace
cents
sense
scents
wear
where
their
there
they're
once
entire

134

© Spelling Grade 3

Student Spelling Support

1. Write this week's words categorized by patterns on a large piece of paper and attach to the Word Wall.

2. Duplicate **BLMs SP3-34F–G Lesson 34 Spelling Words I and II** on CARD STOCK for students to use as flash cards at school or at home.

3. Use **BLM SP3-01A A Spelling Study Strategy** in instructional groups to provide assistance with some or all of the words.

4. Assist students in writing the Challenge Words, numbers 21 and 22, in the section called My Words for Writing, in the back of their textbook.

5. For auditory and visual learners, dictate sentences with **homophones** and invite students to identify each homophone by selecting the correct flash card from **BLMs SP3-34F–G Lesson 34 Spelling Words I and II**.

6. For advanced learners, use **BLMs SP3-34H–I More Homophones I and II** to extend the homophone lesson by introducing the homophone list as a resource for writing. Invite students to write a journal entry describing their imaginary journey on the *ISS*, utilizing as many **homophones** as possible.

Day 3 Word Study

Objective

The students will utilize dictionary skills by answering questions about the different components of a dictionary entry. They will write **homophones** and high-frequency words in shape boxes to complete sentences.

Introduction

Display **T-6 Dictionary Entry**—from Lesson 5—to review and remind students that a dictionary entry consists of the following five parts: entry word, pronunciation, part of speech, definition, sample sentence. Point out that an entry word may have more than one part of speech and more than one definition. Words with more than one definition may have more than one sample sentence. Words can also have multiple pronunciations. Remind students that **homophones** have the same pronunciation.

Directed Instruction

1 Have students look up *piece* in their Spelling Dictionary. Select a volunteer to identify the two parts of speech for *piece* in this lesson. (**noun** and **verb**) Have students chorally read each definition and sample sentence.

2 Invite students to look up *peace*. Have a volunteer read the definition and sample sentence.

3 Proceed to page 135. Encourage students to use their Spelling Dictionary to complete exercises 1–9 on their own. In exercises 2 and 6, students are asked to write one pronunciation for two differently-spelled words; teach that this is possible because each set of homophones has one pronunciation but different spellings. Complete exercises 10–11 together. Review the page, as a class, when complete.

Day 4 Writing

Objective

The students will correctly write **homophones** according to sentence usage in several paragraphs. They will identify high-frequency words and use them in context in a story starter.

Introduction

Read the text on **T-34 Homophones** aloud to the class. Keep the text from their view. When finished, ask students if the paragraphs made sense. (**Yes.**) Display **T-34 Homophones** on the overhead and point out to students that the **homophones** are in bold. Read the paragraphs again and direct students to follow along as you read. When complete, ask students if the written paragraphs are correct. (**No.**) Have students identify what is wrong. (**Homophones are being used incorrectly in sentence context.**) Invite students to read the sentences aloud and to correct the homophone in each sentence. Write the correct **homophones** on the lines below the paragraphs. Refer to **BLM SP3-34E T-34 Answer Key** for guidance.

Directed Instruction

1 Proceed to page 136 and read the directions aloud. Invite students to listen as you read the paragraphs aloud. Have students reread the paragraphs and correctly replace the **homophones** in bold. Assist students as they complete the page independently.

2 Ask students to share the definition of *homophone*. (**Homophones are words that sound the same but have different meanings and spellings.**)

3 Challenge students to locate the High-Frequency Words, *once* and *entire*, in the paragraphs. Invite students to complete the following story starter: "I traveled to the *ISS* when I was ___ years old to prepare for writing a project. Once my entire project was completed, I was very excited because now I would have time to ___."

4 Homework suggestion: Read the paragraphs about the *International Space Station* on page 136 to an adult. Take a practice spelling test at home or use **BLM SP3-01A A Spelling Study Strategy** for additional practice.

Day 5 Wrap Up

Objective
The students will correctly write dictated spelling words and sentences.

Introduction
Provide a review, utilizing WHITEBOARDS or Student Spelling Support suggestions.

Directed Instruction

1 Dictate the list words by using the Warm Up sentences or developing original ones. Reserve *to*, *too*, and *two* for the dictation sentences.

2 Follow this procedure for the dictation sentences: read the sentence, invite the class to say the sentence with you, then read the sentence again. Dictate the following sentences:
- I am going to ride the shuttle tomorrow.
- I built the rockets and telescopes, too.
- The two heroes walked into the building.

3 If assigned, dictate Extra Challenge Words. Score the test.

Notes

Student Day 3

Name _____

Lesson 34
Word Study

Homophones

Use your Spelling Dictionary to look up the bold words. Answer each question.

1. What guide words are on the top of the page for the entry word **wear**?
   vision - windy
2. What is the pronunciation for **wait** and **weight**? /'wāt/
3. What is the part of speech for **two**? adj.
4. What is the definition for **weight**? heaviness
5. What is the sample sentence for **entire**? The entire space station is very large.
6. What is the pronunciation for **piece** and **peace**? /'pēs/
7. What are the parts of speech for **piece**? n. and v.
8. What are the two definitions for **too**? 1 very. 2 besides; also.
9. What are the sample sentences for **too**? 1 The mission in space was not too long. 2 An astronaut has to go to school and study hard, too.

Write Pattern Words and High-Frequency Words to complete each sentence.

10. O n c e the astronauts are in space, they feel no w e i g h t the e n t i r e time.

11. T h e y ' r e going to w e a r special suits during t h e i r space walk.

to
too
two
wait
weight
rode
road
rowed
piece
peace
cents
sense
scents
wear
where
their
there
they're
once
entire

© Spelling Grade 3   135

Student Day 4

Read the paragraphs below about the *International Space Station*. The homophones in bold are used incorrectly. Write the correct homophone for each bold word below.

Lesson 34
Writing

Homophones

The U.S. National Aeronautics Space Administration (NASA) announced a program in 1984 to establish a permanent space station called *Freedom*. In 1994, the *Freedom* project was combined with the *Russian Mir 2* project and produced the *International Space Station (ISS)*. Crews are currently building the *ISS* and conducting experiments on board the station. Some astronauts live on the *ISS* for long periods, and others visit when bringing supplies from Earth.

Each **peace** of equipment is important **two** the *ISS* and sometimes is in need of repair by the astronauts. **There** responsible for repairing and constructing the *ISS* so that crews can continue to live and work in space. When repair or construction is needed, astronauts will perform a space walk. They **where** special suits during **they're** entire space walk. These suits are designed to protect the astronaut while in space.

Astronauts are sometimes attached to a space arm while on a space walk. The robotic arm will take them **wear** they need to go during their time outside the *ISS*. **Their** are many procedures to follow during this time. Usually, **to** astronauts perform a space walk at one time. Once the crew has completed the space walk mission, they return to the *ISS*.

Do you think that you would like to be an astronaut? Would you be nervous or would you **cents** God's **piece** while floating in space?

to
too
two
wait
weight
rode
road
rowed
piece
peace
cents
sense
scents
wear
where
their
there
they're
once
entire

1. piece   2. to   3. They're
4. wear   5. their   6. where
7. There   8. two   9. sense
10. peace

136

© Spelling Grade 3

Student Pages
Pages 137–140

Lesson Materials

BLM SP3-35A
T-36
BLM SP3-35B
T-35
BLM SP3-01A
Whiteboards

Transportation

The theme of this lesson is the Shuttle Carrier Aircraft (SCA). The SCA is a modified 747 jetliner that carries the space shuttle back to the Kennedy Space Center in Florida when the shuttle is forced to land somewhere else due to adverse weather conditions. For this reason, the SCA is often referred to as the piggyback jet.

Day 1 Warm Up

Objective

The students will accurately spell and write words with **final syllables -sion** and **-tion**. They will spell and write high-frequency words and challenge words.

Introduction

Before class, select Challenge Words for numbers 21 and 22 from a cross-curricular subject, words misspelled on previous assignments, or words that interest your students. The word *revolution* has **-tion** and is suggested for number 21. Administer the Warm Up.

Directed Instruction

1 Say each word, use it in a sentence, and then repeat the word.

Pattern Words

1.	station	The train <u>station</u> is busy.	station
2.	nation	Canada is a <u>nation</u>.	nation
3.	action	The player's <u>action</u> was fast.	action
4.	motion	The shuttle is in <u>motion</u>.	motion
5.	vision	<u>Vision</u> is one of our five senses.	vision
6.	mission	The space shuttle is on a <u>mission</u>.	mission
7.	position	The shuttle's <u>position</u> is upright.	position
8.	location	What is the space center's <u>location</u>?	location
9.	addition	I know how to do <u>addition</u>.	addition
10.	subtraction	It is important to know <u>subtraction</u>.	subtraction
11.	conclusion	I liked the <u>conclusion</u> of the story.	conclusion
12.	confusion	In my <u>confusion</u> I made a mistake.	confusion
13.	division	<u>Division</u> is a math concept.	division
14.	permission	Mom gave me <u>permission</u> to stay.	permission
15.	exploration	The <u>exploration</u> of space is exciting.	exploration
16.	education	We are getting a good <u>education</u>.	education
17.	television	Dad watches the news on <u>television</u>.	television
18.	multiplication	Do you know <u>multiplication</u>?	multiplication

High-Frequency Words

19.	silent	One should be <u>silent</u> during prayer.	silent
20.	science	Doug's favorite subject is <u>science</u>.	science

Challenge Words

21. _____

22. _____

2 Allow students to self-correct their pretest, following this procedure:

a. Write each word on the board. Discuss the letter/sound relationships in each word. Point out that the final syllable **-sion** can be pronounced two ways—/zhən/ as in *vision* and /shən/ as in *mission*. When **-sion** comes after a vowel, it usually says /zhən/; when **-sion** comes after a consonant, it usually says /shən/. The final syllable **-tion** also makes the sound /shən/.

b. As a class, read, spell, and read each word again. Direct students to circle misspelled words with a colored pencil and rewrite them correctly.

3 Proof each student's Warm Up.

4 Homework suggestion: Use **BLM SP3-35A Piggyback** to practice the Pattern and High-Frequency Words in this lesson.

Day 2 Phonics

Objective
The students will sort words by **final syllables -sion** and **-tion**. They will supply the missing syllables in pattern words and sort words by syllables. They will write high-frequency and challenge words.

Introduction
Remind the students that **-sion** can be pronounced two ways—/zhən/ as in *vision* or /shən/ as in *mission*. Write the words *vision* and *mission* on the board. Circle **-sion** in each word and underline the letter that precedes it—*i* in *vision* and *s* in *mission*. Explain that the sound /zhən/ usually comes after a vowel; the sound /shən/ usually comes after a consonant. Instruct the students that **-tion** also says /shən/ as in *action*. Words with final syllables **-sion** and **-tion** are often confused. The spelling pattern for each word must be memorized.

Directed Instruction

1 Display **T-36 Lessons 31–35 Study Sheet** on the overhead and refer to Lesson 35 words.

Write the following two column headings on the board:

-sion		-tion		
vi|sion	con|fu|sion	ac|tion	po|si|tion	ex|plo|ra|tion
di|vi|sion	con|clu|sion	na|tion	lo|ca|tion	sub|trac|tion
mis|sion	per|mis|sion	sta|tion	ad|di|tion	mul|ti|pli|ca|tion
te|le|vi|sion		mo|tion	e|du|ca|tion	

2 Select volunteers to read a word from the overhead, name the final syllable, and come to the board to write the word in the appropriate column. When finished, chorally read each column, clapping out the syllables in each word.

© Spelling Grade 3

Differentiated Instruction

- For students who spelled all the words correctly on the Warm Up, select and assign three Extra Challenge Words from the following list: modified, jetliner, scissors, punctuate, luminous, Zechariah.

- For students who spelled less than half correctly, assign the following Pattern and High-Frequency Words: vision, action, nation, station, motion, position, television, permission, silent, science. On the Wrap Up, evaluate these students on the ten words assigned; however, encourage them to attempt to spell all the list words to the best of their ability. They are also responsible for writing the dictated sentences.

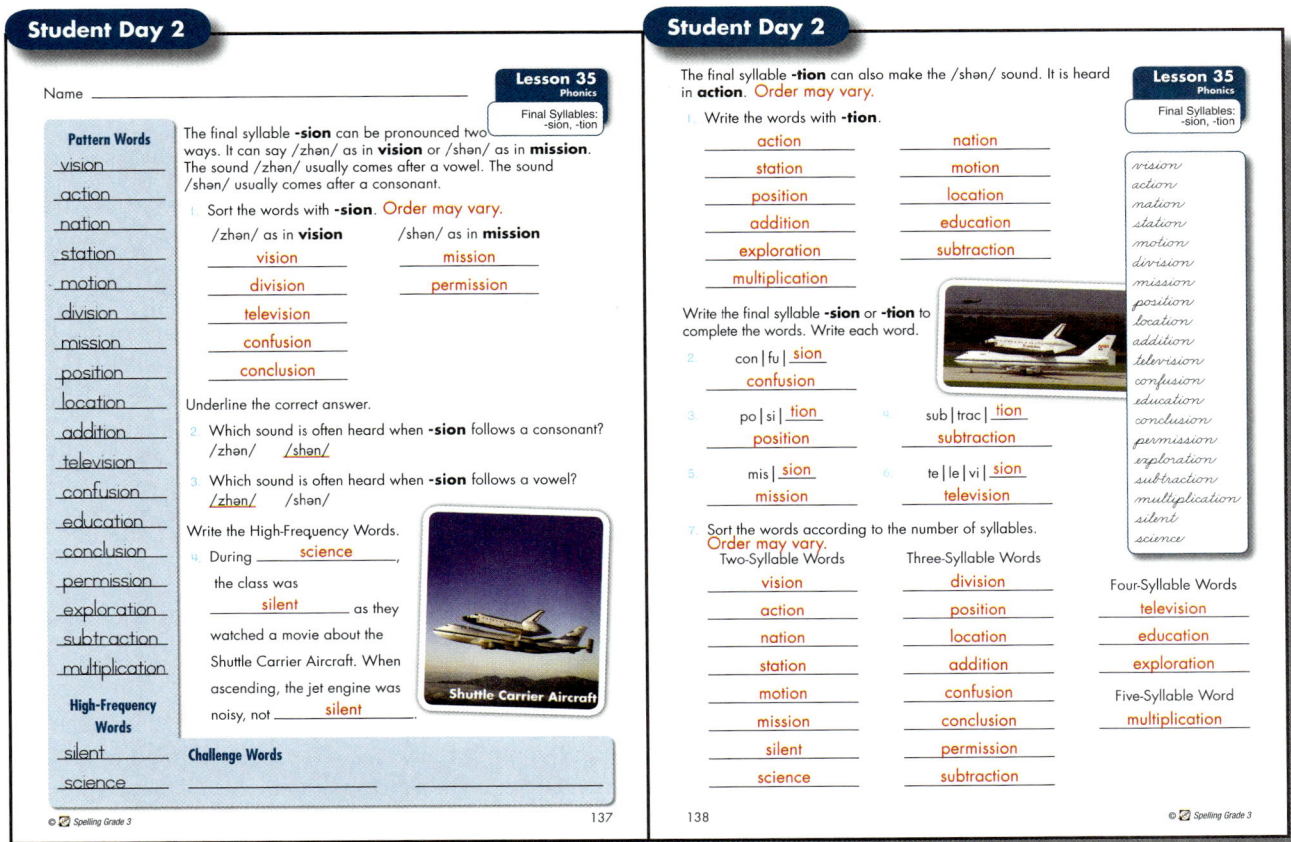

Student
Spelling Support

1. Write this week's words categorized by patterns on a large piece of paper and attach to the Word Wall.

2. Duplicate **BLMs SP3-35C–D Lesson 35 Spelling Words I** and **II** on CARD STOCK for students to use as flash cards at school or at home.

3. Use **BLM SP3-01A A Spelling Study Strategy** in instructional groups to provide assistance with some or all of the words.

4. Assist students in writing the Challenge Words, numbers 21 and 22, in the section called My Words for Writing, in the back of their textbook.

5. For visual learners, write each Pattern Word using a BLACK MARKER on a 3" X 5" INDEX CARD, omitting **-tion** or **-sion**. On eleven additional index cards write **-tion** with a RED MARKER. On seven more index cards write **-sion** with a BLUE MARKER. Have students shuffle all the cards together and place facedown on the table. Students take turns turning over two cards. If the two cards form a word, he/she places the cards next to himself/herself. If the two cards do not form a word, they are placed facedown on the table again. Students may check their accuracy by looking at the list of words in Lesson 35.

Cont. on page 141

3 Divide each word into syllables, explaining that both **-sion** and **-tion** are considered syllables. Include the High-Frequency Words by writing them on the board and dividing them into syllables—si|lent, sci|ence. Point out that each long *i* is in an open syllable.

4 Proceed to page 137. Say, spell, and say each Pattern and High-Frequency Word. Provide this week's Challenge Words and have students write them in the spaces provided. Select a student to read the sentences at the top of the page and the directions. Allow students to complete the page independently.

5 Continue to page 138. Assist students as needed.

6 Homework suggestion: Use **BLM SP3-35B Match Me** to review **final syllables** with **-sion** and **-tion** and High-Frequency Words.

Day 3 Word Study
Objective

The students will match list words with their definitions. They will write the pattern words that name the mathematical operations used in story problems. They will write operations that use the symbols.

Introduction

Inform the students that the class is going to play a dictionary drill game with this week's words. Instruct students to place their spelling book on top of their desk, listen for the list word, locate the word in the Spelling Dictionary, and stand when they find it. Call on a student to say-spell-say the entry word and read its definition. After each word is spelled aloud and its definition is read, have students close their book and sit down before the next word is given.

Directed Instruction

1 Proceed to page 139. For exercises 1–12, remind students to read each definition carefully and to use the Spelling Dictionary as needed.

2 For exercises 13–14, select volunteers to read each story problem and its answer. The students write the mathematical operation that was used to solve the problem. Provide needed assistance.

Day 4 Writing
Objective

The students will read an invitation and write a thank-you note.

Introduction

Display **T-35 Invitation/Thank-You Note** on the overhead showing the invitation and covering the thank-you note with a piece of paper. Explain that an invitation usually consists of the five W's—who, what, when, where, and why. Read the invitation. Define a *planetarium* as a building in which there is a large room with a domed ceiling. Images of the night sky are projected onto the ceiling for an audience to see the location and position of stars and planets. Have students tell about any invitations they may have received. Explain that if you have been invited as a guest to an event, it is courteous to write a thank-you note. Read the thank-you note and point out the following components: the date in the upper right-hand corner, a comma after the greeting, each indented paragraph, the person being thanked for the gift or invitation to a special event, something especially nice about the gift or event, the indented closing, the comma after the closing, the name of the person writing the note.

Directed Instruction

1 Proceed to page 140. Select a volunteer to read the sentences at the top of the page and the invitation. Hold a class discussion about what it would be like to attend such an event. Ask students to name things that they might see, hear, smell, and touch. Lead a discussion about their favorite part of the imaginary field trip that they could include in the thank-you note.

2 Direct the students to complete the page, reminding them to include as many spelling words as possible in the thank-you note.

3 Homework suggestion: Read the invitation and thank-you note on page 140 to an adult. Take a practice spelling test at home or use **BLM SP3-01A A Spelling Study Strategy** for additional practice.

Day 5 Wrap Up

Objective
The students will correctly write dictated spelling words and sentences.

Introduction
Provide a review, utilizing WHITEBOARDS or Student Spelling Support suggestions.

Directed Instruction

1 Dictate the list words by using the Warm Up sentences or developing original ones. Reserve *nation*, *position*, and *permission* for the dictation sentences.

2 Follow this procedure for the dictation sentences: read the sentence, invite the class to say the sentence with you, then read the sentence again. Dictate the following sentences:
- There are fifty states in our nation.
- Which position does Bill play in baseball?
- Mrs. Smith gave me permission to leave early.

3 If assigned, dictate Extra Challenge Words. Score the test.

Student Spelling Support

Cont. from page 140

6. For a social studies and math connection, inform the class that when the space shuttle is transported on the Shuttle Carrier Aircraft, the SCA is so heavy that it can only fly 1,000 miles before having to land and refuel. Using a RULER and the map scale on a UNITED STATES MAP, plot every 1,000 miles from Los Angeles to Florida, simulating the possible flight pattern from Edwards Air Force Base to the Kennedy Space Center. Edwards Air Force Base is located northeast of Los Angeles in the Mojave Desert. The Kennedy Space Center is located on Merritt Island on the east coast of the Florida peninsula. As a "pretend" flight pattern is plotted, have students tell how many times the aircraft would have to land and refuel. Have students also name the possible states that the SCA may fly over.

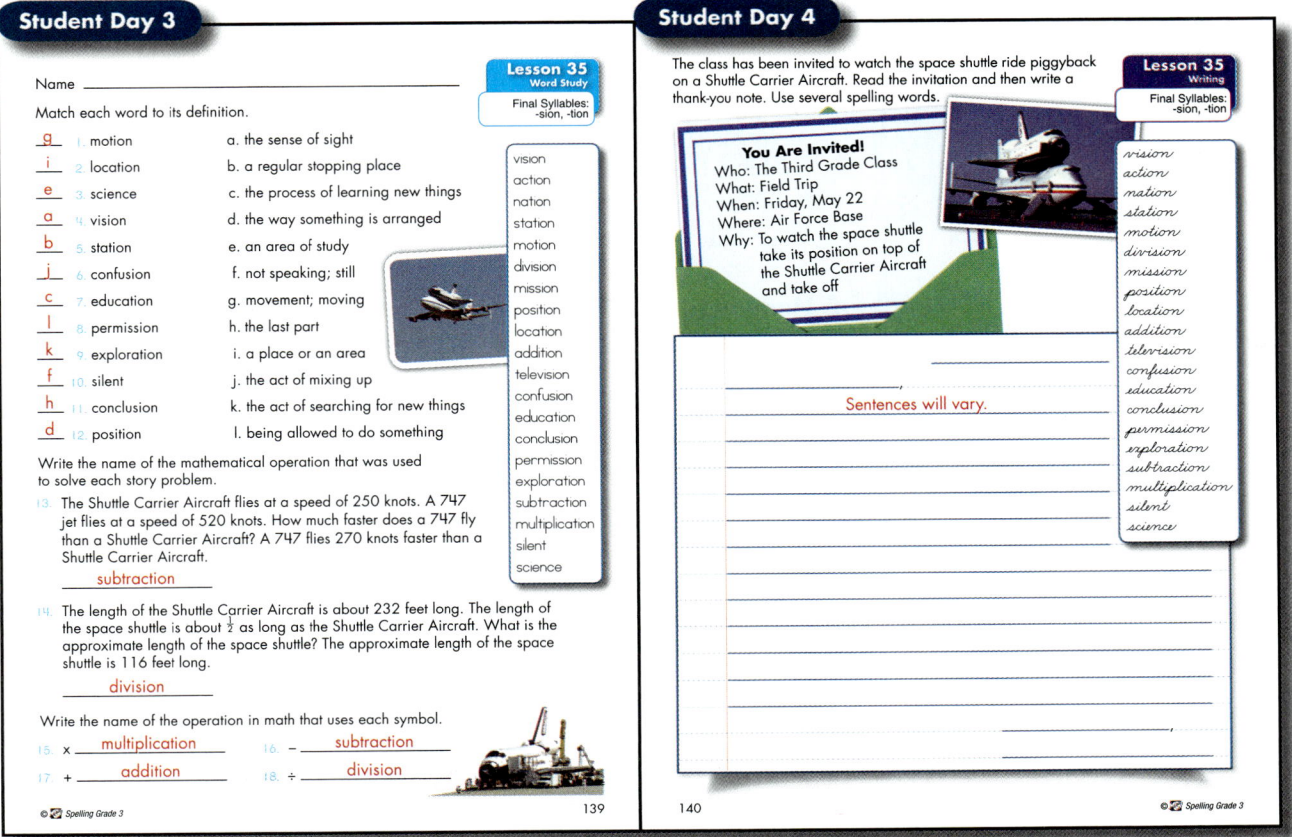

Student Day 3

Name _____

Match each word to its definition.

g	1. motion	a. the sense of sight
i	2. location	b. a regular stopping place
e	3. science	c. the process of learning new things
a	4. vision	d. the way something is arranged
b	5. station	e. an area of study
j	6. confusion	f. not speaking; still
c	7. education	g. movement; moving
l	8. permission	h. the last part
k	9. exploration	i. a place or an area
f	10. silent	j. the act of mixing up
h	11. conclusion	k. the act of searching for new things
d	12. position	l. being allowed to do something

Write the name of the mathematical operation that was used to solve each story problem.

13. The Shuttle Carrier Aircraft flies at a speed of 250 knots. A 747 jet flies at a speed of 520 knots. How much faster does a 747 fly than a Shuttle Carrier Aircraft? A 747 flies 270 knots faster than a Shuttle Carrier Aircraft.
    subtraction

14. The length of the Shuttle Carrier Aircraft is about 232 feet long. The length of the space shuttle is about ½ as long as the Shuttle Carrier Aircraft. What is the approximate length of the space shuttle? The approximate length of the space shuttle is 116 feet long.
    division

Write the name of the operation in math that uses each symbol.

15. × __multiplication__   16. − __subtraction__
17. + __addition__   18. ÷ __division__

Lesson 35 Word Study
Final Syllables: -sion, -tion

vision
action
nation
station
motion
division
mission
position
location
addition
television
confusion
education
conclusion
permission
exploration
subtraction
multiplication
silent
science

139

Student Day 4

The class has been invited to watch the space shuttle ride piggyback on a Shuttle Carrier Aircraft. Read the invitation and then write a thank-you note. Use several spelling words.

You Are Invited!
Who: The Third Grade Class
What: Field Trip
When: Friday, May 22
Where: Air Force Base
Why: To watch the space shuttle take its position on top of the Shuttle Carrier Aircraft and take off

Sentences will vary.

Lesson 35 Writing
Final Syllables: -sion, -tion

vision
action
nation
station
motion
division
mission
position
location
addition
television
confusion
education
conclusion
permission
exploration
subtraction
multiplication
silent
science

140

© Spelling Grade 3

Student Pages
Pages 141–144

Lesson Materials

P-9
P-10
T-36
BLM SP3-36A
BLM SP3-36B
BLM SP3-36C
Transparency pen
BLM SP3-36D
BLMs SP3-36E–F
3" × 5" Index cards

Day 1 Plural Nouns

Objective
The students will spell, identify, and circle words that are **plural nouns**.

Introduction
Teacher Note: This week's lesson incorporates the Pattern and High-Frequency Words taught in Lessons 31–35 using a variety of activities such as sorting, a crossword puzzle, silly song titles, shape boxes, and a word search.

Display **P-9 Spelling Rules** to review the following rules: For most nouns, add **-s** to make them plural (rule number 11). For nouns that end with *ch*, *sh*, *s*, *x*, *o*, or *z*, add **-es** to make them plural (rule number 12). Display **P-10 Spelling Rules** to review the following rules: For nouns that end with a **consonant** and **y**, change **y** to **i** before adding **-es** to make them plural (rule number 13). For nouns that end with **f** or **fe**, change **f** or **fe** to **v** before adding **-es** to make them plural (rule number 14).

Directed Instruction
1 Display **T-36 Lessons 31–35 Study Sheet** on the overhead to review Lesson 31 words in unison, using the say-spell-say technique.

2 Read the words in Lesson 31 again, this time pausing after each word to ask students to write the singular form of each plural noun on the board.

3 Ask students to identify Lesson 31 words that add **-s**, add **-es**, change **y** to **i** before adding **-es**, change **f** or **fe** to **v** before adding **-es**, or change several letters to form the plural. Have students identify words that are spelled the same in both the singular and plural forms.

4 Proceed to page 141. Explain that the box contains all the Pattern and High-Frequency Words in Lessons 31–35. This list is the same list of words that were previously displayed on the overhead. Encourage students to use this list as a review tool. Allow students to complete the page independently.

5 Distribute one copy of **BLM SP3-36A Lessons 31–35 Study Sheet** to each student to take home for study.

6 Homework suggestion: Duplicate one copy of **BLM SP3-36B Rocket Launch** for each student to practice words from Lessons 31 and 32.

Day 2 Schwa Before n Syllables and Final Syllables with -le

Objective
The students will spell and write words with **schwa before n syllables**. They will spell and write words that contain **final syllables with -le** in a crossword puzzle.

Introduction
Display **T-36 Lessons 31–35 Study Sheet** on the overhead. Point out that each of the words in Lessons 32 and 33 contains both stressed and unstressed syllables. Review that stressed syllables are the syllables that are pronounced the loudest in each word; unstressed syllables are not spoken as loudly. Vowels in an unstressed syllable have the schwa sound /ə/, which is the same sound as **short u** as heard in *sun*.

Read several words from Lesson 32 and clap out the syllables. Have students give a louder clap to each stressed syllable.

Directed Instruction

1 Draw this simple diagram on the board. Tell students that the letters surrounding the circle spell a word from Lesson 32, but that they must first find the correct beginning letter and then read the other letters in a clockwise direction. Choose a volunteer to find the first letter (**f**) and spell the word (**frozen**).

2 Display **T-36 Lessons 31–35 Study Sheet** to review Lessons 32–33 words in unison, using the say-spell-say technique. Have students identify and circle the vowels with a schwa sound in Lesson 32 words.

3 Proceed to page 142. Allow students to complete the page independently. Encourage them to use their Spelling Dictionary as needed.

4 Homework suggestion: Distribute a copy of **BLM SP3-36C Planets** to each student to practice words that contain **final syllables with -le** and **homophones**.

Day 3 Homophones and High-Frequency Words

Objective

The students will find and circle **homophones** that have been used incorrectly in the context of song titles. They will write the correct homophones. They will write high-frequency words in shape boxes.

Introduction

Before class, write the sentences below with **homophones** that have been used incorrectly. Read each sentence aloud and tell students that there is a word in each sentence that is a homophone, but that it is the wrong word for the context of that sentence.

• Sam would like two go into space. (**to**)
• He'll have to weight until he is older to be an astronaut. (**wait**)
• Astronauts where special space suits. (**wear**)
• They will use they're suits in airless environments. (**their**)

Have students raise their hand when they have found the incorrect homophone. Call on volunteers to identify and write the correct homophone for each sentence. Conclude the lesson by asking students why each incorrect homophone did not fit the sentence.

Directed Instruction

1 Display **T-36 Lessons 31–35 Study Sheet** to review Lesson 34 words and High-Frequency Words in unison, using the say-spell-say technique.

2 Select several High-Frequency Words and write them on the board. Have volunteers trace around each word and tell how many tall letters or tail letters are in each word.

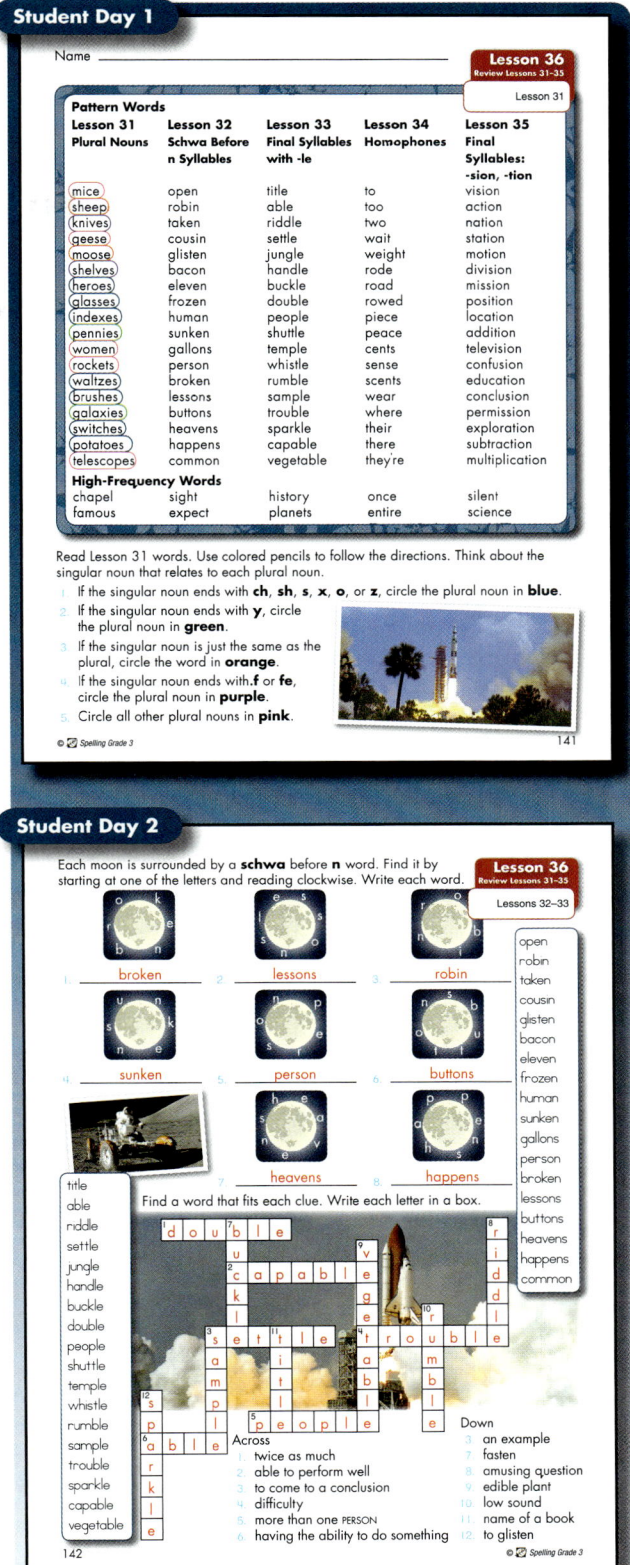

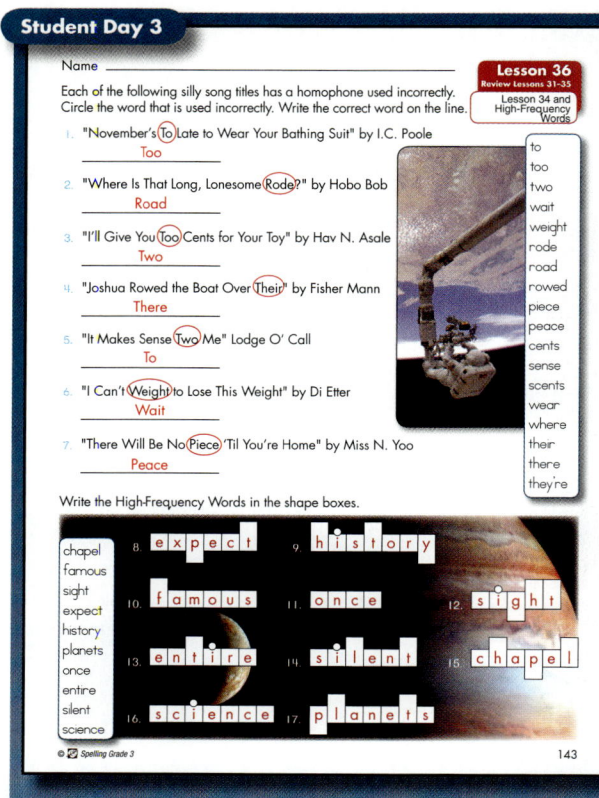

Name _____

Each of the following silly song titles has a homophone used incorrectly. Circle the word that is used incorrectly. Write the correct word on the line.

Lesson 36
Review Lessons 31–35
Lesson 34 and
High-Frequency
Words

1. "November's (To) Late to Wear Your Bathing Suit" by I.C. Poole
   Too

2. "Where Is That Long, Lonesome (Rode)?" by Hobo Bob
   Road

3. "I'll Give You (Too) Cents for Your Toy" by Hav N. Asale
   Two

4. "Joshua Rowed the Boat Over (Their)" by Fisher Mann
   There

5. "It Makes Sense (Two) Me" Lodge O' Call
   To

6. "I Can't (Weight) to Lose This Weight" by Di Etter
   Wait

7. "There Will Be No (Piece) 'Til You're Home" by Miss N. Yoo
   Peace

to
too
two
wait
weight
rode
road
rowed
piece
peace
cents
sense
scents
wear
where
their
there
they're

Write the High-Frequency Words in the shape boxes.

chapel
famous
sight
expect
history
planets
once
entire
silent
science

8. e x p e c t
9. h i s t o r y
10. f a m o u s
11. o n c e
12. s i g h t
13. e n t i r e
14. s i l e n t
15. c h a p e l
16. s c i e n c e
17. p l a n e t s

© Spelling Grade 3   143

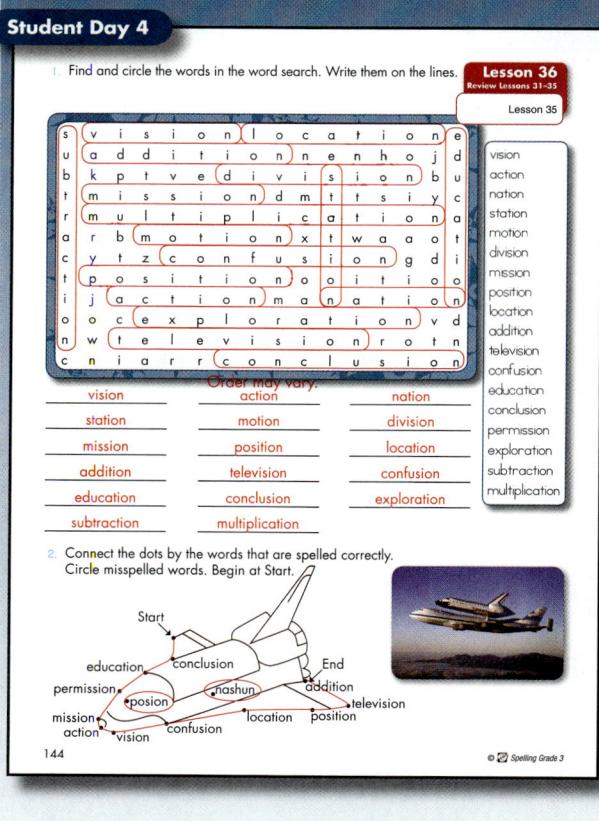

1. Find and circle the words in the word search. Write them on the lines.

Lesson 36
Review Lessons 31–35
Lesson 35

vision
action
nation
station
motion
division
mission
position
location
addition
television
confusion
education
conclusion
permission
exploration
subtraction
multiplication

Order may vary:

vision	action	nation
station	motion	division
mission	position	location
addition	television	confusion
education	conclusion	exploration
subtraction	multiplication	

2. Connect the dots by the words that are spelled correctly. Circle misspelled words. Begin at Start.

Start
education   conclusion   End
permission   nashun   addition
posion   television
mission   location   position
action   confusion
vision

144   © Spelling Grade 3

---

3. Draw students' attention to Lesson 34 words. Select volunteers to use each word correctly in a sentence. Be sure to clarify and reinforce the meaning of each homophone.

4. Proceed to page 143 and allow students to independently complete the page.

Day 4 Final Syllables: -sion, -tion

Objective

The students will find words with **final syllables -sion** and **-tion** in a word search. They will complete a dot-to-dot puzzle by connecting the dots near the words that are spelled correctly and circle misspelled words.

Introduction

Display **T-36 Lessons 31–35 Study Sheet** to review Lesson 35 words. Use a TRANSPARENCY PEN to underline **-sion** or **-tion** in each word. Divide the class into two groups. Tell one group that they will stand when you read a word that ends in **-tion**. The other group will stand for **-sion** words. Read each word, invite the appropriate group to stand, and pronounce each syllable. Have students say and spell each syllable and then say and spell the entire word. The list below is provided for reference.

vi|sion	ac|tion	na|tion	sta|tion
mo|tion	di|vi|sion	mis|sion	po|si|tion
lo|ca|tion	ad|di|tion	te|le|vi|sion	
con|fu|sion	e|du|ca|tion	con|clu|sion	
per|mis|sion	ex|plo|ra|tion	sub|trac|tion	
mul|ti|pli|ca|tion			

Directed Instruction

1. Refer to **T-36 Lessons 31–35 Study Sheet** to review Lesson 35 in unison, using the say-spell-say technique. Remind students that **-sion** has two sounds; /shən/ and /zhən/. The letters **-sion** usually make the /shən/ sound when they come after a consonant and the /zhən/ sound after a vowel. The letters **-tion** also have the /shən/ sound.

2. Select a few words from Lesson 35 to design an abbreviated word search on the board. Choose words with similar letters so the words can intersect one another. Select a volunteer to identify and circle the hidden words.

3. Proceed to page 144. Allow students to complete the page independently.

4. Homework suggestion: Duplicate one copy of **BLM SP3-36D Shuttle Piggyback** for each student to practice words that contain **final syllables -sion** and **-tion**. Prepare for the Assessment by studying the words on **BLM SP3-36A Lessons 31–35 Study Sheet** that was sent home on Day 1.

Day 5 Assessment

Objective

The students will accurately select the appropriate answer circle within the context of a sentence and fill it in.

Introduction

Teacher Note: The Test makes provision for Differentiated Instruction. The first ten sentences include the words assigned to students with shortened lists. Encourage these students to try all the sentences, but only grade the first ten sentences. The Sample will be dictated and the sentences are provided below for reference. The Test is found on two blackline masters.

Prior to handing out the Test, read through the sentences and select words that may be confusing or challenging for students. Inform students that the Test will not be a teacher-dictated test, but that you will be reviewing some difficult words that are in sentences on the test. Write the words on the board and sound them out with students before the Test.

Directed Instruction

1 Distribute a copy of **BLMs SP3-36E–F Lessons 31–35 Test I** and **II** to each student and a 3" × 5" INDEX CARD to be used as a marker. Remind students to fill in each answer circle completely and to erase completely if they wish to change an answer.

2 Lead students to correctly place their marker below the Sample, listen to the following dictation, and find the correct answer choice:

Sample

The janitor will <u>handel</u> repairs to the <u>broken</u> <u>shelves</u>. <u>All correct</u>
● Ⓑ Ⓒ Ⓓ

Say, "The circle below the first underlined word has been filled in to show that it is the misspelled word. You will continue the test now on your own. Move your marker below each sentence and read each sentence. Choose the word that you think is misspelled and fill in the circle below it. If all the words are spelled correctly, fill in the fourth circle underneath *All correct*."

3 Assist students as needed while they read the sentences and complete the Test on their own.

1. The heroes were able to lift off in the shuttle.
2. People have used rockets to launch television satellites.
3. Telescopes provide improved vision of distant galaxies.
4. It's common to see a robin in the springtime.
5. Two mice ate an entire slice of cheese.
6. Jan got permission to open the sample of soap.
7. Our science book tells the history of the discovery of the planets.
8. They're ready to settle on a title for the book.
9. One person can take action to bring peace to others.
10. The chapel in Paris is a famous sight.
11. Eleven geese started across the dirt road.
12. We'll use knives to slice the bacon and potatoes.
13. My cousin had to take lessons before she could dance waltzes.
14. The stars sparkle and glisten in the heavens.
15. Mom helped me learn addition with pennies and buttons.
16. Once we arrived at the station, we had to wait a few hours.
17. The moose crossed the frozen lake without trouble.
18. It shows good sense to check your division by using multiplication.
19. No one knew the exact location of the sunken temple.
20. Where will the astronauts go on their next mission?

Manuscript Handwriting Models

Aa Bb Cc Dd Ee

Ff Gg Hh Ii Jj Kk

Ll Mm Nn Oo Pp

Qq Rr Ss Tt Uu

Vv Ww Xx Yy Zz

. ? ! , '

bullet train

Cursive Handwriting Models

Aa Bb Cc Dd

Ee Ff Gg Hh

Ii Jj Kk Ll

Mm Nn Oo Pp

Qq Rr Ss Tt

Uu Vv Ww Xx

Yy Zz

. ? ! , '

skiing

© *Spelling Grade 3*

My Words for Writing

A *a*

_____
_____
_____
_____

_____
_____
_____
_____

_____
_____
_____
_____

aircraft carrier

B *B*

_____
_____
_____
_____

_____
_____
_____
_____

_____
_____
_____
_____

C c

_____

_____

_____

_____

car

D d

_____

_____

_____

E e

_____

_____

_____

F *F*

freighter

G *G*

H *H*

I *i*

_____ _____
_____ _____
_____ _____
_____ _____

J *j*

_____ _____
_____ _____
_____ _____

K *k*

_____ _____
_____ _____
_____
_____

kayak

L *L*

M *m*

motorcycle

N *n*

O *O*

P *P*

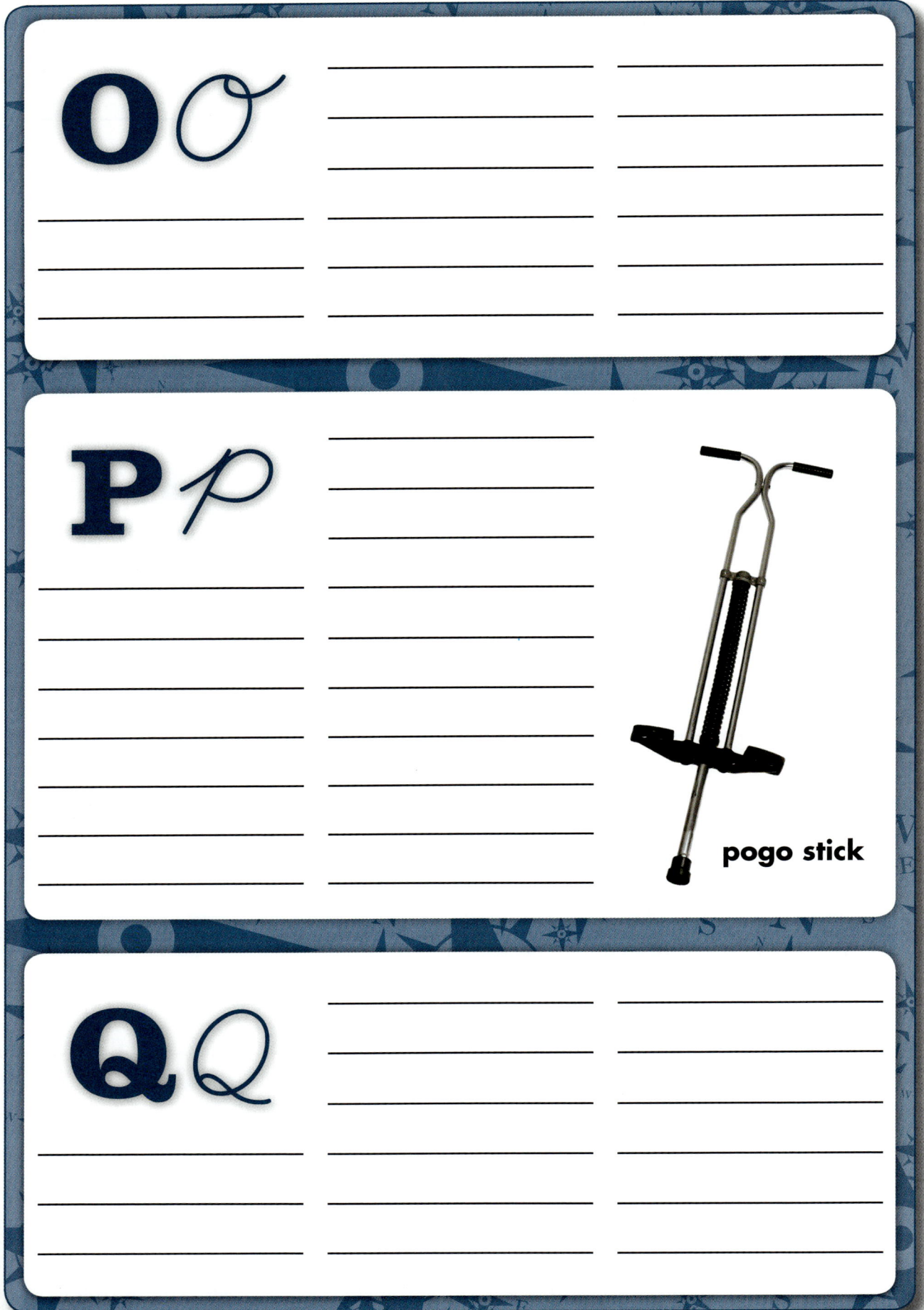

pogo stick

Q *Q*

R *R*

S *S*

space shuttle

T *T*

U $\mathcal{U}$

unicycle

V $\mathcal{V}$

W $\mathcal{W}$

X *x*

Y *y*

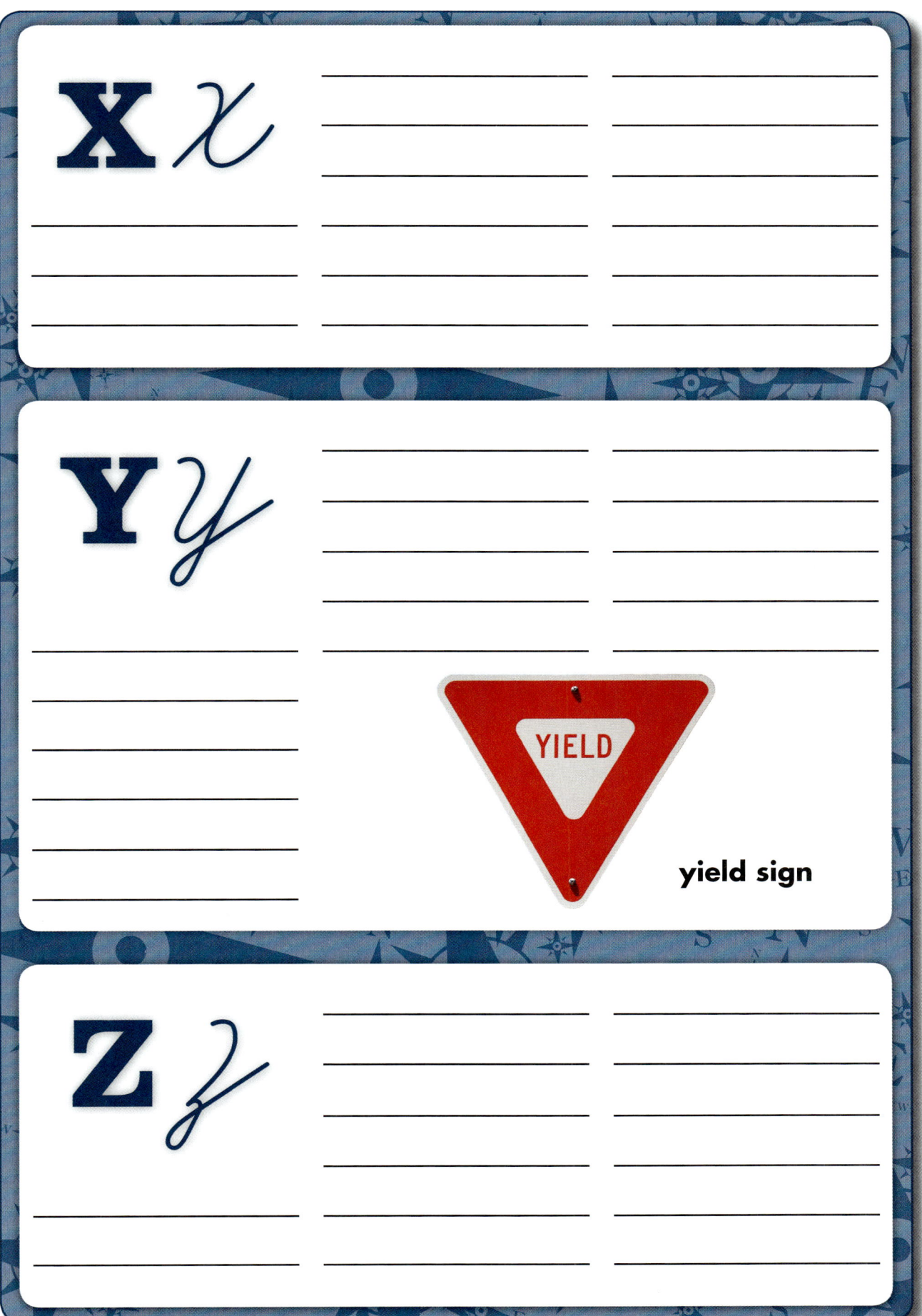

yield sign

Z *z*

Pronunciation Key

Letters written within slashes on this key represent common phonemes, the smallest units of distinct sound in English. Listed to the right are variant spellings for these sounds.

Consonants

/b/	**b**i**b**, **b**a**b**y, **b**u**bb**le
/ch/	**ch**ild, mu**ch**, pa**tch**, na**t**ure, ques**ti**on
/d/	**d**ay, sa**d**, la**dd**er
/f/	**f**ish, o**f**ten, o**ff**, **ph**one, cou**gh**
/g/	**g**o, bi**g**, wi**gg**le, **gh**ost, lea**gue**
/h/	**h**ot, **h**urry, **wh**o
/j/	**j**ump, **j**u**dge**, **g**ym, ran**ge**
/k/	**k**eep, **c**up, si**ck**, ti**ck**le, pi**c**nic, anti**que**, **sch**ool
/l/	**l**ook, ta**ll**, **l**i**l**y, a**ll**ey, penci**l**
/m/	**m**y, co**m**e, **m**o**mm**y
/n/	**n**o, **n**i**n**e, wi**nn**er, **kn**ow
/ng/	ri**ng**, si**ng**i**ng**
/p/	**p**ie, ho**p**e, a**pp**le
/kw/	**qu**een, **qu**iet, **ch**oir
/r/	**r**ed, **r**ose, nea**r**, a**rr**ow
/s/	**s**ee, le**ss**on, mi**ss**, **c**ity, dan**ce**
/sh/	**sh**e, wi**sh**, **s**ugar, ma**ch**ine, na**ti**on, spe**ci**al
/t/	**t**ie, ea**t**, **t**a**tt**le, walk**ed**
/th/	**th**ink, bo**th** (breath)
/<u>th</u>/	**th**is, ei**th**er (voice)
/v/	**v**ase, sa**v**e
/w/	**w**e, **w**ell
/hw/ or /w/	**wh**at, **wh**y, **wh**ether
/y/	**y**es, **y**ellow, on**i**on, mill**i**on
/z/	**z**oo, fu**zz**y, ma**z**e, ha**s**
/zh/	mea**s**ure, vi**s**ion

Vowels

/ā/	**a**ble, d**a**te, **ai**d, p**ay**, **eigh**t, gr**ea**t
/a/	p**a**t, **a**pple
/ä/	f**a**ther (same sound as /o/)
/är/	f**ar**m, **ar**m, sp**ar**kle, h**ear**t
/ē/	m**e**, b**ee**, m**ea**t, ch**ie**f, c**ei**ling, lad**y**, vall**ey**
/e/	b**e**t, **e**dge, m**e**ss, r**ea**dy, fr**ie**nd
/ī/	**I**, f**i**ne, n**igh**t, p**ie**, b**y**
/i/	h**i**s, **i**t, g**y**m
/ō/	b**o**ne, **o**pen, c**oa**t, sh**ow**, s**ou**l
/o/	t**o**p, **o**tter, b**o**ther (same sound as /ä/)
/ò/	s**o**ft, **o**ften, **a**lso, h**au**l, c**augh**t, dr**aw**, b**ough**t
/oi/	j**oy**, f**oi**l, r**oy**al
/oo/	b**oo**k, p**u**ll, sh**ou**ld
/o͞o/	p**oo**l, t**u**be, t**o**, st**ew**, fr**ui**t, gr**ou**p
/yo͞o/	**u**se, f**ue**l, p**ew**, **you**, b**eau**ty
/ou/	**ou**t, n**ow**, t**ow**el
/u/	h**u**t, l**o**ve, c**ou**ple, an**o**ther (used in stressed syllables)
/âr/	**air**, **c**are, b**ear**, Janu**ar**y
/ôr/	f**or**, t**or**n, c**or**n, ch**or**e, w**ar**m
/îr/	**ear**, p**ier**ce, w**eir**d
/ûr/	t**ur**n, w**or**d, th**ir**d, t**ur**tle, fert**i**le, h**ear**d (used in stressed syllables) furth**er**, col**or** (used in unstressed syllables)
/ə/	schwa—the /u/ sound in unstressed syllables: **a**like sudd**e**n penc**i**l cott**o**n circ**u**s

Spelling Dictionary

The Guide Words are two words at the top of the page in a dictionary. These two words are the first and last words defined on a page.

fields   **glisten**

fields   **glisten**

fields /ˈfēldz/ n. pl. open areas of land that do not have buildings or a lot of trees. *Farmer Jon picked the crops in*

fields

fruit /ˈfroot/ n. an edible part of a plant. *The mango is my favorite fruit.*

fruit

fifth /ˈfith/ adj. the o[...] following fourth. *Tr[...]*

finally /ˈfi nəl ē/ adv[...] [...] our math c[...] [...]/ adv. befo[...] [...]lse. Alex [...] [...]ō lō/ v. to [...] "*Come, fo[...]* [...]foo lish/ adj. no[...] [...]ble. It is [...] behave rude[...] [...]/fôr ˈgāv/ v. p[...] [...]ense of [...] to no longer[...] [...]me or hold a grudge against so[...] [...]ne. *Mindy forgave Anna for te[...] g a lie.*

forgetful /fôr ˈget f[...] adj. not likely to remember. *The fa[...] etful child did [...] have a lunch.*

forgotten /fôr ˈg[...] ən/ v. not reme[...] bered. *I had forgotten [...] send her birth[...] ay card.*

fourth /ˈfôrth/ [...] dj. the ordina[...] umber following thir[...] *My friend [...] in fourth grade.*

fracture /ˈfrak chûr/ n. **1** a break in something. *There was a fracture in the cable line.* v. **2** to break something. *For the [...] rt projec[...] we will fracture the glass [...] ith a hamme[...]*

frie[...] ly /ˈfrend lē/ adj. k[...]d, pleasant. *M[...] Rideout is a friendly [...] dy.*

f[...]ght /ˈfrīt/ n. sudden fear. *I r[...] way [...] fright from the angry dog.*

[...]own /ˈfroun/ v. to make a displease[...] expression. *The odd situation caused [...] Ava to frown.*

gases, [...] ogether [...]axies

[...]quid [...] gallons

garage /gə ˈräj/ n. a shelter or repair shop for cars. *Rosa parked her car in*

and without handles. *Gwen filled the glasses with apple juice.*

glided /ˈglī dəd/ v. past tense of GLIDE;

The Pronunciation shows how to say the word.

/ˈfrak chûr/

An Entry Word is a word being defined.

fracture

A Definition is the meaning of the word. A word may have more than one definition.

fracture /ˈfrak chûr/ n. **1** a break in something. *There was a fracture in the cable line.* v. **2** to break something. *For the art project, we will fracture the glass with a hammer.*

An entry word may have more than one Part of Speech.

fracture /ˈfrak chûr/ n. **1** a break in something. *There was a fracture in the cable line.* v. **2** to break something. *For the art project, we will fracture the glass with a hammer.*

A Sample Sentence helps in understanding the definition.

fracture /ˈfrak chûr/ n. **1** a break in something. *There was a fracture in the cable line.* v. **2** to break something. *For the art project, we will fracture the glass with a hammer.*

A

able /'ā bəl/ *adj.* having the ability to do something. *Are you able to attend the concert?*

acorn /'ā kôrn/ *n.* a nut containing the seed of an oak tree. *An acorn can grow into a big oak tree.*

action /'ak shən/ *n.* something that is done. *The player's action was fast.*

actor /'ak tûr/ *n.* one who acts in plays or movies. *An actor played the part of the king.*

addition /ə 'di shən/ *n.* combining two or more parts to find the whole, or sum. *I know how to do addition.*

address /'a dres/ *n.* the number, street name, or other description of where a person lives when written on an item of mail. *My address includes the zip code.*

adventure /əd 'ven chûr/ *n.* an exciting experience. *My adventure began on the seashore.*

advice /əd 'vīs/ *n.* information about what to do that is given to one person from another person. *The doctor gave the patient helpful advice.*

afraid /ə 'frād/ *adj.* scared. *When I am afraid, I will trust God.*

afternoon /af tûr 'noon/ *n.* the part of the day between noon and evening. *It rained yesterday afternoon.*

against /ə 'genst/ *prep.* **1** alongside. *Mack put his finger against his forehead.* **2** in competition with. *Our team will play against the red team.*

aglow /ə 'glō/ *adj.* in a state of glowing. *The candle was aglow in the darkness.*

airplane /'âr plān/ *n.* a vehicle with attached wings used to transport people, luggage, mail, and other things from one place to another through the air. *The airplane landed safely at the airport.*

airplane

airport /'âr pôrt/ *n.* a place where planes take off and land. *Our plane landed safely at the airport.*

almost /'ȯl mōst/ *adv.* nearly. *I almost forgot your birthday!*

aloft /ə 'lȯft/ *adv.* in a state of being above the ground. *The hot-air balloons went aloft.*

alone /ə 'lōn/ *adv.* away from others. *It is not wise to stay home alone.*

also /'ȯl sō/ *adv.* in addition to. *I like salt, but I also like pepper.*

always /'ȯl wāz/ *adv.* constantly. *God is always with us.*

angle /'ang gəl/ *v.* **1** to turn or move at an angle. *Joe will angle his jet sharply.* *n.* **2** a sharp course. *Trigger uses an angle to move his jet quickly.* **3** a figure formed by two lines meeting at a point. *There is more than one angle in a triangle.*

annoy /ə 'noi/ *v.* to bother or disturb. *Talking out in class will annoy teachers.*

answer /'an sûr/ *n.* a reply to a question, letter, or invitation. *What is the answer to five times eight?*

anybody /'e nē bə dē/ *pron.* any person. *Can anybody help me fix the chair?*

anywhere /'e nē hwâr/ *adv.* to, at, or in any place. *Fernando can fall asleep anywhere!*

apply /ə 'pli/ *v.* to bring or put something into contact with something else. *Mr. Larry will apply fresh paint to the wall.*

aren't /'är ənt/ contraction for ARE NOT. *My brother and I aren't twins.*

ascend /ə 'send/ *v.* to rise or move upward. *Airplanes ascend into the air after takeoff.*

asks /'asks/ *v.* to pose a question. *Marcus always asks good questions.*

authors /'ȯ thûrz/ *n. pl.* those who write. *That book has two authors.*

away /ə 'wā/ *adv.* gone from a place. *My family went away on vacation.*

awesome /'ȯ səm/ *adj.* amazing; wonderful. *God's power is awesome!*

B

bacon /'bā kən/ *n.* fried pork; meat that is often eaten at breakfast. *Doug likes to eat bacon and eggs for breakfast.*

badge /'baj/ *n.* an emblem that is usually worn as a pin. *A pilot's badge has wings on it.*

badge

balance /'ba lənts/ *v.* to make equal in weight or number. *Mom will balance the checkbook.*

beat /'bēt/ *v.* to defeat somebody. *Will Tara beat the other contestants?*

beautiful /'byo͞o ti fəl/ *adj.* full of beauty; pretty. *Al saw the beautiful sunset.*

because /bi 'kȯz/ *conj.* the reason why. *We love God because he first loved us.*

before /bi 'fȯr/ *prep.* prior to. *We will practice our song before chapel.*

behind /bi 'hind/ *prep.* in back of. *My best friend sits behind me in class.*

believes /bə 'lēvz/ *v.* to place one's faith in. *Whoever believes in Jesus has eternal life.*

below /bi 'lō/ *prep.* lower than something else in place, rank, or value. *The air is cold when it is below zero.*

beside /bi 'sīd/ *prep.* next to. *My Bible is beside my bed.*

between /bi 'twēn/ *prep.* in the space that separates. *Can you run between the cones?*

beyond /bē 'ond/ *prep.* past. *Do not go beyond the safety line.*

bicycles /'bī si kəlz/ *n. pl.* vehicles with two wheels. *My parents bought us new bicycles.*

bicycles

bigger /'bi gûr/ *adj.* greater in size. *Goliath was bigger, but David won!*

biggest /'bi gəst/ *adj.* greatest in size. *A blimp is the biggest thing I've seen.*

blind /'blīnd/ *adj.* unable to see. *Jesus healed a blind man.*

block /'blok/ *n.* houses bordered by streets. *Can you ride around the block on a scooter?*

bottom /'bo təm/ *n.* the lowest part or place. *We drove toward the bottom of the hill.*

bought /'bȯt/ *v.* past tense of BUY. *Pat bought a new motorcycle.*

branches /'branch əz/ *n. pl.* **1** parts of something larger. *There are branches of the military.* **2** parts of a tree. *The tree branches are full of leaves.* *v.* **3** to spread out. *The river branches out near Clarksville.*

break /'brāk/ v. to damage something so that it no longer works or is in one piece. *"Did you break this cup?" asked Phil.*

breeze /'brēz/ n. a gentle wind. *The cool breeze felt wonderful.*

brighter /'brī tûr/ adj. having more light. *We need a brighter light for reading.*

broken /'brō kən/ adj. separated into parts. *The old chair has a broken leg.*

brook /'brook/ n. a stream. *Blake caught a fish in the brook.*

brownie /'brou nē/ n. a chocolate dessert. *Jan chose to eat a brownie for dessert.*

browse /'brouz/ v. to look over or through something casually. *Annette will browse through the books.*

brushes /'bru shəz/ n. pl. sweeping devices made of bristles that are set into a handle. *Astronauts use brushes to clean lenses.*

buckle /'bu kəl/ v. to fasten. *Don't forget to buckle your seatbelt.*

building /'bil ding/ n. **1** a structure with walls and a roof. *The tall building is fifty stories high.* v. **2** making something. *He is building a new boat.*

built /'bilt/ v. to have made something. *Noah built the ark according to God's plans.*

business /'biz nəs/ n. **1** a commercial company or organization. *The business opened on time today.* **2** commercial activity. *New York City receives a lot of daily business from their subway system.*

busy /'bi zē/ adj. occupied. *Martha was busy with many things.*

buttons /'bu tənz/ n. pl. parts that are pushed to work a switch. *Have you pushed the buttons on an elevator?*

buying /'bī ing/ v. purchasing; to get by paying for. *Mom is at the store buying groceries.*

C

cabin /'ka bən/ n. **1** the place where passengers travel in an airplane. *The passengers took their seats in the cabin.* **2** a small structure for dwelling. *We drove to our cabin in the woods.*

cages /'kā jəz/ n. pl. more than one CAGE. *There were five cages for sale.*

calf /'kaf/ n. a young cow, moose, elephant, or whale. *Did you know a baby whale is called a calf?*

calf

calmed /'kämd/ v. past tense of CALM; to make quiet or peaceful. *Jesus calmed the storm on the Sea of Galilee.*

cannot /'ka not/ a form of CAN NOT. *Jenna cannot come to the movie.*

capable /'kā pə bəl/ adj. able to perform well. *Third graders are capable of spelling well!*

captain /'kap tən/ n. a leader of a group of people. *The captain sailed the ship across the ocean.*

careful /'kâr fəl/ adj. taking care. *Be careful when riding your bike on the road.*

careless /'kâr ləs/ adj. without care; not taking care of something. *The builders did a careless job.*

catcher /'ka chûr/ n. a baseball player who catches. *Ed played catcher on his baseball team.*

caught /'kȯt/ v. past tense of CATCH. *The fisherman caught a large fish.*

cents /ˈsents/ *n. pl.* coins that each represent one cent. *How many cents make one dollar?*

chair /ˈchâr/ *n.* a piece of furniture used for sitting. *You should never lean back in your chair.*

chair

chapel /ˈcha pəl/ *n.* **1** a place of worship. *Tad went to the chapel and prayed to Jesus. adj.* **2** a worship service. *Buzz Aldrin held a communion chapel service on the moon!*

checking /ˈche king/ *v.* inspecting or examining. *The mechanic is checking the engine.*

cheerful /ˈchîr fəl/ *adj.* full of cheer. *Jesus wants us to have cheerful hearts.*

chief /ˈchēf/ *n.* the leader of a crew. *A fire chief directs the operations at a fire.*

childhood /ˈchĭld hood/ *n.* the years in which a person is young. *Riding a tricycle is a childhood pastime.*

children /ˈchil drən/ *n. pl.* young people. *People brought children to see Jesus.*

choice /ˈchois/ *n.* **1** a selection. *We have a choice to do right or wrong. adj.* **2** high quality. *Prime rib is a choice piece of meat.*

choose /ˈchoōz/ *v.* to decide. *Will you help me choose a dessert?*

chosen /ˈchō zən/ *v.* selected. *I have chosen two helpers today.*

Christian /ˈkris chən/ *adj.* describes the followers of Christ. *Let's say the pledge to the Christian flag.*

Christmas /ˈkris məs/ *n.* a holiday celebrating Christ's birth. *Have you read the story of Christmas?*

circle /ˈsûr kəl/ *n.* a round, geometric shape; ring. *Coins are in the shape of a circle.*

cities /ˈsi tēz/ *n. pl.* areas made up of large numbers of people and businesses, larger than towns. *Airplanes land in many cities.*

clasp /ˈklasp/ *v.* **1** to join together. *The girls will clasp hands.* **2** to take hold of. *Chris will clasp the handlebars of his bike tightly.*

cleaned /ˈklēnd/ *v.* past tense of CLEAN; to make something free of dirt. *The volunteers cleaned up after the race.*

climber /ˈkli mûr/ *n.* a person who climbs. *Does a mountain climber wear hiking boots?*

climber

¹**close** /ˈklōz/ *v.* to shut. *"Please close the door," said the pilot.*

²**close** /ˈklōs/ *adv.* to be nearby. *Tommy likes to sit close to the window.*

clothes /ˈklōz/ *n.* items of cloth to be worn. *I packed my clothes in the suitcase.*

cloudy /ˈklou dē/ *adj.* covered with clouds. *Yesterday was a cloudy day.*

clue /ˈkloō/ *n.* an aid in solving a mystery or crossword puzzle. *Do you understand the clue?*

coach /ˈkōch/ *n.* **1** a person who instructs a person or a team. *My soccer coach is also my dad. v.* **2** to instruct. *Dad told me he would coach me in how to fish.*

coast /ˈkōst/ *n.* **1** the land near the ocean or sea. *Oceanside is a city on the coast. v.* **2** to move along without power. *It's easy to coast downhill on my bike.*

coins /'koinz/ *n. pl.* money made from metal. *Sue's piggy bank is full of coins.*

colorful /'ku lûr fəl/ *adj.* bright; full of color. *The colorful sunset was beautiful.*

common /'ko mən/ *adj.* usual. *It has become common to own a computer.*

conclusion /kən 'kloo zhən/ *n.* the last part. *I liked the conclusion of the story.*

confusion /kən 'fyoo zhən/ *n.* the act of mixing up. *In my confusion I made a mistake.*

corner /'kôr nûr/ *n.* the junction of two streets. *Min lives in the house on the corner.*

cornstalk /'kôrn stȯk/ *n.* the stem of a corn plant. *The cornstalk held six ears of corn.*

couldn't /'koo dənt/ contraction for COULD NOT. *Mom couldn't open the jar of pickles.*

count /'kount/ *v.* to say numbers in order so as to find a total sum. *How many police cars did you count?*

courage /'kûr ij/ *n.* mental strength against danger. *A fighter pilot needs to have courage.*

course /'kôrs/ *n.* a series of lessons on a particular subject. *Dr. Gordon teaches a Bible course.*

cousin /'ku zən/ *n.* the child of a person's aunt or uncle. *My cousin lives in Mobile, Alabama.*

cove /'kōv/ *n.* a small inlet in the shoreline of a sea, river, or lake. *We rowed past the cove.*

cove

covered /'ku vûrd/ *adj.* **1** coated. *Rachel likes chocolate-covered strawberries.* **2** topped. *The silver covered casserole dish belongs to my grandmother.*

craft /'kraft/ *n.* a type of artwork often made with paper. *Origami is a Japanese paper craft.*

crew /'kroo/ *n.* the workers on a ship; a group of people working together. *The ship's crew stood on deck.*

crooked /'kroo kəd/ *adj.* not straight. *Freda straightened the crooked picture.*

crowd /'kroud/ *n.* a large group of people. *There was a crowd in front of the door.*

cruise /'krooz/ *n.* **1** trip by sea. *Vivian went on her first cruise.* *v.* **2** to travel at an easy rate. *The police car will cruise the parking lot.*

crumb /'krum/ *n.* a small piece of baked food. *Mark picked up the crumb on the floor.*

crush /'krush/ *v.* to press forcefully. *Please don't crush the pages of your book.*

curve /'kûrv/ *n.* a bending without angles. *The curve in the road was very wide.*

cycle /'sī kəl/ *n.* an order of events that repeat themselves. *Evaporation is part of the water cycle.*

D

danger /'dān jûr/ *n.* harm or risk. *A fighter pilot's job is full of danger.*

darkness /'därk nəs/ *n.* the condition of being dark. *The helicopter flew in the darkness.*

dashboard /'dash bôrd/ *n.* the section of a vehicle cab just in front of the windshield. *Mom's sunglasses are on the dashboard.*

dashboard

daughter /ˈdȯ tür/ *n.* a female offspring. *Mary's daughter gave her a card.*

daughter

deceive /di ˈsēv/ *v.* to trick or mislead somebody. *It is not good to deceive anyone.*

deer /ˈdȋr/ *n.* **1** a woodland animal. *A young deer walked along the stream.* *n. pl.* **2** woodland animals. *I drove by some deer grazing in the field.*

delay /di ˈlā/ *n.* a waiting period. *The storm caused a delay to our trip.*

depart /di ˈpärt/ *v.* to leave. *The train will depart on time.*

descend /di ˈsend/ *v.* to go down; to lower. *Airplanes descend when beginning to land.*

destroy /di ˈstroi/ *v.* **1** to ruin the condition of something. *An earthquake can destroy buildings.* **2** to tear up. *The puppy will destroy the shoe.*

different /ˈdi fə rənt/ *adj.* **1** distinct. *A siren can make many different sounds.* **2** another. *I have a different idea for the story.*

direct /də ˈrekt/ *v.* to show or tell the way to a place. *Can you direct me to the office?*

directions /də ˈrek shənz/ *n. pl.* instructions on how to get somewhere or do something. *Alexis wrote down the directions.*

distance /ˈdis tənts/ *n.* **1** an expression of length. *He rode his bike a long distance.* **2** a far-off place. *I could see the sunset in the distance.*

divided /də ˈvi dəd/ *v.* **1** past tense of DIVIDE; to be separated into parts. *The teacher divided the class into teams.* *adj.* **2** separated. *Mr. Almond drove down the divided highway.*

division /də ˈvi zhən/ *n.* separating a number into equal amounts. *Division is a math concept.*

dodge /ˈdoj/ *v.* to make a sudden movement or move quickly in another direction. *Jeremy will dodge his jet quickly.*

double /ˈdu bəl/ *v.* to make twice as much. *Mom will double the cookie recipe.*

downstairs /ˈdoun stȧrz/ *n.* **1** the lower floor of a building. *The downstairs has windows.* *adv.* **2** down the stairs. *Passengers enter the subway by going downstairs toward the platform.*

downtown /doun ˈtoun/ *adv.* the business center of a city. *Ivan drove downtown to work.*

downtown

drifted /ˈdrif təd/ *v.* past tense of DRIFT; floated along. *The boat drifted along the river.*

drown /ˈdroun/ *v.* to cause something to not be heard by making a loud noise. *The music will drown out the city noise.*

during /ˈdoor ing/ *prep.* at some time. *Nicodemus came to Jesus during the night.*

E

eager /ˈē gûr/ *adj.* excited. *Sean was eager to begin his project.*

early /ˈûr lē/ *adv.* **1** before the expected time. *Mr. Fikse gets up early every morning.* *adj.* **2** occurring near the beginning. *The Japanese railroads added more trains in the early 1980s.*

earth /'ûrth/ *n.* **1** the planet on which we live. *God made the heavens and the earth.* **2** the ground. *The hot-air balloon returned to the earth with a bump.*

Earth

easy /'ē zē/ *adj.* not hard to do. *The math problem was very easy.*

edge /'ej/ *n.* a border. *The jet was at the edge of the runway.*

education /e jə 'kā shən/ *n.* the process of learning new things. *We are getting a good education.*

eighty /'ā tē/ *adj.* the number written as 80. *Grandpa Brown is eighty years old.*

electric /ē 'lek trik/ *adj.* of, related to, or operated by electricity. *Subways run off of electric power.*

eleven /i 'le vən/ *adj.* the number written as 11. *Conner found eleven tadpoles in the pond.*

engine /'en jən/ *n.* **1** motor. *The engine on the train is loud.* **2** locomotive. *Sometimes more than one train engine will pull the train cars.*

enjoyed /in 'joid/ *v.* past tense of ENJOY; had a good time; liked. *Steven enjoyed eating the apple pie.*

entire /in 'tī ûr/ *adj.* whole. *The entire space station is very large.*

equal /'ē kwəl/ *adj.* the same as. *Five plus five is equal to ten.*

errand /'âr ənd/ *n.* a short trip taken to perform a task. *Anya went on an errand to the store.*

error /'âr ûr/ *n.* a mistake. *Isaac made an error on his paper.*

everyone /'ev rē wən/ *pron.* every person. *Everyone is invited to the party.*

except /ik 'sept/ *prep.* not including. *Everyone is going except Mark.*

exercise /'ek sûr sīz/ *v.* moving the body to help keep it healthy. *Robert will exercise for twenty minutes.*

expect /ik 'spekt/ *v.* to believe that something will happen; to look forward to. *Do you expect to see the moon tonight?*

explain /ik 'splān/ *v.* to tell how, so something is easily understood. *Will you explain how to do this?*

exploration /ek splə 'rā shən/ *n.* the act of searching for new things. *The exploration of space is exciting.*

eye /'ī/ *n.* the organ of sight. *If dirt gets in your eye, do not rub it.*

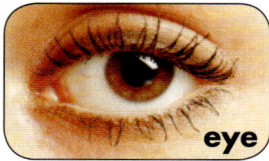
eye

F

facts /'fakts/ *n. pl.* pieces of true information; things known to be true. *Joshua knew his math facts very well.*

famous /'fā məs/ *adj.* well-known. *Many astronauts are famous and respected.*

fault /'folt/ *n.* one's responsibility for a mistake. *He was at fault in the accident.*

favorite /'fā və rət/ *adj.* preferred. *My favorite ice-cream flavor is chocolate.*

fearful /'fir fəl/ *adj.* scared. *Many people are fearful of spiders.*

fearlessness /'fir ləs nəs/ *n.* the condition of being without fear; courage. *The fireman showed fearlessness.*

fewer /'fyo͞o ûr/ *adj.* not very many people or things. *Fewer people came to the pool today.*

fields /ˈfēldz/ *n. pl.* open areas of land that do not have buildings or a lot of trees. *Farmer Jon picked the crops in his fields.*

fields

fifth /ˈfith/ *adj.* the ordinal number following fourth. *Tristin is in fifth grade.*

finally /ˈfi nəl ē/ *adv.* at last. *We finally finished our math assignments.*

first /ˈfûrst/ *adv.* before anything or anyone else. *Alex raised his hand first.*

follow /ˈfo lō/ *v.* to be led or guided by someone. *"Come, follow Me," Jesus said.*

foolish /ˈfoo lish/ *adj.* not sensible. *It is foolish to behave rudely.*

forgave /fôr ˈgāv/ *v.* past tense of FORGIVE; to no longer blame or hold a grudge against someone. *Mindy forgave Anna for telling a lie.*

forgetful /fôr ˈget fəl/ *adj.* not likely to remember. *The forgetful child did not have a lunch.*

forgotten /fôr ˈgo tən/ *v.* not remembered. *I had forgotten to send her birthday card.*

fourth /ˈfôrth/ *adj.* the ordinal number following third. *My friend is in fourth grade.*

fracture /ˈfrak chûr/ *n.* **1** a break in something. *There was a fracture in the cable line.* *v.* **2** to break something. *For the art project, we will fracture the glass with a hammer.*

friendly /ˈfrend lē/ *adj.* kind; pleasant. *Mrs. Rideout is a friendly lady.*

fright /ˈfrīt/ *n.* sudden fear. *I ran away in fright from the angry dog.*

frown /ˈfroun/ *v.* to make a displeased expression. *The odd situation caused Ava to frown.*

frozen /ˈfrō zən/ *adj.* affected by freezing. *The pizzas were frozen in the freezer.*

fruit /ˈfroot/ *n.* an edible part of a plant. *The mango is my favorite fruit.*

fruit

G

galaxies /ˈga lək sēz/ *n. pl.* stars, gases, and dust clouds that are pulled together by gravity in large groups. *Galaxies are classified by their shapes.*

gallons /ˈga lənz/ *n. pl.* units of liquid measurement. *Mom bought two gallons of milk at the store.*

garage /gə ˈräj/ *n.* a shelter or repair shop for cars. *Rosa parked her car in the garage.*

gasoline /ˈga sə lēn/ *n.* automobile fuel. *Jeff put gasoline into the car's tank.*

gather /ˈga thûr/ *v.* **1** to form into a group. *Chris will gather his flight gear.* **2** to collect data and information. *Rex has learned to gather and use the information to fly his jet.*

geese /ˈgēs/ *n. pl.* large, freshwater birds. *A flock of geese flew overhead.*

giant /ˈjī ənt/ *adj.* large; gigantic. *A jet does not have a giant fuel tank.*

gifts /ˈgifts/ *n. pl.* things given as presents. *The wise men brought gifts to Jesus.*

glasses /ˈgla səz/ *n. pl.* containers for drinking that are usually made of glass and without handles. *Gwen filled the glasses with apple juice.*

glided /ˈglī dəd/ *v.* past tense of GLIDE; moved smoothly over. *The sailboat glided over the lake.*

gliding /ˈglī ding/ *v.* to move smoothly over. *The skaters were gliding on the ice.*

glisten /ˈgli sən/ *v.* to give off a sparkle. *The clean window began to glisten.*

gnat /ˈnat/ n. a small, biting fly. *A gnat has two wings.*

grabbed /ˈgrabd/ v. past tense of GRAB; snatched. *Mom grabbed her purse before leaving.*

grabbing /ˈgra bing/ v. to snatch. *We were grabbing treats from a piñata.*

graceful /ˈgrās fəl/ adj. full of grace; displaying grace, balance, and beauty. *Katie is a graceful skater.*

great /ˈgrāt/ adj. very large. *A great crowd came to see Jesus.*

grief /ˈgrēf/ n. sadness. *Mary experienced grief when Jesus died.*

guard /ˈgärd/ v. to protect. *Fighter jets protect and guard our country.*

guess /ˈges/ v. to suppose something. *Can you guess how much it cost?*

guest /ˈgest/ n. a visitor to whom hospitality is given. *Paige was a guest at the Air Force base.*

guide /ˈgīd/ v. to lead or steer. *Jesus will guide you in all that you do.*

gulped /ˈgulpt/ v. past tense of GULP; to have swallowed quickly. *Justin quickly gulped the glass of water.*

gutter /ˈgu tûr/ n. the edge of the street below the curb that serves as a channel for water. *Water filled the gutter.*

H

halftime /ˈhaf tīm/ n. the time between two halves of a game. *The band played during halftime.*

handle /ˈhan dəl/ v. able to perform a task. *Our secretary can handle the book orders.*

hangar /ˈhang gûr/ n. an enclosed and covered shelter used for housing and repairing aircraft. *David's jet is parked in the hangar.*

happens /ˈha pənz/ v. takes place. *Do you know what happens when the sun sets?*

happier /ˈha pē ûr/ adj. gladder. *His words made me happier than ever!*

happiest /ˈha pē əst/ adj. gladdest. *JoAnn is happiest of all the girls.*

happiness /ˈha pē nəs/ n. the condition of being happy. *Jesus fills our lives with happiness.*

haul /ˈhȯl/ v. to pull something. *Will the tow truck haul the wreck?*

heard /ˈhûrd/ v. past tense of HEAR; listened. *Have you heard the story of Ruth and Boaz?*

heavens /ˈhe vənz/ n. the area of space surrounding the earth. *The heavens were created by God.*

helper /ˈhel pûr/ n. a person who assists another person. *Mandy is a good helper.*

heroes /ˈhîr ōz/ n. pl. men admired for their courage and achievements. *David and Samson are heroes in the Bible.*

herself /hûr ˈself/ pron. her own self. *Shirley made the gift all by herself.*

himself /him ˈself/ pron. his own self. *Jesus Himself died for our sins.*

history /ˈhis tə rē/ n. **1** the order of events. *The Bible records the history of Israel.* adj. **2** describes a course of study. *We'll attend history class.*

honey /ˈhu nē/ n. the sweet, sticky substance made by bees. *Honey is sweet and golden.*

hood /'hood/ *n.* **1** an engine cover. *The hood on the old truck is rusty.* **2** a head covering. *Nancy pulled the hood of her sweatshirt over her head.*

hoped /'hōpt/ *v.* past tense of HOPE; longed for. *Teresa hoped to win a prize.*

hoping /'hō ping/ *v.* longing for. *I am hoping to receive a birthday gift.*

hopped /'hopt/ *v.* past tense of HOP; jumped. *My rabbit hopped all over the lawn.*

hopping /'ho ping/ *v.* to jump. *Lee was hopping in the hopscotch game.*

household /'hous hōld/ *n.* people who live together in a home. *Jason has five members in his household.*

however /hou 'e vûr/ *conj.* yet or but. *I slept well, however, I am still tired.*

huge /'hyo͞oj/ *adj.* very large. *Ricky saw the huge ship in the harbor.*

human /'hyo͞o mən/ *n.* a person. *Each human is created by God.*

hundred /'hun drəd/ *adj.* the number written as 100. *A century is one hundred years.*

hurry /'hûr ē/ *v.* **1** to rush. *Do not hurry me while I'm driving.* *n.* **2** in a rush. *Mom was in a hurry and forgot to lock the door.*

I

icicle /'ī si kəl/ *n.* dripping water that is frozen in the shape of a cone. *Jim broke off an icicle from the eave.*

icicle

icy /'ī sē/ *adj.* covered with ice. *Will the icy roads make driving dangerous?*

I'm /'īm/ contraction for I AM. *I'm going to draw a picture.*

inactive /i 'nak tiv/ *adj.* not active. *Bears are inactive during the winter.*

incomplete /in kəm 'plēt/ *adj.* not complete. *The math problems were incomplete.*

incorrect /in kə 'rekt/ *adj.* not correct. *The answer was incorrect.*

indexes /'in dek səz/ *n. pl.* lists used to organize specific data. *The indexes listed the correct information.*

interesting /'in tə res ting/ *adj.* able to hold one's interest. *The Bible is the most interesting book.*

invisible /in 'vi zə bəl/ *adj.* not visible. *God is invisible, but He's always here.*

it's /'its/ contraction for IT IS or IT HAS. *It's Zachary's birthday this week.*

J

jacket /'ja kət/ *n.* a light coat. *Antonio zipped his jacket before leaving.*

jeans /'jēnz/ *n.* a pair of pants. *Alyssa bought a new pair of jeans.*

jeans

joining /'joi ning/ *v.* becoming a member. *Is anyone interested in joining the choir?*

judge /'juj/ *v.* to assess or evaluate. *The pilot will need to judge his landing.*

jungle /'jung gəl/ *n.* the rain forest. *Kipling wrote stories about the jungle.*

K

kept /'kept/ *v.* past tense of KEEP. *Sam kept his promise to be ready.*

keys /'kēz/ *n. pl.* more than one KEY; metal objects used to unlock locks. *I'll loan you the keys to the storage room.*

kitchen /'ki chən/ *n.* room where food is prepared. *Dad went to the kitchen to get a snack.*

kneel /'nēl/ *v.* to get down on one or both knees. *Sometimes I kneel when I pray to Jesus.*

knew /'nōō/ *v.* past tense of KNOW. *Max knew the answer to the riddle.*

knife /'nīf/ *n.* a tool used for cutting. *The butcher sharpened his carving knife.*

knives /'nīvz/ *n. pl.* tools used for cutting. *Judd sharpened the kitchen knives today.*

knock /'nok/ *v.* **1** to make a pounding noise. *Please knock loudly on the door.* *n.* **2** a metallic noise made regularly by an engine. *The engine's knock needed to be repaired.*

knotted /'no ted/ *adj.* tied or tangled in a knot. *The ribbons were all knotted up.*

L

lady /'lā dē/ *n.* a woman. *The nice lady smiled at me.*

lamb /'lam/ *n.* a young sheep less than a year old. *The little lamb lay next to its mother.*

lamb

landmark /'land märk/ *n.* a noticeable object that serves as a guide and identifies a location. *The White House is a landmark.*

larger /'lär jûr/ *adj.* greater in size. *California is larger than Hawaii.*

largest /'lär jəst/ *adj.* greatest in size. *The largest state is Alaska.*

laugh /'laf/ *n.* a happy sound. *A baby's laugh is a delight to hear.*

lawyer /'lȯ yûr/ *n.* one trained in the practice of law. *Ellen's dad is a lawyer.*

lazily /'lā zə lē/ *adv.* done in a lazy way; not willing to work. *The cow lazily swatted at the flies.*

leaf /'lēf/ *n.* a part of a plant. *Emilio found a beautiful oak leaf.*

leaf

learn /'lûrn/ *v.* to get knowledge or gain a skill. *Conner likes to learn about the planets.*

led /'led/ *v.* past tense of LEAD. *Don led the class in a prayer.*

legs /'legz/ *n. pl.* more than one LEG; limbs. *His legs were strong and muscular.*

lessons /'le sənz/ *n. pl.* things that are taught and learned. *Mrs. Powell teaches piano lessons.*

let's /'lets/ contraction for LET US. *Let's sing praises to the Lord.*

lies /'līz/ *v.* to tell something that is not true. *Can a person who lies be trusted?*

listen /'li sən/ *v.* to pay attention. *You should always listen to directions.*

lives /'līvz/ *n. pl.* more than one LIFE. *Lives are changed when people accept Jesus.*

location /lō 'kā shən/ *n.* a place or an area. *What is the space center's location?*

looked /'lookt/ *v.* past tense of LOOK; to have used your eyes to see something. *Julianne looked for her lost coat.*

loose /'lōōs/ *adj.* not fastened or pulled tight. *The rubber band was loose.*

loss /'lòs/ *n.* **1** an instance of losing something. *The loss of his money made him sad.* **2** a defeat. *Our team suffered a loss against the Tigers.*

louder /'lou dûr/ *adj.* higher in volume of sound. *Please speak louder so I can hear you.*

loyal /'loi əl/ *adj.* faithful. *A dog is loyal to its master.*

M

machine /mə 'shēn/ *n.* an object that uses energy, motion, and force to do some kind of work. *Lorraine enjoys her new sewing machine.*

market /'mär kət/ *n.* grocery store. *We buy our fresh vegetables at the market.*

matches /'mach əz/ *v.* **1** to coordinate with. *James' shirt matches his pants.* *n. pl.* **2** sticks used to light a fire. *Never play with matches.* **3** multi-game competitions. *Three soccer matches ended in a tie.*

matter /'ma tûr/ regardless of. *No matter what happens, trust God.*

maybe /'mā bē/ *adv.* perhaps. *Maybe it will rain today.*

mean /'mēn/ *adj.* unkind. *Do not be mean to your friends.*

meant /'ment/ *v.* past tense of MEAN; intended. *She never meant to hurt your feelings.*

melted /'mel təd/ *v.* to have changed from a solid to a liquid. *The chocolate melted in the hot sun.*

merry /'mâr ē/ *adj.* happy. *Mandi was having a merry day.*

mice /'mīs/ *n. pl.* small rodents. *The mice were brown and white.*

mice

might've /'mī təv/ contraction for MIGHT HAVE. *He might've come if he had not been sick.*

mighty /'mī tē/ *adj.* strong; powerful. *We have a mighty God.*

minutes /'mi nəts/ *n. pl.* more than one MINUTE. *How many minutes are in a day?*

mission /'mi shən/ *n.* a special job or assignment. *The space shuttle is on a mission.*

mistake /mə 'stāk/ *n.* an error. *Mike had one mistake on his math test.*

modern /'mo dûrn/ *adj.* now; current; up-to-date. *Modern cars look different from older ones.*

mold /'mōld/ *n.* **1** a fuzzy growth. *The bread with mold was thrown away.* *v.* **2** to shape. *I mold clay into animal shapes.*

monkey /'mung kē/ *n.* a small primate. *The little monkey chattered and chattered.*

monkey

months /'munts/ *n. pl.* more than one MONTH. *How many months equal one year?*

moose /'mo͞os/ *n. pl.* **1** the largest members of the deer family. *Moose wandered into the clearing.* *n.* **2** the largest member of the deer family. *The moose had large antlers.*

mostly /'mōst lē/ *adv.* **1** mainly. *We eat mostly cereal for breakfast.* **2** done almost always. *Ben mostly hits home runs.*

motion /'mō shən/ *n.* movement; moving. *The shuttle is in motion.*

motor /'mō tûr/ *n.* a machine that gives movement and power to an object. *The motor on the lawn mower is loud.*

mountain /ˈmoun tən/ n. very high hill. *Eric plans to climb a tall mountain.*

mountain

Mr. /ˈmis tûr/ n. the title of courtesy used before the name of a man. *Mr. Evans will pray during chapel.*

Mrs. /ˈmi səz/ n. the title of courtesy used before the name of a married or widowed woman. *Danielle saw Mrs. Walker today.*

multiplication /məl tə plə ˈkā shən/ n. repeated addition of the same number. *Do you know multiplication?*

N

nation /ˈnā shən/ n. a country. *Canada is a nation.*

nature /ˈnā chûr/ n. natural scenery. *God created all we see in nature.*

naughty /ˈnȯ tē/ adj. poorly behaved; disobedient. *The naughty dog was covered in mud.*

nearby /nîr ˈbī/ adv. a short distance away. *My grandparents live nearby.*

nearly /ˈnîr lē/ adv. almost. *Robert is nearly as tall as Tyler.*

neighbor /ˈnā bûr/ n. **1** another person; a friend. *God's Word tells us to love our neighbor.* **2** a person who lives next door or near you. *My neighbor likes to ride his bike.*

never /ˈne vûr/ adv. not ever. *Jesus will never leave you nor forsake you.*

noisy /ˈnoi zē/ adj. loud. *That crow is very noisy!*

northwest /nôrth ˈwest/ adv. to the direction between north and west. *The subway train headed northwest.*

nothing /ˈnu thing/ pron. not anything. *There was nothing left in the cookie jar.*

notice /ˈnō təs/ v. to observe; to take note of. *"Did you notice my clean room?" asked Avery.*

nurse /ˈnûrs/ n. **1** a person who cares for sick people. *The nurse rode a cable car to work.* v. **2** to treat a health problem. *I will nurse my sprained ankle.*

O

object /ˈob jikt/ n. something that can be seen or touched. *The broken object will be replaced.*

often /ˈȯ fən/ adv. frequently. *Jesus often prayed for others.*

oily /ˈoi lē/ adj. covered with oil. *The rain caused the road to be oily.*

once /ˈwunts/ conj. as soon as. *Once the mission is complete, we will rest.*

only /ˈōn lē/ adj. just. *She had only five cents in her pocket.*

open /ˈō pən/ adv. not closed. *Who left the door open?*

opening /ˈō pə ning/ v. undoing; removing something that is in the way. *Sue is opening her birthday present.*

outdoors /out ˈdôrz/ adv. any area outside a building. *Megan ate her lunch outdoors.*

outstanding /out ˈstan ding/ adj. excellent. *Hank did an outstanding job today.*

overdue /ō vûr ˈdo͞o/ adj. late or delayed. *The ship was overdue into port.*

P

palm /ˈpäm/ *n.* the front part of a person's hand between the fingers and the wrist. *The pitcher held the baseball in his palm.*

pasture /ˈpas chûr/ *n.* land with plants where grazing animals eat. *The cows were grazing in the pasture.*

peace /ˈpēs/ *n.* a state of quiet or calm. *Jesus gives us peace when we pray.*

peaceful /ˈpēs fəl/ *adj.* full of peace; quiet. *Sophie fell asleep in the peaceful room.*

pencil /ˈpen səl/ *n.* an object used for writing. *Bree used a pencil to complete her homework.*

pennies /ˈpe nēz/ *n. pl.* coins that are valued at one cent apiece. *There are one hundred pennies in a dollar.*

pennies

penniless /ˈpe ni ləs/ *adj.* without a penny; not having money. *The penniless child earned money.*

people /ˈpē pəl/ *n. pl.* more than one PERSON. *Many people brought children to see Jesus.*

permission /pûr ˈmi shən/ *n.* being allowed to do something. *Mom gave me permission to stay.*

person /ˈpûr sən/ *n.* a human being. *Jesus is the only person who has not sinned.*

photograph /ˈfō tə graf/ *n.* a picture made with a camera. *Marcy took a photograph of the lake.*

picture /ˈpik chûr/ *n.* a drawing, painting, or photograph that represents something. *Which picture is your favorite?*

piece /ˈpēs/ *n.* **1** an individual object, item, or part. *Steven will repair the piece of equipment.* *v.* **2** to complete, repair, or make by adding a part or parts. *The astronauts will piece together the International Space Station.*

pieces /ˈpē səz/ *n. pl.* more than one PIECE; parts to a whole. *Does your puzzle have over 500 pieces?*

place /ˈplās/ *v.* **1** to put or set. *We should always place our trust in Jesus.* *n.* **2** a particular location. *An airplane can take you to almost any place!*

planets /ˈpla nətz/ *n. pl.* large bodies in orbit around the sun. *Our solar system has several planets.*

playground /ˈplā ground/ *n.* an outdoor play area. *The playground was full of toys.*

playing /ˈplā ing/ *v.* **1** making music. *Jeanie enjoys playing the piano.* **2** having fun. *The children enjoy playing on the playground.*

please /ˈplēz/ *adv.* to show politeness in asking. *Could you please help me lift the box?*

pliers /ˈpli ûrz/ *n.* a tool used for holding small objects or cutting wire. 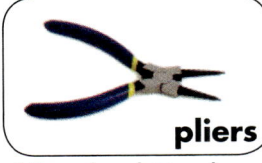 pliers *"Where are my pliers?" asked Dad.*

pocket /ˈpo kət/ *n.* a flap of cloth found in clothing used to hold small items. *My pocket has a hole in it.*

pointed /ˈpoin təd/ *adj.* **1** having a point. *The top of the church steeple is pointed.* *v.* **2** past tense of POINT; to be aimed or turned in a particular direction. *The train was pointed in the wrong direction.*

position /pə ˈzi shən/ *n.* the way something is arranged. *The shuttle's position is upright.*

post /ˈpōst/ *n.* **1** a pole in the ground. *Dad dug a hole in the ground for the post.* *v.* **2** to publish. *I will post the list tomorrow.*

potatoes /pə ˈtā tōz/ *n. pl.* root vegetables that grow underground and are edible. *Ila put butter on her sweet potatoes.*

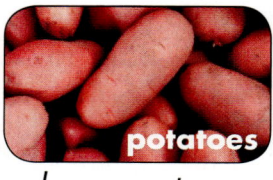
potatoes

pounds /ˈpoundz/ *n. pl.* units of weight. *How many pounds does a car weigh?*

power /ˈpou ûr/ *n.* **1** authority. *Jesus has the power to do all things.* **2** energy to produce electricity. *The electric power was being fixed.*

prepay /prē ˈpā/ *v.* to pay ahead of time. *We will prepay for the field trip.*

preschool /ˈprē skool/ *n.* education before elementary school. *Tessa just finished preschool.*

present /ˈpre zənt/ *adj.* **1** in attendance. *All members of the class were present.* *n.* **2** a gift. *Laurie received a present for her birthday.*

preview /ˈprē vyoo/ *n.* **1** a view in advance. *The movie preview seems interesting.* *v.* **2** to view ahead of time. *We will preview that book before we read it.*

prewrite /prē ˈrīt/ *v.* planning done before writing; write ahead of time. *I'll use an outline to prewrite my story.*

probably /ˈpro bə blē/ *adv.* most likely. *Melissa will probably win the race.*

proofread /ˈproof rēd/ *v.* to read, mark corrections, and fix mistakes in. *Mrs. Lim will proofread my paper.*

Psalms /ˈsämz/ *n.* a book in the Old Testament of the Bible. *There are 150 chapters in the book of Psalms.*

pumpkin /ˈpump kən/ *n.* a fruit related to the squash family. *The large pumpkin weighs seventy pounds.*

purpose /ˈpûr pəs/ *n.* the goal of something. *What is the purpose of your trip?*

purse /ˈpûrs/ *n.* a bag. *Jasmine bought a yellow purse.*

Q

queen /ˈkwēn/ *n.* a king's wife; a female ruler of a country. *Do you know the name of the queen?*

quickly /ˈkwik lē/ *adv.* done in a quick way; fast. *The fire spread quickly.*

R

rack /ˈrak/ *n.* a stand for holding or carrying things. *Lucas placed his bicycle on the rack.*

rack

rainfall /ˈrān fȯl/ *n.* **1** a quantity of rain. *Seattle receives a lot of rainfall.* **2** a shower of rain. *A brief rainfall watered my plants.*

reach /ˈrēch/ *v.* to arrive at a certain place. *Paula will reach the end of the trail soon.*

really /ˈrē lē/ *adv.* truly. *I really wanted to buy the gift.*

rebuilt /rē ˈbilt/ *v.* past tense of REBUILD; built again. *The students rebuilt the block tower.*

receive /ri ˈsēv/ *v.* to get or accept something. *Ian will receive a trophy for first place.*

recess /'rē ses/ *n.* **1** play period during a school day. *We will take a break at recess.* **2** a short break. *The camper stopped for a lunch recess.*

rejoice /ri 'jois/ *v.* to be glad. *The Bible tells us to rejoice in the Lord.*

removed /ri 'mo͞ovd/ *v.* past tense of REMOVE; moved again to another place. *Andrew removed the dead tree limbs.*

reply /ri 'plī/ *v.* to answer. *Mrs. Hansen will reply to my question.*

report /ri 'pôrt/ *n.* **1** a summary of information. *His book report is on Charlotte's Web.* **2** a description. *When we return, we will write a report about our vacation.*

return /ri 'tûrn/ *v.* to come back. *One day Jesus will return again.*

rewrote /rē 'rōt/ *v.* past tense of REWRITE; wrote again. *Jackson rewrote his book report.*

riddle /'ri dəl/ *n.* an amusing question. *Jackie told me a funny riddle.*

risk /'risk/ *v.* to take a dangerous chance. *Soldiers risk their lives for their country.*

road /'rōd/ *n.* **1** an open way for vehicles, people, and animals. *The truck drove down a long road.* **2** the way to an end or circumstance. *The road to becoming an astronaut is full of education.*

roadblock /'rōd blok/ *n.* a temporary road barrier. *The roadblock made us an hour late.*

robin /'ro bən/ *n.* a kind of bird. *The robin caught a worm.*

rockets /'ro kəts/ *n. pl.* self-propelled devices that carry their own fuel and the oxygen needed to burn the fuel. *Special rockets are used as launch vehicles.*

rode /'rōd/ *v.* past tense of RIDE. *Christa rode in a van to the launchpad.*

root /'ro͞ot/ *n.* **1** the part of the plant that absorbs water and nutrients from the soil. *One root of the tree was above ground.* *v.* **2** to cheer or shout. *We will root for our team.*

rope /'rōp/ *n.* **1** a large thick cord. *The rope is very thick and long.* *v.* **2** to fasten with a rope. *The cowboy will rope the runaway calf.*

rowboat /'rō bōt/ *n.* a small boat that is made to be rowed with oars. *We sailed on the lake in a rowboat.*

rowed /'rōd/ *v.* past tense of ROW. *The disciples rowed a boat toward land.*

royal /'roi əl/ *adj.* being related to kings and queens. *The royal family lives in London.*

rumble /'rum bəl/ *n.* a low rolling sound. *The rocket lifted off with a rumble.*

S

safety /'sāf tē/ *adj.* protective. *It is important to wear a safety helmet.*

said /'sed/ *v.* past tense of SAY. *Jesus said to love one another.*

sample /'sam pəl/ *n.* an example. *A free sample of soap came in the mail.*

sandwich /'sand wich/ *n.* two pieces of bread with something between them. *I like cheese on my sandwich.*

says /'sez/ v. present tense of SAY. *The sign says, "Keep out!"*

scale /'skāl/ n. a device used for weighing. *The fish weighed twelve pounds on the scale.*

scale

scared /'skârd/ v. **1** to be afraid or frightened. *The loud noise scared the baby.* adj. **2** frightened. *Major Jess is not scared of flying a fighter jet.*

scents /'sents/ n. pleasant and sweet aromas. *Sweet and spicy scents smell good!*

school /'skool/ n. a place of teaching and learning. *School is a place for learning.*

science /'si ənts/ n. an area of study. *Doug's favorite subject is science.*

score /'skôr/ n. points in a game or on a test; touchdown. *The final score was Chargers 41, Broncos 24.*

scratch /'skrach/ v. to make a scraping movement. *My dog began to scratch a flea.*

seashore /'sē shôr/ n. the beach. *The seashore is a wonderful place to play.*

secret /'sē krət/ n. **1** hidden fact. *It's no secret that Jesus loves you!* adj. **2** hidden. *The door led to a secret room.*

sense /'sents/ n. **1** an awareness or sensation of something. *They felt no sense of heaviness in space.* **2** intelligence; understanding. *An astronaut will use sense to carry out his mission.*

service /'sûr vəs/ n. work done to help others. *The project was done as a service to a family.*

settle /'se təl/ v. to come to a conclusion. *They'll soon settle on a name for their team.*

shaky /'shā kē/ adj. the condition of something that shakes; likely to fall down. *The shaky straw house collapsed.*

share /'shâr/ v. to divide between one another. *Will you share your snack with me?*

sheep /'shēp/ n. pl. **1** animals that are related to goats and are raised for their meat and wool. *The group of sheep followed the shepherd.* n. **2** an animal related to a goat that is raised for its meat and wool. *A young sheep is called a lamb.*

shelter /'shel tûr/ n. a protected area. *Let's eat lunch at the picnic shelter.*

shelves /'shelvz/ n. pl. flat surfaces that are used to display objects. *Tiffany and Sara built the wooden shelves.*

shepherd /'she pûrd/ n. a person who takes care of sheep. *A shepherd takes care of his sheep.*

shine /'shīn/ v. **1** to give forth light. *The sun will shine all day.* **2** to polish something. *Mabel will need to shine the trophy.*

shoes /'shooz/ n. pl. coverings for feet. *Rachel wore her new shoes.*

shoes

shortest /'shôr təst/ adj. the one least in length. *December 21st is the shortest day of the year.*

shouldn't /'shoo dənt/ contraction for SHOULD NOT. *Children shouldn't disobey their parents.*

shrimp /'shrimp/ n. pl. small crustaceans. *Shrimp are my favorite seafood.*

shrink /'shringk/ v. to decrease in size. *Some clothes shrink in the dryer.*

shuttle /ˈshu təl/ *n.* a spacecraft. *The orbiter is part of the space shuttle.*

sight /ˈsīt/ *n.* something that is worth seeing. *A full moon is a pretty sight.*

sign /ˈsīn/ *n.* a board with information, directions, or warnings. *The highway sign posted the speed limit.*

silent /ˈsī lənt/ *adj.* not speaking; still. *One should be silent during prayer.*

silky /ˈsil kē/ *adj.* soft and smooth. *Mom wore a red, silky scarf with her suit.*

silver /ˈsil vûr/ *n.* **1** a precious metal like gold and bronze. *The beautiful ring was made from silver.* *adj.* **2** a color similar to gray. *Many trains are painted silver.*

skateboard /ˈskāt bôrd/ *n.* a board with wheels, shaped like a small surfboard,  that one stands on and rides. *Billy likes to ride on his skateboard.*

skill /ˈskil/ *n.* an ability. *It takes lots of skill to juggle.*

skipper /ˈski pûr/ *n.* the commander of a ship or boat. *The skipper commanded the crew.*

skirts /ˈskûrts/ *n. pl.* more than one SKIRT; clothing that hangs from the waist. *Mom bought three new skirts for me.*

skyline /ˈski lin/ *n.* an outline of buildings, mountains, and other objects seen from a distance with the sky in the background. *The San Diego skyline looks pretty at night.*

sleepy /ˈslē pē/ *adj.* wanting to sleep; drowsy. *Jeff felt sleepy after taking a warm bath.*

slick /ˈslik/ *adj.* **1** slippery. *The roads were very slick after the storm.* **2** glossy or shiny. *We put a slick coat of paint on the old car.*

slowly /ˈslō lē/ *adv.* in a slow way; not fast. *The dog walked slowly across the yard.*

sniff /ˈsnif/ *v.* to smell. *The puppy began to sniff its food.*

snowy /ˈsnō ē/ *adj.* covered with snow. *He saw footprints on the snowy ground.*

soldiers /ˈsōl jûrz/ *n. pl.* more than one SOLDIER; men and women who serve in 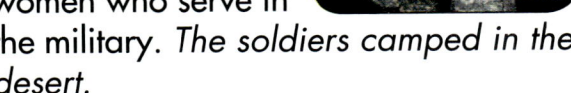 the military. *The soldiers camped in the desert.*

something /ˈsum thing/ *pron.* an unspecified action, feeling, or thing. *I would like something to eat.*

sounded /ˈsoun dəd/ *v.* past tense of SOUND; to have made noise. *The school bell sounded every hour.*

sparkle /ˈspär kəl/ *v.* to glisten. *Diamonds sparkle in the sunlight.*

special /ˈspe shəl/ *adj.* precious. *God thinks that you are very special.*

speech /ˈspēch/ *n.* a talk given to a group. *Mr. Davis gave a nice speech in chapel.*

speed /ˈspēd/ *n.* a rate at which something moves. *The track team ran at a good speed.*

splashed /ˈsplasht/ *v.* past tense of SPLASH. *Water splashed against the boat.*

splinter /ˈsplin tûr/ *n.* tiny piece of wood or metal. *Jana got a splinter in her finger.*

spoiled /ˈspoild/ v. **1** ruined. *The rainy weather spoiled our trip.* adj. **2** lost freshness of something. *Milk becomes spoiled when it is left out.* **3** bratty; self-centered. *The spoiled child cried until he got the new toy.*

spotless /ˈspot ləs/ adj. without a spot; clean. *The clean floor was spotless.*

spray /ˈsprā/ v. to apply tiny droplets of water. *I will spray the plants with water daily.*

sprinkle /ˈspring kəl/ v. fall lightly. *Rain began to sprinkle down.*

squall /ˈskwȯl/ n. a storm with wind and rain. *A storm at sea is a squall.*
squall

squeak /ˈskwēk/ n. a high-pitched sound. *The little mouse let out a squeak.*

stairs /ˈstârz/ n. pl. steps. *Cindy took the stairs, not the elevator.*

stall /ˈstȯl/ n. **1** an area bordered on three sides, usually by low walls. *The parking stall was very narrow.* v. **2** the sudden stop of a motor. *The motorcycle may stall while going uphill.*

station /ˈstā shən/ n. a regular stopping place. *The train station is busy.*

steak /ˈstāk/ n. meat. *The steak tasted delicious.*

steep /ˈstēp/ adj. sloping very sharply. *The hiking trail was very steep.*

steer /ˈstîr/ v. to guide the direction of a vehicle or ship using mechanical means. *The driver does not steer a cable car.*

stick /ˈstik/ n. **1** a small pole, often wooden. *Anita used a stick to hit the piñata.* v. **2** to cling to something. *The glue will stick to the paper.*

stilts /ˈstilts/ n. pl. more than one STILT; long poles with footrests used for walking. *Akeelah learned to walk on stilts.*

stir /ˈstûr/ v. to mix something with an object such as a spoon. *Jean began to stir the pancake mix.*

stopped /ˈstopt/ v. past tense of STOP; ended. *It stopped raining just as I left.*

stopping /ˈsto ping/ v. to end or cause to end. *The highway worker was stopping cars.*

storms /ˈstôrmz/ n. pl. more than one STORM; much rainfall, snowfall, windy, or rainy weather. *Strong storms can damage crops.*

straight /ˈstrāt/ adj. extending or proceeding in a single direction without bends or curves. *The road was very straight and narrow.*

street /ˈstrēt/ n. a public road. *Rose walked across the street.*
street

stroke /ˈstrōk/ n. **1** a controlled swing. *The golfer has a perfect stroke.* v. **2** to rub gently in one direction. *Julie will stroke her kitten.*

strong /ˈstrȯng/ adj. having strength. *The strong little tugboat towed a barge.*

struggle /ˈstru gəl/ n. a challenge. *It was a struggle to put on the tight pants.*

subject /ˈsub jikt/ n. **1** something studied in school. *The next subject is math.* **2** one who lives under a king's rule. *The palace cook was the king's favorite subject.* **3** the topic of the sentence. *The subject of a sentence is often a noun.*

subtract /səb ˈtrakt/ v. to take away. *Did you subtract to find the difference?*

subtraction /səb 'trak shən/ *n.* finding the difference between the whole and one part. *It is important to know subtraction.*

suddenly /'su dən lē/ *adv.* done in a sudden way; happening quickly. *The helicopter suddenly swerved left.*

suit /'sōōt/ *n.* **1** a set of clothes. *Ken bought a new suit for the trip.* **2** a case brought to a court of law. *Our suit was dismissed by the judge.*

suitcase /'sōōt kās/ *n.* a portable case used to hold clothes and other belongings during travel. *Edward's suitcase is red and black.*

suitcase

sunken /'sung kən/ *adj.* below the ground level. *The craters on the moon are sunken.*

surprised /sûr 'prīzd/ *v.* **1** to cause to feel wonder or amazement. *Ben surprised his mom with a gift.* *adj.* **2** amazed; shocked. *Dad was surprised when I gave him the gift.*

surround /sə 'round/ *v.* to enclose or encircle. *The policemen will surround the area.*

switches /'swi chəz/ *n. pl.* buttons or levers that control electrical circuits. *The switches are on the control panel.*

symbol /'sim bəl/ *n.* something that stands for something else. *The flag is a symbol of the United States.*

T

taken /'tā kən/ *v.* to have put into your body. *Have you taken your vitamins today?*

telephone /'te lə fōn/ *n.* device used for making or taking calls. *Please answer the telephone politely.*

telephone

telescopes /'te lə skōps/ *n. pl.* instruments that are used to observe faraway objects by making them appear larger and closer. *Miss Choi brought two telescopes to class.*

television /'te lə vi zhən/ *n.* a device that receives and projects pictures and sounds. *Dad watches the news on television.*

temple /'tem pəl/ *n.* place of worship. *Jesus went to the temple with His disciples.*

tennis /'te nəs/ *n.* a game played with a net, rackets, and a ball. *You'll need a racket to play tennis.*

than /'than/ *conj.* a word used to compare two things or ideas. *Nathan is older than his brother.*

that's /'thats/ contraction for THAT IS or THAT HAS. *The ball that's red belongs to Everett.*

their /'thâr/ *adj.* relating or belonging to them. *The astronauts wore their space suits.*

then /'then/ *adv.* a word used to tell the order of events. *We'll stop for lunch, then continue on.*

there /'thâr/ *adv.* a function word used to introduce a sentence or a clause. *There are many parts to a space station.*

there's /'thârz/ contraction for THERE IS or THERE HAS. *"There's a bee on me!" screamed Ruth.*

they /ˈthā/ *pron.* more than one person already mentioned. *Mom and Dad said that they were tired.*

they'd /ˈthād/ contraction for THEY WOULD or THEY HAD. *They'd have gone if it had started earlier.*

they'll /ˈthāl/ contraction for THEY WILL. *Tom and Diana said they'll come home.*

they're /ˈthâr/ contraction for THEY ARE. *They're going to perform a space walk.*

they've /ˈthāv/ contraction for THEY HAVE. *They've traveled a long way.*

thirteen /thûr ˈtēn/ *n.* the number written as 13. *A baker's dozen means thirteen.*

thoughtful /ˈthȯt fəl/ *adj.* **1** kind. *Her thoughtful gift made me smile.* **2** full of thought. *Kate gave a thoughtful answer to the difficult question.*

thread /ˈthred/ *n.* a long, thin fiber used for sewing. *Mom will embroider with thread.*

thread

three /ˈthrē/ *adj.* the number written as 3. *Jesus went to pray with three disciples.*

thrill /ˈthril/ *n.* an exciting moment. *It was a thrill to hear the orchestra play.*

throat /ˈthrōt/ *n.* the inside of the neck. *Amesha stayed home with a sore throat.*

throughout /thro͞o ˈout/ *prep.* in or to every part of. *The tunnel runs throughout the city.*

throw /ˈthrō/ *v.* **1** to send an object through the air using the hand. *Will you throw the ball to me?* *n.* **2** a type of thin blanket. *Mom put the throw on the bed.*

tied /ˈtīd/ *v.* **1** past tense of TIE; restrained. *The hot-air balloon was tied down.* *adj.* **2** the condition of being fastened. *The kitten played with the tied shoelace.*

tinier /ˈtī nē ûr/ *adj.* lesser in size. *From up high, many things seem tinier.*

tiniest /ˈtī nē əst/ *adj.* least in size. *Even the tiniest child is precious to Jesus.*

tiny /ˈtī nē/ *adj.* very small. *The tiny baby fell asleep.*

tired /ˈtī ûrd/ *adj.* very weary; worn out. *After a long day, I feel tired.*

title /ˈtī təl/ *n.* the name of a book, story, or other written work. *The title of the book is* The Borrowers.

to /ˈto͞o/ *prep.* **1** a function word used to indicate direction or position of something. *Seven astronauts headed to the spacecraft.* **2** indicates purpose. *Ralph is going to do his homework.*

toe /ˈtō/ *n.* a part of the foot. *I stubbed my big toe on a rock.*

together /tə ˈge thûr/ *adv.* **1** at one time. *Our class recites Bible verses together.* **2** with each other. *Uncle Ralph and Billy spend the day together.*

tomorrow /tə ˈmär ō/ *adv.* the day after today. *Tomorrow we will go on a field trip.*

too /ˈto͞o/ *adv.* **1** very. *The mission in space was not too long.* **2** besides; also. *An astronaut has to go to school and study hard, too.*

toward /tə ˈwôrd/ *prep.* in the direction of. *The little dog made its way toward home.*

towels /ˈtou əlz/ *n. pl.* absorbent cloths or paper. *Torrey folded the towels neatly.*

towels

training /'trā ning/ *n.* the act of practicing and learning how to be better. *An athlete spends hours in training.*

tried /'trīd/ *v.* past tense of TRY; to make an effort to do. *Molly tried to lift the heavy box.*

trouble /'tru bəl/ *n.* difficulty. *Chris didn't expect any trouble with the car.*

truthful /'trōōth fəl/ *adj.* honest. *It pleases God when you are truthful.*

tube /'tōōb/ *n.* **1** a hollow pipe. *Anne slid down the tube into the pool.* **2** a container with a cap. *The tube of lotion was in my purse.*

tube

turns /'tûrnz/ *v.* to move to face in a different direction. *A cable car turns around on a turntable.*

two /'tōō/ *adj.* the number written as 2. *Two astronauts performed a space walk.*

U

unable /ən 'ā bəl/ *adj.* not able. *Max is unable to climb a large tree.*

underground /'un dûr ground/ *adj.* located beneath the earth's surface. *The underground tunnel was long.*

underneath /ən dûr 'nēth/ *prep.* below; under. *My cat sleeps underneath my bed.*

understand /ən dûr 'stand/ *v.* to grasp the meaning of something. *I cannot understand Spanish.*

understood /ən dûr 'stood/ *v.* past tense of UNDERSTAND; to have known thoroughly. *Christy understood the rules of the game.*

unfair /ən 'fâr/ *adj.* not fair. *It is unfair to refuse to take turns.*

uniform /'yōō nə fôrm/ *n.* **1** an outfit of work clothes. *Her uniform was clean and ironed.* *adj.* **2** the same in color or design. *The deck was covered with uniform chairs.*

unknown /ən 'nōn/ *adj.* not known. *The unknown sound startled Karl.*

unspoken /ən 'spō kən/ *adj.* not spoken aloud. *God hears unspoken prayers.*

unthinkable /ən 'thing kə bəl/ *adj.* **1** not open to consideration. *For Jim to tell a lie was unthinkable.* **2** cannot be thought of. *The glory of God is unthinkable.*

upstairs /əp 'stârz/ *adv.* on an upper level. *Rebecca walked upstairs to her room.*

useful /'yōōs fəl/ *adj.* beneficial or having value. *A compass is a very useful tool.*

usual /'yōō zhə wəl/ *adj.* typical or normal. *We will drive the usual way to school.*

V

valley /'va lē/ *n.* a low area often between mountains. *The valley is lower than the mountains.*

valley

vegetable /'vej tə bəl/ *adj.* an edible plant. *Aunt Sophie's vegetable soup tastes great!*

very /'vâr ē/ *adv.* extremely. *It gets very hot in the summertime.*

village /'vi lij/ *n.* a small community in a rural area. *The tiny village was on the mountain.*

vision /ˈvi zhən/ *n.* the sense of sight. *Vision is one of our five senses.*

voice /ˈvois/ *n.* the sound of speaking, shouting, or singing that is made through a person's mouth. *Mrs. Brown has a lovely singing voice.*

W

wait /ˈwāt/ *v.* to do nothing until something happens. *We had to wait for permission to launch.*

waltzes /ˈwȯlt səz/ *n. pl.* ballroom dances in triple time. *Waltzes are danced in many ballets.*

warm /ˈwȯrm/ *v.* **1** to make hotter. *Mom will warm the cinnamon rolls.* *adj.* **2** somewhat hot. *It will be a warm day today.*

warning /ˈwȯr ning/ *n.* an alarm. *A blue jay will call a warning to other birds.*

watched /ˈwächt/ *v.* **1** past tense of WATCH; to take care of. *Al watched his sister one afternoon.* **2** to keep track of. *Cassie watched her diet, so she lost weight.* **3** to exercise care over. *Kevin watched his manners at the fancy restaurant.*

watercolors /ˈwä tûr kə lûrz/ *n. pl.* paints whose liquid is part water. *Diana used the watercolors.*

watercolors

wavy /ˈwā vē/ *adj.* the condition of having a wave. *Chloe's hair is wavy, not straight.*

wear /ˈwâr/ *v.* to have something on the body. *The astronauts wear special space suits.*

weather /ˈwe thûr/ *n.* condition of the air at any point in time. *Will the weather be warm and sunny?*

weigh /ˈwā/ *v.* to be a certain weight. *Do you know how much you weigh?*

weight /ˈwāt/ *n.* heaviness. *Astronauts feel no weight while in space.*

we'll /ˈwēl/ contraction for WE WILL. *We'll leave for church in five minutes.*

we're /ˈwîr/ contraction for WE ARE. *We're going on a field trip next week.*

weren't /ˈwûr ənt/ contraction for WERE NOT. *Doug and Lisa weren't able to come.*

wheel /ˈhwēl/ *n.* **1** a round device used for turning a vehicle. *The steering wheel became hot.* **2** object that allows a vehicle to roll. *The wheel of the car hit the curb.*

where /ˈwâr/ *adv.* in, at, or to what place. *Where will this mission take us?*

whether /ˈwe thûr/ *conj.* whichever one of two choices. *We're not sure whether or not we'll go.*

which /ˈhwich/ *adj.* used to ask or identify one out of a group. *Which way is the rest stop from here?*

whistle /ˈhwi səl/ *v.* to make a noise by blowing air through one's lips. *Manuel likes to whistle while he works.*

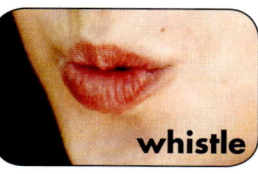
whistle

whole /ˈhōl/ *adj.* entire. *Henry bought a whole new set of tires.*

whom /ˈhōōm/ *pron.* what person. *Whom did you expect to see?*

whose /ˈhōōz/ *adj.* belonging to whom; of which. *Whose car shall we use tonight?*

windy /ˈwin dē/ *adj.* the condition of strong winds blowing. *On Saturday it was very windy.*

without /wi 'thout/ *prep.* used to indicate the lack of something or someone. *Denny left home without his lunch.*

wobble /'wo bəl/ *v.* to move shakily back and forth. *The baby may wobble when learning to walk.*

women /'wi mən/ *n. pl.* ladies. *Are there any women who are astronauts?*

worker /'wûr kûr/ *n.* one who works. *The highway worker wore a hard hat.*

world /'wûrld/ *n.* the earth. *Jesus said, "You are the light of the world."*

worry /'wûr ē/ *v.* to be very concerned about something. *Jesus told the people not to worry.*

wouldn't /'woo dənt/ contraction for WOULD NOT. *Annie wouldn't tell a lie.*

wrecker /'re kûr/ *n.* a tow truck. *A wrecker came to the accident scene.*

wrecker

wrench /'rench/ *n.* a tool used for gripping and turning. *Jaye used a wrench to hold the bolt.*

wrist /'rist/ *n.* the joint between the hand and arm. *Amber twisted her wrist when she fell.*

writing /'rī ting/ *v.* composing words. *Rico is writing a poem for the contest.*

wrong /'rȯng/ *adj.* incorrect. *The wrong car part was ordered.*

Y

yawned /'yȯnd/ *v.* past tense of YAWN; inhale slowly when one is tired. *The sleepy baby yawned.*

yawned

yellow /'ye lō/ *n.* **1** a light color. *Yellow is a light color.* *adj.* **2** colored yellow. *Ken wore a yellow cap.*

yield /'yēld/ *adj.* **1** the right of way. *A yield sign tells drivers to wait for others.* *v.* **2** to surrender. *The Hebrew slaves had to yield to the cruel Pharaoh.*

you'd /'yo͞od/ contraction for YOU WOULD or YOU HAD. *I knew you'd do just fine on the test.*

you're /'yôr/ contraction for YOU ARE. *You're a precious child of God.*

yours /'yôrz/ *pron.* owned by you. *Are those mittens yours?*

yourself /yûr 'self/ *pron.* the person that is you. *You'll complete the project all by yourself.*

Index

Note: Page numbers refer to the student page inserts in the Teacher Edition. Lesson numbers preceded by TE refer to Teacher Edition content.

Abbreviation
in context, 29–32
defined, TE 8

Adjectives
in context, 111–112
defined, 111

Alphabetical Order, 7, 43, 99, 127

Analogy
in context, 39, 67, 103
defined, 39

Antonyms
in context, 15, 35, 79, 99
defined, 15

Apostrophe
in contractions, 85–88
in possessives, 127

Assessment
cumulative review
Lessons 1–5 Test, BLMs 06E–F
Lessons 7–11 Test, BLMs 12E–F
Lessons 13–17 Test, BLMs 18E–F
Lessons 19–23 Test, BLMs 24E–F
Lessons 25–29 Test, BLMs 30E–F
Lessons 31–35 Test, BLMs 36E–F
weekly
TE lessons 1–5
TE lessons 7–11
TE lessons 13–17
TE lessons 19–23
TE lessons 25–29
TE lessons 31–35

Auditory Discrimination, 6, 38, 42, 50, 58, 74, 81; TE 24

Auditory Learning. *See* Learning Modality Activities.

B

Base Word
in context, 105–108
defined, 105
with prefixes, 117–118
with suffixes, 113–116, 117, 119–120

in syllables, 75

Blends. *See* Consonant(s).

Cartoon
in context, 112
defined, TE 28

Cause and Effect
in context, 44; TE 11
defined, TE 11

Classifying, 59, 79, 123

Cloze Activities
defined, TE 1
e-mail, 44
flow chart, 68
helicopter tour, 116
journal, 4, 84
letter, 56
paragraph, 20, 128
poem, 64
sentences, 1, 5, 9–10, 13–14, 18, 26, 29–30, 33, 35, 37, 41–42, 49, 53, 57, 61–62, 65, 73, 78, 81, 85, 89, 91, 97, 101–102, 105, 107, 109, 114, 117, 121–123, 125, 129, 131, 133–134, 137

Cognitive Skills
auditory discrimination, 6, 38, 42, 50, 58, 74, 81; TE 24
compare and contrast, 40
context clues, 3, 8, 11, 16, 28, 36, 40, 52, 76, 87–88, 92, 112
multiple meanings, 27, 31, 55, 59, 83
visual discrimination, 23, 30, 38, 48, 53, 66, 71–72, 77–78, 82, 87, 95–96, 110, 118, 120, 135, 143–144; TE 24

Compare and Contrast
in context, 40
defined, TE 10

Compound Words
in context, 89–92, 93, 96
defined, 89
in syllables, 7, 53, 89–91

Consonant(s)
blends
in context, 33–36, 37–40, 45–47
defined, 33; TE 9, 21
and silent letters, 37–40, 45, 47
digraphs
in context, 53–56, 69–70
defined, 53; TE 21
doubles, 1–4, 21
hard c, 97–100, 117
hard g, 101–104, 117–118
soft c, 97–100, 117
soft g, 101–104, 117–118
spelling patterns with three letters, 41–44, 45, 48

Contractions
apostrophe
in context, 85–88
defined, 85
in context, 85–88, 93, 95
defined, 85

Conventions
capitalization, 72, 75; TE 17
punctuation
comma, TE 35
exclamation point, 63
period, 63
question mark, 63

Cross-Curricular
Bible, 9, 10, 34, 38, 54, 78, 103, 111, 126, 131; TE 2, 3, 5, 8, 10, 15, 20, 21, 23, 25, 26, 28, 29, 32
illustration, TE 28, 29, 31, 32, 33
language arts
capitalization, 72, 75; TE 17
punctuation
comma, TE 35
exclamation point, 63
period, 63
question mark, 63
sentence
declarative
in context, 63
defined, 63

Note: Page numbers refer to the student page inserts in the Teacher Edition. Lesson numbers preceded by TE refer to Teacher Edition content.

© Spelling Grade 3